Marcel Minnaert

Light and Color in the Outdoors

Translated and Revised
by Len Seymour

With 223 Figures and 49 Color Plates

 Springer

Author
Prof. Dr. Marcel Minnaert †

Translator
Len Seymour
16 Gorsecliff Court
Boscombe Spa Road
Bournemouth
BH5 1AW, United Kingdom

Title of the original Dutch edition:
De natuurkunde van 't vrije veld. I. Licht en kleur in het landschap
© 1974: B. V. W. J. Thieme & Cie, Zutphen

Hardcover:
ISBN 0-387-97935-2 Springer-Verlag New York Berlin Heidelberg
ISBN 3-540-97935-2 Springer-Verlag Berlin Heidelberg New York SPIN 10702832
Softcover:
ISBN 0-387-94413-3 Springer-Verlag New York Berlin Heidelberg

Library of Congress Cataloging-in-Publication Data
Minnaert, M. G. J. (Marcel Gilles Jozef), 1893– . Light and color in the outdoors / M.
Minnaert ; translated and revised by L. Seymour. p. cm. Includes bibliographical refer-
ences and index.
ISBN 0-387-97935-2. –ISBN 3-540-97935-2 (hard) ISBN 0-387-94413-3 (soft)
1. Light–Popular works. 2. Color–Popular works. I. Seymour, L. II. Title.
QC358.5..M56 1992 535−dc20 92-33748

Caution: Contrary to what Minnaert suggests in a few places in this book, the only
filters that block damaging radiation sufficiently to allow safe viewing of the sun are shade
13 or 14 arc-welder's glass or metallized filters made specifically for viewing the sun.

9 8 7 6 5 4 3

© 1993 Springer-Verlag New York, Inc.
Printed in the United States of America.

From *Song of the Open Road*

Afoot and light-hearted I take to the open road,
Healthy, free, the world before me,
The long brown path before me leading wherever I choose.

Henceforth I ask not for good-fortune, I myself am
    good-fortune,
Henceforth I whimper no more, postpone no more, need
    nothing,
Done with indoor complaints, libraries, querulous
    criticisms,
Strong and content I travel the open road.

I think heroic deeds were all conceiv'd in the open air, and
    all free poems also,
I think I could stop here myself and do miracles,
I think whatever I shall meet on the road I shall like, and
    whoever beholds me shall like me,
I think whoever I see must be happy.

I inhale great draughts of space,
The east and west are mine, and the north and the
    south are mine.

I am larger, better than I thought,
I did not know I held so much goodness.

Now I see the secret of the making of the best persons,
It is to grow in the open air and to eat and sleep with the
    earth.

Allons! whoever you are come travel with me!
Traveling with me you find what never tires.

The earth never tires,
The earth is rude, silent, incomprehensible at first, Nature
   is rude and incomprehensible at first,
Be not discouraged, keep on, there are divine things well
   envelop'd,
I swear to you there are divine things more beautiful than
   words can tell.

Camerado, I give you my hand!
I give you my love more precious than money,
I give you myself before preaching or law;
Will you give me yourself? will you come travel with me?
Shall we stick by each other as long as we live?

Walt Whitman, *Leaves of Grass*

Foreword

Light and Color in the Outdoors by the Dutch astronomer Marcel Minnaert (1893–1970) is a classic among books on the physics of nature. In its pages Minnaert will show you where to find the extraordinary array of light and color phenomena that may be seen in the open air; in every case he discusses their physical explanations and connections to other related phenomena. His book is intended for everybody who loves the outdoors: many of the treasures of nature presented here may even be observed in a crowded city.

The first edition of the book appeared in 1937, and by 1940 it had been followed by two other works, *Geluid, Warmte, Electriciteit* (*Sound, Heat, Electricity*) and *Rust en Beweging* (*Rest and Motion*), forming the series *De Natuurkunde van 't Vrije Veld* (*Physics in the Outdoors*). The first English translation of Volume 1, *Light and Colour in the Open Air*, was published by G. Bell and Sons in 1940 and was reprinted in 1954 by Dover Publications Inc.

Over the years, Professor Minnaert made many corrections and additions to the work, and the present Dutch edition of Volume 1 is the fifth (1968), reprinted unabridged in 1974. This translation, prepared for the 100th anniversary of Minnaert's birth (12 February 1893), closely follows the latest Dutch edition.

In the 1980s the work was translated into Finnish under the auspices of the Finnish astronomical association Ursa. The latest research on halos and related phenomena was used to update Minnaert's Chapter 10 and has been incorporated here, as has a brief biography of Minnaert by Pekka Kröger. In addition, the outstanding photographic records of several Finnish observers, principally Pekka Parviainen, were drawn upon. Many of these, as well as a completely new color section, are now used here to illustrate more vividly than was possible in earlier editions the magical and often awesome sights that would escape the attention of the rest of us but for Minnaert.

This book is an invitation to rejoice in nature and science. Join Professor Minnaert here on an odyssey that will change completely the way you see the natural world.

February 1993   *Translator*

Through the foliage, the sun throws countless spots of light on to the road.
(Photo by Lauri Anttila)

Preface

If you love nature, you respond to her phenomena as naturally as you breathe. Whether it's sunny or raining, warm or cold, you'll find something of interest to observe. Wherever you are, in town, at or near the sea, or in the countryside, there is something new and important happening all the time. Impressions come at you from all directions and affect all your senses: you smell the aroma of the air; you feel the difference in temperature; you hear the birds and insects at work; you see the colorful butterfly. And all these impressions make you fully conscious of the richness of life.

Never think that the poetry of nature's moods in all their infinite variety is lost on the scientific observer, for the habit of observing refines our sense of beauty and adds a brighter hue to the richly colored background against which each particular fact is outlined. The connection between events and the relation between cause and effect in different parts of the landscape unite harmoniously what would otherwise be but a chain of unrelated scenes.

The phenomena described in this book are partly things you can observe in everyday life, and partly things as yet unfamiliar to you, though they may be seen at any moment, if only you will touch your eyes with that magic wand called 'knowing what to look for'. And then there are those rare, remarkable wonders of nature that happen only occasionally in a lifetime, so that even trained observers may wait year after year to see them. When they do see them, they are filled with a sense of extraordinary and deep happiness.

However remarkable it may seem, it remains a fact that we do not observe much more than the things we are already familiar with; it is very difficult to see something new, even if it stares us in the face. In ancient times and in the Middle Ages, innumerable eclipses of the sun were observed, and yet the corona was hardly noticed until 1842, although nowadays it is regarded as the most striking phenomenon of an eclipse and may be seen by anyone with the naked eye. In this book, I have tried to collect and draw to your attention all those things that in the course of time have become known through the activities of many outstanding and able naturalists. No doubt there is much, much more yet to be observed in nature; every year sees the publication of a number of treatises concerning new phenomena. It is strange to think how blind and deaf we must be to so many things around us that posterity is bound to notice.

By 'observation of nature' is normally understood the study of flora and fauna: as if the spectacle of wind and weather and clouds, the thousands of sounds that fill the air, the waves of the sea, the rays of the sun, and the rumblings of the earth were not part of nature, too! A book containing notes of all that is to be seen that is of particular interest to the student of inanimate physical science is just as necessary to him or her as a book on flora and fauna is to the biologist. Inevitably, you will be led into the domain of the meteorologist, and into regions bordering on astronomy, geography, and biology, but I hope to have found a certain unity in which the connections between all these subjects can be perceived.

Since we are concerned with a simple, direct way of observing nature, we must systematically avoid:

- anything that can be found only with the help of instruments (concentrating instead on our senses, our chief helpers, whose characteristics we ought to know);
- anything deduced from a long series of statistical observations;
- theoretical considerations not directly concerning what we see with our eyes.

You will see that a surprising abundance of observations even then remains possible; indeed, there is hardly a branch of physics that is not applicable out of doors, and often on a scale exceeding any experiments in a laboratory. Bear in mind, therefore, that everything described in this book lies within your own powers of understanding and observation. Everything is meant to be seen by you and done by you! Where the explanations offered are perhaps too concise, I suggest that you refresh your memory of fundamental physics by turning to an appropriate elementary textbook.

The importance of outdoor observations for the teaching of physics has not yet been sufficiently realized. They help us in our ever increasing efforts to adapt our education to the requirements of everyday life; they lead us naturally to ask a thousand questions, and, thanks to them, we find later on that what we learned at school is to be found again and again beyond the school walls.

But this book is also aimed at anyone who loves nature; at young people going out into the world and gathering together around the globe; at the painter who admires, but does not understand, the light and colors in the landscape; at those living in the country; at all those who delight in traveling; and also at town-dwellers for whom, even in the noise and clamor of our dark streets, the manifestations of nature remain. I hope that even for the trained physicist it will contain something new, for the field it covers is vast and often lies outside the ordinary course of science. It will therefore be understood why very simple as well as more complicated observations have been chosen, grouped according to their interrelationships.

This book is very probably the first attempt of its kind and as such it is not perfect. I feel more and more overwhelmed by the beauty and extent of the material, and more and more conscious of my inability to explain it according to its merits. I have been experimenting systematically for more than twenty years and I have collected in this book the essence of some thousands of articles from every possible periodical, although only those articles that give a comprehensive survey or throw light on very special points have been quoted. I am, however, well aware how incomplete this collection still is. Many things already known are still unknown to me, and much remains a problem, even to a professional.

1937   *M. Minnaert*

Preface to the Fifth Edition

For too long *Light and Color* has been out of print, but unfortunately a new edition had to wait till I had found time to revise the text. As little as possible has been changed, but new subjects are discussed in §§ 5, 6, 11, 46, 59, 67, 70, 71, 88, 113, 149, 178, 186, 197, 204, 207, 215, and 233. Many small additions and revisions were found necessary in a number of places. Many of the older literature references have been deleted and newer, more up-to-date ones added. The reader is directed particularly to large reference books and surveys, but also to a number of smaller articles that are not generally known.

Spring 1968   *M. Minnaert*

Foreword to the Fifth Edition (Reprint)

This reprint is unchanged from the Fifth Edition and was prepared by Professor Minnaert in late 1968. Only a number of printing errors have been removed.

Spring 1974   *J.G. van Cittert-Eymers*

Professor Marcel Minnaert

M. G. J. Minnaert (1893–1970)

Marcel Gilles Jozef Minnaert was a scientist, in particular a specialist in solar research. For more than forty years he was associated with the Utrecht Observatory in the Netherlands. But Minnaert was more than a prominent astronomer: he was a spiritual descendant of the Enlightenment, someone who spoke his mind.

Marcel Minnaert was born on 12 February 1893 in Bruges, Belgium. His parents were teachers. One of the important influences on the young Minnaert was his uncle Gerard D. Minnaert, who played an important role in the Flemish language movement, which worked toward equality of the Flemish (Belgian Dutch) language with the (then official) French language.

After the death of his father in 1902, Minnaert and his mother moved to Ghent, where he later started his university studies. He read biology and in 1914 he completed a thesis on the effects of light on plants ('Contributions à la Photo-Biologie Quantitative'). However, Minnaert wanted to know more about the physical basis of his work, and in 1915 he moved to the University of Leiden in the Netherlands to study and teach physics. A year later he returned as a physics teacher to the University of Ghent, which by then had become completely Flemish.

During the First World War the Germans occupied a large part of Belgium; toward the end of the war it became clear that the Belgian government was to regard the language activists of the University of Ghent as German collaborators. To escape judgment, many of the leading figures of the Flemish Movement fled to the Netherlands. Minnaert moved to Utrecht, where in 1918 he started work on solar spectroscopy at the University's physics laboratory under the directorship of Professor Julius. In 1925 he completed a second thesis, this time on abnormal dispersion.

In his scientific works Minnaert considerably advanced the interpretation of the spectral lines of the sun and stars. He was also an excellent observer. During the 1927 eclipse at Gällivare in northern Sweden he and A. Pannekoek obtained the first flash spectra of the sun that could be used for quantitative photometry.

In 1927 Minnaert was appointed to succeed Nijland as Director of the Utrecht Observatory. A large solar research project culminated in 1940 in the publication of a monumental work, the *Utrecht*

Photometric Atlas of the Solar Spectrum (Minnaert, Mulders, and Houtgast).

After the outbreak of the Second World War, Minnaert did not hide his opposition to fascism, and he was arrested by the Nazis in May 1942. He remained in prison until April 1944.

After the war, Minnaert carried out research in many other subjects in addition to the sun: comets, photometry of Venus, and the Orion nebula. He also published a work on astronomical methods based on practical exercises he had developed (*Practical Work in Elementary Astronomy*, 1969).

The influence of Minnaert extended far outside the range of his actual research. Many amateurs know him best for the series *De Natuurkunde van 't Vrije Veld* (*Physics in the Outdoors*) (first editions 1937–1940), three magnificent books.

Minnaert was also very fond of music and he was an accomplished pianist. His home contained a collection of exotic musical instruments, which on his retirement he donated to the University of Utrecht. His primary interest, however, was traveling: the simpler the means, the better. Many of his landscape paintings have their origin in these travels.

Minnaert's book *De Sterrekunde en de Mensheid* (*Astronomy and Mankind*) (1946) reflects on the intimate relationship between astronomy and mankind. Astronomy and poetry meet in the multilingual anthology *Dichters over Sterren* (*Poets on Stars*) (1949) compiled by Minnaert. This book is also indicative of Minnaert's interest in languages. He was an enthusiastic Esperantist and understood almost twenty languages.

Minnaert received many international honors. He retired from the Utrecht Observatory in 1963, but even in retirement he remained active as the chairman of many committees of the International Astronomical Union.

Minnaert died in Utrecht on the morning of 26 October 1970. In accordance with his wish, there was no funeral: his body was donated to scientific research. There is no gravestone, but the work remains. One part of it is in front of you.

Contents

The sun shines brightly through the foliage.
(Photo by Matti Martikainen)

Light and Color in the Outdoors

First and foremost, we consider our relevant experiences in broad daylight. We take the observer into the open air before we lead him into the restrictions of the dark room.

Goethe, *Farbenlehre*

Chapter 1
Light and Shadows

1. Images of the sun

Oh, sun, when you move through the foliage of
the high lime trees,
You drop splashes of light on the ground,
So beautiful that I dare not tread on them.

E. Rostand

In the shade of a group of trees the ground is dappled randomly with spots of light, some small, some large, but all regularly elliptical. If you hold a pencil in front of one of these spots, the line connecting pencil and shadow will indicate where the rays of light that form the spot come from; they are, of course, sunlight that falls through some opening in the foliage: all we see here and there between the leaves is a blinding ray of light.

Random dappling of spots of sunlight beneath trees. (Photo by Veikko Mäkelä)

Fig. 1. The sun's rays penetrating dense foliage.

The surprising thing is that all these images have the same shape, although it is obviously impossible that all the holes and slits in the foliage happen to have the same shape. If you intercept one of these rays on a piece of paper held at right angles to the ray, the image is no longer elliptical but round. Hold the piece of paper higher and higher and you will note that the spot of light gets smaller and smaller. This shows that the beam of light causing the spot is conical: the image is only elliptical because the ground cuts the cone at an angle.

The origin of the phenomenon lies in the fact that the sun is not a point source. Each tiny opening P in Fig. 1 gives a sharp image of the sun AB, a somewhat larger opening P' gives a slightly displaced sharp image $A'B'$ (dashed lines); a wider opening that contains both P and P' gives a slightly hazy but clear image $A'B$. And indeed we see spots of light of all kinds of brightness: of two equally large spots the brighter one is also the less sharp.

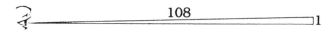

Fig. 2. We see the sun's disk at an angle of $\frac{1}{108}$ radian.

When clouds move in to hide the sun, you will also see them moving across the images of the sun, but in the opposite direction; during a partial solar eclipse, all spots of light are crescent-shaped. When there is a large sunspot, it is visible on the clearest of the spots of light. Get a clear image of the sun by making a tiny round hole in a sheet of thin cardboard. Then examine the images of the sun formed by a square opening at a number of distances between the cardboard and the ground.

The angle subtended at our eye when we view the sun must be the same as angle APB of the cone forming the image of the sun. Such small angles are measured in radians. We say, for example: 'This is an angle of $1/108$ radian', which means that the sun looks to us as large as 1 cm (⅜ in) at a distance of 108 cm (3 ft 6 in), or 10 cm (4 in) at a distance of 1080 cm (35 ft)—see Fig. 2. In the same way, the diameter of a sharp spot of light must be $1/108$th of its distance to the opening in the foliage; if the image is hazy, the size of the opening in the foliage must be added. Catch faint but sharp images of the sun on a sheet of paper, hold it at right angles to the rays, measure the diameter k of the spot of light, and determine the distance L from the paper to the opening in the foliage with the aid of a length of string. Is it true that $k = L/108$?

Measure the minor axis, k, and the major axis, b, of the elliptical spots of light formed on the liquid of a spirit level; their ratio will be same as that of the height of the tree, H, and the distance L. From this it follows that $H = (k/b)L = 108k(k/b)$. A conspicuously large spot of light under a beech had axes of 53 cm (20 ⅞ in) and 33 cm (13 in); the height of the opening in the foliage above the ground was thus $108 \times 33 \times (33/53) = 2200$ cm or 22 m (24 yd). Note that the images of the sun are more elongated in the morning and toward the evening, and rounder at midday.

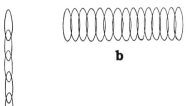

Fig. 3. Shadows of metal wires in slanting rays of the sun: (**a**) distinct shadow; (**b**) indistinct shadow.

Fine images of the sun are found in the shade of beeches, lime trees, and sycamores, but seldom in that of poplars, elms, or plane trees.

Pay particular attention to the spots of light formed by trees at the banks of shallow water: they are outlined wonderfully at the bottom of the water!

2. Shadows

When you look at your shadow on the ground, you will notice that the shadow of your feet is clearly defined, whereas that of your head is not. The shadow of the bottom part of a tree or post is sharp, while that of the higher part becomes increasingly unclear toward the top.

Hold your hand spread out in front of a piece of paper: its shadow is sharp. Move it away from the paper and note that the umbra (the dark part of the shadow) of the fingers becomes narrower, while the penumbras (the lighter parts of the shadow) get broader and finally merge.

Again, these findings are a consequence of the sun not being a point source and correspond to what we have observed earlier with the spots of light. Look at the shadow of a butterfly or a bird (how often do we do that?) and note that it looks more or less like a round spot: a shadow image of the sun.

Particularly noteworthy is the shadow of a wiremesh fence when the sun is low in the sky: only the vertical wires throw a shadow, the horizontal ones do not. Hold a piece of paper with a small hole in it at right angles to the sun and note the resulting elliptical spot of light on the ground. Think of the shadow of the wire netting as being caused by a number of such ellipses in juxtaposition, but dark ones, not light ones; this shadow becomes sharp when the wire lies along the major axis and hazy when it lies along the minor axis (Fig. 3).

Hold a piece of paper horizontal behind the fence on the side opposite the sun and then move it away, so that the gradual development of the remarkable shadows can be observed. Try this with the sun falling on to the wire netting at different angles, tilt the piece of paper, etc.

Shadows have played an important role in popular beliefs. It used to be considered a terrible punishment for anyone to lose his shadow, and anyone possessing a headless shadow would die within a year! Tales like these, which are common among all peoples and throughout history, are also of interest to us, because they show how careful one has to be with statements of untrained observers, however numerous and unanimous they may be.

3. Images of the sun and shadows during solar eclipses and at sunset

During a solar eclipse, the dark moon is seen to move in front of the solar disk until only a thin crescent is left. At that instant it is worth while noting that all spots of light under a tree resemble crescents, large or small, bright or dim.

Again, the shape of shadows corresponds to the crescent shape. For instance, the shadows of our fingers take on an extraordinary claw-like shape. Each small dark object throws a crescentlike shadow; the shadow of a small rod consists of a number of such crescents, while a curvature appears at its ends.

A good example of a single dark object is an air balloon; it has been observed that during a solar eclipse both its shadow and that of its basket are crescent-shaped. An aircraft at a given height also throws a curved shadow.

Solar eclipses, even partial ones, are rare. It is therefore interesting to know that similar distortions of shadows can be seen to be caused during sunset in clear weather at the seaside if you stick coins or disks of cardboard of varying sizes to a window or suspend them from a thin thread. The shape of the shadows and the distribution of light vary according to the size of the coins or disks and how far the sun has sunk below the horizon.

4. Double shadows

When the trees have lost their leaves, you may happen to see the shadows of two equally thick branches covering each other. The shadow of the branch closer to you is sharp and black; that of the other is broader and grayish. There is something peculiar here: where the shadows cover each other exactly, a bright thin line is visible within the narrower shadow, which gives it the appearance of being doubled. Why should this be so?

Assume that your eye is successively at A, B, C, D, and E in Fig. 4. Every time it will see the solar disk with the two branches in front as shown in the lower part of the figure. In order to distinguish between them, assume that the more distant of the branches appears somewhat thicker than the other. It is clear that in positions B and D your eye will see the solar disk covered in two places, but in position C in only one place, because the branches then cover each other exactly. This explains the existence of the thin line of light.

It appears that this phenomenon will occur whenever the angle between the two branches subtended at the eye is smaller than that of the solar disk. This occurrence may also be seen when the shadows of two telephone wires cover each other.

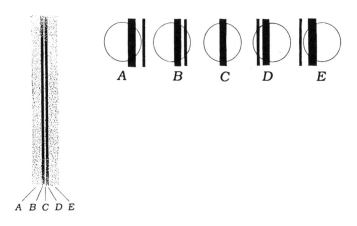

Fig. 4. How double shadows arise.

The shadows in spots of light on the ground underneath tall trees vary in a typical manner. Hold a book in such a way that its shadow falls in the dim light of a large spot of sunlight: the shadow will be much clearer than usual. Now look for a situation where high, thin twigs throw a faint shadow and hold a pencil above it: you will note that you get double or multiple shadows, of which one component is sometimes fainter and sometimes clearer than the other. In this situation a book will throw a shadow with exceptionally clear penumbra. All these typical events are easily explained.

> I once strolled along the beach on an evening, late in March. The sun set in the west across the sea and the moon was bright in the east. The sunset, which lasted for quite a while, made my shadow fall eastward. *But then there was a period when I had no shadow* until the brightness of the moon became stronger than the light from the red evening sky and my shadow fell westward.
>
> From the Icelandic *Alfur of Windhael* by S. Nordal

Is this an accurate observation?

5. The shadow of an aircraft trail

During certain weather conditions, an aircraft leaves an ever-widening vapor trail against a clear sky. It is sometimes possible to see the shadow of this trail on a lower layer of cloud. Note how the distance between trail and shadow slowly changes.

Vapor trail of an aircraft and its shadow on a cloud layer. (Photo by Pekka Parviainen)

6. Lengthening shadows

At night when you pass a streetlight you can see how your shadow lengthens faster and faster as you walk away from the light. Faster and faster? It cannot be true: the speed of lengthening is constant—see Fig. 5.

For more about shadows, see §§ 59, 111, 115, 208, 247, 251, and 261.

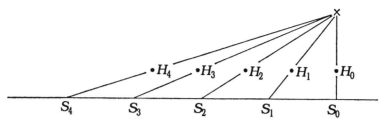

Fig. 5. The lengthening of our shadow when we pass a streetlight.

Chapter 2

Reflection of Light

7. The laws of reflection

Find a place where the moon is reflected in a smooth surface of water. Compare the angle between the moon and the horizon with that between the reflection and the horizon: within the tolerances of observation, the angles are equal. If the moon is not too high in the sky, you may guess at the angles with the aid of a stick: holding the stick with a straight arm, make the tip just 'touch' the lower edge of the lunar disk and make the tip of your thumb 'touch' the horizon. Then, using your arm as the axis, turn the stick upside down, hold your thumb so that it continues to touch the horizon, and check whether the tip of the stick touches the edge of the reflected disk. Similar measurements, carried out by the author on clearly visible constellations, give the most practical confirmation of the laws of reflection.

Clouds reflected in water. (Photo by Pekka Parviainen)

Fig. 6. Sunlight reflected by an inset window.

An inset window is lit by the sun when the sun is not too high in the sky—see Fig. 6. The direction of the incoming rays of light is indicated by the shadow *AB*; the reflected light is seen as a clear spot of light in the direction *BC*. You will note that the two directions are symmetrical with respect to the normal *BN*, that is, $\angle ABN = \angle CBN$. This is not the same as the law of reflection, but follows from it. Prove this!

Why do windows of distant houses reflect only the rays of the rising or setting sun?

8. Reflection by wires

If you walk parallel to a number of telephone wires that reflect the light of the sun, you will note that the spot of light moves at the same speed as you walk. At night, a streetlight will be reflected by the overhead wire of a train, tram, or trolley bus. What determines the exact location of the reflections? Imagine an ellipsoid that has foci at your eye and at the source of light and which touches the wire as shown in Fig. 7. The point of contact is the light spot: it is a well-known property of the ellipsoid that lines from any point on its surface to the foci subtend equal angles with the tangent plane.

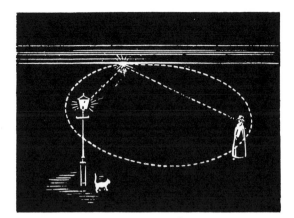

Fig. 7. Reflection of a street-light by telephone wires.

9. Differences between an object and its reflection

Most people think that the reflection of a scene in calm water resembles the scene itself upside down. Nothing could be further from the truth. You only have to look at night how streetlights are reflected—see Fig. 8. The reflection of a bank sloping toward a river (see Fig. 9) appears shortened, and even disappears when we look from high enough above the water. When we see in a picture that the reflection of a riverbank resembles a narrow dark edge, we get the impression that we are looking straight down at it. You will never see the reflection of the top of a stone lying in the water. The closer the objects are to us, the lower their images with respect to that of the background.

Fig. 8. Reflections of a number of distant street-lights.

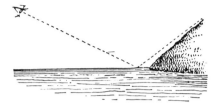

Fig. 9. Shortening of the image of a riverbank.

Some more examples of this general law are shown in Fig.10. Fig.10(a) shows why it is that an observer can see the moon direct, whereas its reflection is hidden by the tower. The effect is represented in Fig. 10(b): the reflection of the tower is lowered with respect to that of the distant moon; note also that the reflection of the tree appears taller with respect to that of the tower than it is in reality. Furthermore, in Fig. 10(c) compare the image of the tree against the distant hills with the direct view of it; the effect here is particularly pronounced and makes our subconscious throw up a number of similar views that we must have seen in the past.

These phenomena are quite natural when you realize that although the reflection is identical to the object, it looks different in perspective because the two are shifted with respect to each other. We see the landscape as if we were looking at it from a point beneath

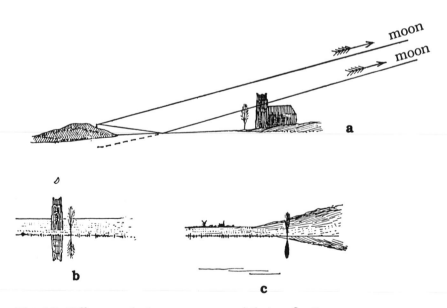

Fig. 10. Differences between scenes and their reflections.

the water's surface where the image of our eye is. The differences become smaller the closer we bring our eyes to the water and the farther away the objects are (cf. § 152).

However, it appears that something else also plays a role here. The reflections of trees and shrubs in small ponds and puddles at the roadside sometimes have a more pronounced clarity, sharpness, and warmth of color than the objects themselves. Clouds are never as beautiful as when they are reflected in a mirror. The reflection of a street in a shop window against a dark background is surprisingly clear and sharp. The cause of these differences is more psychological than physical. It has been suggested that the reflected view is always sensed as a picture that lies in one plane (physically, the reflections lie in a number of planes, of course, just as the objects themselves). Another reason put forward is that the 'framing' makes us uncertain about the position of the object in space, which gives rise to a strong impression of relief. It appears to me more important that our eyes remain protected from the large bright area of the sky that surrounds the observed scene: an effect not unlike looking at something through a tube (§ 197). The reduced brightness of the mirror image is in itself beneficial for looking at the sky and clouds, which otherwise are somewhat too bright for our eyes. Furthermore, the reflection is polarized, so that it may attenuate the luster of certain objects and saturate colors.

10. Light beams reflected by ditches and canals

During sunny weather, any smooth water surface reflects a beam of sunlight, and all these beams rise over the landscape like those of gigantic searchlights. Yet we seldom notice them; to do so apparently requires a combination of favorable conditions that happen only once in a while. The greatest likelihood appears to be early in the morning or late in the evening when the sun is low and the reflected light is strong (cf. § 63). Evidently, the air should be hazy so as to give a clear outline to the beam; fog or mist is not suitable because it attenuates the rays and scatters the light all over the countryside: any differences in brightness are then erased. The ditch or canal should preferably run in the direction of the sun and that is also where we should look to, not in the opposite direction; haziness disperses light rather better in a forward direction (§ 208). The water surface should not ripple; the wind should preferably be slight or gentle and blow across the water; high banks are favorable, unless they screen the incident and reflected light too much. The rising belt of light will be seen better the longer and straighter the stretch of water is, since the lighting haze is then seen under a thicker layer. It should also be considered that the left flank of the rising beam is more clearly

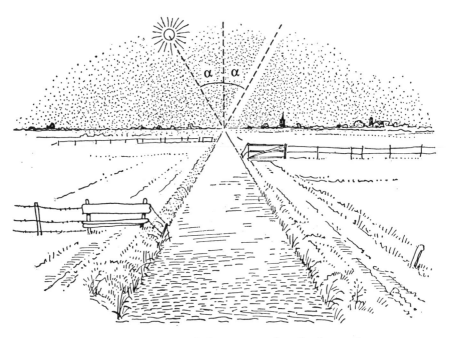

Fig. 11. Beams of reflected sunlight portrayed in the hazy air.

defined than the right one if you are standing on the left bank of the canal, and vice versa. Observations prove that this is so. In favorable conditions it is sometimes possible to view this imposing scene over a number of successive, parallel-running ditches: a frequent occurrence in low lands; you have to be close to the ditches, of course.

11. Sunlight reflected on a layer of clouds

Sometimes a spot of stationary light has been seen on a layer of clouds while the clouds were drifting away. This was apparently caused by light reflected by the water surface of a nearby lake on to the cloud layer like a searchlight. This phenomenon appears to happen only during windstill weather (smooth water surface) and when the sun is low (not higher than 7°: strong reflections), while the lake should have a diameter of not less than 1 km (⅔ of a mile)[1].

---

[1] Zamorski, *Izv. Vses. Geogr. Obschestva*, **86**, 104, 1954.

12. Freak reflections

A row of houses throws a dark shadow on to the road, but in the middle of this you often see spots of light—see Fig. 12. How does that light get there? Hold your hand in front of one of the spots and from the direction of the shadow deduce where the light comes from: you will find that it is reflected by the windows of the houses on the other side of the road.

The spots of light caused by standard window glass are irregular, whereas those caused by plate glass are far more uniform. The farther away, or the smaller or more even, the windows are, the more the spot of light looks like a hazy circle (or ellipse—see § 1). Similarly, light may be seen shimmering on the surface of a canal that itself lies in shadow: the houses on the other side reflect the light.

Close to the edge of the water is a row of houses of which the facades are totally in shadow; yet, light plays over them: a shimmer with uniform, more or less parallel, lines that move along in it. They are reflections of the waves of the water—see Fig. 13. The part *AB* of the undulation acts as a concave mirror that gives a focus at *L*; part *BC* is much less curved and concentrates the rays at a far greater distance. In this way, there is for each and every distance from the facades a part of the water surface that provides a clear beam of light; other parts cause the general shimmering.

Fig. 12. Spots of sunlight in a dark street.

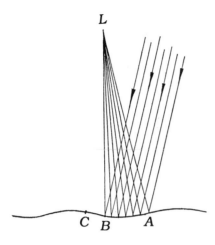

Fig. 13. Formation of faint lines by reflection from gently undulating water.

A similar playing of light may be seen along quaysides and against the arches of bridges. This is a small-scale model of the twinkling of stars (cf. § 51).

A lovely scene is created when sunlight is reflected by the water of a canal that is whipped up by a stiff breeze. Thousands of bright sparks flare up rhythmically, say five times a second, almost simultaneously from the entire water surface. One reader wrote to say that the flickering appears quicker when he accommodates his eyes.

The mathematical analysis is fairly complex. It appears, however, that the rhythm of the flickering is faster the higher the observer is above the surface of the water[2].

13. Shooting at a reflection

Near Salzburg, Austria, is a lake, the Königsee, which is enclosed by high mountains and is therefore always very calm. Shooting competitions are held there, in which the competitors aim at the reflection of the target in the water; the bullet is 'reflected' by the surface and hits the target. The likelihood of a hit appears to be just as great as when the shot is aimed directly at the target.

The extraordinary thing is that the bullet is not reflected by the surface of the water, but actually penetrates the water. According to a hydrodynamic theorem, the curvature of the water is then such that the bullet moving in the water is 'attracted' by the surface, approaches it, and finally leaves the water at the same angle as it en-

---

[2] Longuet-Higgins, *J. Opt. Soc. Am.*, **50**, 851, 1960.

Diffuse reflections on a wall caused by windows of houses opposite. (Photo by Veikko Mäkelä)

tered. It has been possible to follow the trajectory of the bullet by suspending screens submerged in the water.

14. Gauss's heliotrope

Place a mirror in such a position that it reflects sunlight; close to the mirror, the reflection has the same shape as the mirror; a little farther away it is less well defined; still farther away it becomes round; and at a fairly large distance it becomes a true image of the sun. If you then cover a part of the mirror, the reflection remains round but becomes less bright. You will not be able to see the spot of light farther away than about 50 m (165 ft), but an observer at that distance will see the mirror shine brightly.

In the open, fix the mirror on a tripod or some other suitable support so that the reflected sunlight is horizontal. Then move away from the mirror in the same direction as the reflected light until you can only just see the light. It is not easy to keep the beam in sight, but fortunately its diameter increases with distance. This can be seen when you move at right angles to the direction of the beam and determine within which limits you can still see it: you will note that at a distance of about 100 m (330 ft) it is already 1 m (3 ft) wide. Bear in mind that the sun moves in the sky and it is therefore best to carry out this experiment at noon, because the reflected beam will

Fig. 14. Signaling with a mirror.

then remain horizontal for some time so that the mirror needs very little, if any, readjustment.

It is amazing how far away the reflected light can be seen. The reflection of the sun from the windows of a tower has been seen at a distance of 50 km (31 miles). A mirror of only 5×5 cm (2×2 in) is visible at up to 13 km (8 miles) and a standard pocket mirror (about 9×6 cm—3.5×2.5 in) at up to 30 km (18.5 miles). It is for this reason that small mirrors form part of the kit found in lifeboats and rafts[3]. A simple way of pointing the beam in a given direction is shown in Fig. 14. Here, a small circle of the silver coating at the center of the back of the mirror has been scratched away; this makes it possible to look 'through' the mirror and take aim at the distant target just over the edge of a small board held at a little distance by a helper. Incline the mirror until the circle of reflected light on the board is bisected by the upper edge of the board. Gauss used this method to

---

[3] *J. Opt. Soc. Am.*, **36**, 110, 1946.

obtain sources of intense light for use in triangulation; these sources could be seen in the viewers of the measuring instruments at distances of up to 100 km (62 miles). Such a heliotrope (a form of the heliostat used in surveying) has a special sighting mechanism that enables the light beam to be directed accurately to any spot one wishes. When a heliotrope is fitted with a special spring device, which enables the mirror to be deflected, it can be used for morse signaling.

15. Reflections in a spherical mirror

The convex mirrors we were taught about at school are normally small and only slightly curved; they resemble arc AB of a spherical mirror shown in Fig. 15. Such a mirror is a very interesting object: in it we see the entire surface of the celestial sphere (more correctly, the sky and the earth) compressed in a small circle; in other words, it behaves as an optical instrument with an ideally large aperture. This is, of course, only possible because the images are distorted: they are compressed in the direction of the beam, and the more so the closer they are to the mirror. Suppose for simplicity's sake that both the object and the observer are a fairly long distance (compared with the radius R) away from the mirror. If the object makes an angle α with the line CE, its image lies at a distance $r = R\sin(\alpha/2)$ from the center, C, of the mirror. Note that r approaches R when α approaches 180°, which shows that indeed the whole of the earth and the sky are shown on the mirror. The only piece missing is that immediately behind the mirror and that becomes smaller the farther away we are from it.

Helmholtz once said that a scene distorted by a spherical mirror would become normal again if the standard used to measure the scene were similarly distorted. This piece of wisdom is akin to the fundamentals of the theory of relativity.

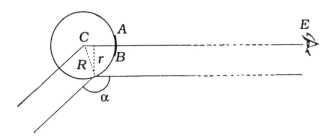

Fig. 15. How a spherical mirror reflects the universe.

The reflection of clouds in the water is clearer than the clouds in the sky. (Photo by Arja Kyröläinen)

A spherical mirror may be used for the most interesting observations in the area of meteorological optics because it gives such a good view of a large part of the sky. If you have the opportunity, stand a few meters away from such a mirror so that your head covers the image of the sun and you will see with exceptional clarity: rings, halos, iridescent clouds, Bishop's ring, the colors at twilight, the separation of brightness across the sky, Haidinger's brush, and the polarization of the light from the sky. These phenomena will also be discussed in later sections. Because of the reduction of the image, the slowly changing tints are transformed into much stronger gradients, so that the differences in brightness and color are far more pronounced. I have often seen the reflection of wispy clouds in the shining (convex) surface of my bicycle bell that I had not noticed by direct observation.

On a smaller scale, the same reflections may be seen in one of those beautiful Christmas-tree balls.

16. Reflections in and on soap bubbles

Try blowing soap bubbles in the open air in a well-sheltered position when there is little or no wind: reflections from the delicate spherical surfaces are then at their best. The side turned toward us acts as a convex mirror and shows the same upright images as the spherical mirror, more curved and compressed the closer they are to the edges. At the same time, we look through the front of the bubble at the inside back which acts as a concave mirror and inverts the images. The upright and inverted images are virtually the same size; they cover each other and we might confuse them were it not that the upright one is closer to our eyes. The upright image floats $r/2$ in front of the center of the bubble, and the inverted one $r/2$ behind it (at least as far as the central parts of the scene are concerned).

Note particularly the double reflection of the clear sky; the silhouette of your head, which is dark against a light background; the peculiarly distorted roofline of the houses; the greatly magnified image of your hand that holds the pipe from which the bubble is suspended (clearer on the concave side); the reflection of the point where the bubble is connected to the pipe (only on the concave side); and the outstanding clearness of the clouds that are so indeterminately hazy in the sky. But also enjoy the magnificent shades of color, the changing tints that become richer and richer ... until the bubble bursts. They arise through interference: they are the famous colors of Newton (§ 177).

17. Irregularities of a water surface

Imagine a pool of water in a hollow in the dunes on a windstill day when the water is unruffled. Here and there a stalk of grass or a reed sticks out of the water. The stalk acts as a capillary so that the surface tension of the water causes it to heap up around the stalk: the mound of water so formed reflects the sunlight so that it can be seen from a long way off. If one part of the pool reflects a nearby dark slope of a dune and the other the bright sky, you can see how, near

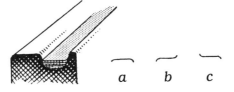

Fig. 16. Rainwater in a tram-rail forms a curved mirror.

a b c

the dividing line, those tiny mounds of water show up light or dark depending on the direction in which you are looking.

In a similar way you can detect eddies anywhere where a river has a current worth mentioning. Inside each eddy (diameter typically 4 cm— 1.5 in) the tension is a little less and its surface is slightly hollowed out to a depth of a few mm. In the vicinity of the boundary between light and dark reflections, you can see clearly even the tiniest eddies. This is an application of natural 'schlieren'.

When it has been raining, water lies along the rails of a tram and you can see a horizontal cross-line, e.g. the wire supporting the over-head trolley cable, reflected in it. If you look along the vertical plane of the rail, you will see that the reflection is symmetrically distorted— see Fig. 16: clear evidence that the water surface is curved and forms a capillary meniscus. If we stand to the left of the rail, the image is distorted as in Fig. 16b; if we stand to the right, as in Fig 16c.

Consider why the reflection assumes this shape.

Images reflected by a curved water surface may be studied with great effect from on board a powered boat, because all along you are looking from the same position and in the same direction at the waves moving along with it. Note especially how the reflections are immediately distorted by the first bow waves. The images are strongly compressed: they are upright or inverted according to whether they are formed by a convex or a concave part of the surface.

18. Window glass and plate glass

The reflections from windows indicate whether they are of normal window glass or plate glass: if the latter, the images are fairly clear; if the former, they are so irregular that the unevenesses of the glass can be seen clearly.

It is remarkable how different even in this respect houses in well-to-do suburbs are from those in the city center! Right in the middle of a row of houses with plate-glass windows we notice one with window glass. We can see that two adjacent plate-glass windows are not in the same plane, because their reflections of a line of roofs are shifted with respect to each other. Somewhere else we see that an otherwise perfect plate-glass window has a flaw in one of its corners; yet another one is ever so slightly, but unmistakably, curved.

19. The poor traffic mirror

Traffic mirrors are often fitted at dangerous bends or exits. Invariably they are of very poor quality; at night they distort, stretch, and shift reflections of streetlights. The surprising thing is that close by, the

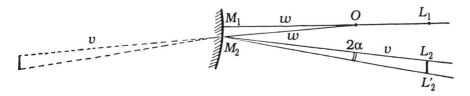

Fig. 17. Distortion of images caused by a poor mirror.

same mirror does not look too bad. It is instructive to look at it from close quarters and from afar. The explanation is that an object is reflected by only a small part of the mirror when you are close to it, but by a large part when you are standing some distance away. The larger the part, the more it becomes noticeable that the mirror is not smooth. A simple calculation with the aid of Fig. 17 makes this clearer.

Observer O at a distance w from the mirror sees object L_1 at a distance v from the mirror, reflected by surface M_1. An object L_2 next to it is reflected by M_2. If the surface of the mirror there is out of plane by an angle α, the light beam is deflected by an angle 2α and it appears as if the object is shifted by $L_2L_2' = 2\alpha v$. But the observer sees the reflection at a distance v behind the mirror, that is, at a distance $v+w$ from his eyes. This means he sees the shift as an angular deflection equal to $2\alpha v/(v+w)$. Now consider that α increases roughly in proportion to the distance $M_1M_2 = L_1L_2w/(v+w)$. The distortion is proportional to $L_1L_2vw/(v+w)^2$. The relative distortion is the elongation divided by the angle $v + w$ over which we would see the undistorted object, and is thus proportional to $vw/(v+w)$. All this appears to tally: at close quarters the distortions are negligible; at greater distances they reach a maximum when $v = w$, while the relative distortion continues to increase.

20. Irregular reflection by a slightly rippled surface[4]

To me, the long streaks of reflected light from streetlamps are inseparable from the quiet mood of the evening. I see the moon reflected in the sea in a broad stream of light. I recall the houses and churches of my birthplace reflected in the silent waters: every spot of light, every color stretched to a vertical line and all those lines, some long, some short, quivering in the changes of light and indescribable hues.

---

[4] Van Wieringen, *Proc. Acad. Amsterdam,* **50**, 952, 1947. Y. Le Grand, *Bull. Inst. Océanogr. Monaco,* No. 1002, 1952.

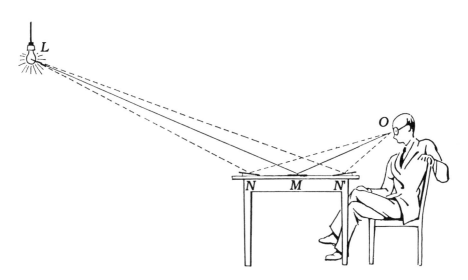

Fig. 18. Formation of a light column.

A chimney or a thin mast is reflected clearly, but the strong lines of the roofs have disappeared: only the vertical lines are found back in the reflections. Vertical trunks of trees are clearly recognizable, but those that lean over are much less so, while slanting branches have disappeared completely. The slender neck of a swan is reflected as a clear dab of light, but the body of the bird is lost in the movement of the water.

Observing a streetlight at night gives us the 'elementary phenomenon'; the landscape by day may be considered as being composed of a number of such spots of light, each of which is drawn to a vertical column in the reflection. In the case of an upright line, the columns are neatly stacked together and magnify each other; in the case of a horizontal line, they lie side by side and broaden the line to a hazy surface (compare Fig. 3).

The drawing out of a spot of light to a column directed toward our eyes, while the waves are wholly irregular and occur equally in all directions, is therefore the fundamental and intriguing phenomenon that must be explained. The moon or a streetlamp reflected in gently moving water nearby shows us that each wave gives a separate image. All lighted waves together form on average an elongated spot whose major axis lies in the vertical plane between eye and light source.

A simple experiment will make clear how the column of light comes into being (Fig. 18). Sit at a table on which a mirror is laid and shift this in such a way that it reflects the light from lamp L into your eyes and assume that it is then in position M. Then place a strip of card-

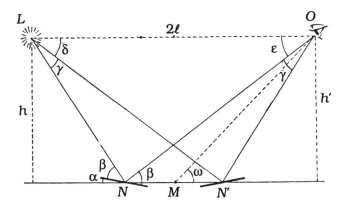

Fig. 19. How to compute the long axis of a light column.

board under one of the ends of the mirror to make it tilt toward you: it will then reflect objects higher than the lamp. To get the light of the lamp reflected into your eyes again, the mirror has to be moved to position N. If now the strip of cardboard is put under the other side of the mirror to make it tilt away from you, the mirror has to be moved to position N' to get the light back in your eyes. The mirror in those two positions resembles the wave; the distance NN' is the length of the column of light. There will be a number of positions between N and N' where the slope is not sufficient to reflect the light into your eyes.

To be correct, therefore, one should consider and compute the average distribution of the intensity of light over a path of this kind as

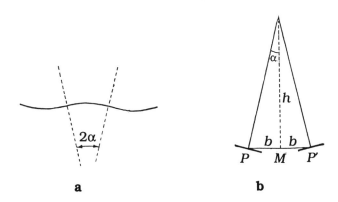

Fig. 20. How to compute the short axis of a light column **(b)**.

When the sun gets lower, its beam of light becomes narrower. This photo and the one on the opposite page also show that, when there is a light breeze, the beam of light straightens itself obliquely along the bank of the water. (Photo by Arja Kyröläinen)

a probability problem[5]. Let us therefore simplify things by assuming that the slopes of the waves do not exceed an angle α and find out only what are the boundaries of the patch of light formed in this way. Or, to express it in another way: if at each location there are a large number of little waves sloping at an angle α, but in all directions of the compass, what is the locus of the waves that will be illuminated? Even when stated like this, the problem is complicated enough.

1. The simplest case: $h = h'$; observer and source of light are at equal heights above the water (see Fig. 19). A small horizontal mirror throws light in the eye of observer O when it is exactly halfway, at M, the place of regular reflection. A small mirror inclined at angle α must be shifted a little from the midpoint if it is to send light to the observer. How far?

---

[5] Cox and Munk, *J. Opt. Soc. Am.*, **44**, 838, 1954.

(Photo by
Arja Kyröläinen)

For a shift in the vertical plane through eye and light source, this question is easily answered. Call the required position N if the mirror slants in the one direction and N' if it slants in the other. For reasons of symmetry, $MN = MN'$. Now consider the angles:

$$\beta + \alpha = \gamma + \delta \quad \text{and} \quad \beta - \alpha = \varepsilon = \delta.$$

Thus

$$\gamma = \alpha + \beta - (\beta - \alpha) = 2\alpha.$$

This is an important result. The angle subtended at the eye by the longest axis of the patch of light is equal to the angle between the two largest inclinations of the wavelets (see Fig. 20a).

Let us now shift the mirror in the plane through M, perpendicular to the line connecting eye to light source and call P, P' the points where the favorable reflection occurs (see Fig. 20b).

Obviously, $MP = MP' = h \tan\alpha$. The width of the patch of light is therefore $2h \tan\alpha$, and the short axis subtends at the eye the angle

$$PP'/OM = 2h \tan\alpha/\sqrt{(l^2 + h^2)}.$$

The ratio of the apparent axes of the patch of light is therefore

$$h \tan\alpha/\alpha\sqrt{(h^2 + l^2)},$$

or about

$$h/\sqrt{(h^2 + l^2)} = \sin\omega$$

if the patch is not too large. Therefore, when we look down at the water from a hill, the patch is only slightly oblong (ω large, $\sin\omega$ nearly 1). The more obliquely we look across the water, the more oblong the patch. If we let our glance graze the surface, it becomes infinitely narrow.

We must always distinguish the 'primary oval', the curve that can be imagined as being drawn on the rippling water, indicating the boundary of the patch of light, from the 'secondary oval', which arises from the former by projection on the plane at right angles to the direction of our gaze. The axes of the primary oval may simply be calculated, but the entire figure is a complicated curve of the sixth degree, symmetrical with respect to M. The secondary oval becomes slightly asymmetrical; the greatest width lies in reality more toward us than the point M at which we calculated the cross-axis. This asymmetry is particularly noticeable when we look at the surface at a small angle.

2. The general case: $h \neq h'$ (Fig. 21).

By similar arguments we can prove the two fundamental properties

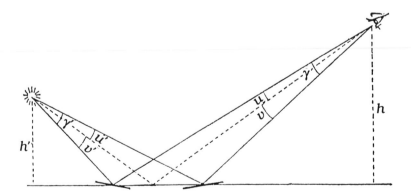

Fig. 21. Observation of a light column from a height different from that of the light source.

$$u + v' = 2\alpha \quad \text{and} \quad u' + v = 2\alpha.$$

Hence

$$u + v + u' + v' = \gamma + \gamma' = 4\alpha.$$

Further computation proves that the patch remains more or less elliptical in outline, but the results are complicated. Practically speaking, the difference in height between h and h' influences only the dimension of the patch of light, not its proportions; approximately,

$$\gamma/\gamma' = h'/h$$

so that

$$\gamma = 4\alpha\, h'/(h + h').$$

3. Special case: $h' = \infty$. This holds for the sun, the moon, and very high lights.

The formulas are now $\gamma = 4\alpha$ and $PP' = 2h \tan 2\alpha$ (as can be proved). The axes of the oval subtend at the eye angles of about 4α and $4\alpha \sin\omega$. The ratio of the apparent length to the breadth of the light path is therefore $\sin\omega$, precisely the same as in Case 1, except that *all the dimensions are twice as large.*

Let us sum up the results of our calculations from the point of view of a practical observer. First, if we suppose ourselves to be at the same height above the water as the light source, the angle subtended by the longer axis of the patch is at the same time the angle 2α between the two steepest slopes of the wavelets (Fig. 19). Relative to this, the transverse axis of the patch is smaller the more obliquely we look at the surface of the water. Second, if the source is higher above the water than our eye, all the dimensions of the light patch become larger (in angular measure); they approach twice what they were originally if the source recedes to infinity. However, the ratio between the long and short axes remains about the same.

Compare the patch of light formed by the moon with that of a lamp whose reflection lies more or less in the same direction. The light patches are generally larger the farther away they are from the light source. Objects quite close to the water give an almost pointlike, not elongated, image. Compare the patches of light seen at different angles with the water's surface.

Determine angle 2α from the length (in angular measure) of the patches at various strengths of the wind.

A general idea of the distribution of light in these reflections is obtained without computation by the following argument (Fig. 22). Imagine the reflecting

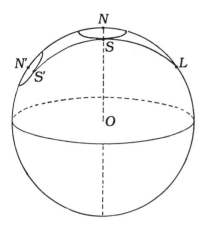

Fig. 22. Origins of light columns illustrated by a construction on a spherical mirror.

surfaces on a very small scale to be close to the center of a large sphere; the normal to the undisturbed surface of the water ends at N; the normals to the slanting sides of the wavelets end therefore in a small circle at angular distance α from N; the light source at infinity is represented by point L on the sphere. To find how, for example, the surface with normal OS reflects the rays, it suffices to draw the arc of the large circle LS, and to extend it to S', so that $SS' = SL$. This shows at once that the rays reflected by all the wavelets form a cone with an oval cross section, which becomes more oblong the more obliquely we look at the water's surface. It is also easily understood why the cone formed by the directions of the gaze of the observer, that is, from the eye to the boundaries of the light path, has the same shape.

Notice how beautifully long, regular, and vertical the light patches are when it rains; the waves, though small, slant sharply.

There is still one more peculiarity in perspective connected with these patches of light. Each patch always lies in the vertical plane through my eye and the light source (for exceptions, see § 22). When I am drawing or painting, I project everything on to a vertical plane in front of me, and for this reason every patch of light is bound to run in a vertical direction, even when outside the center of the scene.

In a painting by Claude in the Uffizi the sun is close to the side of the canvas, and the painter has represented a column of light which falls obliquely from the sun to the middle of the foreground. But this is wrong!

21. Detailed examination of light columns

It is also worth while watching the shapes of the reflections on each separate wavelet. Each wavelet bears a spot of light, spread out in a

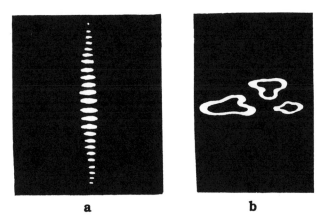

a   b

Fig. 23. (a) light column on gently undulating water; (b) reflection of advertizing lights as closed coils.

horizontal direction, which is reduced more and more to a small line as the sun sinks lower; and all these little lines together form the vertical column as shown in Fig. 23a. At the end directed toward us we see how the column sometimes gets longer, sometimes shorter, depending on the rippling of the water. At the other end, however, the spots of light tend to merge.

Remarkable is the appearance of *closed coils of light* (Fig. 23b), seen when the water surges gently, the waves have short crests, and the light source is high (for instance, a neon-light advertisement).

When you then look at the water at a sufficiently large angle, you will see the light source L reflected by *two* separate spots of light on each wavelet, for instance, one at the crest and the other at the trough of the wavelet: in general, at two points S_1 and S_2 where the

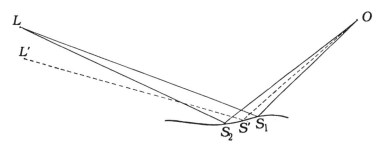

Fig. 24. Origin of closed coils in the reflection of a point of light.

Light coils on gently undulating water. (Photo by Pekka Parviainen)

tangents have the correct angle—see Fig. 24. In between, say at S', the slope of the wavelet is steeper and you will see the reflection of a lower, unilluminated, point L'.

The associated reflections, S_1 and S_2, are always in the same plane of the wavelet, of course. When you look slightly to the left or right,

Fig. 25a. A strange sight: the light column does not lie in the vertical plane through eye and light source!

you will see the reflections getting closer and closer together until they fuse into one closed coil whereby an irregular annulus is formed. After all, the wavelets not only have a given wavelength, but also a certain crest length; when two crests merge, the tangent is horizontal. But before that, a point must have been reached where the slope was still steep enough to reflect the light source to our eyes: at that point, S_1 and S_2 coincide.

Conversely, a thin object outlined darkly against the background of the sky may be reflected as a series of twisting dark rings: the bow of a ship or a ridge of hills in the distance.

In the wavelets closest to you, you see the reflections twisted and distorted, moving to and fro in the oddest manner; masts, poles, the dark vertical outlines of a ship's hull all change into capricious kinks, knots, and coils.

22. Reflection from the rippled surface of a stretch of water with preferred direction

Columns of light frequently show distinct asymmetry: when you look obliquely at a light across a canal, say, toward the right, *they no longer lie in the vertical plane through your eye and the source of light,* but are inclined toward the direction of the canal, that is, to the right (Fig. 25a).

If you look obliquely at a light toward the left, the columns are again inclined toward the direction of the canal, that is, to the left.

And yet, our theory is not wrong, for if it rains and there is no wind, the columns are perfectly vertical in whichever direction you

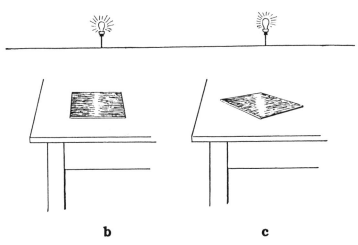

b   **c**

Fig. 25b, c. How to form leaning light columns.

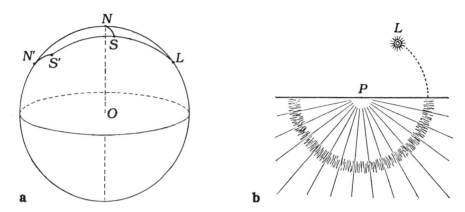

Fig. 26. (a) How leaning light columns arise when the waves have a preferred direction; (b) light columns on directed waves.

look. The cause of the deviations is the wind, which shows a preference for blowing ripples across the direction of the canal, so that we can no longer take the ideally irregular wave formation as our starting point. The following observations may serve to prove this:

(a) In a *very* wide river, the direction is much less systematic, the waves do not show a predominating direction at right angles to the banks.
(b) When the water is covered by a layer of ice, it appears that this layer has a lot of little lumps and gives a distinct patch of light, which, however, is vertical.
(c) On a Tarmac road, wet after a shower, the same deviations as those on a canal in windy weather can be observed in the reflections of street lights or the headlights of a car. In fact, irregularities are caused in the asphalt by the traffic (how they arise is in itself an interesting phenomenon!); if we examine the surface we can see these roughnesses at once, and notice that they are just like real waves, with their crests at right angles to the direction of the road.

The phenomenon may be observed indoors by lightly greasing a sheet of glass with Vaseline, using parallel strokes (see Fig. 25a), and placing this on a table (greased side up). The light of a lamp that is not too high above the table will then be reflected as a column. When the glass is shifted by 45°, the column leans only a little, perhaps about 10°. Only when the glass is shifted even more will the column tend to coincide with the normal to the Vaseline ripples again.

A detailed treatment of this subject has not yet been given, but we can get some idea of its main features with the aid of our projection on the sphere, at least for the case of a light source at infinite distance (Fig. 26). If the normals are distributed over the planes as represented by the curved line surrounding N, the mirrored rays will be directed toward the various points of the curved line around L'; the axis of the column, therefore, no longer lies in the plane LNN', but deviates sideways.

If the normals lie on the arc NS, the reflected rays will be directed toward the individual points of the curved line $N'S'$; the axis of the column, therefore, no longer lies in the plane LNN', but deviates sideways[6].

The geometry becomes clear from the following reasoning. All rays that are reflected by one wave form the surface of a cone whose axis is the crest of the wave. Conversely, the eye, taking in the extended field of the parallel waves, sees all points of light on the surface of the cone whose axis is the horizontal line through the eyes and which is parallel to the wave crests directed at a point, P, on the horizon where they appear to converge—see Fig. 26b. If you imagine the arc of light completed to a circle, the light source itself lies on that circle. At each point you will see the column of light at right angles to the waves (and both projected at right angles to the direction of observation).

23. Reflection from large rippled surfaces of water

Reflection in a mildly choppy sea is accompanied by a phenomenon that we shall call 'the shifting of reflected images toward the horizon' (Fig. 27). The reflection $A'B'$ of the boundary AB between cloud and blue sky lies much closer to the horizon than does the boundary itself. The first 25° or 35° of the sky above the horizon are, however, hardly visible in the reflection. All the images are, of course, formed irregularly, but the effect is very clear all the same, and so striking that it dominates the entire distribution of light on the sea. This explains why one never sees trees, dunes, etc., on the coast reflected in the sea: they are not high enough. Ships, too, are hardly ever seen in these circumstances, as the dark spot they ought to produce is forced, by this effect, close back to the ship.

The reflection of the sun in the waves is a dazzlingly bright patch, which, as the sun sets, is more or less triangular in shape, showing the shift toward the horizon (Fig. 28).

These phenomena are easily explained: at a great distance we can see only the sides of the waves turned toward us. This makes it seem as if we see all the objects in the sky reflected in a slanting mirror (Fig. 29).

---

[6] Van Wieringen, *Proc. Acad. Amsterdam*, **50**, 952, 1947.

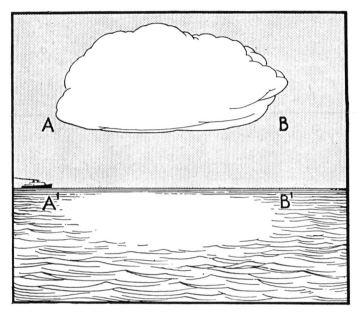

Fig. 27. Reflections at sea: the image of the cloud is shifted toward the horizon.

Fig. 28. Sunlight over the sea.

Fig. 29. Explanation of the shifted images: the beam of light enters at a fairly large angle, but is reflected at a smaller one.

This accounts for the shifting of the reflections toward the horizon. It follows from the disappearance of the lowest 30° or so in the reflection that the waves show average slopes of about 15° in each direction (if the sea is neither calm nor rough).

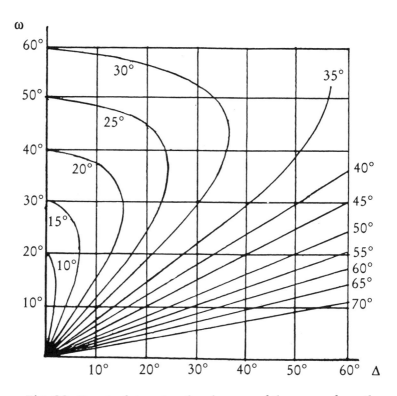

Fig. 30. How to determine the slopes α of the waves from the width Δ of the light column at the horizon. For each observed value of ω and Δ, there is a certain point: judge the position of this with respect to the curves, each of which corresponds to a certain value of α.

Fig. 31. Can the curvature of the earth be observed in the reflection of the rising sun in a calm sea?

Why was this phenomenon not mentioned in our theory in § 20? Because we were not considering the case where $\omega < 2\alpha$, that is, where we look very obliquely across the surface of the water. This case, for which our calculations do not hold, occurs whenever the surface of the water is very wide, and especially where the sea is concerned. The calmer the surface, the more obliquely one has to look.

You can see at once whether this condition is fulfilled on gazing at the sunlit sea: the pathlike patch of light then reaches the horizon. We can no longer measure the inclinations of the waves from the length of the light column, but must apply another method; if the inclinations of the waves get steeper, an increasingly broader part of the horizon is covered by sparkling light.

Measure this angle Δ, which is the breadth of the patch on the horizon; measure also the height of the sun ω and determine from this the inclination α of the waves with the help of the graph in Fig. 30, or with Spooner's formula, simplified for when the sun is below 15°:

$$\alpha = \Delta 2\omega \text{ radians (1 radian} = 57.3°).$$

In a very calm sea, the rising and the setting sun show an almost linear reflection, which merges into the fiery disk of the sun and forms a kind of Ω (Fig. 31). Sometimes, when the sea is exceptionally calm, the elliptical reflection can still be seen when the sun is as much as 1° above the horizon, but usually the transition into the triangular spot of light mentioned earlier is soon visible. In such cases, the influence of the curvature of the earth's surface also comes into play; if there were no waves at all, one might say that the roundness of the earth was directly observable. In the most favorable case hitherto investigated, however, the observed shifting toward the horizon still remains twice as large as might be expected from the curvature of the earth.

24. Visibility of very slight undulations

Very slight undulations can be seen better by looking at the crests of the waves at right angles than by observing them in a direction parallel to themselves. Therefore, to see how the wind makes the water ripple on a canal, one must as a rule look in the direction parallel to the canal. This explains, too, why the magnificent cross-waves behind a ship can be observed from the bridge, while they are practically invisible from the shore. The explanation of this is the same as that of the elongation of the image of a lamp into a column of light. If you look at the waves at right angles, you can see, so to speak, the long axis of the patch of light; if you look at them in a parallel direction, the short axis is seen. It amounts to this: a wave causes a greater deviation in the direction at right angles to its crest line than in the direction parallel to it.

25. Pillars of light on the surface of dirty water

Even when the surface of water is as smooth as glass, you can often see columns of light around the reflections of streetlights at night. These plumes of light do not show the lovely sparkles of columns of light on waves; they are perfectly calm and motionless. They occur everywhere where the surface is not quite clean; evidently, the small particles of dust on the water form so many minute irregularities on its surface that optically they act as wavelets. You would expect to see these columns grow thinner the more obliquely you look at the surface, and indeed this turns out to be so.

At more or less vertical incidence, the light patches can hardly be seen; at grazing incidence they are very noticeable and give a clear indication of the presence of dust on the surface. The difference in intensity is so striking that there must be some special cause. The particles are so small that we are justified in speaking of the *scattering* of light, and we shall see later that the scattering by such particles is by far the strongest in the neighborhood of the direction of the incident beam of light (§ 194). This explains, no doubt, why the scattering and the whole patch get stronger and stronger the more obliquely you look.

26. Columns of light on snow

Sometimes snow is covered with a layer of beautiful, small flat disks and stars, all more or less horizontal. If you look for the reflection of the low-lying sun in the layer of snow, you will see a beautiful column of light that must be ascribed to small irregular deviations of the snow disks from the horizontal plane. The sun must be low at the time, because then the column of light contracts laterally and becomes more distinct.

The formation of pillars of light is still more striking at night when the streetlights are on and each light is reflected in the fresh snow.

27. Pillars of light on roadways

Columns of light similar to those seen on undulating water also appear on roads, most clearly when it has been raining and everything is wet and shining. They are splendid not only on modern roads, but also on old-fashioned cobbled and gravel roads. Even without rain, roads often reflect so well that paths of light can be seen almost always, if only you look at them *obliquely enough* (cf. § 22).

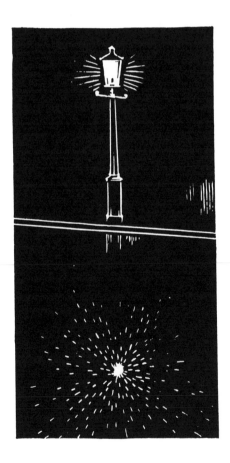

Fig. 32. Raindrops draw fiery sparks around the reflection of a streetlight.

28. Reflections during rain

When you look at the reflection of a streetlight in a puddle at night when it is raining, you will notice that it is surrounded by a lot of sparkles arising wherever a drop of rain has fallen, and that all of them look like small *lines of light radiating from the reflection* (Fig. 32). Forel noticed a similar phenomenon when he looked through dark glasses at the sun's image reflected in calm water, in which air bubbles rose here and there.

The explanation is that each drop makes a set of concentric wavelets, and the reflections from their sides must always lie on the line connecting the center of the waves and the image of the light source (Fig. 33). This may be seen at once when the source *L* and the eye *E* are at the same height above the surface of the water, and drop *D* falls at an equal distance from both of them. The points D_1 and D_2 lie on the line *MD*; if a wavelet expands in a circle around *D*, the reflected light travels over part of the line *DM*, and does this so rapidly as to make us think we see a line of light. The theory is equally obvious when the drop of rain falls in the plane *EML*, either in front of, or behind, *M*.

This phenomenon can be reproduced if, over a glass plate in which a light is reflected, you move an object that is concentrically ribbed, such as the lid of a sugar bowl or a disk of brass ground on a lathe.

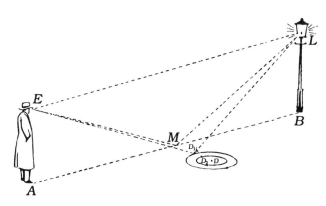

Fig. 33. How sparkles arise around the reflection.

29. Circles of light in treetops

At night, when a streetlight shines just behind a tree, you may see that the light is reflected here and there by the twigs; these shining

A streetlight behind a tree causes circles of light on the branches around the lamp. (Photo by Veikko Mäkelä)

patches are in reality shorter or longer lines of light, and all these lines lie in concentric circles round the light source.

The best way to see this phenomenon is to stand in the shadow of the tree trunk if the light is quite close to the tree. But it may be seen in sunlight, too, if, for instance, the branches are wet after rain, when the glistening twigs form a delicate pattern of dancing lines against a dark background. To prevent your being dazzled, the sun should be screened off by a wall or roof. The effect of glazed frost is also exceptionally beautiful.

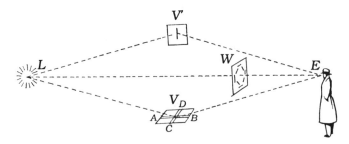

Fig. 34. How circles of light arise in treetops. The plane *ELV* is vertical.

This is explained as follows (Fig. 34): consider a small plane *V* that reflects the light toward your eyes. You will see all the little branches in that plane glisten. But, owing to perspective, you will see branches like *AB* greatly shortened, whereas those like *CD* show their full length. Since there are as many branches to be found in either direction, you will see light lines mainly at right angles to the plane *ELV*. A similar statement is true for other small planes like *V'*, which are seen above, to the right or left, of the light source. In this way you get the impression of concentric circles. It is easily seen that the effect of the direction is accentuated the smaller the angle your line of sight makes with the line *EL*, and that the effect will be slightly greater if the source is at infinity, like the sun, than if it is a light close to you.

A similar phenomenon can also be observed when you see the setting sun shining on a cornfield, or in misty weather when the cobwebs are sprinkled with little drops of dew, and when you look at a streetlight through one of these cobwebs. The scratches on the windows of a train show the same effect (cf. § 182). In all these cases, it is mainly the little lines at right angles to the plane of incidence of the light that glisten, so that you get the impression of concentric circles round the source of light.

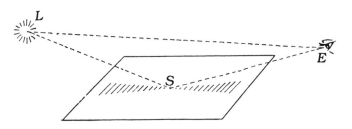

Fig. 35. Compare the circles of light in treetops with a light column on undulating water.

Columns of light on undulating water are a simplification of this (Fig. 35). Imagine that the branches here do not appear everywhere in space and in all directions, but only in the horizontal plane, *S* (the surface of the water). The only lines lying in this plane and yet roughly forming part of concentric circles round *EL* lie, each of them, at right angles to the plane *ESL*, but together form a column of light in this plane. This is entirely analogous to the case of the water wavelets.

(Photo by Veikko Mäkelä)

Chapter 3
Refraction of Light

30. Refraction of light when it passes from air into water

The pole used by the boatman to push his boat along looks as if it were broken just where it enters the water; this impression is caused by the fact that rays of light bend when they go from the air into water, or vice versa. Notice, however, that this 'broken stick' by no means represents the image of the broken ray of light, for the latter is bent in just the opposite direction. The connection between the two is seen in Fig. 36.

Place a pole upright in clear water and mark it where its height above the surface appears to be the same as that under the surface. Upon measuring the two, you will find that the two lengths are quite different.

Gauge by eye the depth of an object under water and try to catch hold of it quickly. As a rule, you will miss it because, owing to the refraction of the light rays, the object seems to have been raised (cf. Fig. 36). It lies deeper than you thought. And yet, the phenomenon is not so simple as to be correctly described by stating that the refrac-

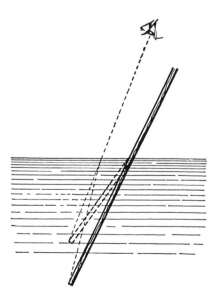

Fig. 36. Refraction of the rays of light makes the pole look bent.

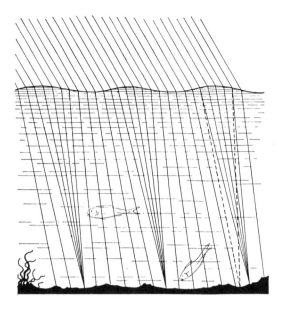

Fig. 37. Rays of sunlight penetrate the water and are collected into lines of light by the refraction of the wavelets. The blue rays (*dashed*) are refracted to a larger degree.

tion of the light replaces, as it were, an object by an image lying in a higher plane. When, for instance, you are walking or cycling along the side of a ditch in which the water is clear, you will see that the positions of plants under water seem to undergo a peculiar change; their displaced images keep moving and the more obliquely you look at them, the higher they are raised.

When the sun casts bright lines of light through the clear water on to the bottom of a shallow pool, or close to the banks of a river, the crests of the wavelets act as lenses and unite the rays of light into focal lines that move on slowly with the waves (Fig. 37). We have met a similar phenomenon in reflected light (§ 12) and now find its counterpart in refraction. When the rays are incident obliquely, the lines of light are edged with colors: blue toward the sun and reddish away from the sun, because blue rays are refracted more strongly than red ones. This is the phenomenon of dispersion or color shifting.

If you throw a white pebble into deep, transparent water and look at it from some distance, it will appear blue at the top and red underneath. This, too, is caused by color shifting.

31. Refraction by an undulating water surface

When a water surface is not perfectly smooth, this is revealed by a change in direction of broken rays of light and an uneven brightness at the bottom.

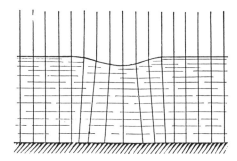

Fig. 38. Rays of light spread at the center and then close up concentrically.

Note the tiny eddies that move to and fro at the surface of little streams and ponds. Each eddy causes the surface to hollow out slightly and we can see how corresponding dark patches at the bottom move in unison. On closer inspection, it appears that each of these dark patches is surrounded by a border of light. Why this is so is clear from Fig. 38: the rays of light spread at the center and then close up concentrically.

Something similar is caused by the shadow of water boatmen, and pond skaters, tiny insects darting across the surface of water carried on the capillary boundary. Each of their legs causes a little dent in the water surface and, however tiny the dent may be, a shadowy image is caused on the bottom: six dark flecks with faint aureoles.

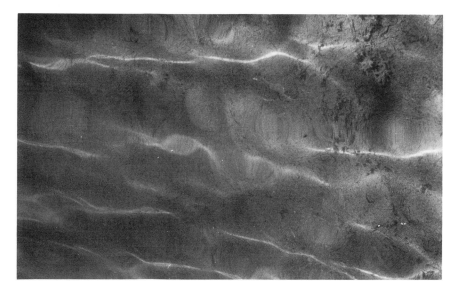

Light is refracted at the surface of the water and forms stripes on the sandy bed. (Photo by Pekka Parviainen)

Another form of surface occurs at the edge of floating leaves, like those of the water lily, where the water creeps up the curled-up edge of the leaves through capillary action. Irregular flecks of light occur within the shadows (cf. § 73); this makes the shadows look like those of palm leaves.

32. Refraction through uneven panes of glass

Windows of poor glass in older houses deform the images of the landscape. If the sun shines through such a window on to a sheet of paper, bright and dark streaks will be seen on the paper. If you move the paper farther away from the window, each streak will become a fairly sharp line of light.

The window pane is evidently not a parallel plate, but has thinner and thicker parts that act as irregular lenses, spreading out or collecting the rays of light and giving fanciful focal lines (cf. § 30). Even small deviations of the rays cause appreciable differences in brightness, so that virtually every window of standard glass exhibits the streaks.

Although windows of plate glass are much purer, even they show streaks at a distance: you can often see in what direction the glass was rolled during manufacture.

The streaks become very noticeable when rays of sunlight fall through a small opening in dense foliage to form an image of the sun (see § 1) that then falls through the window. This is because the beam of light is highly directional: the slightest deviation of the rays is immediately visible.

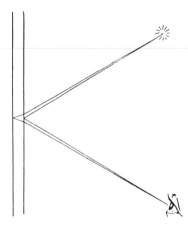

Fig. 39. A sheet of absolutely parallel plate glass produces double images, but these lie very close together.

33. Double images reflected by plate glass

Look at a distant lamp or the image of the moon reflected in a window along the road. You will see two images, one moving irregularly
in relation to the other according to whether the reflection falls on
one or another part of the pane. A 'philosopher' once stated that this
was a case of effect without cause. Physicists, however, must see if
they can discover a cause!

Notice that the beautifully polished slabs of black glass adorning
parts of some shops and offices do not show double images. It is
clear, then, that one image is reflected by the front surface of the
plate glass, and that the other is formed by the rays that have penetrated the glass and are reflected by the back surface, reaching our
eye through the glass. In the case of black glass, the rays of the second image are absorbed.

Refraction causes a slight deviation in the direction of one of the
rays—see Fig. 39. Can this be the cause of the double images? No,
because in that case (a) they would not draw so much closer to each
other on some parts of the same pane than on others; (b) they would
not lie farther apart than the thickness of the glass, which would hardly
be observable; (c) the shifting or displacement would be zero for very
small and very large angles of incidence (with a maximum near 50°,
as can be easily computed), while in the case of normal incidence we
also observe double images; (d) for a source of light at infinity, such
as the moon, the distance of the double images would always be
zero.

The conclusion is that *a plane parallel glass plate cannot produce
double images of this kind. If, however, the pane of glass should be at
all wedge-shaped, they may occur*, owing to the surfaces being slightly
undulating. But before we can feel quite satisfied with this explana-

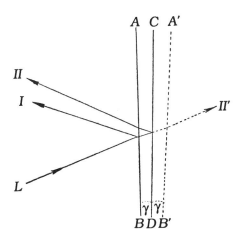

Fig. 40. How double images arise
from a window pane that is not
of uniform thickness.

tion, we must first calculate how large the angle must be between the front and the back surfaces to account for the distance observed between the double images, for it is not likely that, in good plate glass, the deviations from the parallel would be large.

Suppose first that the planes are parallel, and then follow one ray after it is divided; the two reflected rays are still parallel, only slightly shifted relative to each other.

Now let the face AB be inclined at a small angle γ as in Fig. 40. Ray I will then have turned through an angle 2γ. To follow ray II on its path, imagine CD to be a mirror, giving a reflected image of AB at $A'B'$, and an image of ray II along II'. Notice that the ray $L\,II'$ has passed through the small prism $ABB'A'$, with the small refracting angle 2γ. Geometrical optics teaches us that such a prism causes an angular deflection $(n-1)\,2\gamma$ in the path of the ray, provided the angle of incidence is not too large. The total angle between I and II is therefore $2\gamma+(n-1)2\gamma$. In the case of glass, the refractive index $n = 1.52$, so that the angle in question amounts to about 3γ.

Figure 41 shows what follows from this when a person at E looks at the source L when it is very far away; the two rays I and II arising from that distant source, in, practically speaking, parallel directions, enter the observer's eye at an angle 3γ. A proof on different lines is given in § 34.

From this, it may be concluded that if the angular distance between the two reflections is estimated, *the angle between the two glass surfaces is one-third of that amount.* The estimate may be made, for instance, by determining the distance a of the reflected images on the glass, dividing this by the distance R between eye and glass and multiplying by $\cos i$.

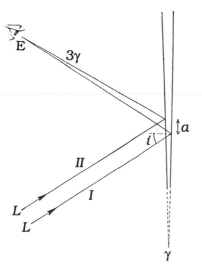

Fig. 41. Determining the wedge shape of a sheet of plate glass from the angle 3γ between the two images.

The angles obtained in this way amount, in ordinary plate glass, to a few thousandths of a radian (see § 1) or a few minutes of arc. Thus, the thickness of the pane changes over a length of, say, 12.5 cm (5 in) only 0.25 mm ($1/100$ in). This is so slight that, but for careful measurements of the thickness, we would not notice it at all. When these measurements were actually carried out, the above estimate was confirmed.

Is it not splendid to be able to evaluate such extremely minute faults in the glass without any further auxiliary means, simply as you walk along? And, moreover, you have seen now that our explanation of the double image is indeed correct. Whenever we are unable to find the cause of any natural phenomenon, it is our own ignorance that is to blame!

A more general and more accurate formula for the angular distance between the two images is $2m\gamma R'/(R+R')$, where R' is the distance from light source to glass, R is the distance from eye to glass, and $2m$ has the following values:

Angle of incidence $i =$	0°	20°	40°	60°	80°	90°
$2m =$	3.0	3.1	3.6	5.0	13.3	∞

It has been assumed so far that the incident ray lies in the plane V, which is perpendicular to the refracting edge of prism γ formed by the two planes of the pane. At a given wedge shape and a given angle of incidence i the angular distance between the two images is then a maximum. In general, the plane of incidence will form an angle ϕ with the plane V and the angular distance between the images becomes $\cos\phi$ times the above calculated amount.

Ordinary window panes cannot be used for the investigation of multiple images because they distort them very badly owing to their uneven surfaces; the method is too sensitive.

34. Multiple images shown by plate glass in transmitted light

One evening, look sideways through a *good-quality* window in a train or car at a distant light or the moon. You will see various images at pretty well equal distances apart, the first one quite clearly, the following ones fainter and fainter; the more obliquely you look through the window, the greater their distances become and the less they differ in brightness from one another.

It is clear that phenomena of this kind arise from repeated reflections from the front and back of the glass. They really resemble very closely the phenomenon of the doubly reflected images, and we have the same reasons for believing that the front and back surfaces are

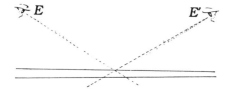

Fig. 42. The brightest of the multiple images is always on the same side as the observer (in this case at the right).

not parallel. But there is an additional reason: *in a parallel plane, the brightest image would necessarily always lie on the side nearest to the observer*, no matter whether you look through the pane in the directions from *E* or from *E'*; experiment, however, teaches us that *the brightest image lies invariably on the same side* (always to the right or always to the left), so long as you look through one definite point of the pane—see Fig. 42. But in one and the same pane, parts can be found where the brightest image lies to the right, and other parts, where it lies to the left: in the first case, there is a wedge-shaped region of which the greatest thickness is turned toward your eye; in the second case, the greatest thickness is turned away from your eye.

Let us compute the angular distance in a way slightly different from that in § 33. From Fig. 43, we see that the angles at which the rays L_1, L_2, L_3, ... emerge from the back surface are $r+\gamma$, $r+3\gamma$, $r+5\gamma$, ... Now,

$$\sin\alpha_1 = n\sin(r+\gamma),$$

or, since γ is a small angle,

$$\sin\alpha_1 = n\sin r + \gamma n\cos r.$$

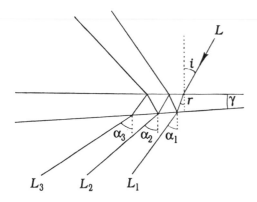

Fig. 43. Multiple images in transmitted light.

Similarly,

$$\sin\alpha_2 = n\sin r + 3\gamma n\cos r.$$

Subtracting,

$$\sin\alpha_2 - \sin\alpha_1 = 2\gamma n\cos r.$$

Now, α increases only slightly, so we may put $(\sin\alpha_2 - \sin\alpha_1)$ equal to the differential of $\sin\alpha$, that is,

$$\sin\alpha_2 - \sin\alpha_1 = \delta(\sin\alpha)$$

$$= \cos\alpha\,\delta\alpha$$

$$= \cos\alpha(\alpha_2 - \alpha_1),$$

so that

$$\alpha_2 - \alpha_1 = \gamma(2n\cos r)/\cos\alpha.$$

Using Fig. 43, a similar argument would also hold for the images formed by multiple reflections. The distances between the successive images are exactly the same, whether you observe them in reflected or in transmitted light; the factor by which γ is multiplied is, in fact, the same as the one denoted by $2m$ in § 33, where its values are given.

35. Reflection of crowns of trees in plate glass

The foliage of a tree reflected by a wedge-shaped plate-glass window has an odd stripelike appearance. Now we have seen how each point of light has a double image, we can understand that all leaves, all spaces in the crown of the tree, have a double image and that all these double images have been shifted into the same direction, at least within a certain portion of the window. The direction of the stripes is determined by those whose front and rear areas are tilted toward one another the most (that is, the area V, mentioned toward the end of § 33).

Compare this observation with the following simple test, which you can conduct with any fairly thick mirror. Sprinkle drops of water over the mirror and you will see a stripelike pattern, but this time the stripes originate at the same point: the reflection of your eye. In this case, the displacement of the two images is determined primarily by the thickness of the glass: the reflection of each droplet is

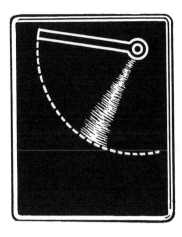

Fig. 44. Light column in the tracks of a windscreen wiper.

shifted into the direction of the area of incidence. The shift is the greater the larger the angle from which you look at the droplet, whence the characteristic irradiation.

36. Tracks of a windscreen wiper

Windscreen wipers cause numerous concentric segments of circles on the windscreen of a car or boat and these refract the light of the sun when it is low or of a streetlight at night. You then see a column of light emanating from the center of rotation and pointed at the sun or streetlight. This column is really part of a hyperbole, but it appears straight over the small distance we see it. The theory of this phenomenon is the same as that of the reflections of light in rainbows (§ 28). It does not matter whether the rays of light are bent by reflection or refraction: the important thing is that in both cases they remain within the plane of incidence.

Nevertheless, there is something interesting and special about this. If you alternately close your left and right eye, you will notice that the column points into a slightly different direction for both eyes. This, of course, is because your left eye sees the sun through a different point of the windscreen from your right eye. If you look with both eyes open, these two slightly different impressions merge into a spatial view. You will see a beam of light that points from the center of rotation obliquely rearward to the sun, or that comes forward at the opposite side. This is an example of stereoscopy, which we will meet again in § 125.

37. Drops of water as lenses

Raindrops on the windows of the compartment of a train or those of
a car produce very tiny images, just like a strong lens, but these images are, of course, deformed, because raindrops are not shaped at
all like perfect lenses. They are upside down, and, whereas the scenery
outside seems to move in the opposite direction to the train or car, the
images are seen to move in the same direction as the train or car.

The image of a post is much thicker at the top than at the bottom,
because the lens makes the images smaller according as its focal length
is smaller, and therefore its curvature greater: since the top part of a
raindrop is much flatter than its lower part, it gives a larger image.

If the inside of the windows is misted up, and some fairly large
drops roll downward like little streams, refraction may be studied in
the cylindrical lenses thus formed—see Fig. 45. It can be clearly
seen how left and right in the image have been transposed and how
everything moves in the opposite direction to the landscape.

38. Iridescence in dewdrops and crystals of hoarfrost

Who does not know the colorful gems of light in the morning dew?
See how steadily and brilliantly they glitter on the short grass of the
lawn, and how they twinkle like stars on long and waving blades.

Look more closely at the dew on a blade of grass. Don't pick it!
Don't touch it! The tiny spherical drops do not wet it, they are quite
close to it, but at most places there is still a layer of air between the
dewdrop and the blade of grass.

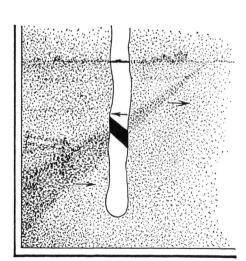

Fig. 45. Light is refracted by
the tracks of drops of water
that behave like cylindrical
lenses.

Superior mirage above cold water: a tanker below the horizon appears upside down in the mirage. (Photo by Veikko Mäkelä)

The grayish aspect of the bedewed grass is caused by the reflection of the rays of light in all the tiny drops, inside as well as outside; a great many of the rays do not even touch the blade of grass (cf. § 191). Large flattened drops have a beautiful silver sheen when seen at fairly large angles, because the rays are then totally reflected at the back surface.

Select one large drop and look at it with one eye, and you will see colors appear as soon as you observe it in a direction making a sufficiently large angle with the direction of incidence. First you see blue, then green, and then, particularly clearly, yellow, orange, red. This is, of course, the same phenomenon as that seen on a large scale in any rainbow (§ 143).

Similar sparkling colors are seen in the crystals of hoarfrost and freshly fallen snow.

A fine observation was reported from a pine forest. The observer looked in the direction of the sun, which was at an altitude of about 15°, and saw that the floor of the forest was covered in crystals of hoarfrost, each twinkling like a tiny source of colored light. Not one was white! There were all sorts of color. When he stood on tiptoe, the colors shifted toward the blue end of the spectrum and vice versa. The remarkably lovely colors can be explained by the fact that the crystals were not illuminated by the whole sun but only by sunlight falling through tiny gaps in the crowns of the trees. The incident rays must therefore have been highly directional, otherwise one point of the solar disk would have thrown red light on to the observer's eyes, another point, blue or green light, and all these colors would have merged into white. The angle of the solar disk we see is about twice as large as the angle between blue and red rays. The shifting of the colors is understood by considering that when the eye is placed higher up, it receives rays that have undergone a larger diffraction. Compare with § 176.

> You must ask Professor Clifton to explain to you why it is that a drop of water, while it subdues the hue of a green leaf or blue flower into a soft grey, and shows itself therefore on the grass or the dock leaf as a lustrous dimness, enhances the force of all warm colours, so that you can never see what the colour of a carnation or a wild rose really is until you get dew on it.
>
> Ruskin, *The Art and Pleasures of England*
>
> Hoar frost of gold ... see the dew on a cabbage leaf or, better still, on grey lichen in the early morning sunshine.
>
> Ruskin, *Arrows of the Chase*
>
> When this hoarfrost flew off the branches, it glittered in a richness of colors in the sunlight.
>
> M. Shokolov, *And Quiet Flows the Don*

(Photo by Pekka Parviainen)

Chapter 4
Curvature of Light Rays in the Atmosphere

39. Terrestrial ray curvature

The celestial bodies appear to us slightly higher above the horizon than they really are, and this displacement increases the nearer they get to the horizon. This accounts for the flattening of the sun and the moon on the horizon. At sunset, the lower edge of the sun's disk appears, on average, 35 minutes of arc higher than it actually is, but the top edge, which is farther from the horizon, only 29. The flattening amounts, therefore, to 6 minutes of arc, or about $\frac{1}{5}$ of the sun's diameter.

This phenomenon, which shows us by direct observation how the apparent rise increases near the horizon, is simply a consequence of the increase in the density of the atmosphere in the lower layers. As the density becomes greater, the refractive index of the air increases and the velocity of the light decreases, so that, when the light waves emitted by a star penetrate our atmosphere, they move somewhat more slowly on the side nearest the earth and bend round gradually. The light rays, which indicate how the wavefronts are propagated, curve

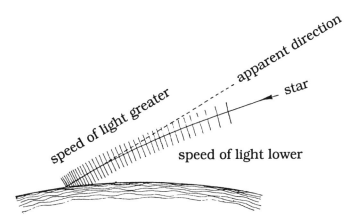

Fig. 46. Owing to terrestrial ray curvature, the altitude of a celestial body appears greater than it is.

too, therefore, and distant objects appear to be raised—see Fig. 46.

The terrestrial curvature of rays changes from day to day, owing to the varying distribution of temperatures in the atmosphere. It would be very interesting to note for a number of days the time the sun rises and sets, and to compare the results with the times calculated from almanacs and tables. You would have to aim at an accuracy of one second, which is quite possible with the help of radio signals. It appears that differences in time of one or two, or even five, minutes can be expected. Anyone living at the seaside could carry out this experiment very well, since there the sunset may be observed above a clear and open horizon. An experiment of this kind might be combined with observations of the height of the horizon, of the shape of the sun's disk, and of the green ray—see §§ 40, 45, and 47. The flattening of the solar disk may be so pronounced that an axes ratio of 1:2 is obtained!

40. Abnormal curvature of rays without reflection

Notice how often, when on the beach, you can see the waves in the distance standing out against the horizon, while waves of the same kind near to you do not reach the line of the horizon, although the line connecting equally high crests ought to be level and therefore meet the horizon, too. This phenomenon can also be studied during a sea voyage in stormy weather, if you keep watch on one of the lower decks, where you can see how the waves near to you do not quite reach the horizon, and compare them with the waves a long way off. It will be clear that the observation can be explained only by the curvature of the earth, which you can see demonstrated here, before your very eyes—see Fig. 47.

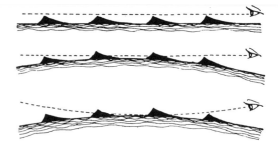

Flat earth: no curvature of rays.

Curved earth: no ray curvature.

Curved earth: curvature of rays.

Fig. 47. How to observe sea waves against the horizon.

Distant objects become invisible: the surface of the water appears convex.

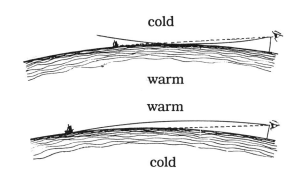

Abnormal sighting of distant objects: the surface of the water appears concave.

Fig. 48. (The curvature of the light ray is shown exaggerated.)

The phenomenon just described is, however, altered by the terrestrial curvature of the rays. This is very pronounced on days when the horizon seems quite near, and ships seem farther off than usual and bigger, and it seems as if the curvature of the earth were increased. On other days, the calm sea resembles a huge concave dish. Objects normally beyond the range of vision become visible and seem near to you and smaller than might be expected. Distant ships, which to your eyes should have been on or beyond the horizon, still seem to move in a valley of water. They look as if they were compressed more or less in a vertical direction, the line of the horizon running above

Fig. 49. Measuring changes in the terrestrial ray curvature.

their hull, while, as a matter of fact, your eye is lower than the top of the hull. The horizon seems abnormally far away.

In these two characteristic conditions, the surface of the water appears convex or concave—see Fig. 48. The first condition arises when the density decreases upward in the atmosphere abnormally slowly from below or even (in the bottom air layers) increases; the second condition arises when the density decreases upward with abnormal rapidity from below. Anomalies of this kind are a consequence of exceptional temperature distribution. If the sea is warmer than the air, the lowest air layers become warmer than the upper layers and therefore optically more rarefied and less refracting, and the light rays curve away from the earth. If the sea is colder, the curvature is the other way round. On such days it is desirable to measure the temperature at different heights to see whether this may account for the observations.

There is yet one more characteristic by which these two optical conditions may be distinguished, namely, the apparent height of the horizon. To measure this without instruments, you must choose a fixed point of reference, A, near the shore, and a variable point of reference, B, on a post or tree trunk a few hundred meters (yards) inland—see Fig. 49. Take B as your post of observation, and find the height at which you have to keep your eye so as to see the horizon pass exactly through point A. If the water is colder than the air, the horizon seems higher and B descends, but if the water is warmer than the air, the horizon appears lower and B ascends. Differences of 6–9' occur at times in one direction or the other, especially when there is no wind. If AB = 100 meters, these differences amount to ±20 to ±30 cm (±8 to ±12 in). The use of binoculars makes this method of observation more accurate.

In very rare cases, the curvature of the rays is abnormally strong and gives rise to the most remarkable optical phenomena. There are days when everything can be seen with extraordinary clarity, and a faraway town or lighthouse suddenly becomes visible which in ordinary circumstances would be impossible to see at all because it lies below the horizon. Very often, it gives the impression of being surprisingly near. Two very striking cases of this kind were once observed along the English Channel. Once, the whole of the French coast opposite Hastings could be seen from the beach there with the naked eye, whereas in ordinary circumstances it cannot even be seen with good binoculars. Another time, the whole of Dover Castle was seen from Ramsgate to appear from behind the hill that usually covers the greater part of it[1].

---

[1] *Hemel en Dampkring*, **51**, 12, 1953.

And, conversely, there are cases where distant objects that usually project above the horizon disappear as if they lay below it. These conditions, too, give a strong impression of proximity.

Observations of this kind should always be done in combination with measurements of the temperature of the surface of the sea and that of the air.

> According to her wishes, the dying, nearly 90-year-old Trin Jans had been sat propped upright against pillows so that she could look through the small leaded-glass windows into the distance. There had to be a rarefied (warmer) layer of air above a colder (denser) one, because the horizon appeared high and the refraction had elevated the sea like a glittering, silvery strip above the edge of the dike, so that the light shone blindingly into the room; even the southerly point of Jevers was visible.
>
> Th. Storm, *Der Schimmelreiter*

41. Mirages on a small scale

The well-known mirage of the desert can be seen quite easily on a small scale. Find an even, south-facing wall or stone parapet at least 8 meters (10 yards) long on which the sun is shining. Lay your head flat against the wall and look along it sideways, while someone, as far away as possible, holds some bright object, shining in the sun, for instance an ordinary key, closer and closer to the wall. As soon as the object is within a few centimeters (an inch or so) of the wall, its image becomes strikingly deformed and a reflected image from the surface of the wall seems to approach the object. Often, the whole hand holding the object can be seen reflected, too. Once this phenomenon has been properly observed, it can be noticed with every distant object that can be seen by looking grazingly along the surface of the wall. When the wall is shorter, this reflection can also be perceived if the eye is placed quite close to the wall, which may be managed if there is enough room at the end of the wall to stand in.

If a very long wall is heated strongly, a second reflection, as well as the first one, can sometimes be seen, not inverted with respect to the

Fig. 50. Mirage along a wall in sunlight. Vertical measurements are not to scale.

Mirage on a stone wall heated by sunlight. The sig-
nal appears to continue to the right; the rails in the
distance are bent, which proves that this is a case
of a mirage. (Photo by Markku Poutanen)

reflected object but erect. This is in agreement with a general law which
states that the successive images of a mirage must be alternately
upright and upside down.

The reflection occurs as a consequence of the air near the heated
object being warmer and therefore more rarefied, so that its refractive index is diminished. This causes the rays of light to bend until
they are parallel to the surface and afterward to diverge from it—see
Fig. 50. This is sometimes called 'total reflection', but this expression
is wrong because the transition between the different layers is gradual everywhere. On the other hand, you must bear in mind that the
curving of the ray takes place almost entirely in close proximity to
the heated object. Near to the wall there is probably a layer of air
some millimeters (a small fraction of an inch) deep which has approximately the temperature of the wall itself; beyond this, the temperature falls at first rapidly, and then more slowly.

It would be worth while measuring the temperature of the wall and of the neighboring layers of air and showing how the observed curvatures of the rays may be explained quantitatively by these measurements.

Similar mirages on a small scale used to be noticed sometimes along the hot funnels of steamships. The moon, Jupiter, and the rising sun were reflected as in a silver mirror; the mast of the ship, on the contrary, did not show this effect.

Above the roof of a car that has been standing in the sun for some time, the images of distant objects are distorted noticeably, provided you look closely along the heated surface.

When you look over a small board, not longer than 50 cm (20 in), lying in the sun, you can often see every distant object, as it were, 'elongated' and attracted by it.

42. Mirages on a large scale above hot surfaces ('inferior mirages')

A flat surface and observation at a large distance are at least as essential as excessive heating of the ground for the formation of a mirage. This is why flat countryside is especially suitable for observations of this kind: in Holland and Flanders, for instance, the reflections in the air are often as fine as those shown by the scorched desert of the Sahara. Often these mirages can be seen only when you

Mirages of the sky on Tarmac roads on hot days are a familiar sight. (Photo by Pekka Parviainen)

bend down; when you use binoculars, it is amazing how very much clearer they become, and how often they may be seen.

Three cases will now be described in which this phenomenon occurs with extraordinary clarity and frequency.

First of all, it may be seen on any sunny day above flat asphalt (Tarmac) roads. The thermometer shows a fall in temperature of as much as 20° or 30° in the first centimeter (half inch) above the surface, after which the fall becomes a few degrees per centimeter (half inch)[2]. My own experience is that the mirage is still finer above concrete roads. It is true that the radiation of the sun is not absorbed as much by these as by asphalt roads, but the re-emission of heat is less, too. When the weather is sunny, this sort of road appears to be covered with pools of water that grow larger and clearer when you bend down to look at them, and which appear to reflect the bright and colored objects in the distance. What we take for water is nothing but the reflection of the clear sky in the distance. It is remarkable how this reflection remains undisturbed by the traffic, while paper, leaves, and dust are whirled up by it. Note accurately at what angle the mirage is visible, and calculate the temperature of the air that is in contact with the ground by the formula given later in this section.

Second, the mirage is a usual phenomenon in the wide meadows of flat regions, and can almost be called a characteristic of the landscape, at least in spring and summer when the weather is bright and there is not too much wind. Along the horizon you can see a white strip, above which towers and treetops in the distance seem to float apparently without any foundation. If you bend over, you see the landscape nearer to you distorted, with large shining pools of water, reflecting the houses and clear sky in the background. This is particularly clear in the direction of the sun.

Toward midday, the curvature of the rays is often so strong that, even when you stand upright, it seems as if there are pools everywhere, and by bending down for a moment or by climbing a few meters (yards) higher, you will be surprised to see how the pools seem to expand or to shrink. Note how the images become distorted and elongated in a vertical direction, whenever the eye is just a little too high to see the reflection. If the eye is very low, the base of objects in the distance is no longer visible: they are suspended in empty space. On the side away from the sun, the pools are less bright and therefore less noticeable, but the distortion and reflections of distant objects can be seen all the better.

It is interesting to note down a few temperatures in the lower air-layers, at heights of, say, 0–100 cm (0–40 in). In the morning, if the sun is shining, the temperature will invariably be found to be high-

---

[2] S.E. Ashmore, *Weather*, **10**, 336, 1955.

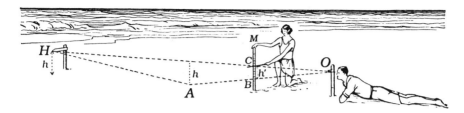

Fig. 51. How to determine the paths of light rays in a mirage. All horizontal dimensions are not to scale.

est close to the ground; if the difference between 0–100 cm (0–40 in) amounts to 3 °C (5.5 °F), there is little or no reflection. If it rises to 5 C° (9 °F), the reflection is moderate, and at a difference of 8 °C (14 °F) the phenomenon is marked. The greatest differences occur in the spring on bright sunny days following chilly nights.

It was over the vast meadows near Bremen in north-western Germany that Busch, who was the first to make a scientific and thorough study of this phenomenon, was able to observe (in 1779) the mirage of the faraway city clearly.

Third, the most beautiful and most evenly produced mirage is seen on the beach, across firm and smooth sands, when the weather is warm and there is no wind. When you lie flat on the ground with your eyes as close as possible to the surface of the sand, you see no clearly reflected image, but if you raise your head a little it seems suddenly as if you are surrounded by a reflecting lake, and you can even see objects 10–20 cm (4–8 in) high, 30 m (35 yd) away, reflected in it. Pick out one clear, bright object H (see Fig. 51), and keep your eyes fixed at a point O, just as high from the ground as the object is, which may, for instance, be indicated by a twig or a stick.

Let us now determine by experiment the path of the ray of light by which the mirrored image is seen. At C, a known distance, an assistant holds a small measuring rod M upright, and moves a little lath (strip of wood) along until it intercepts (a) the image in question at B and (b) the top of the object itself. We may assume that the direct ray of light HO from H toward our eye is a straight one, so that we are able to determine successively the height of each point of the deflected ray of light HAO and therefore, point for point, the path of the ray itself. In this way, it appears that close to the sand it must have suffered a rather sudden deflection. If this is true, we may expect $h/AO = h'/BO$ to be constant and equal to the angle between the surface of the sand and the ray traversing the longer path. This proves to be so and angles of up to 0.01 rad = 0.5° are found. From this angle and the known refractive index of air for various temperatures, the difference in degrees between the temperature of the air immediately next to the ground and that at the height of the eyes is deduced.

Since the curvature is so sudden, it holds, as in the case of total reflection, that $\sin i = n'/n$. The angle h/AO is the complement of the angle of incidence i, so that

$$\cos(h/AO) = 1 - \tfrac{1}{2}(h/AO)^2 = n/n',$$

from which

$$\tfrac{1}{2}(h/AO)^2 = 1 - n/n' = (n'-n)/n'.$$

The refractive index of air at normal temperatures is 1.00029. The amount by which the refractive index of air exceeds that of a vacuum is directly proportional to the air density, that is, inversely proportional to the absolute temperature:

$$(n-1)/(n'-1) = T'/T,$$

whence

$$(n-n')/(n-1) = (T-T')/T.$$

Since $n-n' = 29\times10^{-5}\times273/\Delta t$,

$$\Delta t = 273/29\times10^{-5}\times\tfrac{1}{2}(h/OW)^2,$$

which is normally 5–35° C (41–95 °F).

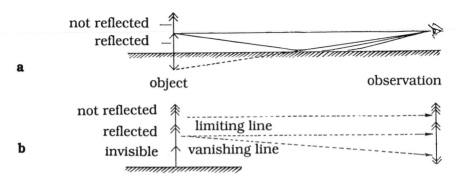

Fig. 52. Only part of an object is seen in a mirage; **(a)** at small distances; **(b)** at larger distances.

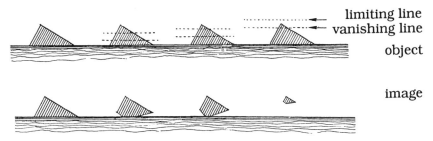

Fig. 53. An island seen, at increasing distances, in a mirage.

In the foregoing case, the origin of the mirage is very simple. As soon as you direct your gaze to a point on the ground beyond a certain limit, the visual ray impinges on the hot layers at a sufficiently inclined angle to suffer a sudden deviation. The effect is about the same as if a mirror were lying on the ground at that point. In this way, distant objects are divided into two parts: the top part is seen single, and the bottom part shows an inverted reflection—see Fig. 52a.

The curvature of the earth and the ordinary curvature of the rays have a very marked influence on distant mirages. Below a certain vanishing line, the foot of distant objects is invisible owing to the curvature of the earth. Between this vanishing line and a still higher limiting line lies that part of the object that is seen reflected, and its reflection is usually compressed in a vertical direction. Finally, above the limiting line, we see those objects that have no reflection—see Fig. 52b.

Instead of the rapid rise in temperature at the earth's surface, there are many much more complicated temperature distributions, each of which has its own peculiar optical consequences. In a very clear mirage above the beach, it is possible by an experimental investigation, as described above, to find out the course of the vanishing line and limiting line, and from that to deduce the temperature distribution. Direct temperature measurements may be compared with this. But the likelihood of the beach not being quite level makes investigations of this kind very difficult.

On any sea voyage, numbers of mirages can be seen that can be explained by the preceding consideration—see Figs. 53 and 54. If the phenomenon is only partly developed, as usually happens, the (inverted) reflected image becomes so flattened that it looks merely like a small horizontal line, merging into the base of the object itself. The only striking thing then is the bright streak of light of the reflected sky: the fact that this is similarly compressed is normally not noticed. Faraway objects, therefore, seem to float, as it were, at a short

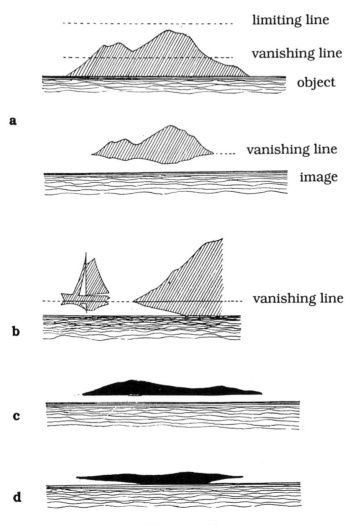

Fig. 54. Observations of a mirage during a sea voyage.

distance above the horizon. This optical phenomenon, which is nothing but a partly developed mirage, can be seen at sea almost every day, especially when binoculars are used. If the different parts of an island are at different distances from you, those farthest away are touched higher up by the limiting line and vanishing line, and the condition in Fig. 54d results.

Measuring the height of the vanishing line above the apparent horizon is a simple means of expressing the 'intensity' of the mirage numerically, and may be carried out by one of the methods given in Appendix A. Angles of a few minutes of arc will be found.

There is another phenomenon that produces an effect which may sometimes be mistaken for this one: the formation of a layer of fine drops of water by the foam from surf. These drops float in the air above the sea, and cover the lowest parts of distant objects with a light layer of mist.

Mirages with their deformation and reflection of images have been observed also in the following circumstances:

- while bathing, when the water is warmer than the air;
- on large lakes in favorable atmospheric conditions;
- above railway lines, where, by bending down, you can see how completely distorted an engine looks in the distance;
- above flat sandy tracts or flat farmland;
- along the slopes of dunes if you look parallel to the slope;
- along a stone-paved street, especially if you can look very closely along the highest point of a rise in the street;
- above an expanse of ice when the air is appreciably colder than the ice.

43. Mirages above cold water ('superior mirage' or 'looming')

Just as a downward reflection occurs mostly above heated land, upward reflection is seen mainly over the sea, although far less often. This occurs when the sea is much colder than the air, so that the temperature in the lowest strata of air increases very rapidly with increase of height above the sea; this type of temperature distribution is called a temperature inversion by meteorologists—see Fig. 55.

Some classic observations of magnificent 'superior' mirages were carried out from the south coast of England by looking through a telescope across the Channel, sometimes in the evening after a very hot day, sometimes while a mist was lifting. Superior mirages may also be seen under quite different conditions, for instance, in the spring over the Baltic when it has just thawed, or above a frozen surface when it suddenly begins to thaw and the air close to the ice is colder than higher up; however, to see it, you have to bend down and look closely along the frozen surface.

Sometimes, the bending of the rays upward causes multiple reflections, free to develop since there is nothing to cut off the light rays (as the earth does when the reflection is downward), and strange images arise, upright and inverted, varying from one moment to the next, changing in accordance with the distance of the object and the distribution of temperature in the atmosphere.

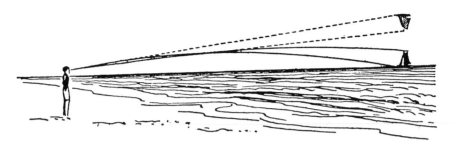

Fig. 55. Superior mirage caused by a temperature inversion.

44. Castles in the air

In a few very rare cases, most remarkable mirages have been seen by reliable observers, who describe them as landscapes with towns and towers and parapets, rising above the horizon, transforming, crumbling, fairylike scenes, producing a deep sense of happiness and an endless longing: *fata Morgana!** No wonder that these observations, already so beautiful in themselves, have been adorned by the fancies of poetry and folklore.

Forel observed simpler forms of this phenomenon time and again above Lake Geneva and, after fifty years of study, described it in detail. A calm surface of water, 10–30 km (6–20 miles) across, is essential; the eye must be 2–4 m (6–12 ft) above the water, after which, and this is important, the exact height must be found by experiment.

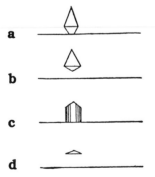

Fig. 56. A *fata Morgana* as transition between refraction of light above warm water and above cold water.

---

* A mirage often seen in the Strait of Messina (southern Italy), which was believed to be caused by Morgan le Fay (It. *fata Morgana*), the fairy sister of King Arthur in Celtic and Arthurian legend—Translator.

In the afternoon on bright days, Forel saw four consecutive stages develop gradually along the opposite shore, the one succeeding the other, and remaining in the same place for not longer than 10–20 minutes.

The stages were—see Fig. 56:

(a) the mirage above warm water, reflection below the object;

(b) the abnormal mirage above cold water, a very strange phenomenon in which the object is seen quite normally, with its reflection below very compressed (probably an unstable, temporary transition stage);

(c) the castles in the air; the distant coast line is distorted over a distance of 10–20° (in angular measure) and elongated vertically into a row of rectangles (the 'streaked zone');

(d) the normal curvature of the rays above cold water; no reflection is visible, but the object itself is strongly compressed in a vertical direction.

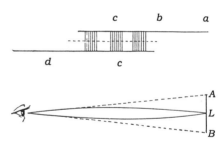

Fig. 57. How a *fata Morgana* arises.

The upper horizon in stages a and b and the lower horizon in stage d are the boundaries between which the vertical shading of the streaked zone is developed—see Fig. 57. The shifting of the castles in the air is a result of refraction of type a being gradually replaced by type d. The theory that the density of the air, in a transition region of this kind, is greatest in layers of average height seems quite acceptable. The path of the rays is that shown in Fig. 57 and, as will be seen, every point of light L is drawn out vertically into a line AB.

The *fata Morgana* has been observed over a frozen, snow-covered lake during sunny weather[3].

---

[3] *J. R. Astron. Soc. Can.*, **61**, 74, 1967.

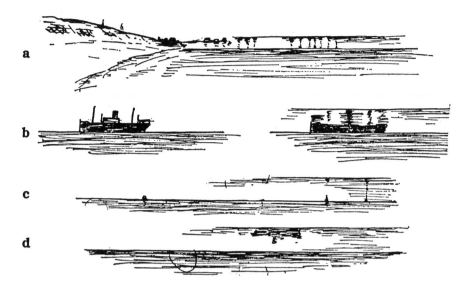

Fig. 58. Castles in the air observed at the Dutch coast.

But gradually the landscape loses
Its cheerlessness before her eyes;
And she sees how in the distance
A large, bright expanse of water begins to undulate.
The shrubs and aquatic plants
Surround the flooded landscape
And grow and drape their tops in shadows.

It is a scene fresh and heavenly,
A wondrous dream from the East!
Gradually, in the distance along the blueing lake
Arises a town with its walls,
Its ring of proud, reinforced ramparts,
Its churches, roofs and fountains,
And its towers that grow in the light of the sun!

The large ships and the small,
With their slender white sails,
Are inward bound;
The flags and colorful pennants on their masts
Flutter gaily in the playful wind.

Fr. Mistral, *Mireio*

45. Distortions of the rising and setting sun and moon

When the sun is low, the most curious distortions may be seen at times. The corners of the visible segment are often rounded off, or the disk appears to consist of two pieces joined together, or there is a strip of light below the sun that rises as the sun's disk sinks. In other cases, the sun does not set exactly behind the horizon, but a few minutes of arc above it. These distortions seem to vary more in the evening than in the morning, and this must be ascribed to meteorological factors (cf. § 223). On still, cloudless days, the layers of different density are less disturbed during their formation, so that the distortions of the sun's edge may be taken to indicate that the atmosphere is steady, and are a sign of fine weather. If the sun is too blinding, it is advisable to hold a sheet of aluminium foil (ordinary paper will do) with a small round hole pricked in it, in front of one of your eyes, or to use good sunglasses. Binoculars are not necessary, but they facilitate observation. When they are used, hold a piece of blackened glass or a pinhole diaphragm in front of your eyes (not the objective).

The phenomena enter their most interesting stage usually only 10 minutes or so before sunset (or last 10 minutes or so after sunrise). Note, too, the different shades of color in the sun's disk: dark red on the side nearest the horizon, gradually changing to orange and yel-

Owing to instability in the atmosphere, the moon appears notched while it slowly sinks to the horizon over the sea. (Photo by Pekka Perviainen)

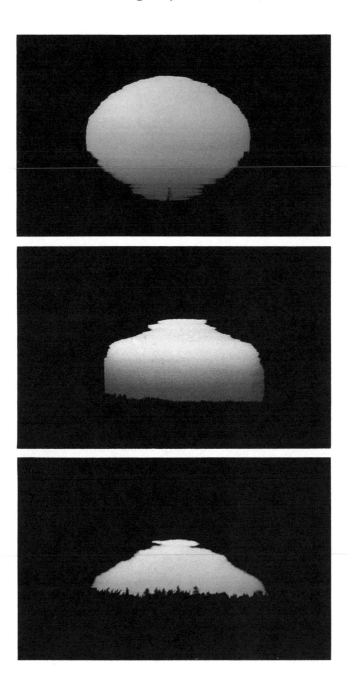

The sinking sun strongly distorted by the atmosphere. In the bottom photograph, a narrow segment is just about to split off the upper edge of the sun. (Photo by Pekka Parviainen)

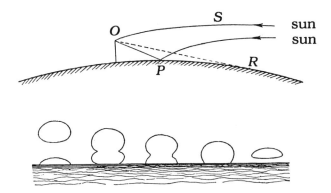

Fig. 59. Sunset with distortions caused by a mirage as in Case A.

low on the upper part. Observe also the large sunspots, present on the disk at all times, which are drawn into the shape of a short rod.

It would be interesting, although difficult, to take photographs, but see Appendix B.

These optical distortions are caused by nothing but the ordinary mirage, and distinction must be made between an upward mirage and a downward one. A fairly good approximation is obtained if you assume that there is a sudden bend in the light ray coming from the sun when it strikes a layer of discontinuity. Remember that such a layer follows the curvature of the earth. However, the light ray must be assumed straight before it reaches the layer and after it has passed through it.

Case A. A thin stratum of warm air, *PR*, rests on the earth—see Fig. 59. You then see the sun in the direction *OS* and, at the same time, underneath it, the reflected image in the direction *OP*, with the horizon *OR* lying in between. At sunset, a flattened 'counter-sun' rises from the apparent horizon *OP* as the sun sets, and they unite at the spot where the real sun is about to disappear (*OR*). The two disks glide more and more into one another, while balloonlike shapes, and so on, are formed.

Case B. Assume that in Fig. 60 the air near the ground is cold, while a warmer layer, *ABCD*, lies above it (inversion). Point *M* is the center of the earth, round which two arcs are drawn to represent the level of the sea and of the layer of discontinuity. Imagine observer *O* to be looking in directions nearer and nearer to the horizontal; in direction *OA* his gaze touches the upper rim of the sun; in direction *OB* he sees a point a little lower down, but his gaze is more inclined in relation to the discontinuity layer; in the horizontal direction *OC* it is incident on the layer at such a large angle that the visual ray is

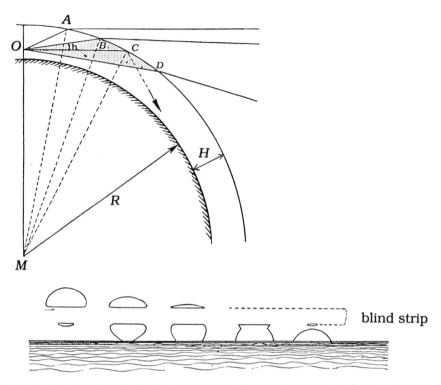

Fig. 60. Sunset with distortions caused by a mirage as in Case B.

curved and can no longer leave the earth. If the observer stands on a slight elevation above the earth's surface, he will also be able to look downward at a small angle: thus, if he looks in the direction *OD*, the angle of incidence of his line of sight on the layer of discontinuity is decreased and is once more sufficiently small for the visual ray to be able to escape. Within the dotted angle on both sides of the horizontal direction, therefore, no rays from outside the earth reach the observer: he sees a 'blind strip' as high as 2*h*. This is a consequence of the following theorem.

Of all the chords through *O*, the horizontal chord *OC* is the one that makes the smallest angle with the circle.

Proof: In triangle *MOB* we have

$$\sin\angle OBM / OM = \sin\angle MOB / MB,$$

so that

$$\sin\angle OBM = R/(R+H)\sin(90°+h) = R/(R+H)\cos h.$$

Fig. 61. Distortion of the sun owing to the presence of several layers of discontinuity.

It is clear from this that $\angle OBM$ attains its maximum value when $h = 0$. In the limiting case of total reflection,

$$\sin\angle OB = 1/n,$$

where n denotes the refractive index of one layer relative to the other.

Writing ε for H/R and δ for $(n-1)$, and replacing $\cos h$ by its approximate expression $1-\frac{1}{2}h^2$, the result for h will be

$$h = \pm\sqrt{[2(\delta-\varepsilon)/n]}$$

or, since for all practical purposes $n = 1$,

$$h \approx \pm\sqrt{[2(\delta-\varepsilon)]}.$$

We see, therefore, that the blind strip extends just as far above as below the horizon (double sign). For $H = 50$ m (55 yd), $\varepsilon = 78\times10^7$. If we put $\delta = 100\times10^7$, $h = \pm0.0021$ radian $= \pm7'$.

The width of the blind strip is therefore $14'$.

We should, of course, have taken account of the ordinary terrestrial curvature of the rays as well, but we are only concerned here with the main features of the phenomenon.

It is clear now that, considering this structure of the atmosphere, the sun sets before it reaches the actual horizon, that is, as soon as it enters the blind strip. If you are standing on top of a hill or on the deck of a ship, you will probably be able to see the lower rim of the sun appear from behind the blind region. The images are, of course, distorted, that is, compressed above the blind region and elongated below it.

In some cases, the sun's image shows several small steps, evidently indicating the presence of more than one layer of discontinuity—see Fig. 61. Occasionally, one of the notches between these steps becomes so deeply indented, on both sides, that a strip is cut off, as it were, from the top of the sun, remains afloat in the air for a moment, and then vanishes, often with a magnificent display of the green flash (§ 47) phenomenon. This may be followed by another strip being cut off in the same way, and so on—see Fig. 68.

46. Double and multiple images of the sun and the moon

Earlier editions of this book mentioned observations of multiple crescents of the moon that were remarkably clear and undistorted — see Fig. 62. The distance between these was so great that I did not dare think of a mirage but rather of a distortion in the eye of the observer. But I was wrong! Nature continually proves to be richer in possibilities than we imagine. A similar phenomenon was seen: beside and above the sun appeared no fewer than seven images of the sun, clear and undistorted. And this time they were photographed, clearly and unambiguously. The sun was about 2° above the horizon at sea and the phenomenon lasted about three minutes. The images were bluish, while the real sun was bright orange.

Furthermore, so many other instances have been reported[4] that there is no longer any doubt about:

(a) double and multiple crescents of the moon, a phenomenon that appears at relatively small refraction: displacements of 0.5° occurred while the moon was at altitudes of 12°, 15°, and 35°;

(b) double suns, one above the other, and cases of one or more mock suns appearing after the real sun had set;

(c) multiple suns shifted randomly with respect to one another;

(d) finally, and different from all the previous cases, observations of sun and mock sun(s) being at exactly the same altitude. The case of a mock sun 3°25' to the left of the nearly set sun sounds incredible but has been recorded photographically.

Fig. 62. Multiple crescents of the moon. The distance between the images seems improbably large. The moon's altitude was 15° and 12° respectively.

---

[4] *Mar. Obs.*, **22**, 125, 1952; **29**, 178, 1959; **34**, 181, 1964; **35**, 66 and 122, 1965. Richard, *La Météor*, **4**, 301, 1953; *Ciel et Terre*, **71**, 350, 1955. *Meteorol. Mag.* **87**, 277, 1958. *Weather*, **21**, 251, 1966.

An explanation of these phenomena has been sought in abnormal refraction of light. Even so, it remains extraordinary that the images of the sun and moon were sharp and of the same size as the real sun and moon. Note that refraction obtains not only vertically, but also sideways, and that the refractive index is often quite large.

47. The green flash[5]

> Have you ever seen the sun set at the seaside? Yes? And did you follow it until the top edge of the sun's disk just touched the horizon and then started to disappear? Probably. But did you observe the phenomenon that occurs at the instant of the last ray of light when the sky is perfectly clear? Perhaps not. Well, the first time that the opportunity for such an observation offers itself (it is very rare), take it and you will see that it is not a red ray, or rather flash, but a green one; a wondrous green that is not found anywhere else in nature. If there is green in Paradise, it must be this green: the true green of hope!
>
> Jules Verne, *The Green Ray*

According to an old Scottish legend, anyone who has seen the green flash will never err again where matters of the heart are concerned.

The green flash may be perceived more frequently than people used to think. During a sea voyage from the Far East to Europe, I observed it more than ten times. The best place to see it is undoubtedly over the sea, either from the deck of a ship or from the shore. It may, however, be seen above land as well, if the horizon is distant enough. It occurs, too, sometimes when the sun is disappearing behind a sharply outlined bank of clouds. It seems that it is visible over mountains and clouds, provided these are not higher than about 3° above the horizon. In a few cases, the green flash has been seen at an amazingly short distance. One observer relates how he once stood at the edge of the shadow of a rock fairly close to him, and by moving his head a little more to one side or the other, he could see the green

Fig. 63. The green segment.

[5] O' Connel, *The Green Flash*, Vatican Observatory, 1958.

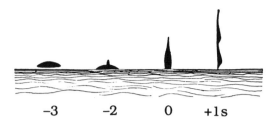

Fig. 64. The real green ray. The times shown refer to the moment of sunset.

flash as often as he liked. Others have seen it along the top of a wall 300 m (330 yd) away, but these are exceptional cases.

All who have observed it agree that the green flash is clearest on evenings when the sun shines brightly up to the moment of setting, whereas it is almost invisible when the sun is very red.

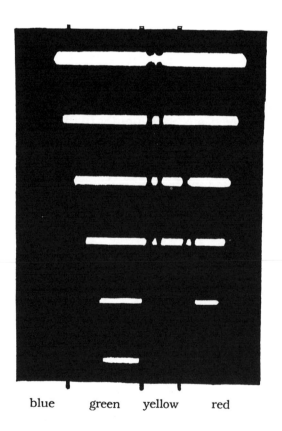

blue   green   yellow   red

Fig. 65. Visually observed spectrum of the setting sun.

Binoculars are generally a help and a telescope still more so. However, care should be taken not to look through these into the sun itself, except during the very last seconds before it sets, for fear of being dangerously dazzled. Nor should you look too soon into the last segment of the sun's disk with the naked eye, but turn your back to it until someone lets you know when it is the right moment for observation.

The phenomenon is very transitory: it lasts only a few seconds. Once, by running up the slope of a dyke, 6 m (20 ft) high, I was able to watch the green ray for 20 seconds; at times it became bluer, and at times whiter, depending on whether my own pace was too slow or too fast. It should be possible to see it occasionally from the different decks of a ship in turn. Some observers have been able to see it several times in succession owing to the movement of the ship they were on. Others have seen it from a plane flying at 12 000 m (39 000 ft)[6]. In one very special case of abnormally strong ray curvature, it has been seen for 10 seconds and longer. During Byrd's expedition to the South Pole, the green ray was observed for 35 minutes, while the sun, rising for the first time at the close of the polar night, was moving exactly along the horizon.

The phenomenon of the green flash may appear in three forms.

1. The green rim, which, as a matter of fact, can always be distinguished along the top of the sun's disk and becomes wider the more it descends toward the horizon; at the same time, the lower part becomes red.

2. The green segment (Fig. 63). The last segment becomes green at the extremities, and this green color shifts gradually toward the center of the segment. This green segment is visible to the naked eye, often for a second or so, and with binoculars sometimes for 4 or 5 seconds.

Fig. 66. How the green flash arises.

6 *J. R. Astron. Soc. Can.*, **59**, 53, 1965.

Fig. 67. The last segment shows upward bent corners: a green flash is likely!

3. The green flash proper. This phenomenon, visible to the naked eye, is seen only rarely. It is a green flash similar in appearance to a flame that shoots up out of the horizon just as the sun is disappearing.

In all three forms, its color is mostly emerald, seldom yellow. Sometimes it is blue or violet. The color was once seen to run from green through blue into violet in the course of the few seconds the phenomenon lasted.

There can no longer be any doubt as to the explanation of the green flash. The sun is low so that its white rays have a long way to travel through the atmosphere. A great part of its yellow and orange light is absorbed by the water vapor and perhaps by O_4 molecules, the absorption bands of which lie in this spectral region. Its violet light is weakened considerably by scattering (cf. § 195), and there remain, therefore, red and green-blue, as can also be seen by direct observation—see Fig. 65.

Now, the atmosphere is denser below than above, so that the rays of light on their way through the air are bent (cf. § 39). This bending is somewhat slighter for red light and somewhat stronger for the more refrangible blue-green rays. This causes us to see two solar disks partially covering one another, the blue-green one a little higher, the red one a little lower, which accounts for the red rim underneath and the green rim at the top—see Fig. 66. You can now understand why the extremities of the segment are green when the sun is low and why the white part disappears gradually behind the horizon while the green covers the whole of the remaining segment. In many circumstances, however, refraction is abnormally strong near the horizon and the green segment is more clearly visible for a longer time. Should mirages arise, it may even be extended into a kind of flame or ray.

The green flash has been photographed. The photograph shows that the green light is noticeably stronger than that in the solar spectrum just before sunset: only abnormal refraction can explain this[7].

It would be very important to find the relation between the green flash and the difference in temperature between the water and the air. Unfortunately, data are conflicting.

---

[7] T.S. Jacobsen, *J. R. Astron. Soc. Can.*, **46**, 93, 1952; *Sky and Telescope*, **12**, 233, 1953.

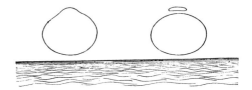

Fig. 68. The green flash arises
because of the separation of the
upper parts of the setting sun.

It is said, too, that the green segment may be seen exceptionally
well when the characteristics of a mirage are present underneath;
that is, when the lower edge is not straight but bent upward at the
corners.

When the sun's disk is indented like a staircase by layers of discontinuity, you can see how a strip at the top is detached now and
then and disappears in a green glare: a very wonderful sight—see
Figs. 61 and 68. Here is yet another fact that speaks strongly for the
considerable influence of abnormal refraction; on two occasions, the
green flash could be observed from one deck of a ship, and not from
another, which shows that it depended on the height at which the
observer was standing. And yet, there are competent observers of
nature who insist that the ordinary terrestrial ray curvature is quite
sufficient to produce the green flash.

The chief problem still to be solved in regard to the green flash,
therefore, is how strong must the refraction be to cause a given intensity of the phenomenon? To solve this, it would suffice if someone
on the shore could determine for a number of days exactly what time
the sun sets and observe the green flash phenomenon at the same
time. The difference between the observed and the computed times
is a good indication of the deviation of ray curvature from the normal
(cf. § 39).

It used to be thought that the green flash might be a physiological
afterimage in the complementary color of the last vestige of the red
setting sun (§ 105). This supposition is refuted sufficiently by the
fact that the green flash may also be seen when the sun is rising, though
it is then more difficult to know where to look in anticipation of the
appearance of the light. You have to find the brightest point or take
as an indication the crepuscular rays or Haidinger's brush (§§ 206
and 221). Another argument is that the green flash can be seen only
when the distance to the horizon is sufficiently great; though this would
not affect the afterimage in any way, it is naturally very important as
regards curvature of the rays.

The green flash has been observed, too, on rare occasions in connection with the moon, Venus, and Jupiter, though seldom with Saturn.
One observer has described how he saw the reflection of Venus rise
toward the planet and how, the moment they met, the color suddenly turned from dull red to green.

48. Green surf

On the coast of Sumatra it was perceived that on the distant horizon the white-crested breakers seemed green and that this applied only to the lower ones, the higher breakers being white as usual. The sea was gray and the line of the horizon dipped clearly.

This phenomenon seems to be identical with the green flash, the gleaming white of the lower waves corresponding to the extreme edge of the setting sun.

49. The red flash[8]

It follows from the explanation of the green flash that there must be a red flash, too, which would occur, for instance, when the sun has gone down behind a heavy, sharply outlined bank of clouds near the horizon and the very lowest edge of it comes peeping out below. This has been observed at times, but very seldom, and it appears to last for an even shorter time than the green flash.

One observer, watching the green flash through an opening in a wall 300 m (330 yd) away, was able to see the red flash on the same occasion.

50. Twinkling of terrestrial sources of light

The phenomenon known as twinkling or scintillation may be seen in its most intense form above the braziers or stoves used to melt asphalt for the surface of roads. The objects in the distance seem to quiver and ripple so much as to be hardly distinguishable, and the air itself appears to be no longer transparent. Also, you can see how everything quivers above a sheet-iron roof, a field of burning stubble, or a stretch of sand heated by the sun.

The phenomenon is shown most clearly by bright and shining objects, the trunks of silver birches, white posts, patches of white sand, or distant windows lit up by the sun. In the summer or on cold days in spring, you can see railway lines twinkling in the distance; they no longer appear straight, but twist and turn. If you lay your head on the ground, the twinkling becomes greater, and you see air striae borne along by the wind. These 'waves' can be higher than the waves of the sea. When wearing sunglasses, you can never see the objects in the distance really distinctly while the sun is shining. (Observe this especially in directions away from the sun.) In winter, a prac-

---

[8] *Mar. Obs.*, **25**, 217, 1955.

ticed eye can see by the quivering vibration of the images of distant objects the warm air ascending above the roofs of the houses.

> For the air through which we look upon the stars is in a perpetual tremor; as may be seen by the tremulous motion of shadows cast from high towers, and by the twinkling of the fix'd stars
>
> Newton, *Opticks*

Have you ever observed this?

All these phenomena can be explained by the curvature of the light rays in the currents of warm air that rise like small fountains from the heated earth. At a height of not more than 2 m (6 ft), they have already mingled considerably with the cold air, and the striae have become smaller.

On a smooth white wall, illuminated by the sun, the ascending striae may often be seen dancing above a window sill, casting shadows as delicate as very thin smoke. The parallel nature of the light rays is disturbed by these striae, light becomes more localized in some parts and less so in others. It is an effect similar to that caused to a much greater degree by an undulating surface of water or by an uneven window pane (§§ 30 and 32).

It is evident that the scintillation will be more intense the farther away the object you look at through the unevenly heated stratum of air is. Lights a few miles away twinkle at night, but as you get closer to them the twinkling becomes less and finally disappears. A stationary car in the road reflects the sun with fierce brilliance, which, at a distance of 500 m (545 yd), is one mass of scintillation; at 200 m (218 yd), it is much more steady, and as you get closer still, the twinkling vanishes completely.

It has been observed that those parts of the light path nearest to the eye contribute most to scintillation. In the same way, a pair of spectacles is most effective when close to the eyes: if you lay them on the printed page you are reading, you will see that they do not change the size of the letters at all, but on moving them toward your eye, the letters are magnified or diminished, the change being greater the closer the lenses are to your eye. Similarly, most of the scintillation arises from temperature variations in the air near the observer. This is confirmed by the fact that if the sun's radiation is obstructed for a short time by a thick cloud, so that the light path in the immediate neighborhood of the observer is overshadowed, the scintillation ceases almost immediately: conversely, it reappears as the cloud moves away. Evidently, the surface temperature of the ground follows any change in the sun's radiation very quickly.

Scintillation may be seen not only above sand or soil or houses but also above a surface of water, above snow, and above the foliage in a wood, which shows that the temperature of all these things can be so affected by radiation as to differ greatly from the temperature of the air. The rows of streetlights along the distant promenades of seaside towns are a fine sight from a ship entering a port, or steaming down the English Channel or through the Strait of Messina.

By observing scintillation repeatedly from the same place, you will soon discover how it varies under different weather conditions. It is always much less pronounced when the sky is overcast. Before sunrise it is rather feeble, becomes fairly strong soon after the sun is up, reaches a maximum about midday, and is much less pronounced toward 4 or 5 p.m. On some days, however, the development is quite different.

Terrestrial sources of light sometimes show color phenomena during twinkling, but only when they are a long way off. On one exceptional occasion, distinct color changes were seen in the light from lamps not more than 5 km (3 miles) away.

51. Scintillation of the stars[9]

Note how Sirius, or any other bright star, twinkles when it is close to the horizon. When looking through a telescope, you will notice slight changes of position. When looking with the naked eye, you will see variations in the brightness and also changes of color.

Needless to say, this flickering is not a phenomenon taking place on the star itself, but is explained in the same way as the scintillation of terrestrial light sources (§ 50). The changes in position are caused by curvature of the rays in the striae of hot and cold air, both of which are always present in the atmosphere, and especially where a warm layer of air passes over a cold layer and air waves with eddies are formed (§ 69). The changes in brightness arise from the fact that at the surface of the earth the irregularly deviated rays of light are concentrated at some places and sparsely distributed at others. If the continually changing system producing this is borne along bodily by the wind, the observer will stand, now in a brightly illuminated region, now in one less bright. The color changes must be ascribed to slight dispersion of the normal terrestrial ray curvature, so that the rays from the star travel along slightly different paths in the atmosphere, according to their color. For a star 10° above the horizon, we compute the distance between the violet and red rays to be as much as 28 cm (11 in) at a height of 2 000 m (1.25 miles) and

---

[9] *Q. J. Theor. Appl. Meteorol.*, **80**, 241, 1954.

Fig. 69. Irregularities in the atmosphere diffract the light rays of a star and cause flickering (scintillation).

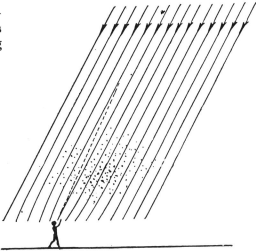

58 cm (23 in) at 5 000 m (3 miles). The air striae are, on average, fairly small, so that it may often happen that the violet ray passes through a striation and is deflected, whereas the red ray passes on without deviation—see Fig. 70[10]. The moments when the light of a star becomes brighter or feebler as a result of scintillation are therefore different for the different colors.

It is now thought probable that refraction of light also plays a role in scintillation, particularly when it concerns small air striae at great heights[11]. Refraction here does not mean curvature of the ray, but the effects that are closely associated with the wave character and interference of light: effects that depart from what geometric optics predict of light rays.

Scintillation is least near the zenith; there, when the atmosphere is calm, you can only just see, now and then, a twinkling of the bright stars. The closer the stars are to the horizon, the more they twinkle, simply because you are then looking through a thicker layer of air, and therefore through more striae. Color changes never occur, apparently, at altitudes of more than 50°, but frequently below 35°. The most beautiful scintillation of all is that of the bright star Sirius, which is visible rather low in the winter sky (in the northern hemisphere).

Scintillation is so rapid that you cannot see what actually takes place, but anyone wearing glasses for short-sightedness can make a

---

[10] *Nature*, **164** and **165**, 1950.
[11] *Q. J. Theor. Appl. Meteorol.*, **80**, 241, 1953; **82**, 227, 1956. C.G. Little, *Mon. Not. R. Astron. Soc.*, **111**, 289, 1951.

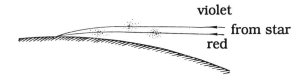

violet

from star

red

Fig. 70. How colors come about when a star twinkles.

splendid study of scintillation by holding his glasses in his hand and moving them slightly up and down in their own plane before his eyes. This causes the image of the stars to be drawn out into a short line. It is even better if you move the glasses in a circle, which can be done readily after a little practice (3 to 4 revolutions per second). As a consequence of the persistence of visual impressions (§ 97), you can now see, distributed along the circumference, all the variations of brightness and color shown in succession by a star: a marvelous sight when the scintillation is strong! Sometimes, dark spots occur in the band of light, which shows that there are moments when we receive hardly any light from the star. You can estimate how many different colors can be seen along the circumference and calculate from that the number of color variations in a second. This method of observation is based on the fact that glasses act not only as a lens but also as a weak prism if you do not look through the center of them.

There are other means of analyzing this scintillation phenomenon: (a) if you have normal sight, you can use a pair of weak glasses in the way indicated, but you will have to accommodate your eye as if the star were nearer; (b) by looking through binoculars while tapping them gently; (c) by looking at the reflection of the star in a pocket mirror while rotating it through small angles; (d) simply by letting your gaze move across the star (this can be done only after much practice, cf. § 99).

There is a simple method of observation that gives you a direct estimate of the dimensions of the air striae[12]. Look at a brightly twinkling star with your eyes slightly converged, that is, focused on some object at, say, a distance of 1.5 m (5 ft) and more or less in line with the star. You will now see not one but two images of the star, and these two images do not scintillate in step, because the eyes are so far apart that a striation, while passing before one eye, has as yet no effect on the other eye. A large proportion of air striae must, therefore, be smaller than 7 cm (3 in), that is, the space between our eyes.

A very beautiful scintillation is that of the Pleiades, whose stars lie so close together that the mutual connection in the twinkling as

---

[12] R.W. Wood, *Physical Optics*, New York, 1962.

a whole makes it possible for us to distinguish the separate air striae as they pass by.

It is often said that older people cannot observe the twinkling because their eyes cannot react rapidly enough. Is this true?

52. How can the scintillation of stars be measured?

1. If you do not know how to measure a phenomenon, you can always begin, by way of introduction, with an arbitrary qualitative scale: for a nontwinkling star I use the number 0; the strongest scintillation I have ever seen near the horizon I call 10; and the steps between these two I distinguish by the other numbers. It is remarkable how useful preliminary scales like this have been in the study of all natural sciences. You get accustomed to the significance of each number of the scale sooner than you would expect, and there very soon comes a time when you find a means of calibrating this qualitative scale quantitatively.

2. Another simple standard for the turbulence in the air is the altitude above the horizon at which colors disappear, or the altitude at which twinkling becomes almost imperceptible.

3. The number of changes of the light per second, determined by rotating glasses, provides also a rough criterion for the nature of the scintillation (cf. § 51).

53. When do stars twinkle most strongly?

Strong scintillation proves only that the atmosphere is not homogeneous, and that layers of different densities are intermingled. Since this inhomogeneous atmosphere is usually accompanied by certain meteorological conditions, however, it would seem as if twinkling were a consequence of a special kind of weather.

In general, scintillation increases with low barometric pressure, low temperature, intense humidity, strong curvature of the isobars, and great change in pressure with altitude, and it is stronger when the wind is of normal strength than when the wind is either slight or very strong. It is clear, therefore, that atmospheric rest or motion depends on so many complicated factors that, for the present, the twinkling of stars cannot be used for weather forecasts.

Scintillation disappears largely when there is rising ground mist; the air is then very stable and the striae have virtually all gone.

Twinkling is also said to increase at dusk, which must either be a physiological optical illusion or a consequence of peculiar atmospheric conditions about that hour. It is even said that the Northern Lights promote scintillation, but this is difficult to understand, considering the great height (110 km—60 miles) at which the Northern Lights are usually formed in the atmosphere.

Scintillation is strongest in the northern sky, which can be explained by slightly more complicated considerations.

54. Scintillation of planets

Planets twinkle far less than stars. This seems so strange, because in other respects they appear quite alike to the naked eye. The cause of this difference lies in the fact that the disks of the stars on account of their tremendous distance appear as mere points even in the largest telescopes (0.05" at most), while the planets show an apparent diameter of, for instance, 10–68" (Venus) and 31–51" (Jupiter). In the case of planets, therefore, there will pass through any small, flat area, high up in the atmosphere, a cone of light rays, a few of which will enter your eyes. A striation which, as we know, deflects a light ray through only a few seconds of arc will cause rays entering your eyes to be replaced by other rays of the same cone, so that the brightness is not altered at all. You will notice only a variation in brightness if it so happens that a bundle of rays, originally falling just beyond your eyes, is now made to enter them. But the variation will be only slight, owing to the fact that there are many striae, some of which bend the rays toward your eyes, while others bend them away. In the case of Jupiter, for instance, at 30° above the horizon, the pencil from your eye toward the planet has, at a height of 2 000 m (7 000 ft), a diameter of 60–100 cm (27–40 in).

You will understand now that the scintillation of a planet will become noticeable as soon as the changes in direction suffered by its light are of the same order of magnitude as its apparent diameter.

That is why Venus and Mercury, which at times are observed as fairly narrow crescents, do occasionally twinkle quite appreciably, and why Venus can even show changes of color when it is very close to the horizon. When the disturbance in the air is very pronounced and the planets are low in the sky, you will almost invariably notice some changes of intensity.

In this way, therefore, twinkling provides us with a means of estimating the size of mere specks of light, which to the naked eye show no trace of a disklike shape. It has even been said that in this manner it would be possible to estimate the diameter of the fixed stars, but for the time being this would seem too optimistic*. Nevertheless, such methods have been applied with the use of radio waves.

---

* Since this book was written, the technique, *speckle interferometry*, has, indeed, become well established—Translator.

55. Shadow bands

The twinkling of stars is caused, therefore, by the irregular fluctuations of density in the ocean of air, at the bottom of which we move and live. It is, properly speaking, the same phenomenon as the localized gathering and spreading of the sun's rays in gently undulating water (§ 30): to fish, the sun twinkles just as stars do to us (see Fig. 37), with only the difference that fluctuations in the thickness of the water layers replace fluctuations in the density of the air layers. The latter are so much less effective that we can see the scintillation of only the sharpest pointlike sources of light.

In the same way as we have shown concentrations of light in clear water, so we can make air striae directly visible!

At night, in a very dark room, with only a small window opened so as to let in the light of Venus, a wispy cloudiness can be seen to pass over the smooth background formed by a wall or a white cardboard screen. These are 'shadow bands'. They can be seen clearly only when the planet is close to the horizon. Each time it twinkles, with only a slight increase in brilliance, a bright band is seen to pass over the screen, and conversely each decrease of brightness has a correspondingly darker band (cf. § 69). That which one observation shows us subjectively is shown by another objectively. These air striae have no preferred direction and they move the same way as the wind prevailing at the time in the layer of air where they originate.

Jupiter, Mars, Sirius, Betelgeuse, Procyon, Capella, Vega, and Arcturus are likewise suitable for this kind of observation, though it may be difficult because the intensity of their light is weaker. Air striae can be seen much better when light from a searchlight at a distance of not less than, say, 25 km (15 miles) happens to fall on a wall near to you.

Very remarkable shadow bands can be seen immediately preceding or immediately following the totality of a solar eclipse on a white wall or sheet. They remind one of the folds of a gigantic curtain. These, too, are air striae, made visible in the light of a linear light source, that is, the last crescent of the sun before it disappears entirely. This causes the phenomenon to be more complicated than with a pointlike source of light, each spot being drawn out into a little arc (§§ 1 and 3) and the cloudlike striae seeming to consist of bands, all of which are parallel to the sun's crescent (at its brightest point). The bands are moved by the wind, but we see only the component of their motion at right angles to their own direction. Sometimes, this phenomenon lasts only a few seconds, often a minute or longer. The distances of the bands give us an idea of the average thickness of air striae: 10–40 cm (4–16 in) is most usually given.

However, it is not necessary to wait for total eclipses of the sun, which are few and far between, to see shadow bands. You can carry out observations in the way described, at sunrise (or sunset), during those brief moments when only a narrow segment of the sun stands out above the horizon. The bands are then horizontal and move up or down according to the direction of the wind. Their velocity is 1–8 m s^{-1} (3–25 ft s^{-1}), according to the force of the wind; the space between them is 3–20 cm (1–8 in). They are generally visible for not longer than 3–4 seconds, because the sun's segment very quickly becomes too broad.

In similar conditions, but only on few occasions, Iven noticed shadow bands on almost horizontal terrain[13]. He looked from a high vantage point or from an aircraft. The bands were several kilometers (a mile or so) wide and lasted for not more than 30 seconds.

(Photo by Pekka Perviainen)

---

[13] *J. Opt. Soc. Am.*, **35**, 736, 1945.

Chapter 5

The Measurement of Intensity and Brightness of Light

56. The stars as sources of light of known intensity

The stars form a natural series of light sources of every intensity. With the aid of photometers, these intensities have been measured with great accuracy and graded in a scale of magnitudes. This scale of 'magnitudes' has, however, nothing whatever to do with the actual dimensions of a star, but refers only to its brightness or luminous intensity.

Correlation between magnitude and light intensity of a star.

m = magnitude	i = light intensity in arbitrary measure	m	i
−1	251		
0	100	0	100
1	39.8	0.1	91
2	14.8	0.2	83
3	6.31	0.3	76
4	2.51	0.4	69
5	1.00	0.5	63
6	0.40	0.6	58
7	0.16	0.7	53
		0.8	48
		0.9	44

Each class is 2.51 times weaker than the one preceding it. Apart from a constant factor, we have $i = 10^{-0.4\,m}$.

In Fig. 71, magnitudes are given for the stars in the neighborhood of the Great Bear, which are visible the whole year round, at least in the northern hemisphere. In Fig. 72, the magnitudes are given for a number of stars near the brilliant winter constellation Orion. The table on p. 96 gives some bright, well-known stars. For other stars, an atlas should be consulted.

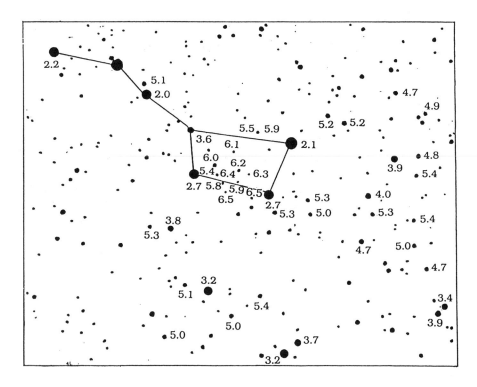

Fig. 71. Magnitudes of a number of stars near the Great Bear.

Most people can observe as far as the 6th magnitude, at least on bright nights and outside built-up areas.

57. Extinction of light by the atmosphere

Close to the horizon, usually only very few stars can be seen owing to the absorption of the rays of light on their way through the air.

Some bright, well-known stars together with their visual magnitudes. (English names of constellations are given in parentheses).

Sirius = α CMa (the Great Dog) = −1.3	Procyon = α CMi (the Little Dog) = 0.6
Vega = α Lyr (the Lyre) = 0.3	Altair = α Aql (the Eagle) = 1.1
Aldebaran = α Tau (the Bull) = 1.1	Pollux = β Gem (the Twins) = 1.3
Capella = α Aur (the Charioteer) = 0.3	Regulus = α Leo (the Lion) = 1.6
Arcturus = α Boö (the Shepherd) = 0.2	Castor = α Gem (the Twins) = 1.7

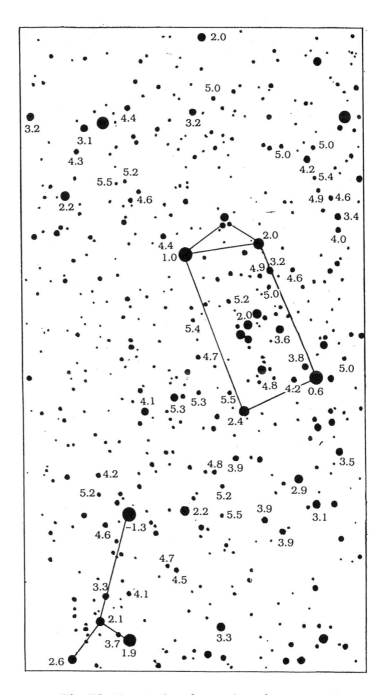

Fig. 72. Magnitudes of a number of stars near Orion.

Rays running almost horizontal have traversed a much longer path than slanting rays and have therefore undergone a greater diminution in brightness.

We will now determine this diminution, if possible, with the aid of a star map supplemented by a list of magnitudes, although our own tables in § 56 are sufficient when Orion is low and the Great Bear high in the sky.

The magnitudes indicated in them refer to when the stars are high in the sky. We take star A, which is not far from the horizon, and compare its brightness with that of the stars round the zenith (stars higher than 45° are almost unweakened). As far as possible, we take stars whose brightness is exactly equal to that of A, or between whose magnitudes A lies. The difference between the apparent and true magnitude of A as given in the tables is noted. At the same time, the altitude of star A is determined as described in Appendix A.

If this process is carried out for different stars at various distances h above the horizon (10 is enough to obtain a first impression), the results will be, more or less, those in the table below.

The numbers in the second column, which represent the extinction caused by the atmosphere, are the average values for northern latitudes and for a very clear sky, but they vary from place to place and still more so from night to night.

The zenith distance $Z = 90° - h$, and sec$Z$ is proportional to the length of the path traversed by the light through the atmosphere—see Fig. 73.

Plot Δ against sec$Z$, and you will find a collection of points, lying more or less close to a straight line, which is drawn so as to fit the various points as well as possible—see Fig. 74. From this graph you can conclude how many magnitudes a star is weakened as the length of the path traveled through the atmosphere increases. An extra-

Z is the zenith distance and Δ is the difference between the apparent and true magnitudes.

h	Δ	Z	sec$Z$
90°	0	0°	1
45°	0.09	45°	1.41
30°	0.23	60°	2.00
20°	0.45	70°	2.90
10°	0.98	80°	5.60
5°	1.67	85°	10.4
2°	3.10	88°	19.8

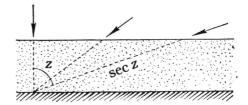

Fig. 73. The more oblique the ray of light, the longer its path through the atmosphere.

ordinarily interesting feature of the graph is that you can find how much brighter the stars would seem to shine if you could rise above the atmosphere surrounding the earth, that is, higher than the stratosphere. A star near the zenith would increase in brightness by as much as 0.2 magnitudes, that is, from about 83 to 100*.

The result is, therefore, that about $\frac{1}{5}$ of the light of rays incident nearly perpendicularly is extinguished, and this is true for the sun as well as for the stars. The extinction is not absorption of light, but scattering, which also causes the blue of the sky—cf. § 194.

The measurements described here give the best results in the case of stars near the horizon, that is, when Z = 80–90°. It is, for in-

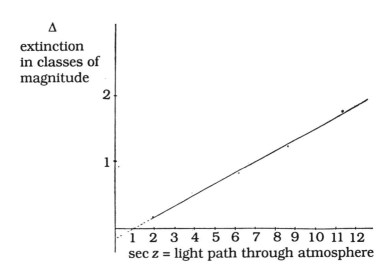

Fig. 74. Reduction Δ in magnitude of a star caused by the length of the path its light travels through the atmosphere.

*Since this book was written, travel to these heights has, of course, become possible, enabling the estimated values to be confirmed—Translator.

stance, possible to follow Sirius as it approaches the horizon. Actually, Sirius is the only star that can be seen to set; none of the others is bright enough.

58. Comparing a star with a candle

At night, choose an open stretch of country and there compare the intensity of a candle with that of a bright star, for instance, Capella. You will be surprised at how great a distance you have to stand from the candle in order to see its light reduced to the same brightness as that of the star: about 900 meters (1000 yards). Thus, Capella gives an illumination of $1/900^2 = 1/810000$ lx (lux).

The experiment can also be carried out with a torch, fixed on the roof of a house or outside the window of a high building, but this requires still greater distances. Note the difference in color.

59. Comparing two streetlights with one another

When at night you approach a streetlight it appears as if your shadow gets darker. This is not so, of course, it is merely that the surroundings get brighter near the light and thus accentuate the contrast between light and shade.

When you hold a pencil vertically in front of a sheet of white paper S (see Fig. 75), it will throw different shadows on to the paper, each corresponding to a different nearby streetlight. It is possible to make two of the shadows identical by standing at the right distance from two streetlights. Then, $A/B = a^2/b^2$, that is, from the distances a and b to the sheet of paper you can compute the ratio of the brightness of lamps A and B. This is only true, however, if both lights shine on

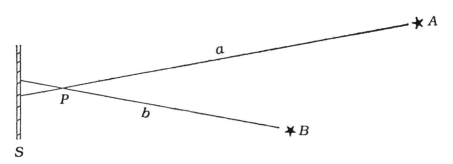

Fig. 75. Comparing two streetlights with one another.

the paper from about the same direction and you look at the shadows also from roughly that direction (cf. § 251). The proof is not simple; it is easy to make errors.

Note the difference in color of the shadows when sodium and mercury lights are compared.

60. Comparing the moon with a streetlight

Find the two shadows cast by the full moon and a streetlight. The one opposite the moon is reddish, that opposite the lamp, dark blue (cf. § 115). Move away from the streetlight; the shadow cast by the moon remains just as strong, whereas that caused by the streetlight grows fainter. Assume that the shadows are equal at a distance of 20 m (22 yd) from the streetlight. Assume that the luminous intensity of the streetlight is 50 cd (candela). At a distance of 20 m, the illuminance will be $50/20^2 = 0.13$ lx. This must also be the illuminance produced by the full moon.

Repeat the experiment during the first or third quarter of the moon. The illuminance is then far less than half that at full moon, because a considerable portion of the surface of the moon is darkened by the oblique shadows of the lunar mountains (cf. § 192).

The exact values are: 0.20 lx for the full moon, and 0.02 lx for the first or third quarter.

61. Brightness of the moon's disk

When Herschel, on a voyage to South Africa, arrived at Cape Town, he saw the moon, at the time nearly full, rise above Table Mountain, which was illuminated by the setting sun. It struck him that the moon was less bright than the rocks, which made him conclude that the surface of the moon must be formed of dark rock.

A similar observation can be made in your own surroundings if you compare the full moon, rising at about 6 p.m., with a white wall illuminated by the setting sun. The distances between sun and moon, and sun and earth, are practically the same. If moon and wall were made of the same material, their brightness would be the same, however much their distances from your eyes might differ (a splendid application of a classical photometric theorem!). The difference observed must be ascribed to the fact that the moon consists of dark rock (volcanic ashes?).

For this observation to be absolutely accurate, the sun and moon should be at the same height above the horizon, so that the reduction in illuminance by the atmosphere is the same for both.

62. A few ratios of brightness in the landscape

The sun's brightness = 300 000 × the brightness of the blue sky.

The brightness of a white cloud = 10 × the brightness of the blue sky.

On a normally sunny day with a blue sky, 80 percent of the light comes directly from the sun; only 20 percent from the sky.

The illuminance of a horizontal plane after sunset, with a cloudless sky, is:

Sun's position	0	–1°	–2°	–3°	–4°	–5°	–6°	–8°	–11°	–17°	
Illuminance	400	250	113	40	14	4	1	0.1	0.01	0.001	lx

The eye adapts itself to every luminous intensity so well and so rapidly that we never realize sufficiently how tremendous are the brightness ratios around us. Let us compare a landscape, illuminated by the sun at its height, with another illuminated by the moon.

Disk of the sun	10^5 cd cm^{-2}	Disk of the moon	3×10^{-1} cd cm^{-2}
Bright white object	2 cd cm^{-2}	Bright white object	5×10^{-6} cd cm^{-2}
Pitch black	4×10^{-2} cd cm^{-2}	Pitch black	10^{-7} cd cm^{-2}

This shows that in one and the same landscape, the greatest brightness ratio is not higher than 50:1, yet, as regards the absolute value, the illuminance changes enormously. The comparison also shows that pitch black in the light of the sun is as much as 8 000 times brighter than a white object in moonlight.

Differences in brightness of various parts of the landscape can be obtained by comparing their power of reflecting sunlight: fresh snow, 80–85%; old snow, up to 40%; grass, 10–33%; dry soil, 14%; moist soil, 8–9%; rivers and bays, 7%; deep oceans, 3%; ponds and puddles, sometimes not more than 2%. When you observe from an aircraft, these brightnesses are modified by scattering in the air through which you look; also, clouds reflect up to 80% sunlight.

63. Reflecting power

> Your soul is a vast expanse of water,
> the stars are not reflected in you.
>
> Kurt Heynicke, *Ferne Frau*

Have you ever seen stars reflected in water? In town, this is hardly possible; in the country, only sometimes—in a pool or lake when there is no wind; on dark nights, it is very striking.

Bright stars of the 1st magnitude, near the zenith, give a feeble reflection, about equal to stars of the 5th magnitude. A difference of four magnitudes corresponds to a ratio of about 40 in luminous intensity, so that water reflects only 2.5 percent of the vertically incident rays. Stars situated lower are better reflected.

The reflecting power is connected with the index of Fresnel refraction. For perpendicular incidence, this is

$$[(n-1)/(n+1)]^2.$$

In the table below, the values of reflecting power of glass and water are given for various angles of incidence.

You will now understand why you can never see stars reflected in water in a town; the sky is not dark enough, stars of the 3rd magnitude are hardly visible, and, moreover, the surface of the water is illuminated too much. Only planets are visible at all by reflection and then only if they are much brighter than the 1st magnitude.

The brightness by day of the reflected blue sky, the houses, and the trees seems much greater than two percent; in some paintings, the difference between the brightness of the objects, and of their reflection, can hardly be seen. This is simply an optical illusion.

There is a superstition that stars are never reflected in deep waters. This is, of course, without any foundation whatever.

Reflecting power of glass and water for various angles of incidence.

Angle of incidence	Reflecting power	
	of water	of glass ($n = 1.52$)
0°	0.020	0.043
10°	0.020	0.043
20°	0.021	0.044
30°	0.022	0.045
40°	0.024	0.049
50°	0.034	0.061
60°	0.060	0.091
70°	0.135	0.175
75°	0.220	0.257
80°	0.350	0.388
85°	0.580	0.615
90°	1.000	1.000

By day, too, it can easily be seen how much the reflecting power of water depends on the angle of incidence. Each puddle at the side of the road looks different, depending on whether you look into it from above or obliquely from a distance—see § 239.

Flying over the sea, you can see clearly how much darker the water directly beneath you is and how it becomes lighter toward the horizon.

It seems improbable that the reflections of the blue sky, of houses and trees, when you look perpendicularly into the water, have only two percent of the brightness of these objects proper; in some paintings, there is hardly a difference between the brightness of the object and its reflection in water. This is caused partly because we almost always observe a surface of water at a very small angle below the horizon (see Fig. 178) and partly because of psychological factors.

A pane of glass reflects 4.3 percent of the light at each surface, that is, 8.6 percent altogether. In many small glass buildings, such as telephone booths, reflections of its lighting can be seen repeated between two parallel and opposite windows; sometimes there are as many as four visible reflections at each side. The first is formed by once reflected light; the second by three times; the third by five times; and the fourth by seven times reflected rays. The brightness of the last reflection is therefore only 0.0867, that is, less than one ten-millionth part of the original brightness. This simple computation is a very good example of the tremendously wide range of brightnesses to which our eye can react.

64. Transmission of light through wire netting

Illuminated advertizing signs on roofs are often fixed on wire netting attached to metal frames.

At a distance, the separate wires are no longer distinguishable, and the netting resembles a sheet of uniformly gray glass. It is interesting to look at the netting at an increasingly acute angle, and to see how it gets darker and darker against the sky. This proves that the wires of which it is made have a round cross section, for if it were built up of small, flat bands, it would remain equally dark at every angle—see Fig. 76.

65. Opaqueness of a wood

Looking through a narrow strip of woodland, you can see between the tree trunks the light sky beyond. There must obviously be some expression indicating what part of the light is allowed to pass unobstructed if it is assumed that the distribution of the trees is acciden-

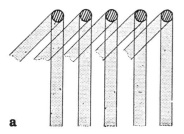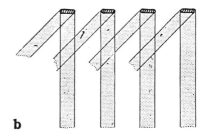

Fig. 76. Transmission of light through wire netting made (**a**) of round wire, and (**b**) of flat wire.

tal, that N trees occur per square meter (1.1 yd²), and that they have a diameter D at a height on a level with your eyes.

Consider a beam of light of width b which has already traveled a distance ℓ through the wood—see Fig. 77. Let i be the amount of light that still remains of the original amount i_0. When the rays of light penetrate a little farther over a short distance dℓ, an amount of light di is removed; hence,

$$di/i = -NDbd\ell/b = -d\ell ND,$$

from which it follows by integration that

$$i = i_0 e^{-ND\ell} = i_0 \times 10^{-0.43ND\ell}.$$

The amount of light let through will therefore become less and less, according as the wood is more extended in the direction of incidence of the light, in exactly the same way as the light transmitted by a dark liquid is less according as the layer increases in thickness. Assume that, in the case of a wood of fir trees, $N = 1$ per m² and $D = 0.10$ m (4 in). Then, approximately:

$\ell = 10$ m (11 yd)	$i/i_0 = 0.37$
$= 25$ m (27 yd)	$= 0.10$
$= 50$ m (55 yd)	$= 0.01$
$= 70$ m (76 yd)	$= 0.001$

The rapidity of the increase in opacity is very striking. From a rough estimate of the fraction of the horizon that is as yet not intercepted by the trees, you can gather the depth of the wood.

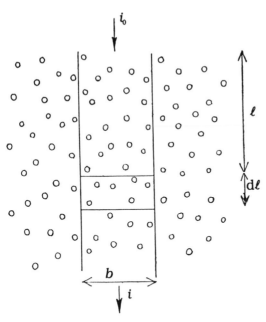

Fig. 77. We compute how much light is visible between the tree trunks.

How much is *ND* in the case of a beech wood, and in the case of a wood of young and one of full-grown fir trees?

Glimpses of the sky in the background through a beech wood.
(Photo by Hannu Karttunen)

This question may be followed by a number of interesting probability considerations. The number of openings, for instance, is directly proportional to $\ell^2 e^{-ND\ell}$, where ℓ is the distance to the edge of the wood. In other words, if you approach the edge of the wood, the number of clear openings at first slowly increases and then rapidly decreases. The number reaches a maximum when $\ell = 2/ND$. Deep in the wood, the number of trees that can still be discerned is $4\pi/ND^2$, that is, 1257 in the example.

66. Beats between two railings

Whenever you can see the posts of one set of railings between the posts of another set, you will perceive broad light and dark bands in the intensity of light that move when you move. These are caused by the apparent distance between the posts of the two sets of railings differing more or less, either because the one has wider spaces than the other, or because they are at different distances from your eyes. In certain directions, the posts seem to coincide, while in others the posts of the first railing fill exactly the space between the posts of the second, so that a difference arises in the average brightness. You might say that they are 'in step' or 'out of step'.

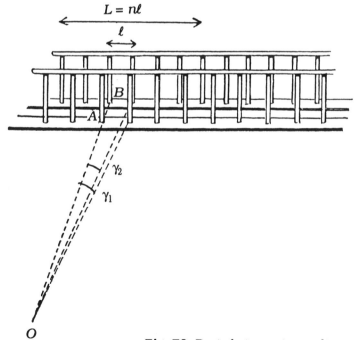

Fig. 78. Beats between two railings.

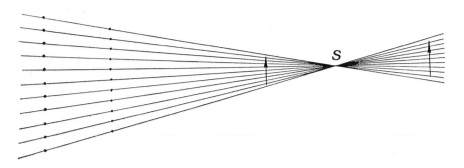

Fig. 79. Beats between two railings with a different period.

When you have noticed these beats once, you will see them in all sorts of place. Every bridge with a parapet in the form of a railing on both sides shows these undulations in intensity when seen from a certain distance. They appear, too, when you see the shadow of a railing between its own posts, in which case the period is the same, but the distance to your eyes is different.

In some stations, a goods lift is surrounded by wire netting, and the combination of the side nearest to us and the side farthest away forms a kind of moiré, such as you see when you lay two pieces of wire gauze, or two combs with unequal distances between the teeth, on one another.

Consider in more detail the simple case (see Fig. 78) of two equal railings seen at unequal distances, $x_1 = OA$ and $x_2 = OB$, from our eyes. Let ℓ be the distance between two successive posts, which subtends the angles $\gamma_1 = \ell/x_1$ and $\gamma_2 = \ell/x_2$ at your eyes. The length of a beat will contain n posts, where n is given by $n = \gamma_1/(\gamma_1-\gamma_2) = x_2/(x_2-x_1)$, that is, the number of beats increases as you move away from the

Fig. 80. Beats between a fence and its shadow; **(a)** position of observer; **(b)** shape of the beat waves.

railings. On the other hand, the angular distance θ covered by a beat, as seen by you, will remain the same, for $\theta = n\gamma_2 = \ell/(x_2-x_1)$. You can determine the true length $L = n\ell = \ell x_2/(x_2-x_1)$ of a beat by moving parallel to the railings; the beats will move with the same speed as you are moving. Now measure the distance you must walk so as to see a beat occupy exactly the same place as the one before. Test the validity of the various formulas. Or, conversely, on determining n, θ, and L, you can solve for x_2, x_2-x_1, and ℓ. In this way, it is possible to obtain all dimensions of the railings at a distance without any further means.

If the periods of the two railings are different, the beats will be seen to move in the most remarkable way whenever your eyes move; now in the same direction as you are moving, now in the opposite one, depending on whether you are in front of, or behind, the radiating point S—see Fig. 79; in other words, depending on whether $\gamma_1 < \gamma_2$ or $\gamma_1 > \gamma_2$. The beats will move faster and faster as you approach S.

When a vertical fence casts its shadow on level ground, the beats look somewhat different—see Fig. 80; at the top they lie closer together than at the bottom, and also a slight curvature is noticeable. But this is in accordance with our earlier considerations, for the distance between the two interfering gridlike systems is greater at the top. Therefore, the angular distance seen by you between successive bars differs considerably, which means that the beats lie close together. At the bottom, it is just the other way round.

67. Measurements with an exposure meter

Many amateur photographers use an exposure meter, and this is, of course, perfectly suitable for measuring light intensities out of doors. Although these measurements are fairly inaccurate, they cover a wide range (1:100 000) and give us the opportunity of getting an idea of the brightness in a large number of places and in all kinds of circumstance, where before we did not even have an idea of the order of magnitude.

There are different kinds of exposure meter. For instance, some are calibrated to the ASA scale, which gives a direct indication of the light intensity, while those calibrated to the DIN scale give ten times the logarithm of the light flux. Thus, 3 DIN units correspond to a factor of 2.

Most exposure meters give the photographer the information he needs: the exposure time, t, and the corresponding aperture diameter, D, or rather the reciprocals of these: $s = 1/t$ and $v = f/D$. These are associated with a certain film speed, so that films need an exposure time, t, aperture (stop), D^2, and light intensity, L, given by $C = tD^2L$. If the camera has been set correctly, $L = C/tD^2 = csv^2$, where

c is a constant. From the values for v and t given by the exposure meter, the incident light flux, except for the constant, c, is found immediately. For instance: a gray sky requires $s = 30$, $v = 4$, so that $L = 480c$, while a blue sky requires $s = 250$, $v = 6$, so that $L = 9\,000c$.

Some tests that can be carried out with an exposure meter are:

1. At night, point the exposure meter at a single light that is not surrounded by walls and then, moving the meter away from the light, find out how far sideways the light can be measured.

2. In the same circumstances as in 1, investigate whether the light intensity is inversely proportional to the square of the distance. It must be possible to use the same settings for v and s at twice the distance when the film speed is 6° DIN higher.

In sunny weather, compare the illumination on a horizontal plane when a shadow is thrown on to the plane and in the absence of a shadow, that is, the illumination caused by direct sunlight and by diffused sunlight.

Compare the illuminations on a plane when this is facing the sky and when it is turned downward; above water the ratio is 6:1, above gravel it is 12:1, and above grass it is 25:1.

In the following tests the object is to measure the light intensity at which different plants grow. The exposure meter should therefore be kept close to the ground, as if it were part of the vegetation.

When the light intensities in a wood and outside it (at least 20 meters (60 ft) away from the edge of the wood) are compared, it will be found that in case of an oak wood the ratio is 0.15–0.20, whereas in case of a coniferous wood the ratio is likely to be only 0.01.

Compare the light intensities in a beech wood in (a) mid-May, (b) when the first leaves begin to unfold, and (c) in early June. In a typical case, it was found that they were respectively $\frac{1}{11}$, $\frac{1}{30}$, and $\frac{1}{64}$ of that outside the wood.

Compare the light intensities in the habitat of waybread, ivy (differentiate between flowering and dead branches), heath, and bracken.

When the light intensity well inside the foliage of a tree, where it is about the lowest at which twigs can still develop, is measured, it will be found that it is about 0.2 (larch), 0.11 (birch), 0.1 (Scotch pine—Pinus sylvestris), 0.03 (spruce), 0.01 (beech) of that outside the tree.

The ratios mentioned are called *daylight factors*. These are commonly used to determine the efficiency of windows and of lighting installations.

Chapter 6

The Eye

The study of nature must necessarily involve the study of the human senses as well. To be accurate in your observations of light and color in the outdoors, you must first of all be familiar with the instrument you use continually: your eyes. It is very enlightening to learn to distinguish between what nature actually shows us and what our eyes add to, or subtract from, it. And no surroundings are more favorable for studying the peculiarities of the eye than those out of doors, to which we are adapted by nature.

68. Seeing under water

Have you ever tried to keep your eyes open under water? A little courage, and it will be easy enough. But every object you look at is then extraordinarily indistinct and hazy, even in a swimming pool with very clear water. In the air, it is the outer surface of the eye, the cornea, that collects the rays of light and causes the formation of the images on the retina, helped only slightly by the crystalline lens. Under water, however, the action of the cornea is neutralized owing to the

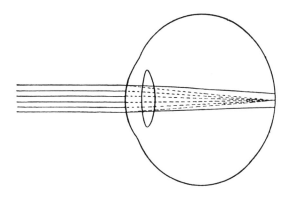

Fig. 81. Under water, the formation of the image in our eyes is all wrong: the path of the light rays under water is shown by the *solid lines* and that in air by the *dashed lines*.

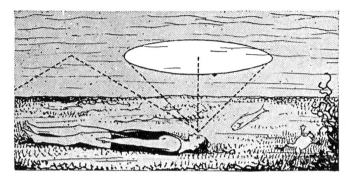

Fig. 82. Looking at things the way fish do.

fact that the refractive indices of the fluid in the eye and in the water outside are nearly equal, so that the rays go straight on at the bounding surface of the cornea—see Fig. 81. This offers an excellent means of judging how insufficient the working of the crystalline lens would be if it alone were responsible for the formation of images. You are at this moment so hopelessly far-sighted that focusing is almost of no use, and a point of light remains equally hazy at whatever distance it may be. The only possible way to distinguish an object at all is to hold it so close to your eye that it subtends a large angle there, while the unavoidable haziness of the outlines is not too much of a disadvantage.

In clear water, a five-pence coin (dime) becomes visible at arm's length (60 cm—25 in), and a piece of iron wire is not visible at any distance at all. On the other hand, anyone swimming past can be observed as far as 9 m (10 yd) off, for such a large object is bound to be noticed. Roughly speaking, the presence of an object of length v is observable at a distance of $30v$ at the most; its shape can, more or less, be ascertained at a distance of $5v$, and you can only speak of seeing it properly when it has come within a distance equal to its own dimensions.

To make your power of vision at all normal, you will require a pair of powerful glasses, but unfortunately glasses are four times less effective under water than in air. And, to make matters worse, such glasses lose their full effect when held a few millimeters (about 80 thousandths of an inch) from the eye! Taking all this into consideration, it will be necessary to use a lens of strength 100, that is, with a focal length of 12 mm (0.5 in). The lens of a linen tester (thread counter) as used for examining cloth and printing would be suitable.

Notice how difficult it is to estimate distances, both with and without water glasses. Most objects look shadowy and almost ghostly.

You should also look upward while submerged in water. Rays of light from above when entering the water make an angle with the vertical smaller than 45° at most, so you will see a large disk of light above your head, and if you look sideways, the ray from your eye will be completely reflected at the surface, and the mirrored image of the feebly illuminated ground will be all it shows—see Fig. 82. This is what the world looks like to fish!

One way of obtaining a very good impression of the view from under water is to hold a slanting mirror beneath the surface while standing upright in the water and taking special care not to cause ripples. Note then how all the objects out of the water appear to be strongly compressed in a vertical direction, the more so the nearer they are to the horizon, and how everything has a beautiful fringe of color.

69. How the interior part of our eye may be made visible

A practiced observer can see the yellow spot of his own eye (the central, most sensitive point of the retina), surrounded by a darker ring in which there are no blood vessels. In the evening, when you have already been outside for a time, look at the vast cloudless sky just when the first stars are making their appearance. Close your eyes for a few seconds, and open them again quickly, looking in the direction of the sky. The darkness will disappear first of all at the circumference of the field of vision, and contract rapidly toward the center where the yellow spot, with its dark edge, becomes just visible and sometimes lights up for a moment.

If you walk beside a high fence, with the bright sun shining through it, the sunlight will flash several times a second in your eyes. If you keep looking straight in front of you, and don't turn your eyes in the direction of the sun, you will be surprised to see that each flash of light is accompanied by an indistinct figure of irregular spots, mazes, and branches, bright on a dark background. It is possible that these are certain parts of the retina made visible to us by this unusual illumination.

70. The blind spot

Another special point on the retina is the 'blind spot', where the optic nerve enters and there are no light-sensitive cells. It is situated 15 degrees from the yellow spot toward the nose. Therefore, if we look at a certain object, anything 15 degrees away from it (to the right in the case of the right eye; to the left in the case of the left eye) is imperceptible. This phenomenon can be tested readily with a clear night sky[1].

---

[1] A.J.M. Wanders, *Hemel en Dampkring*, **51**, 4, 1953.

On a winter's night, look at Vega and β Cygni when they are at about the same altitude. Close your left eye and look at β Cygni with your right eye and you will notice that Vega has become invisible. It may be necessary to tilt your head slightly. Or, in spring, look at the Great Bear; fix your right eye on the feeble star δ and you will note that the bright star η will disappear[2].

71. Night myopia[3]

When out for at walk at dusk, you may notice that you become more and more near-sighted as it gets darker and you are no longer able to see the far-off landscape clearly. In normal light, perhaps with glasses, but in any case with relaxed eyes, you can see distant objects clearly, whereas at dusk you cannot see any objects farther away than, say, one meter (just over three feet) sharply. In other words, you have become 'near-sighted by 1 diopter'. If you can still see clearly up to two meters, your near-sightedness is 1/2 diopter (D). The average is 0.6 D, but in some cases it is as much as 2 D.

The explanation for this is that with decreasing light the pupil opens wider and the periphery of the eye lens begins to play a major role. However, the periphery is 'near-sighted' relative to the center of the lens; in other words, spherical aberration occurs in the eye. During the day, our eyes are most sensitive to yellow, but at dusk to bluish green (§ 92). Therefore, the eye refracts bluish-green light more than yellow light, which means that we are near-sighted as far as bluish-green light is concerned: this is chromatic aberration of the eye. Together, these two aberrations cause near-sightedness of about 0.5 D. A higher degree must be caused by other phenomena, such as the altered convergence of the eye axes.

72. Imperfect images formed by the eye

Stars do not appear to us as perfect points, but as small irregularly shaped figures, often as a spot of light from which rays diverge. The usual representation of five rays is not according to reality. For this experiment, the brightest stars of all should be taken, preferably Sirius or, better still, the planets Venus or Jupiter, because the disk they show us is so small that it is practically a point, and their brightness exceeds that of the brightest stars.

---

[2] These are the stars with magnitude 3.6 and 2.2 respectively in Fig. 71.

[3] M. Koomen, R. Scolnik, and R. Tousey, *J. Opt. Soc. Am.*, **41**, 80, 1951; **43**, 37, 1954. Ivanoff, *J. Opt. Soc. Am.*, **45**, 769, 1955.

Fig. 83. A star or distant light seen by a
slightly myopic person not wearing glasses.

Hold your head on one side, first toward the right, then toward the
left, and the shape slopes accordingly. This is different for each person, and also for each of his or her eyes, but if you cover one eye with
your hand and look with the other eye at various stars you will always see the same shape.

This shows that it is not the stars that look so irregular, but our
eyes that are at fault and do not reproduce a point exactly as a point.

The shape of the rays becomes larger and more irregular when the
eye is in dark surroundings and the pupil is wide open. It becomes
smaller in well-lit surroundings, when the pupil is contracted to a small
hole. And, indeed, Gullstrand has proved that the crystalline lens of
our eye is distorted mostly at the edges by muscles to which it is attached, so that the distinctness of the images diminishes when light
passes near these edges.

Take a sheet of paper, prick a 1 mm ($^{40}/_{1000}$ in) diameter hole in it
and hold this before the pupil. After searching for a while, you will be
sure to find Sirius or a planet, and you will see that the image is perfectly round. Now move this aperture to the edge of the pupil, and
the point of light becomes irregularly distorted; in my case, it stretches
out into a line of light in the direction of the radius of the pupil.

Many people see the cusps of the moon's crescent multiplied.
These deviations from the distinct image must be ascribed mainly to

cornea   retina

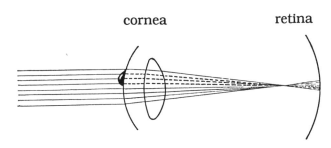

Fig. 84. A myopic person not wearing glasses sees
distant light sources as irregular disks; a raindrop on
the cornea is seen as a small dark spot.

small deformations of the surface of the cornea. Similar deformations appear to anyone who is short-sighted when he removes his glasses—see Fig. 83: every light in the distance becomes a disk of light in which, however, the brightness is distributed very unevenly. Should it happen to be raining, you will see, now and then, a small round spot appear suddenly in the little disk of light: a portion of the cornea is covered by a raindrop—see Fig. 84. You will see that it keeps its shape for a good ten seconds, that is, of course, if you can refrain from blinking for so long!

When the glaring lights of a car in the distance shine toward you, you can see the entire field of view round the intense point of light covered by a haze of light, which is speckled, and sometimes striped radially. This structure is caused by diffraction or refraction of light at a great number of irregularities in the eye. Sodium streetlights also give a diffuse glow round the light source, but this shows fine hatching, the lines of which run exactly parallel to the source of light, for each diffracting grain has produced a line of light instead of a point.

73. Bundles of rays that appear to be emitted by bright sources

Distant lights seem at times to cast long straight rays toward our eyes, especially when we look at them with half-closed eyelids; along the edge of each eyelid lachrymal moisture forms a small meniscus by which the light rays are refracted. Figure 85a shows that the rays are refracted at the upper eyelid in such a way that they seem to come from below; the source gets a downward tail, and the lower eyelid gives, in the same way, an upward tail. The formation of these tails can be followed very well by holding one eyelid open, and clos-

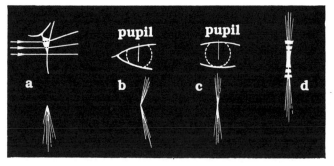

Fig. 85. Formation of light rays around distant lights.

ing the other slowly, or by holding the head up or down while partly closing the eyes. The rays appear at the very moment the eyelid begins to cover the pupil; to a short-sighted observer this is easily visible, for the source of light, which he sees as a broadened disk, is at that moment partly screened off.

The rays are not quite parallel, not even those to one eye. Look at a source of light in front of you, turn your head a little to the right and then move your eyes until you see the source again. The rays are now slanting—see Fig. 85b. The reason for this is evidently that the edges of the eyelids, where they cross the pupil, are no longer horizontal, and each bundle of rays is at right angles to the edge of the eyelid that causes it; the observed directions fit in exactly with this explanation. You will understand now why the rays are not parallel when you look straight ahead, for the curvature of the eyelids is already perceptible even within the breadth of the pupil. Hold your finger against the right-hand edge of the pupil, and the left-hand rays of the bundle will disappear exactly as they should do.

Besides the long tails (Fig. 85c) there are short, very luminous ones, caused by the reflection against the edges of the eyelids—see Fig 85d. Convince yourself by experiment that this time it is the upper eyelid that causes the short upper tail and vice versa. These reflected rays usually show a transverse diffraction pattern.

74. Phenomena caused by eyeglasses

Lines are distorted by ordinary eyeglasses when you look through them slantwise. This distortion is 'barrel' when the glasses are concave and 'pincushion' when they are convex—see Fig. 86. If you wish to judge whether a line in a landscape is perfectly straight or vertical, this deformation is particularly annoying. Astigmatism arises at the outer boundaries of the field so pronouncedly that every kind of

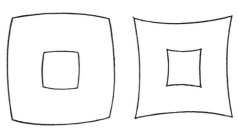

barrel-shaped pincushion-shaped

Fig. 86. Image distortion by spectacles.

minor detail becomes obliterated. These faults in the formation of images are more marked according as the glasses are more concave or more convex. In the case of meniscus glass, they are much slighter.

Anyone looking through his or her glasses at a lighted lamp in the evening will see somewhere in its vicinity a floating disk of light. It is not very distinct, and if you keep staring at it, the accommodation of your eyes changes automatically and you see the disk grow or diminish. If you remove your glasses and hold them away from your eyes a little distance, you will see the disk change into a point of light, which appears to be a much reduced image of the lamp itself. If you look at a group of three lamps, you will see that the image is upright. The explanation for this is that the disk of light is caused by a double reflection on the surfaces of the glasses or at the cornea of the eyes. Actually, three disks should be seen, but you can see these only if they are not too indistinct. In practice, only one kind of double reflection occurs with a given pair of glasses—see Fig. 87.

Unframed glasses, if their edges are beveled, sometimes show a narrow spectrum along their edge caused by distant lights.

For raindrops on eyeglasses, see § 139.

75. Visual acuity

A normal eye has no difficulty at all in distinguishing Mizar and Alcor in the Great Bear, separated by about 12 minutes of arc—see Figs. 71 and 88. The question is how much further this acuity will enable you to go. People with sharp eyes can distinguish points separated by half this amount, as in the double star α Capricorni (the Sea Goat): separation of components 6′, magnitudes 3.8 and 4.5.

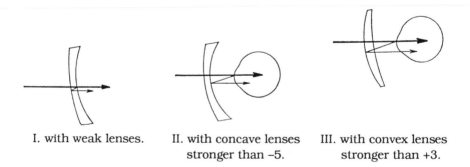

I. with weak lenses.   II. with concave lenses   III. with convex lenses
                            stronger than –5.   stronger than +3.

Fig. 87. How double reflections arise when spectacles are used.

Only a few people can resolve separations smaller than 4′:

α Librae (the Balance or Scales)—separation of components 4′, magnitudes 2.8 and 5.3;

ε Lyrae (the Lyre)—separation of components 3′, magnitudes 5.3 and 6.3.

Exceptionally good observers, of which there are few, can distinguish an incredible amount of detail when the sky is bright and the atmosphere calm. One of them has asserted that with the naked eye he can see α Librae as a double star (distance nearly 4′). Saturn, to him, is distinctly oblong and Venus crescent-shaped, at favorable moments when he looks through a smoked glass or through a cloud

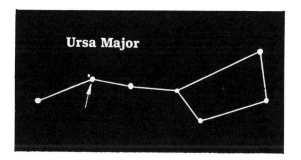

Fig. 88. Some widely spaced double stars.

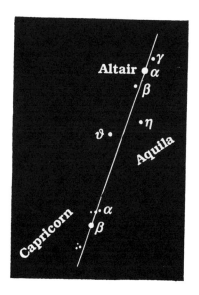
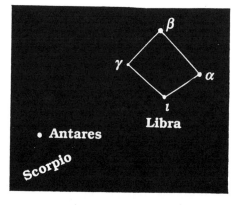

Fig. 89. Some more double stars.

of smoke that happens to be of the right transparency. He is even able to see two of the satellites of Jupiter, though only at dusk when the stars of the first and second magnitude are beginning to appear.

Dusk is the best time, too, for other observations: for example, the characteristics of the moon's surface are then much more clearly visible than at night and one is less dazzled.

It is good fun to observe the narrow crescent of the moon as soon as possible after the new moon, and it has been done by some within just eleven hours[4]. It is, of course, essential to know where to look.

The eye's limited power of discrimination explains the changes in the image of objects from which we move away. At a distance of 50 m (55 yd), the shape of the leaves of a tree can no longer be distinguished, even though they are sharply outlined against the sky; the top of the tree is but a hazy outline. At a distance of 10 km (6 miles), the outline of a wood is very distinct, but cannot be distinguished from the top of a hill. The haze of the air diminishes the contrast of light and dark, but the borders retain their sharpness.

76. Sensitivity of the direct and peripheral fields of vision[5]

When you go into the darkness of the night from a brightly lit room, the eye needs some time to accommodate. The first thing you notice is that, after a few minutes, when you focus clearly, you can see the stars better and better until those of the 3rd and 4th magnitude can be seen: this limit does not change. The accommodation is caused partly by a widening of the pupil and partly by the adaptation to the dark by the cones that occupy the central part of the yellow spot. More important, and longer lasting, is the adaptation of the rods in the peripheral part of the retina: in the indirect field of vision, more and more stars become visible until, after about half an hour, a limit to this is reached also.

The rods have then become much more sensitive than the cones. Moreover, the eye constantly makes tiny, unconscious movements: the cones each work as a unit that must receive enough light to give an impression, whereas the rods work in groups, so that movements of the eye do not attenuate the impression.

When you have been outside for some time in the darkness, which are the faintest stars you can see? Compare this with Figs. 71 and 72. Most people can see stars of the sixth magnitude, some those of the seventh magnitude. Let us try to find out which stars remain vis-

---

[4] *Hemel en Dampkring,* **44**, 217, 1946.
[5] G. Patfoort, *Ann. d'Optique Oculaire,* **2**, 39, 1953. Arden and Weale, *J. Physiol.,* **125**, 417, 1954. Bouman and ten Doesschate, *Ophthalmologica,* **126**, 1953.

ible when you look at them directly and intently. A certain amount of will power is required not to turn away your gaze, but to keep it directed exactly at one star. You will notice, to your surprise, that each faint star disappears as soon as you stare at it intently, but should your gaze move ever so slightly away from it, the star reappears! To me personally, even stars of the fourth magnitude become invisible, but those of the third remain visible. There must, therefore, be a difference of as much as three magnitudes between the threshold value for the yellow spot and that for the surrounding retina, which corresponds to a factor of 16 in luminous intensity. Even experienced observers will be amazed at the magnitude of this effect, so accustomed are we to letting our gaze wander unconsciously away from faint stars so as to see them better[6].

It is well worth while seeing if you can follow a bright star or planet, for instance, Venus, at early dawn. As the sky grows lighter, it becomes more and more difficult to distinguish the point of light, and a peculiar thing is that often you cannot see it, simply because you do not look in the right direction, though it is perfectly perceptible once you have found it again. It is a similar experience to when you are looking in the sky for a lark singing.

If you look carefully, you can often follow Venus until it is broad daylight, and see it the whole day. Sometimes, the same can be done with Jupiter, but it is much more difficult, and it is exceptional to be able to observe it up to the time the sun reaches an altitude of 10°. Mars may be seen when the sun is low. These observations should be made especially when the planet is near the moon, which is an excellent guide in finding the faint luminous points in the vast blue sky. Do these observations not contradict the deduction, made from our experiments with stars, that the yellow spot has the lower sensitivity? By no means, for the rods come into play only in feeble light, and are out of action during the day. By day, the small groove of the yellow spot is most sensitive, while at night the outer parts are.

77. Fechner's experiment

On a day when the clouds are light and hazy, choose a cloud that is only just perceptible against the background of the sky. Hold a piece of smoked glass before your eyes, and you will see that that same little cloud is still only just distinguishable.

This led Fechner to conclude that the eye can distinguish two

---

[6] Edgar Allen Poe states, in *The Murders in the Rue Morgue*, that even Venus can become invisible if you persist in staring at it hard. This is, however, impossible.

brightnesses if their ratio (not the difference between them) amounts to a definite and constant amount (the one about 5 percent greater than the other).

Repeat the experiment with very dark glass: the cloud is no longer visible and all the fine degrees of light have vanished. This shows that the fraction that was only just distinguishable is not absolutely constant.

A counterpart of Fechner's experiment is the daily disappearance of the stars. The difference in brightness between a star and its surroundings is always the same, but the ratio of the brightnesses in the daytime differs greatly from that at night. As a rule, it may be said that our visual impressions are determined mainly by the brightness ratios. This aspect of our sense of vision is of the utmost importance for our daily life. Thanks to this, the objects around us remain definite, recognizable things, even in changing conditions of illumination.

78. The threshold for observing brightness ratios

Windows of buildings reflect sunlight and throw spots of light on to the street (§ 12). If the street itself is also in direct sunlight, these spots are not easily seen. If, however, a window is moved slightly, the spot of light emanating from it is seen immediately. The same happens when we pass by and our shadow skims the spot of light. (Is this not a remarkable psychological peculiarity? Our eyes appear to be eminently suitable for discerning faint light phenomena that move in unison.) A glass sheet reflects 4% from its two surfaces, that is, 8% in all; if the angle of incidence is less than 90°, the reflection increases slightly (§ 63). It appears that an increase in brightness of about 10% is the smallest our eyes can distinguish in normal circumstances and without special precautions.

If there is a small puddle of water in front of a sunlit wall, the light reflected by the water should form a spot on the wall, but unless the wind ripples the water, when lines of light travel across the wall (§ 12), the spot is hardly noticeable. If you move through the rays of reflected light, a faint shadow can be seen. An increase in brightness of 3% can therefore only be discerned in very favorable conditions (§ 104).

79. The landscape by moonlight

If Fechner's law were valid rigorously and the eye could appreciate ratios of intensity only, a landscape by moonlight would convey an impression differing in no way from that of the same landscape in sunlight, for although the light intensities are thousands of times less, objects are illuminated in the same manner and by a light source of practically the same shape and position.

It is clear from this that Fechner's law no longer holds when the brightnesses are very small. You should observe a landscape in the moonlight and note, especially, the differences compared to the illumination in the daytime. The main characteristic is that all the parts not fully illuminated by the light of the moon are almost uniformly dark, whereas, in the daytime, various degrees of brightness are noticeable in these same parts. This explains why, if an underexposed photographic negative of a landscape in sunlight is printed too dark, the print looks like a landscape by moonlight. In a similar manner, painters suggest a nocturnal landscape by painting almost everything equally dark which, owing to the weakening of the contrast, gives us unconsciously the impression that the lighting must indeed be very feeble.

80. The landscape in brilliant sunlight

The brightnesses on a summer's day, particularly at the seaside, are so intense as almost to dazzle you. Here, also, the ratios seem smaller than in average illumination, for everything seems equally glaring in the blazing sunshine. This effect is frequently made use of by painters.

81. White objects by night

A very special and seldom recorded impression is obtained when bright objects, such as a white gravel path, a mass of snow, white flowers, or the foam of the surf, are seen at night. They appear surprisingly bright, much more so than we would have expected in the faint light; it almost appears as if they emanate light. Many a report of phosphorescent hail or snow is due to this phenomenon. It appears that the rods in our eyes are especially sensitive to contrast at this low level of brightness.

82. The veil effect

When you are out for a walk in the sunshine, why is it that a transparent muslin curtain prevents you from seeing what is happening inside the rooms of houses? The veil-like curtain is strongly illuminated, and if the objects in the room have only a small percentage of that brightness, they add to the uniform brightness of the veil a fraction too small to be perceived. This is therefore an application of Fechner's law (§ 77).

At night, when there is a light in the room, you can see through the curtain quite well. The side nearer to you is almost unilluminated and only imposes a very feeble illumination on the objects of various brightness in the room.

For those who are in the room and look outside, the effect is in both cases the other way round. The same phenomenon occurs when an aircraft, clearly visible in the moonlight, can no longer be found when a searchlight is used! The air between our eyes and the aircraft is illuminated by a beam of dazzling light that prevents us from seeing the weak light contrasts behind it.

83. Stained-glass windows

> Poems are like colored church windows:
> If you look inward from the market square,
> Everything is dark and gloomy;
> Enter the holy house, however,
> And everything looks bright and colorful.

Goethe, Gedichte

Goethe describes a very special phenomenon here. Even the most brightly colored stained-glass windows look dull when seen from the outside. This is because they disperse the light much like a curtain: they are covered in dust and full of grains and air bubbles. Most of the light falling on them is therefore reflected, which gives them a generally grayish look; the faintly colored light coming from within can hardly be seen.

84. Stars at dusk and in moonlight[7]

The extinguishing of stars by daylight is a true veil effect. Conversely, each (clear) evening, you can see how the brightest stars appear first and then, gradually, the fainter ones until it is completely dark. It is interesting to follow this gradual transition. On the one hand the brightness of stars is known in magnitudes, which can be converted into brightnesses—see § 56; on the other hand we know how the brightness changes as the sun sinks deeper and deeper below the horizon—see § 62.

---

[7] Tousey and Koomen, *J. Opt. Soc. Am.*, **43**, 177, 1953.

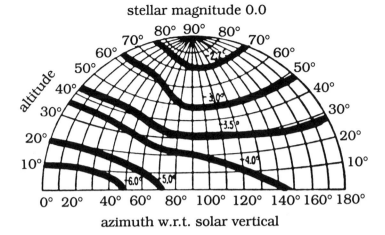

stellar magnitude 0.0

stellar magnitude 2.0

Figs. 90, 91. Visibility of stars at dusk. The numbers on the *bold curves* show at which altitude of the sun (below the horizon) stars just become visible.

The darker the sky, the more stars you can see. However, when the light of the moon spreads a uniform brightness over the heavens, most of them disappear. This, too, is a real curtain effect (§ 82).

Around the moon, so beautiful and full,
The stars conceal again their radiance,
While she spreads her silvery light
Far and wide over the earth.

Sappho

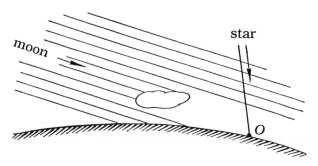

Fig. 92. A cloud in front of the moon is not sufficient
to make stars clearly visible to observer *O*.

Note the excellent observation of detail in 'around the moon' and
'conceal again their radiance', for when the moon rises, the stars
that were visible before now disappear.

A child once thought that a cloud in front of the moon would be
sufficient to make the stars visible again. Why is this not the case?
See Fig. 92.

During a lunar eclipse, the 'extinguished' stars reappear.

85. Visibility of stars by day

By day, the sky is still more brightly illuminated and the stars are
then completely invisible. Moreover, our eyes have then become adapted
to the broad daylight and are therefore thousands of times less sensitive.

A remarkable account[8], dating back as far as the time of Aristotle,
tells us that, seen from the inside of deep wells, mine shafts, and
wide chimneys, the air seems darker than we usually see it, and it
should even be possible to observe some of the brighter stars. This
phenomenon has since been mentioned by a number of writers, who
relied, however, mostly on their memories or on the stories of others.

There is not a single place where this phenomenon has been observed—it is a myth. The whole effect could only consist in the eye
being less dazzled by light entering from its surroundings. This,
however, makes little difference, seeing that the field of light seen directly by us remains illuminated and is the deciding factor.

Still more improbable is the story that the stars can be seen by day
reflected in dark mountain lakes. The 'observers' of this phenomenon

---

[8] Smith, *J. Opt. Soc. Am.*, **45**, 482, 1955.

noticed indeed how dark the reflection of the sky was, but they forgot that the light of the stars diminishes in exactly the same proportion owing to the reflection.

86. Irradiation

It seems as if the setting sun causes an indentation in the line of the horizon—see Fig. 93.

When the first crescent of the moon appears and the remaining part of the moon's disk seems to glimmer feebly in the 'ash-gray light', it strikes us that the outer edge of the crescent seems to be part of a larger circle than the outer edge of the ash-gray light—see Fig. 93. According to Tycho Brahe's estimate, the ratio of the respective diameters is 6:5.

Dark clothes make us look slimmer than white ones do. Leonardo da Vinci, in his writings, says of this phenomenon: 'We can see this when we look at the sun through the bare branches of trees. All the branches in front of the sun are so slender that one can no longer see them, and the same effect can be seen with a spear held between the eye and the sun's disk. I once saw a woman dressed in black

The narrow crescent of the moon appears to belong to a larger disk than the ash-gray light. (Photo by Pekka Parviainen)

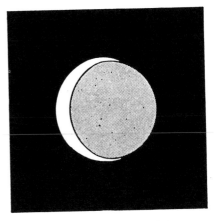

Fig. 93. Examples of irradation: the setting sun and a crescent of the new moon.

with a white shawl over her head. This shawl seemed twice as broad as the darkly clad shoulder. The crenels in the battlements of fortresses are of exactly the same width as the merlons and yet the former appear to be appreciably wider than the latter.'

You can often see two telephone wires apparently intersecting at a very small angle when observed in a certain direction—see Fig. 94a. The remarkable thing about this is that with the sky as background, this point of intersection vanishes in the intense brightness surrounding them, contrasted with the double lines of dark wires to the right and left. Whenever the wind sways the wires, however little, the white gap moves to and fro along the wires—see Fig. 94b.

On the other hand, the appearance is quite different when the background consists of parallel dark lines, such as steps or tiled roofs or brickwork. In this case, the wire seems to be curiously swollen and broken whenever it crosses one of these dark lines—see Fig. 94c. This effect occurs also when wires are seen against the sharp outline of a house (see Fig. 94d), in short, when the straight edge of any solid object cuts acutely across a series of parallel lines.

The origin of all these deformations lies in the fact that the images in our eyes are modified by refraction and imperfect reproduction. Mentally, we place the borders between contiguous areas where the brightness changes most quickly, and if the image is made diffuse by diffraction, this border differs from that given by ideal geometrical considerations. The border line therefore shifts systematically outward in the case of bright fields in dark surroundings, and this shifting is known as 'irradiation', a few instances of which have just been given.

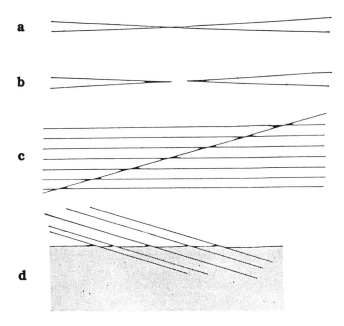

Fig. 94. Examples of irradiation at telephone wires.

87. Dazzling

Where the intensity of the light entering your eyes is too great, dazzling occurs. By dazzling, two things are understood: (a) the appearance of a strong source of light in the field of view, resulting in the other parts of the field of view being no longer clearly observable, and (b) a feeling of giddiness or of pain.

An example of the first condition is given by the headlights of an approaching car shining in your direction. You can then no longer see the trees along the road and run the danger of colliding with them. On closer inspection of the scene before you, you will discover that everything is covered by a haze of light many times stronger than the faint shapes of trees and other objects at night. This general haziness is caused by the scattering of the incident rays in the refractive media of the eyes, which are always sufficiently granular and inhomogeneous to cause scattering[9]. It even appears that daz-

---

[9] G.A. Fry and M. Alpern, *J. Opt. Soc. Am.*, **43**, 189, 1953.

zling light does not enter the eyes through the pupils only, but also partly straight through the sclera. Moreover, in the vicinity of the illuminated part, the retina becomes much less sensitive; at an angle of 10° or more from the dazzling source, the latter effect becomes stronger than the scattering haze.

The second sensation caused by dazzling is felt quite clearly when you gaze at the sky in daytime. You should stand in the shadow of a house to avoid looking straight at the sun. The nearer your gaze approaches the sun, the more intolerable the fierce glare becomes, and if there are white clouds, the brilliance is hardly bearable. It is remarkable how much more sensitive one person is than another to the painful effects of dazzling.

88. Blue bows

When you drive at night behind a car with a very bright red rear light, you will often see a pair of grayish-blue bows in the indirect field of vision. Our eyes look alongside the source of light and see these bows, which appear to extend from the yellow spot toward the blind spot; that is, in the case of the left eye toward the left, and in the case of the right eye toward the right of the field of vision. The most likely explanation for this is that you actually perceive the nerve impulse being passed to the optic nerve via the retina. Some people see these blue bows much more clearly than others.

Chapter 7

Colors

Everything that lives strives for color

Goethe, *Farbenlehre*

89. The mixing of colors

When you look at the scenery from a window of a railway compartment, you can also see the faintly reflected image of the scenery on
the other side of the train. The two images overlap, so that you can
study the color mixture formed. The reflection of the blue sky makes
that of the green fields green-blue, and the resulting color becomes
much paler and less saturated, a phenomenon inherent in color
mixing.

The panes of many shop windows nowadays are made without a
frame, so that from the point *E* in Fig. 95 you can see through the
pane the inside of the window sill *A* and at the same time the reflection of the part outside, *B*. If *A* and *B* are colored differently, you get
a splendid instance of mixed color, and according as the position of
your eyes is higher or lower, the nearer the combined color ap-

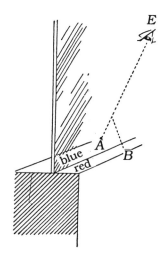

Fig. 95. Color mixing by shop windows.

proaches that of *A* or that of *B*. This shows at the same time that a pane of glass reflects more light at large angles of incidence.

Nature mixes colors for us in yet another way. Flowers in a meadow seen at a distance merge into a single tint, so that dandelions on green grass may give a color mixture of yellow and green. The blossoms of apple trees and pear trees are a dirty white (yes, really, dirty white!), a color mixture arising from pink and white petals, green leaves, red anthers of the pear trees and yellow anthers of the apple trees, and so on. The physical explanation for this mixing of colors is that our eye images every point of light more or less diffusely (cf. § 72) and that the patches of different colors overlap. Painters avail themselves of this physiological fact in their technique of pointillism (cf. § 64).

90. The colors of colloidal metals. Violet window panes

The windows of some old houses have beautiful violet-tinted panes. This violet tint is the result of many years of sunlight shining on the glass. Nowadays, the same process of coloring can be carried out much more rapidly by exposing the glass to the rays of quartz–mercury lamps. The color must be ascribed to a minute quantity of manganese forming a colloidal solution in the glass; the tint depends not only on the optical properties of the metal, but also on the size of the particles. If you heat the glass, the violet color disappears.

Faraday tells us that in his time glass turned violet to a very noticeable degree after the sun had shone on it for as short a time as six months.

91. The color of discharge tubes. Absorption of light by gases

The many colored advertizing signs that at night transform our towns into fairy-tale cities are glass tubes filled with highly rarefied gas with an electric discharge passing through it. Orange light is given out by tubes filled with neon; blue and green, by tubes filled with mercury vapor, made of blue or green glass to weaken the different components of the mercury light; while orange-yellow light is given out by sodium tubes. Sometimes, the inside of the tubes is covered by a fluorescent material that enhances the light intensity and modifies its color.

When the sodium street lighting is switched on, the color of the tubes is at first red, the typical orange-red of neon. Only after 5–10 minutes does the orange-yellow color of sodium light begin to dominate, and after 15 minutes the transformation is complete. The addition of neon is necessary because the vapor pressure of sodium at normal temperatures is much too low. The electric discharge through the neon causes sufficient heat to raise the vapor pressure of the sodium, whereupon the electric discharge passes through the sodium.

Our observations in sodium light are more concentrated because in this monochromatic radiation the chromatic aberration of our eyes no longer plays a role.

92. The Purkinje effect. Cones and rods

> Green and blue are invariably accentuated in the
> half-shadows; yellow and red and white in the lighter parts.
>
> Leonardo da Vinci, *Trattato*

Observe the contrast between the flaming red of geraniums in a border and their background of dark green leaves. In the twilight, and later in the evening, this contrast is clearly reversed, the flowers now appearing much darker than the leaves. You may wonder whether the brightness of red can be compared at all with the brightness of green, but the differences are so pronounced here as to leave no room for doubt.

If you can find a red and a blue in a picture gallery that appear to be equally bright by day, you will see that, in the twilight, the blue becomes by far the brighter of the two, so much so that it seems to radiate light.

These are examples of the Purkinje effect. It is caused by the fact that in normal illumination our eyes observe with the cells in the retina called cones, but with the cells known as rods in very weak illumination. The former are most sensitive to yellow, the latter to blue-green, and this explains the reversal in brightness ratios of various colored objects when the illumination varies in intensity.

The rods provide us with the impression of light only, not of color. Illumination by the moon is so weak that, for practical purposes, the rods only are at work, and colors in a landscape are no longer perceptible: we have become color blind. This color blindness is still more complete on dark nights (cf. § 76).

93. The color of very bright sources of light tends to white

In our towns, you can often see during the evening how various sources of light are reflected in canals and spread out into pillars of light— see § 20. It is surprising how easily differences of color between them can now be observed, for instance, between those from normal light bulbs and mercury-vapor tubes, while the sources of light themselves look nearly equally white. Similarly, the differences between the colors become more distinct when the lights are seen through fog or blurred windows. And by a curious property of our eyes, we see all colors tend to white the fiercer the intensity of the light source. We speak of 'white hot' iron, but stars at that same temperature (about 2 000 °C) appear red. The image of the star in our eye is not sharp: the point of light has become a faint speck.

94. The psychological effect of a landscape seen through colored glasses

With yellow, the eye rejoices, the heart expands, the spirit is cheered and we immediately feel warmed. Many people feel an inclination to laugh when looking through yellow glass. Blue shows everything in a sad light. Red shows a bright landscape in an awful light; this is the color that will be cast over heaven and earth on the Day of Judgment. Green looks very unnatural, very likely because a green sky occurs so seldom.

Goethe, *Farbenlehre*

Vaughan Cornish tried to distinguish between the colors in a landscape giving a sensation of 'warmth' and those giving a sensation of 'cold'. He finds that red, orange, yellow, and yellow-green belong to the former category, and blue-green, blue, and violet to the latter.

95. Observation of color while bending down

There is an old prescription among painters for seeing more life and greater richness in colors of a landscape, and that is to stand with your back to the landscape, your legs wide apart, and bend forward so far as to be able to see between them. The intensified feeling for color is supposed to be connected with the greater quantity of blood running to the head.

Vaughan Cornish suggests that lying on one's side would produce the same effect. He ascribes this to the fact that the well-known overestimation of vertical distances is neutralized (cf. § 130), so that the tints apparently show steeper gradients. The question is whether this applies also to the much stronger effect while bending.

96. Fluorescent paint

If you hold a strip of normal yellow or orange paper alongside a sheet of paper or board that has been painted in the same color but with fluorescent paint, you will see that the sheet will look much brighter, just as if it were illuminated by a powerful source of light. The explanation for this is that fluorescent paints do not just absorb the violet, blue, and green constituents of daylight, but convert them into light of longer wavelength, that is, toward the red. Such paints, therefore, transmit more light than would be the case if the red or yellow were simply reflected.

Chapter 8
Afterimages and Contrast Phenomena

97. Duration of light impressions

When you are sitting in a train and another train races past in the opposite direction, for a few moments you can distinctly see the countryside right through the windows of the other train, almost without flickering, only not quite so brightly.

Or again, you can see right through the window of a passing train while you are standing on a platform, or see the countryside reflected in the windows. In both cases, if you only look steadily in front of you, the images will appear without any flickering.

To ascertain the rate at which light and dark must alternate to eliminate any flickering, walk along the side of a high and long fence regulating your step in such a way as to obtain an impression of uniform lighting, taking care meanwhile to stare through the fence in the same direction all the time.

The speed at which flickering just vanishes depends on the ratio of brightness between 'light' and 'dark', and also on the ratios between duration of lighting and duration of screening. In reality, the light impression does not vanish suddenly but decreases gradually. The continual process of waxing and waning of the light impressions in a cinema must therefore be very complicated.

A classic instance is that of falling snowflakes:

> The flakes nearer to us appear to fall more rapidly; those at a distance rather slower; and the nearer ones appear to be bound together like white cords; but the farther ones seem totally unconnected.

Leonardo da Vinci, *Trattato*

Raindrops, which fall so much faster than snow, always appear lengthened into long, thin lines.

98. The railings or palisade phenomenon

A surprising pattern is shown by the spokes of a fast rotating wheel seen through a railed fence. Strange to say, this pattern is symmet-

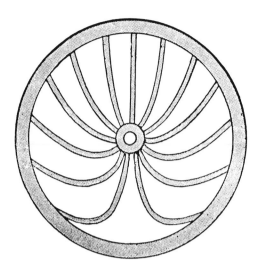

Fig. 96. The railings phenomenon: a rolling wheel observed through a long fence.

rical so that it is impossible to gather from it the direction of rotation—see Fig. 96. Though the wheel possesses a quick forward and rotary motion, the pattern remains almost at rest. When you see a train slowing down at a station and you watch the large wheels of the engine through the railings of a fence, the phenomenon is seen to perfection. It is most striking when the illumination of the rim is strong, that of the spokes rather poor, and when the openings between the bars are narrow. You do not see the pattern if you look through the railings at a wheel that is revolving but not rolling; the combination of both the rotatory and translatory motion is essential.

To explain the phenomenon, we start from the fact that the observer follows the wheel with his eyes, to which he therefore refers everything he sees. This is the condition that has to be fulfilled and which is brought about by the mode of lighting, and so on, mentioned earlier. Imagine, therefore, that the wheel revolves around a fixed axis O, but the openings in the railings move uniformly past it—see Fig. 97a.

Suppose that in their initial positions a certain opening cuts a certain spoke at A: the part of the spoke at A will then be seen through the opening. A few moments later, the spoke will lie along OB, while the opening will also have shifted so that they intersect at B. Still later, the point of intersection will have moved to C. In this way, the whole of the curve $ABCO$ will be described point by point. Each curve of the pattern is therefore the locus of the points at which you see, for a very short time, the intersection of one definite opening and one definite spoke. It is because of the persistence of the visual impres-

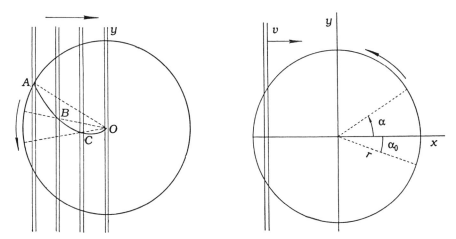

Fig. 97. How the railings phenomenon comes about.

sion that the whole of the curve appears to be seen simultaneously, provided the wheel is moving sufficiently fast.

Each following spoke, after becoming visible in its turn through the same opening, will describe a curve of the same family, but with a different parameter; this means that a complete pattern will arise. If the next opening reaches the position of the one preceding it in exactly the same time as that in which the next spoke reaches the position of the spoke preceding it, the same set of curves will evidently be described again, and the whole pattern is then at rest. But if the distances between the openings are slightly different, each spoke will arrive at the opening just slightly too early (or too late). In this case, each curve is transformed into another one, belonging to the same family, but characterized by a different parameter. You will then see a pattern, slowly changing, in the same or opposite direction as the rotation, but this change is not a rotation of the pattern as a whole, for this remains symmetrical about the vertical. Finally, there is the possibility of the distances between openings being much too large or too small, say, twice as small. You will then see twice as many curves as there are spokes and the pattern will once more be at rest, provided the spacing is regular.

It will be clear from this argument that, generally speaking, the slowly changing pattern will occur most frequently. In reality, the railing is often so short that the whole phenomenon is over in a second or less, so that there is hardly time to realize this changing of the pattern at all.

The equation of the set of curves is easily deduced. Choose the axes of co-ordinates as in Fig. 97b and let v be the velocity of the openings in the railings. Let α_0 be the initial inclination of the radius vector, that is, a spoke, to the x-axis, and α the inclination after a time t. The coordinates of the point of intersection of spoke and opening at the instant t are then

$$x = vt \quad \text{and} \quad y = x\tan\alpha.$$

Also, from the connection between rotatory and translatory motion, we have, if r is the length of a spoke,

$$vt/r = \alpha-\alpha_0,$$

or

$$x = r\,(\alpha-\alpha_0).$$

Eliminating α gives for the equation of the family of curves

$$y = x\tan(x/r+\alpha_0).$$

As appears from this expression, y remains the same when α_0 and x change their sign simultaneously, that is, the pattern is symmetrical about the y-axis.

More complicated patterns arise when one of the large wheels of a cart is seen through the other wheel. As soon as the direction of vision is slightly to the right or to the left, so that the one wheel no longer covers the other one entirely, the most curious curves can be observed. They were noticed by Faraday, and they reminded him of magnetic lines of force. They are the loci of the points where two spokes cross.

Also of interest is the image of two wheels, one immediately behind the other, that revolve in opposite directions, as can be seen at certain coal pits. It is as if you see a 'ghost wheel': if each wheel has n spokes, the 'ghost wheel' has $2n$ spokes. Now and then, the 'ghost wheel' moves slightly forward or backward: this results from the small difference in rotational speed of the wheels. This phenomenon was also observed, reproduced, and explained by Faraday.

99. Sources of flickering light

Among the illuminated advertizing signs flaming so fantastically at night in towns the world over, the orange neon tubes are the most conspicuous. They are fed invariably by an alternating current (a.c.)

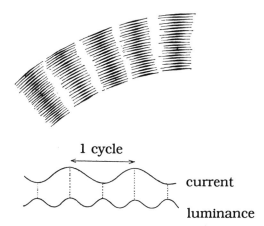

1 cycle

current

luminance

Fig. 98. Showing the rapid flickering of light bulbs and neon tubes.

supply at a frequency of 50/60 Hz (cycles per second). This means that the light intensity alternates 100 or 120 times a second, since two maxima of light correspond to a cycle. The flickering is so rapid that, as a rule, we do not notice it at all.

However, if you move some shining object to and fro in the light of neon tubes, you will see its light track as a rippled luminous plane. The faster you move the object, the farther apart the ripples will be. The number of ripples enables you to compute the frequency of the alternating current. When, for instance, you describe a circle four times a second with, say, a shiny pair of scissors and the light track shows 12 maxima, the frequency of the current pulses is 12×4 = 48, and that of the alternating current itself is 24 Hz (cycles per second).

This experiment can also be carried out by reflecting the source of light in a rapidly oscillating mirror or piece of glass (of your watch, for instance); or you can rapidly move one of the lenses of your glasses in a small circle in front of your eyes (cf. § 51).

Finally, the flickering can be seen with the naked eye by fixing your gaze first on a point in the neighborhood of the neon tube and then looking into another direction quite suddenly; the image of the source of light moves in this case over the retina and each maximum is perceived separately. This sudden looking into a different direction, while continuing to concentrate your attention on the source of light, is surprisingly difficult. Sometimes you succeed; sometimes you do not.

Also investigate incandescent lights fed by alternating current. When you swing a silver pencil in the light, the ripples will be clearly visible, proving that the light from, and the temperature of, the filament increase slightly at every current pulse and decrease in between— see Fig. 98. When the light is fed by direct current, no ripples will be seen.

Sometimes, when you look out of the window of a railway compartment at night at sodium street lights, a very distinct rippling can be seen in the following conditions. You should be about 2 m (6 ft) away from the window, which should be wet or blurred and the wet film smeared slightly in a vertical direction. As soon as the light from the lamp reaches certain parts of the pane, the rippling becomes visible. The explanation is that the wet film is not of the same thickness all over; owing to the wiping, a series of thin prisms has been formed with vertical edges and refracting angles that change from point to point. This causes irregular and sometimes sudden displacements of the images of the lamp and, since these lamps are fed by alternating current, ripples can be seen exactly as in the case of the rapidly moving glass.

100. The merging frequency for the central and peripheral fields of view

The following remarkable experiment can be performed when an a.c. supply of low frequency (20–25 Hz) is available to power a lamp. Look first at the lamp and you will see a steady light, while a wall illuminated by the lamp flickers. Then look at the wall; its illumination becomes steady, but now the lamp flickers.

It is clear that the perceptive power of our direct and of our peripheral field of view must be different. It might be possible that the fluctuations in the intensity of the lamp are very slight and that the differential threshold for intensities is lower for the peripheral field of view. To ascertain this, describe in the light of the same lamp a circle with some shining object. The fluctuations in brightness at regular distances in its light track are now easily visible, even when you watch the track intently (cf. § 99). This means that our direct field of view is sufficiently sensitive to small differences of intensity, but that it is not capable of keeping pace with the fluctuations. Laboratory experiments have proved the existence of this peculiarity of our eyes.

The most remarkable thing, however, is that not only can we not see the flickering in the peripheral field of view, but we also underestimate its frequency: we assume that this is not higher than 10 Hz (cf. § 103).

A similar phenomenon can be seen with certain television tubes and neon lights. When you are at a distance of not less than 50 times the diameter of the TV screen, the flickering disappears.

101. The bicycle wheel apparently at rest

The wheels of a passing bicycle look more or less as shown in Fig. 99. Our eye can follow the motion of those parts of the spokes that are near the center, because there they move slower.

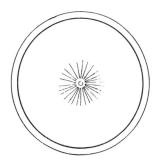

Fig. 99. How we see a rapidly
revolving bicycle wheel.

However, settle down comfortably at the side of a road where many
bicycles are likely to pass. Look intently at a fixed point in the road.
The moment the front wheel of a bicycle enters your field of view, you
suddenly see a number of spokes quite clearly, even when the bicycle is moving quickly. It is a very striking phenomenon. The important thing is to look steadily in one direction and not to watch the approaching bicycle.

The explanation is that the point of the circumference where the
wheel touches the ground is momentarily at rest, because there the
ground grips the wheel—see Fig. 100. The ends of the spokes near
this point will then be nearly at rest, too, whereas points farther from
the ground will move rapidly along curved tracks owing to their combined rotation and translation. If, therefore, you can manage to look
steadily at a definite point on the ground, the lower parts of the
wheel should appear to be more or less at a standstill, and this is indeed what you actually observe.

It is my belief that we can see the spokes clearest of all when they
appear in our peripheral field of view. It is therefore quite possible
that the capacity for perceiving rapid fluctuations of light plays a
part in this matter, too.

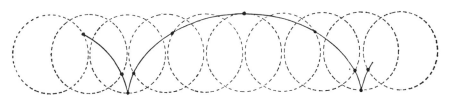

Fig. 100. Trajectory of a point on the circumference of a revolving wheel.

102. The car wheel apparently at rest

When a car comes along, even at a moderate speed, the individual parts of its wheels (spokes, cutouts, and the like) cannot be distinguished. At each fixed point of the retina, the flickering of light and dark is so rapid that the impressions merge into each other; the muscles of your eye cannot make the direction of our gaze describe a cone at the rate required to follow the separate parts.

Now and again, however, it happens that the wheel parts become visible for an infinitesimal instant as in a photograph. As a rule, only a few of the spokes or cutouts can be seen, but at times I seem to see the whole wheel clearly. In this case, the explanation of the bicycle wheel at rest would not be satisfactory. This is such a striking phenomenon that it has been held that the wheel is actually at rest at certain moments, which is obviously a sheer impossibility!

One realizes very soon, however, that the momentary visibility of the spokes or cutouts of the car wheel occurs in practice when we set our foot firmly on the ground; you can also see it when you tap your glasses (assuming you wear them) or jerk your head. Perhaps, in these cases, the eye, or the direction of your gaze, is set into very rapid, damped vibrations, which happen to follow exactly some of the moving parts, so that their images on the retina will be at rest for a very short time. Is it, perhaps, the axis of the eyeball that carries out a slight to-and-fro movement, or does the eyeball as a whole shake in its socket (vibratory motion)? May we assume that the eye, on receiving little shocks such as these, is capable of performing very rapid random rotations round its axis?

A direct proof of the theory that the eye vibrates is the following. If you walk at night with a vigorous, swinging stride, and fix your gaze steadily on a distant light, you will notice that the light describes at every stride a little curve, more or less like that in Fig. 101.

At times, the phenomenon is also visible when, standing still, you look at a passing car. The explanation of this must be found in sudden, slight, unconscious movements of the eye. The fact that the eye frequently moves with such little jerks can be proved by looking for an instant, and very cautiously, into the setting sun. The afterimages will then turn out to consist of a number of black spots, not of a black, continuous band (cf. § 105).

Fig. 101. Curve described by a distant light source when observed by someone walking.

103. The flickering aircraft propeller[1]

It's not often nowadays that you can fly in a propeller-driven aircraft, but if you do, observe the propeller. When the engine is started, you will notice a number of flickerings, caused by the light of the background being intercepted a couple of times a second. Soon, the speed of the propeller is so high that you observe a regular, even field. Turn your eyes sideways, but notice the propeller in your peripheral vision: the flickering is visible again. The flickering becomes clearer particularly when you momentarily shift your gaze. When I cover one eye, I normally see the flickering best with my right eye, looking in a direction just to the right of the propeller, or with my left eye when I look just to the left of the propeller. The flickering may also be observed during the flight, even though the propeller than moves at 50–100 rev s^{-1}.

The phenomenon is particularly interesting when the propeller moves at a relatively low speed, that is, during tests or when the engine is being started. We all make mistakes in estimating the number of flickerings: whereas this appears to be fairly large in the central field of vision, say, 25 per second, we think that it is hardly 10 per second in the peripheral field. This is the same observation as discussed in § 99.

104. Observations of a rotating bicycle wheel

As a rule, the spokes of a rotating bicycle wheel are not visible separately: they are blurred into a thin veil, darkest close to the hub and lighter toward the rim. The shadow of the wheel on an even road shows a similar distribution of light. How dark is this shadow? The spokes are each 2 mm (0.08 in) thick, and their distance apart at the rim is, on average, 50 mm (2 in). The period during which a point on the road is in the shadow is thus 2/50 = 0.04 of the time of a complete revolution. According to Talbot's law, this makes the same impression on our eye as if the shadow cast by the revolving wheel had a constant brightness equal to $^{100}\!/_{04}$ of the brightness of the unshadowed road. But the sun does not shine at right angles to the wheel, so that in the shadow the spokes are closer together, although their thickness remains the same. It will be clear that, even near the rim, the shadow will be as much as 4–8 percent less bright than the surrounding ground, and that nearer to the center this reduction is probably as great as 10–20 percent. And yet, it is difficult to perceive

[1] H.P.H. Hovnanian, *J. Opt. Soc. Am.*, **50**, 1960. I.J. Le Grand, *Light, Colour and Vision*, London, 1968, p. 312.

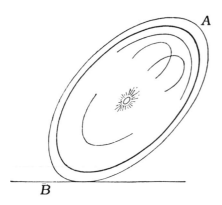

Fig. 102. Light curves and shadow
curves of a revolving wheel.

any difference in brightness at all, since the dark shadow of the tire
forms too marked a separation between the two fields being compared. The gradual decrease in brightness toward the center is hardly
noticeable, because we are always inclined to see a clearly circumscribed, coherent figure as a whole, and this psychological tendency
overlooks the actual difference in brightness.

On closer inspection, however, you will, as a rule, discover one or
more light rings in the shadow of the wheel—see Fig. 102. They are
often open curves of limited length. Get off your bicycle and investigate carefully where the light arc is formed. It corresponds to where
two spokes cross; indeed, at each of these points one spoke has, so
to speak, disappeared, so that the average shadow must be less.
Although the difference is slight, your eye clearly perceives it, be-

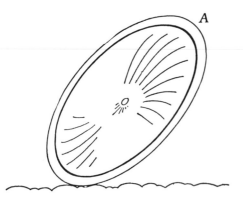

Fig. 103. Peculiar bent lines in the
shadow of a bicycle wheel moving on
a rough road.

cause the two brightnesses to be compared now meet without a line of separation between them. It is difficult to describe the intertwining of the spokes. Mostly, four at a time form a group, which is repeated around the wheel. The crossing of two spokes describes a definite curve, which becomes visible as a small, bright arc. After the wheel has rotated over four times the distance between two spokes, the small arc will be formed again. If, moreover, in each group two crossings should occur, one of which happens to follow the track of the other, the small arc would appear particularly bright. In the former case, it would be one percent brighter than the shadow around it, in the latter case, two percent. Since, however, the spokes in the shadow are, as a rule, projected closer together and the small, bright arc is, moreover, very often at some distance from the rim, these percentages will probably be three and six. These amounts are therefore the smallest differences of brightness still perceptible when two fields are directly adjacent. Though the unevenness of the road, which here acts as a projection screen, is a serious drawback, the result agrees well with our former estimates (§ 78).

Try to account for the fact that the arcs and rings of light are usually at their brightest near the end *A* of the elongated wheel shadow, and investigate why the pattern at *A* is not the same as at *B*.

When, instead of looking at the shadow of your wheel, you look directly at the wheel of someone cycling at your side, you will see these same arcs and rings still better, because they now stand out quite sharply without any blurring (cf. § 2). Against a bright background, the spokes appear dark, so that the rings are brighter; when, however, the wheel is illuminated by the sun against a dark background, the rings are darker.

This is by no means the last of the remarkable effects exhibited by rapidly rotating bicycle wheels. It may happen when you look at the shadow of the wheel that you see the sharp lines of the spokes flash out as quick as lightning, if your eyes happen to make a rapid circular movement, so that, involuntarily, you follow the shadow exactly at its own speed (cf. § 102). If you wear glasses, small sudden displacements of the glasses will suffice to make you see the separate spokes move in an odd, jerky manner.

The most remarkable shadow of all is to be seen when you cycle on an unevenly paved road with clear joints between the paving stones. Notwithstanding the roughness of the background, you perceive clearly a set of radial but curved lines—see Fig. 103. In this phenomenon you can recognize the *railings* or *palisade phenomenon* discussed in § 98. This is most clearly seen from the shadow cast by someone riding beside you. Evidently, the joints between the paving stones play the same optical role as the rails of a fence. At the same time, it is more than likely that in this case you will keep your eyes glued to the wheel itself.

Quite apart from the curves already mentioned, there is still one more peculiar light figure, which, however, can be seen only when the sun shines on a bicycle with glittering new spokes.

105. Afterimages

> When the wanderer had a last look at the sun just before she set, he could afterward still see her image floating against the background of the darkened wood and slope of the rocks; when he turned his gaze, the image had also moved and glittered and vibrated in magnificent colors; in the same way, Hermann saw the image of the lovely maiden ...
>
> Goethe, *Hermann und Dorothea*

Take care during the following observations! Do not overstrain your eyes! Do not carry out more than two tests in succession!

Look carefully and briefly at the setting sun and then close your eyes. The afterimage consists of several small, round disks: proof that your eyes must have moved with little jerks during the short time your gaze lasted. The disks will strike you as remarkably small, for, owing to the fierce brightness of the sun, you are accustomed to 'seeing' it looking larger than it really is; its true dimensions are shown in the afterimages.

Open your eyes again and you will see afterimages everywhere you look. The farther away the objects are on which you project them, the larger the afterimages appear. The angular diameter is always the same, of course, but if you know that a certain object is a long way off and yet you see it subtend the same angle as another closer to you, you conclude subconsciously, on the grounds of daily experience, that in reality the object in the distance must be the larger of the two (cf. § 137).

An afterimage on a dark background is light (a positive afterimage), as can be seen very well by closing your eyes and, because the eyelids are transparent, covering them with your hand. Vice versa, an afterimage on a light background becomes dark (a negative afterimage). The fierce light has apparently stimulated your retina locally and the impression remains, but at the same time that part of the retina has become less sensitive to new light impressions.

> I stared into the large, red sun as intently as I could; and everywhere I looked afterward I saw suns, vague and pale. From

everything there emerged a dark, menacing loop. On the ground, the wall, and in the air a crawling flight of suns. They stream from my eyes and remain in my heart. The last one that I saw hung high and black in the sky.

René de Clercq, *De Noodhoorn*

Sources of light feebler than the sun give correspondingly feebler afterimages. Within seconds, or even fractions of a second, a condition is reached that took a much longer time when fierce sources of light were observed: all that is seen is a negative afterimage.

The change from white to black corresponds, in the case of colored light sources, to the change of the afterimage into its complementary color, so that red changes to green-blue, orange to blue, yellow to violet, green to purple, and vice versa.

Twilight is the best time in which to see afterimages; all Goethe's typical examples of afterimages were observed in the evening. The eye is well rested then, and the contrast between the light in the west and the dark in the east is at its sharpest.

Goethe in his *Farbenlehre* writes: 'One night as I entered the room of an inn, a fine girl came toward me. Her face was of a dazzling whiteness, her hair was black and she was wearing a scarlet bodice. I looked at her intently in the dim twilight while she was standing some distance away from me. When, after a moment, she left me, I saw on the white wall opposite me a black face, surrounded by a bright glow, and the dress of the very well-defined figure was a beautiful sea green.'

It has been recorded that to people who had been gazing for half an hour at the orange-yellow flames in a fire, the rising moon seemed blue.

The afterimage of a flash of lightning seen during a thunderstorm at night can sometimes be observed as a fine, black, snakelike line against the background of an illuminated white wall or of the feebly diffused light of the sky.

When you stare into the distance and scan the horizon while standing on the beach at nightfall, there comes a moment when the difference between the light sky and the dark sea is no longer really visible. This is clearly caused by the fact that the longer a light excites the eye, the weaker its stimulating effect becomes; the retina grows tired. That this is indeed true is shown the moment you turn your gaze a little higher; the negative afterimage of the sea then takes the form of a light streak against the sky. If you then let your gaze descend a little, you can see the dark afterimage of the sky against the sea.

106. The phenomenon of Elisabeth Linnaeus

Elisabeth Linnaeus, the daughter of the famous botanist, noticed one evening that light was emitted by the orange-colored flowers of the nasturtium (Tropaeolum majus). It was thought to be an electric phenomenon. The observation was confirmed by Darwin with a kind of South African lily; also by Haggrén, Dowden, and earlier explorers, whose observations took place always during the dusk of dawn or twilight. Canon Russell repeated the observation with the marigold (Calendula officinalis) and the burning bush (Dictamus fraxinella), remarking at the same time that some people see it better than others. And yet, it seems that this phenomenon, concerning which a whole series of treatises was published at the time, must be ascribed simply to afterimages. Afterimages were seen by Goethe when he stared intently at brilliantly colored flowers and then at the sandy road. Peonies, oriental poppies, marigolds, and yellow crocuses gave lovely green, blue, and violet afterimages, especially at dusk, and the flamelike flash became visible only on glancing sideways for a moment; all of these are details to be expected from afterimages.

When anyone thinks he can see this phenomenon very clearly, he should hold brilliantly colored paper flowers close to the real ones and see whether the former show the same phenomenon.

Has the observation described in § 81 something to do with this phenomenon?

107. Changes of color in afterimages

The speed at which afterimages fade differs for different colors, particularly when the light impression has been very strong. This explains why the afterimages of the sun and intensely white objects are colored. As a rule, the afterimage on a dark background is green-blue at first, and afterward purple colored.

In his *Farbenlehre*, Goethe says: 'Toward evening I entered a smithy, just when the glowing lump of iron was placed under the hammer. After watching intently for some time, I turned around and happened to look inside an open coal shed. An enormous purple-colored image floated before my eyes, and when I looked away from the dark opening at the light woodwork, the phenomenon appeared to be half green, half purple, according to whether the background was dark or light'.

When looking at snow in the sun, or reading a book while the sun is shining on it, every bright object near us looks purple; afterward, in the shadow, every dark object looks a lovely green. Here also, the afterimage on a bright background has the complementary color of that on a dark background. Some observers speak of 'blood red' instead of purple.

108. Sunlight penetrates the wall of the eye

When you walk in the direction of the low-lying sun, you will notice that all dark objects seem to glow in a reddish haze. This is because the sun not only shines into our eyes, but also on to them; the light that falls on to them penetrates through the eyelid and the wall of the eye and in the process it is colored blood red. Our entire field of view is filled with reddish light that is seen clearest on dark objects. This effect is very noticeable when, continuing to look at the landscape, you alternately cover your eyes and let the sunlight fall on to them. When you then enter a shadow or go indoors, the retina remains tired to red light for a little while, manifested by your seeing everything around you in a greenish tint. This is particularly noticeable when you have been lying in the sun for a while with your eyes closed: when you open them again, the landscape appears greenish or greenish blue.

Goethe observed that black letters looked red in the evening when the setting sun was shining in his eyes. Guido Gezelle observed a similar phenomenon while reading his breviary: to him red letters appeared green. This seems to indicate a merging with an afterimage.

> I can scarcely perceive it any more;
> My eyes want to wander;
> The words that are printed black
> In my book appear as if they're red;
> While red seems as if it's green.

> G. Gezelle, *De Dageraad*

> In hollows and in pits,
> In the uneven ground,
> I saw a shadow hiding
> That had found a resting place;
> But although Nature had decreed
> That it be black as coal,
> It ignited before my eyes
> And became as fire and blood.

> J. v.d. Waals, *Zonsondergang*

109. Concurrent contrast

Take a sheet of white art or good-quality writing paper, hold it upright in front of you and stand at right angles to an open window that is not in direct sunlight. Look at the paper, which is brightly illuminated. Then move the paper so that it partly covers the bright sky at the horizon and you will notice that all of a sudden the paper looks black. Yet it is illuminated exactly as before, perhaps even more brightly. This phenomenon is caused by the change in background against which you view the paper: at first, the background was dark and the paper looked very bright in contrast; afterward, the background was much brighter and the paper looked dark in comparison.

This simple test is of fundamental importance, since contrast phenomena of this nature play a significant role during a variety of observations in the outdoors. For instance, a fountain seen against the sun appears dark.

110. Contrast borders

The outlines of a dark row of houses seen against the lighter sky appear to be edged with light, particularly in the evening. This can be explained by assuming that small involuntary movements are made by the eye and the bright afterimages of the houses cover the surrounding sky and make it lighter. Only a small part of the effect, however, is explained in this way: the decrease in sensitivity in the retina surrounding an illuminated part is of much greater importance—see § 89.

> I was once sitting in a field talking to a man standing a little way off, his figure outlined against the gray sky. After looking at him for some time intently and steadily, I turned away and saw his head surrounded by a dazzling glow of light.

> Goethe, *Farbenlehre*

Father Beccaria, while carrying out some experiments with a kite, perceived a small cloud of light surrounding it and also the string attached to it. Every time the kite moved a little faster, the small cloud seemed to fall behind and float for a moment to and fro.

A very striking example of optical contrast can be seen on undulating moors, whose successive ridges become lighter and lighter owing to aerial perspective, and finally become lost to sight in the hazy distance. Each ridge looks darker along the top and along its base: the effect is so convincing that everyone is bound to notice it. And yet it is only an illusion, arising from the fact that each ridge is bounded at the top by a lighter strip and along the base by a darker one. To prove this, use a piece of paper to screen off the upper part of the landscape: this will be quite sufficient to make the contrast effect disappear.

Sharpe noticed that two days after new moon the ash-gray light showed a light rim at the edge of the disk opposite the bright crescent of the moon. This is not a contrast phenomenon, however, but a consequence of the greater whiteness of the moon near the edges. The same observation may be made during the last quarter.

111. Contrast edges along the boundaries of shadows

Everyone knows that a piece of cardboard held in sunlight will cast a shadow on a screen, and that between the light and the shadow there exists a half-shadow caused by the finite dimensions of the sun's disk—see § 2. But does everyone know that this half-shadow has a bright edge near the transition from light to half-shadow?

Experiment while the sun is low and therefore not too bright; hold the screen about 4 meters (4½ yards) behind the piece of cardboard, and move it slightly to and fro to smooth out local unevenesses. The effect is very clear. The distribution of light observed is shown by the solid line in Fig. 104.

Can you understand this? The distribution of light to be expected can be deduced from the following considerations.

From the successive positions 1–5 of the illuminated screen, the sun's disk is seen to be covered less and less by the cardboard. The brightness at the points is in proportion to the increasingly uncovered part, and should therefore follow the dashed curve of Fig. 104.

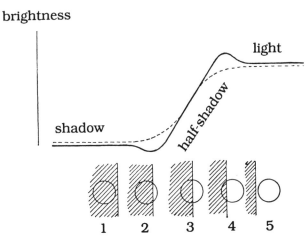

Fig. 104. Contrast edges at the boundary of a shadow; the real brightness division is shown by the *dashed line*, and the apparent brightness division by the *solid line*.

There cannot, therefore, be a brighter edge at all, and the whole thing must be caused by optical illusion.

Indeed, all the circumstances tend to favor this. Mach showed that contrast bands invariably become visible when the brightness does not change at a uniform rate, that is, where the brightness graph is curved. The contrast band always appears to be an exaggeration of the curvature. That this is so can be easily understood either by assuming that small movements are continually being made by the eye, or from the weakened sensitivity of the retina in the neighborhood of its illuminated parts.

The instances mentioned in § 110 also agree completely with the theory of Mach; we need only regard an angle in the brightness curve as an increase of the curvature.

And, finally, from time to time a very special opportunity occurs to test this theory: during a partial eclipse of the sun. Repeating the experiment, you will then obtain various unusual distributions of light along the edge of the half-shadow, according as the sun is screened off by the moon and as the position of the shadow-casting cardboard is altered. Each of these distributions shows its (apparent) contrast bands and in each of these cases Mach's law is satisfied. It is no wonder that the shadows look so unusual as to arouse the interest of even the most casual observers (cf. § 3).

112. Black snow

Watch the snowflakes drifting down out of a gray sky. Seen against the sky, the flakes look decidedly dark. You must bear in mind that the only quality in which black, gray, and white differ is their brightness for which the surrounding background provides the standard of comparison. In this case, we refer all brightnesses to that of the sky, and the sky is much brighter than would have been thought, much brighter, anyhow, than falling snowflakes seen from below. The phenomenon was mentioned by Aristotle.

Compare this with the black-looking leaves against the background of the evening twilight (§§ 109 and 253).

113. White snow and gray skies

When the sky is an even gray, snow-covered fields look much brighter than the sky. This appearance has long been considered a contrast phenomenon, a delusion, because the illuminated object cannot be brighter than the source of light. This, however, overlooks the fact that an evenly overcast sky is not necessarily evenly bright: in fact, near the zenith it is 3 to 5 times brighter than near the horizon

(§ 235). In the illumination of the snow surface, the sky above plays the major role, whereas the observer compares the snow surface with the sky near the horizon. This is beautifully seen when a mirror image of first the sky above, and then of the sky near the horizon, is held near the snow.

Note that paintings which portray snow as darker than the sky look decidedly unnatural.

114. Color contrast

In a variety of cases in which one definite color in the surroundings predominates, the complementary color, in its turn, will appear to be more accentuated. Sometimes this can be explained in the same way as the contrast border, that is, by the involuntary motions continually performed by the eye. But the fact that those parts of the retina that have been stimulated by the predominating color make the adjoining parts less sensitive to that color is much more important in this connection. It is the same as if your eye were now more sensitive to the complementary color, which therefore gives us an impression of greater freshness and saturation. When considered in this way, the color contrast is one more example of the general law that color and brightness are judged only in connection with the complex of all the images delineated on our retina.

Goethe related how, in a courtyard paved with gray limestone and grass growing in between, the grass became an infinitely beautiful green when the evening clouds cast a reddish, scarcely noticeable glow on the pavement.

When you walk through fields under a moderately clear sky and the color green predominates on all sides, the trunks of trees, mole hills, and paths will look reddish.

A gray house seen through green blinds looks reddish. Again, when the waves of the sea show a beautiful green, the parts in shadow look purple (cf. §§ 241 and 243).

If your surroundings are lighted by paraffin lamps or candles, of which the light is reddish, the light of the moon will appear greenish-blue. When the sources of light are not too fierce, this contrast is particularly striking, as, for example, when you see simultaneously reflections of the moon and of gas flames in water.

The spots where sunbeams, after penetrating the green foliage of the wood, strike the ground seem light pink compared with the general green of the surroundings.

Leonardo da Vinci noticed how 'black clothes make a face appear whiter than it is, white clothes darker, yellow clothes bring out the colors in it, and red clothes make it paler'.

The color contrast is most pronounced when the brightnesses of areas do not differ much. What the result is when brightnesses do differ can be seen splendidly in the evening twilight when rows of houses stand out darkly against the blazing orange of the western sky. From a distance, you can see only their uniformly dark silhouettes: all details and differences of brightness have disappeared. Branches and the foliage of trees are outlined in the same way: like dark velvet, their own colors gone (cf. § 253); and this is not because the illumination in itself is too slight, for at the same time the color of every detail on the ground, for instance, can be distinguished clearly.

After you have walked in the snow for a few hours, during which time white and gray were about the only colors to be seen, other colors give the impression of being particularly saturated and warm. Your eyes were 'rested for colors'.

> For the rest, these phenomena occur to the observant everywhere, even to the point of annoyance.

> Goethe, *Farbenlehre*

115. Colored shadows

When a pencil, held perpendicularly on a sheet of paper, is illuminated on one side by candlelight and on the other by moonlight, the two shadows exhibit a striking difference of color; the former is bluish, the latter yellowish.

It is true that here there is a physical difference of color, for where the first shadow falls, the paper is illuminated only by the moon, and where the second shadow falls, only by the candle; and moonlight is whiter than candlelight. But, in any case, it is not blue. The real difference of color between the two shadows is evidently accentuated and modified by physiological contrast.

Similarly, at night you can observe the difference in color between two shadows, one cast by the moon and the other by a streetlamp.

How relative the 'orange' of incandescent lamps is in comparison with the light of sodium lamps can be observed in places where the two illuminations are mixed. The shadow cast by the sodium lamp is beautifully blue; that cast by the incandescent lamp is orange. As soon as you are illuminated by sodium lamps only, your shadow appears black; walking on, you will see it suddenly turn into blue when you approach an ordinary electric bulb; and vice versa, you will see your shadow cast by the electric light change suddenly into orange when you come close to a sodium lamp. The eye evidently adapts itself to its surroundings, and has a tendency to take the predominating color there for 'white'; every other color is then judged relative to this 'white'.

Goethe remarks that the shadows of canary-colored objects are violet. Physically speaking, this is most certainly not true, but, owing to the phenomenon of physiological contrast, it may appear to be so, for instance, when the illuminated side of such objects is turned toward the observer, so that, to him, its shadow is in juxtaposition to a fierce yellow.

You may ask why shadows cast by the sun at midday show practically no colors, since the blue of the sky differs so widely from the color of the sunlight. The answer is that the difference between the brightnesses of shadow and light is too great. When, however, the screen on which the shadow is cast is inclined so much that the sun's rays strike it almost grazingly, the color contrast will become much more pronounced.

A classic case is that of shadows on snow, when the purity of their colors is particularly evident. They are blue because they receive only the light of the blue sky; their blueness equals even the blue of the sky itself. And considering that we see them next to the snow in the yellowish light of the sun, they ought to look even more blue. But their hue is less pronounced than you might expect owing to the great difference in brightness. But watch the shadows when the sun sets over a landscape, especially the last few minutes before it disappears. As the sun turns orange, then red, then purple, the shadow becomes blue, green, and green-yellow. These tints are so pronounced because, at this time of day, the difference in brightness between the shadow and the surrounding snow is much less than in the daytime, for the rays of the sun strike the snow at very small angles and the diffuse light from the sky becomes relatively more important. Moreover, the sun's colors become more and more saturated.

Goethe relates: 'During a journey in the Harz, in winter, I descended the Brocken at nightfall; there was snow on the white fields above and below me and the heath was covered with snow; all the sparse trees and projecting cliffs, all the groups of trees and masses of rock were completely covered with hoarfrost; the sun was just setting over the lakes of the Oder. By day, when the snow was tinged with yellow, the shadows were only a faint violet, but now, when the illuminated parts reflected an intenser yellow, they were decidedly bright blue. When, however, the sun was at last on the point of setting and its light, toned down by the atmosphere, colored everything around me a most glorious purple, the tint of the shadows was seen to change into a green which for purity could compete with the green of the sea, for beauty with that of the emerald. The phenomenon became increasingly vivid, the surroundings changed into a fairy world, for everything was covered with these two bright and beautifully matched colors, until finally, the sun having set, the gorgeous scenery changed to a gray twilight and afterward to a clear night with moon and stars.'

The phenomenon of colored shadows on snow is partly, and in a curious way, of a psychological nature. In daytime, when the sky is blue, the shadows show a much more saturated blue if you are not aware that it is snow. A shaded patch of snow in the distance can give the impression of 'white snow in the shade', as well as of 'a blue lake'. An observer who, from a dense, dark fir wood, saw the hoarfrost on some distant shrubs, was evidently unbiased, for the hoarfrost did indeed appear blue to him; the circumstances were identical to those when you look through a tube with an opening at the end (§ 197).

Psychologists know very well that colors can be reduced to their true hue by looking at them through a small aperture. The moment, however, you imagine an object in its own surroundings and illuminated in the ordinary way, you compensate for their influence automatically, so that one and the same object appears remarkably constant even under changing conditions.

A very curious description of this same phenomenon as observed by children, that is, by unprejudiced observers, is given in the following extract:

> "Galja, look! ... Why is there blue snow falling ...? Look! ... It is blue, blue! ..."
>
> The children became excited and began to shout to each other in sheer delight:
>
> "Blue! Blue! ... Blue snow! ..."
>
> "What is blue? Where?"
>
> I looked round at the snow-covered fields, the snowclad mountains, and felt excited, too. It was extraordinary; the snow came whirling and floating down from all sides—in the distance and quite close in blue waves. And the children shouted in happy excitement:
>
> "Has the sky come down in pieces? Yes, Galja?"
>
> "Blue, blue!"
>
> And once more I was struck by the keen and poetical power of perception of the little mites. Here was I, walking along with them without noticing that floating blue. I had lived through many winters, had many times reveled in the delight of falling snow and not once had I realized this immeasurable azure flight of the snow circling above the earth.
>
> Fj. Gladkow, *New Ground*

116. Colored shadows arising from colored reflections

When colored objects are illuminated by the sun, they often cast so much light around them that this gives rise to shadows, which then show the complementary color. A little pocketbook is the ideal instrument for tracing these light effects. Open it so as to form a right angle; one side of this dihedral angle screens off the sunlight, while the other side catches the colored reflection. Hold the pencil belonging to the pocketbook in front of the paper: its shadow assumes a complementary color and is therefore an extremely sensitive indicator as to whether the incident light is colored. Green paint on a wall or a green shrub casts pink shadows. A yellow wall casts blue shadows (these were once traced as far as 400 meters—420 yards), and the ocher-colored side of a mountain did the same.

117. The contrast triangle

An observer tells us that on a clear night he saw from his ship the moon, which was 20° above the horizon, reflected by the waves in the shape of a light triangle, extending from the ship to the horizon.

Fig. 105. The contrast triangle.

The remarkable thing, however, was that he saw a similar triangle, upside down and dark, descending from the moon to the horizon— see Fig. 105. The effect was, beyond doubt, a physiological and not a true one, because it disappeared when the lower triangle of light and the moon were screened off.

This story seemed to me so fantastic that I was seriously considering omitting it from this edition, when I learned of several similar observations in Norway and in the Netherlands[2]. It was also discovered in paintings and advertizing posters. Moreover, it proved to be fairly simple to imitate it in the laboratory. There is no longer any doubt that it occurs frequently and that it is a contrast phenomenon, because it disappears when the bright light source is screened off. When the moon is screened, only the upper part of the apex of the triangle disappears. For a clear observation, it is necessary for the sky near the horizon to have a general, diffuse illumination, for instance, when there is haze about.

Evidently, the contrast triangle comes about in a manner similar to the contrast borders. The reason that a triangle is seen is facilitated by our tendency to put symmetry and diagrammatic representation in our observations.

Similar phenomena have been observed with sunlight, but these were far less clear.

---

[2] J. Hospers, *Hemel en Dampkring*, **46**, 93, 1948. *Mar. Obs.*, **30**, 193, 1960.

Chapter 9
Judging Shape and Motion

118. Optical illusions regarding position and direction

Suppose that we can distinguish in our field of vision two groups of objects and that within each group the objects are either parallel or at right angles to each other, but that the two groups are inclined relative to each other. Then one group appears to be 'dominant', and we tend to regard it as the true standard for determining horizontal and vertical directions.

If a train happens to stop or to move slowly on a bend in the line, so that the compartment is inclined sideways, all posts, houses, and other buildings appear to us to be tilted the opposite way. We are evidently aware of the inclined position of our compartment, but only to a certain extent.

In the corridors of a ship, heeling under a wind blowing from one side, a man meeting you seems to be inclined relative to the vertical.

When cycling, you will have similar experiences in judging slight inclines in the road. That part of the road where you are cycling will appear to you invariably too horizontal; if you cycle down a steep hill, a sheet of water at the side of the road will not give you the impression of being horizontal, but of sloping toward you. On a gentle downward slope, the road seems to rise farther on, whereas in reality it is flat; a distant rise in the road appears too steep; a downward slope, on the other hand, appears too slight. What your eyes show you particularly is the way the slope in front of you changes, and the visual impression is often at variance with what you gather from the resistance felt while pedaling.

Just south of Ayr in Scotland is a famous slope, the Electric Brae, down which you can 'freewheel', although you get the visual impression that you are cycling up the slope. This impression is caused by the background of woods and mountains that all slope in the same direction.

You can observe a remarkable illusion in a train that is braking. Fix your attention on chimneys, houses, the frames of the windows, or any other vertical objects; the moment the train slows down appreciably, you will get the impression that all these vertical lines are tilted forward and most distinctly of all just when the train comes to an abrupt standstill; immediately afterward, they stand upright again. Under these conditions, even a horizontal meadow appears to

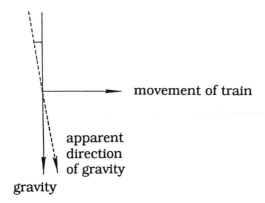

movement of train

apparent
direction
of gravity

gravity

Fig. 106. Apparent change of direction
of the force of gravity when the train or
car you are in brakes.

incline and then to become horizontal again. The explanation is that,
while the brakes are applied, you feel yourself sway slightly forward
as if the direction of gravity were altered. Relative to our muscular
sense of this new 'vertical', the real objects are inclined forward—see
Fig. 106.

119. How movements are seen

As a rule, people think that movements are made apparent when a
change in the position of an object relative to a fixed point is observed. But this is not invariably true: a velocity can be observed as
a single impression, just as well as a length or a duration of time.
When you watch moving clouds, you get at once an impression of
their direction and of their velocity.

It has been found that speeds as low as one or two minutes of arc
per second are perceptible, but only when there are fixed points of
reference in the field of vision (though you may be unaware that you
are referring to them). Without such points, the observation of speed
is about ten times as uncertain. The fixed system for comparison in
this case is your eye, the muscles of which make you feel that it is at
rest, and relative to this frame of comparison you realize by your
sense of vision that the images move over your retina.

Study the passing clouds and try, during the first quiet moments of watching, to determine at once the direction in which they move. Vary the condi-

tions: high clouds, low clouds, gentle wind, strong wind, moon, no moon. A velocity of two minutes of arc means that it takes the edge of a cloud 15 seconds to pass completely over the disk of the moon.

If you watch a net with large mesh hanging out to dry, you can plainly see each gust of wind that passes over it, but when you fix your gaze on one of the meshes, hardly any movement is perceptible at all. It appears that the eye is very sensitive to a complex of small, mutually connected movements.

120. Moving stars

Around the year 1850, much interest was aroused by a mysterious phenomenon: when one looked intently at a star, it sometimes seemed to swing to and fro and to change its position. The phenomenon was said to be observable only during twilight, and then only when the stars in question were not more than 10° above the horizon. A brightly twinkling star was first seen to move in little jerks, parallel to the horizon, then come to a standstill for five or six seconds and to move back again in the same way, and so on. Many observers saw it so plainly that they took it to be an objective phenomenon, and tried to explain it as a consequence of the presence of hot air striae.

However, any real physical phenomenon is entirely out of the question here. A real motion of $\frac{1}{2}°$ per second, seen with the naked eye, would easily be magnified to 50° by even a moderately powerful telescope; that means that the stars would swing to and fro and shoot across the field of vision like meteors. Every astronomer knows that this is sheer nonsense. Even when atmospheric unrest is at its worst, the displacements caused by scintillation remain below the limit of perceptibility of the naked eye. Psychologically speaking, however, the phenomenon has not lost any of its importance. It may be caused by there being no object for comparison, relative to which the star's position can be easily observed. We are not aware that our eyes continually perform little involuntary movements, so that we naturally ascribe displacements of the image over our retina to corresponding displacements of the source of light.

Somebody once asked me why a distant aircraft appears invariably to move in little jerks when followed intently with the eyes. Here, the same psychological cause obviously comes into play, as in the case of the 'moving' stars, and 'distant' seems to point to the fact that this phenomenon, too, occurs most of all near the horizon.

How can we account for the fact that, suddenly and simultaneously, a number of people saw the moon dance up and down for about thirty minutes?

121. The revolving landscape and accompanying moon

When we look at two trees or houses that are at different distances from us and we begin to move toward them, the farther of the two moves with us, whereas the nearer stays in place. This is a simple case of parallax, a phenomenon of geometry rather than of physics.

> The landscape framed in windows hurries by at speed; and whole areas with puddles, fields, trees, a piece of sky, throw themselves into the maelstrom ...

> P. Verlain, *La Bonne Chanson*

One of the first things that struck me as a child when traveling in a train is that peculiar revolving movement the landscape appears to make. It is as if the whole landscape revolves around an imaginary point: the point at which you happen to be looking. Whether you look at a distant or a nearby point, it seems to stand still, while farther points appear to travel with the landscape and nearer ones seem to lag.

It is clear that these visual impressions are caused by parallax; additionally, we refer everything to the point at which we are looking: this is a psychological peculiarity of our visual observations. When at night we walk or cycle, we see that the moon faithfully follows us. The same is true of the sun and the stars, but we do not notice those so much. This proves that we focus our attention on the landscape; the more distant heavenly bodies appear to move with us because of parallax.

122. Illusions concerning rest and motion

> When I cross a bridge and look into the water,
> It's not the water that moves, but the bridge.

> Chinese proverb

A very familiar illusion arises when, from the stationary train in which you are sitting, you see the train next to yours begin to move. You think for a moment that it is your own train that is slowly leaving the station. Or again, after looking for some moments past a high tower at passing clouds, it seems as if the clouds are standing still and the tower is moving. In the same way, some people can see the moon racing through motionless masses of clouds. Take care when crossing a narrow plank over a brook not to look at the water underneath for fear of dizziness; here, your judgment of rest and motion is upset because an unusually large part of your field of vision is in motion. On one's first sea voyage, one sees the things hanging in one's cabin swing to and fro while the cabin itself is at rest.

In all these cases, the illusion is closely connected with the one in § 118. A closer psychological investigation has shown that we have a tendency to consider those things in motion which we know from experience to be usually the moving elements in the landscape. There is, however, another very important and more general law: the notion of rest is, for us, subconsciously connected with the wider frame that encloses elements in our field of vision, whereas motion is connected with the enclosed elements. In several cases mentioned above, this second law clashes with the first one, and, as our illusions prove, completely overrules our common everyday experience.

When you are sitting near the window in a train, gazing dreamily at the ground as it races past, and the train stops, you will get the irresistible impression that it is gliding slowly backward, but not in such a way as to make the whole field of view shift at the same rate! Close to you, the motion appears to be fairly quick, but farther away, rather slower; slightly to the right and left of the point at which you are gazing, the motion will also be somewhat slower. The entire landscape seems to rotate slowly around the point where you are sitting, but, in the manner of some elastic substance, it stretches and shrinks while it rotates. This rotation takes place in a direction contrary to the one when the train was in motion (see § 121). It would be amusing to go and sit quickly at the opposite window the moment the train stops; the rotation ought then to go on in the same direction.

It may be possible that unconsciously our muscles have grown accustomed to following the objects that are racing past and that, when the train stops, these involuntary movements of the eyes do not stop at once, so that for some time we add, so to speak, a constant 'compensating velocity' to the actual velocities. But it is impossible ever to explain by one single movement of the eyes the manner in which the velocity changes toward the boundaries of the field of view. Experiments have been carried out in which an observer watched for some time small objects continually moving away from a central point in every direction; when the movement ceased, the points of light seemed to move back again toward the center from all sides. This cannot possibly be explained by a single movement of the eye. It is, therefore, more than likely that our 'mind', which has been taught to reduce the velocity by a definite amount in every part of the field of vision, continues to do so after the movement has ceased.

The above phenomenon occurs also when we look steadily at a little spot on the window of the compartment, thereby eliminating the movement of the eyes, provided the train does not go so fast as to make the outside objects resemble mere streaks.

On the other hand, however, an old observation of Brewster points very positively to involuntary movements of the eyes. Once, when he looked out of a train window, little pebbles nearby seemed drawn out into short streaks, but when he looked quickly at the ground somewhat farther away, the pebbles appeared at rest for a short moment, as if illuminated by an electric spark. In my opinion, this proves definitely that our eyes do indeed follow the moving objects, though not at exactly the same rate.

Brewster made yet another observation while looking through a narrow slit in a piece of paper at the pebbles flying past; he noticed that when he suddenly turned away his eyes, while still looking through the slit, so that the image of the pebbles fell in his indirect field of vision, everything became clearly visible for a moment. What is the explanation?

When passing by a playground on your right, with a very long fence, keep your head turned to the right while looking at the children. After one or two minutes, look straight ahead again, and see the paving stones and other objects in front of you move from right to left. When you repeat the experiment, looking steadily at the railing this time instead of at the children, the phenomenon will be much less striking.

When carrying out observations of this kind, you will generally notice that you need not follow the rapidly moving objects themselves with your eyes, but that it is better to gaze at some neutral background while images with strong contrasts of light and dark move across the retina.

Watch falling snowflakes and fix your gaze on one of them as it falls, then look up quickly and select another flake, and so on for several minutes. If you then look at the snow-covered ground, you will see it rise and feel as if you yourself are sinking.

Look for a few minutes at the surface of a fast-flowing river or at floating blocks of ice as they drift, all the while fixing your gaze on the top of a mooring post, for example, or on some detail on an island. When you then look at the firm ground again, you see an 'anti-current movement'. Similarly, after admiring a waterfall for a time, the banks seem to move upward. Purkinje, after looking out of his window for some time at a procession of men on horseback, had the impression that the row of houses across the road was moving in the opposite direction. When you walk along a narrow path through corn and look at the distant moon, the conditions are again particularly favorable for the occurrence of this illusion.

Briefly, these conditions are: (a) the movement should last at least one minute; (b) it should not be too fast; and (c) the eyes should look steadily at an object either moving or stationary, and always in such a manner that the images moving over the retina show contrasts and well-defined details.

Fig. 107. Apparent oscillation of double stars seen through moving binoculars.

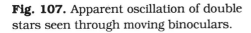

123. Oscillating double stars

The phenomenon of oscillating double stars was observed by the famous Herschel. Look through ordinary binoculars at the last but one star of the Great Bear: you will clearly see a faint star close to the bright one—see Figs. 71 and 88. Carry out the experiment preferably when the faint star is more or less vertically under the bright one (though you may also succeed when it is in other positions). Move the binoculars gently a little to the left, then to the right, and back again to the left, and so on, just fast enough for the images of the stars to remain visible as little dots of light. It will then seem as if the faint star lags slightly behind the bright one each time, as if it were attached to it by a piece of string, and performs an oscillatory motion—see Fig. 107.

The explanation lies in the fact that it takes some time for the light to stimulate our retina, and the brighter the star is, the shorter the time required; by the time we locate the fainter star, the brighter one has already moved a little farther.

This phenomenon was used by Pulfrich for the design of a photometer.

124. Optical illusions concerning the direction of rotation

When the sails of a windmill turn in the twilight and you look at their silhouette (see Fig. 108a) from a direction inclined relative to the plane of the sails, you can imagine their rotation to be clockwise just as well as counterclockwise—see Fig. 108b. The change from one rotation to the other requires a momentary concentration of attention, but it is usually sufficient simply to go on looking at it quietly, when the rotation will appear to change of its own accord. Most meteorological stations are equipped with Robinson's anemometer, that is, a little windmill with a vertical axis of rotation. When I look from a distance at its rotating vanes, without any conscious effort of my will they appear to reverse the direction of their rotation every twenty-five or thirty seconds. A wind vane swinging to and fro can cause us to doubt in the same way, especially if it is not too high up—see Fig. 108c.

In all these cases, our judgment of the direction of rotation depends on which parts of the track appear closer to us and which parts farther away. Those parts that happen to attract our attention

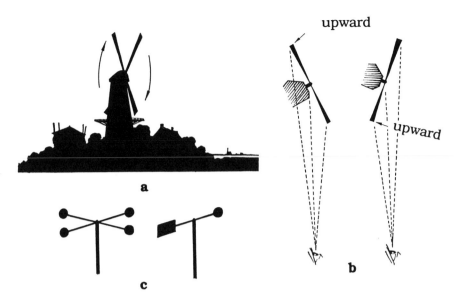

Fig. 108. Silhouette of a windmill at night: (**a**) what the observer sees; (**b**) what image he may associate with it; (**c**) other deceptive silhouettes.

most seem, generally speaking, nearer to us. The reversal of the apparent direction of the rotation must, therefore, be ascribed to a sudden change in our attention.

125. Stereoscopic phenomena

Looking through a window of inferior-quality glass, you can observe an amusing phenomenon. Look attentively at the surface of the ground. Keep your eyes close to the glass and your head steady, and shake off the preconceived idea that the ground must be flat. You will suddenly perceive that it seems to undulate, even to undulate very strongly. If you move your head slowly parallel to the window, the undulations seem to shift over the ground in the opposite direction; if you move away from the window, they seem to remain about equally high, but to become wider.

The explanation is that the windowpane is not perfectly flat, but of a very slightly varying thickness. As a rule, these undulations run parallel to some definite direction as a result of the pane having been made by rolling out the red-hot molten glass under steel rollers. Such an undulation is equivalent to a prism with a small refracting angle, and causes the rays of light to deviate slightly. In Fig. 109, the eyes L and R are assumed to look at the point A of the ground, so that the uneven thickness is not apparent. When they look at B,

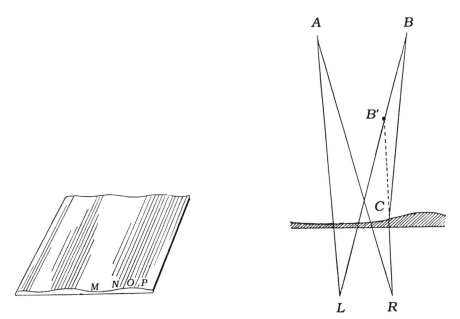

Fig. 109. If you look through an uneven window pane, it appears as if the ground is uneven.

however, the ray *BR* is no longer straight, but broken along *BCR*. The result is that the eyes are directed as if they were looking at *B'*, which lies nearer to them than *B*. In another part of the pane, the deflection of the rays will be different, so that then the object apparently recedes. This enables us to understand that a slight unevenness of the pane can cause the illusion of a strong undulation of the objects outside, though sometimes the way in which the effects on the separate eyes combine is fairly complicated.

If, for example, the left eye looks through a flat part and the right eye through an uneven part of the pane, the details of the way in which the stereoscopic effects arise can easily be traced. Shut your left eye and rock your head slightly to and fro; the pattern on the ground will rock in the same direction for those parts where the pane is concave *M* (see Fig. 109) and in the opposite direction where it is convex *O*. Why? If you now open both eyes, the parts *M* and *O* correspond to places on the ground that we see at normal distances. Looking with your right eye through *N*, you will see a crest; looking through *P*, a trough. Try to account for all the details.

A phenomenon closely related to this can be observed when you stand very near a slightly rippled surface of water. Let your eyes try to fix the reflected image of, say, a branch of a tree; as your eyes do not look at the same point of the undulating surface, two images are seen at a continually changing angular distance from each other and it is impossible to adjust the axis of the eyes on it properly. This causes a very peculiar sensation, difficult to describe. As soon as you close one eye, the surface of the water is scarcely perceptible and you can imagine that you are seeing the tree itself moving in the wind, instead of its reflection. When you look with both eyes, you suddenly become aware of the rippled surface itself, but this surface glistens; this is a characteristic phenomenon when your eyes receive widely differing images, the one light, the other dark.

126. Delusions caused by distance and size

When a weathercock is brought down from a steeple for repair, it looks unexpectedly large. When a painter is at work high upon a block of flats or steeple, he looks minute. Big Ben does not look to have a diameter of seven meters (23 ft); nor does the torch-bearing arm of the Statue of Liberty appear to be 13.1 meters (43 ft) long. In these cases we underestimate the distance of the objects high above us and that is why they look so much smaller than they are.

In a similar manner, we are struck by the minuteness of people and cars we see way below us when we are at the top of a high tower. Here again we underestimate the height at which we are; there are no yardsticks between them and us to give guidance.

In an aircraft we have no impression of the height at which we are flying. The fact that we appear to move relatively slowly indicates that we underestimate the height by a considerable factor.

We shall encounter similar phenomena when we discuss the sun and the moon, when even more complex matters become evident.

127. The man in the moon

The man in the moon is an excellent warning to us to carry out our observations with due objectivity! The dark and light spots on the moon are really flat plains and mountains, and their distribution is obviously very haphazard. Unconsciously, we try to distinguish in this fantastic distribution of light forms that are more or less familiar; we fix our attention on certain peculiarities so that these become clearer and more striking, whereas shapes to which no attention is paid become less distinct. Thus, in the full moon at least, three aspects of a human face can be seen: side view, three-quarter face, and full face. Also, a woman's figure, an old woman with a bundle of twigs, a hare, a lobster, and so on can be seen.

Delusions of this kind have played tricks on the best observers, the famous case of the canals on Mars being one instance out of many. It is as well to bear this in mind in connection with many a fantastic description of mirages or *fata Morgana.*

128. The searchlight phenomenon and cloud bands

A searchlight casts a slender beam of light horizontally over a wide open space. Although I know that the beam runs in a perfectly straight line, I cannot get rid of the illusion that it is curved, highest of all in the middle and sloping down to the ground on both sides. The only way to convince myself that the beam is really straight from one end to the other is to hold a stick in front of my eyes.

What is the cause of this illusion? This tendency of mine to see the path of light as a curve is because on one side I see it slope downward to the left, and on the other side toward the right; as if the straight lines of an ordinary horizontal telephone wire did not behave in the same way! However, looking at the beam of light at night, I have no point of reference in surrounding objects to enable me to estimate distances and nothing is known to me, a priori, of the shape of the beam.

A similar phenomenon can be seen at night along a row of high streetlights, especially when there are no parallel rows of houses, or when these are hidden by trees. The row of lights then looks curved just like the beam of a searchlight.

Immediately related to this is the observation that the line connecting the horns of the moon, between its first quarter and full moon, for instance, does not appear to be at all perpendicular to the direction from sun to moon; we apparently think of this direction as being a curved line. Fix this direction by stretching a piece of string taut in front of your eyes: however unlikely it may have seemed at first, you will now perceive that the condition of perpendicularity is satisfied.

The rows of clouds which seem to radiate from a point on the horizon and meet again on the other side of the celestial sphere run in reality straight, horizontal, and parallel to each other. See also § 221.

If you stand near a lighthouse at night with your back toward it, you can see a most impressive sight. As the great beams sweep over the landscape, they seem to converge on an imaginary 'anti-light-source point' a little below the horizon, and to rotate about this point. Observing one of these beams of light, I conclude that it lies in a definite plane determined by its true position in space and the point occupied by my eye. When the beam revolves, the position of this plane in space changes continually, but continues to pass through the line joining the lighthouse, my eye, and the 'anti-light-source point'. Instead, therefore, of seeing the beams as horizontal lines radiating from a point behind me, I can imagine them to be 'rays with their lower part cut off, revolving about an anti-light-source point that lies below the horizon'. The fact that I involuntarily adhere to the second point of view is psychologically remarkable and arises from my tendency to regard converging lines as belonging together and to extend them up to their vanishing point. Also at play here is the 'underestimation of faraway distances' (§ 134), because of which the beam of light does not appear to extend into infinity, but seems to approach a point at a finite distance from my eye.

When I turn into a direction at right angles to the beams and look upward, each of the beams is strongly curved; it is almost as if the beams of light and antilight shoot upward to meet at the zenith.

129. The apparent flattening of the celestial sphere

When you are outside and look up at the sky, you do not get the impression of a limitless space above you, nor that of a hemisphere hovering above you and the earth. It looks more like a vault whose height above you is much less than the distance between you and the horizon—see Fig. 110. It is an impression, no more, but to most people a very convincing one: its explanation is psychological and not physical.

Measuring this apparent flattening is, of course, impossible but we can estimate it.

1. If we ask what the ratio of the distances eye-to-horizon and eye-to-zenith appears to be, we find that, depending on observers and circumstances, most people seem to think that this lies somewhere between 2 and 4.

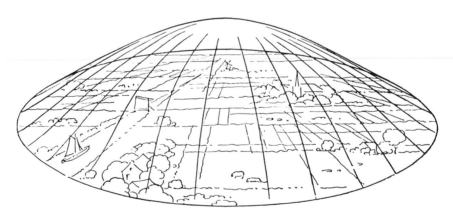

Fig. 110. The sky seems to cover the world immediately around us like a vault.

2. If we estimate as accurately as possible the direction of the center of the arc zenith-to-horizon and then measure it (see Appendix A) we find that this does not lie at 45° (as most of us would expect), but rather lower: about 20–30°; few of us obtain values as low as 12° or as high as 45°. Observers must try to be unbiased and be clear in their minds that they must bisect the arc and not the angle. It is very important to estimate the position of the zenith as accurately as possible: this is best done by first looking into one direction and then into the opposite one until the two estimates coincide or very nearly do so.

Take the average of about ten estimates obtained under each of 1 and 2.

The apparent flattening of the vault of heaven depends on a number of circumstances. It increases greatly when the sky is cloudy, particularly if the cloud is of the altocumulus or altostratus type, since this gives an impression of depth and can be followed right up to the horizon. It also increases at twilight, but decreases with a dark, starry sky. On average, the bisecting angle is 22° during the day and about 30° at night. Note that observations at sea are of greater value, since the view there is generally unhindered and there are no other factors that may affect the estimates.

Differences between individual observers are generally much greater than those resulting from external conditions.

It is difficult to accept the contention that the sky looks flatter in a north–south direction and more curved in an east–west direction[1].

When you look through a piece of red glass, large enough to prevent its size distracting you, the sky looks flatter; through blue glass, it looks higher and closer to a spherical shape.

More elaborate assessments have given us a more accurate picture of the curvature we unconsciously ascribe to the sky. Many observers see it as a kind of helmet or shell—see Fig. 110.

Fig. 111. Bisecting the apparent arc between zenith and horizon.

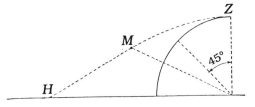

[1] Gietze, Z. Meteorolog., **16**, 286, 1962.

130. Overestimating the angle of elevation

In addition to the sky appearing flattened to us, we generally overestimate heights above the horizon. Evidently, we subconsciously confuse measuring the arc with measuring the angle—see Fig. 111. The point *M*, located at a position where *HM* = *MZ*, is well below 45° above the horizon, yet looks halfway up the arc to us.

At noon in winter, the sun appears to be fairly high in the sky, yet, at our latitudes (about 50° N), it is only just about 15° above the horizon. During summer, it seems to be nearly at the zenith, whereas, in fact, it never gets higher than 61°.

In the same way, we overestimate the height of hills and the steepness of a slope ahead of us. It even happens that observers describe the aureole around the sun or moon (see § 157) as higher than it is wide.

At night, look at a star that you think is at, or very near to, the zenith. Turn around (about 180°) and look at the same star: you will be surprised how far from the zenith it now appears. At your first observation, it was probably not much higher than 70° or thereabout.

An explanation of the influence of the direction we look into is offered by Quix's theory about the operation of our organ of balance, the semicircular canals of the ears, which states that we constantly misjudge the position of our heads.

131. Apparent enlargement of the sun and the moon at the horizon

Astronomers tell us that the sun and the moon subtend (accidentally) the same, virtually constant, angle at our eye of, on average, $32' = \frac{1}{108}$ rad. It seems hard to believe. The moon may look awesomely large when it rises in coppery splendor and it may look insignificantly small high in the sky.

And the sun:

> Above us, the sky turns a watery green;
> While lower down the sun still glows
> and smolders and sinks and grows.

> G. Gezelle, *Avondrood*

Is this a delusion? Let us create an image of the sun and measure it. Take a lens with a focal length of 2 m (6 ft 6 in)[2], mount it in a cork

---

[2] Opticians call this '+0.50' (diopter). Get a round, unpolished one with rough edges.

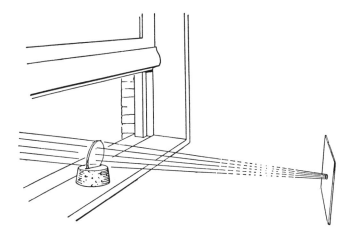

Fig. 112. Obtaining an image of the sun with the aid of a long-focus lens.

in which a suitable cut has been made (see Fig. 112), and let the light of the setting sun fall on to it. This test should be carried out outside or at an open window to prevent distortion by the window glass. Project the rays on to a sheet of paper about 2 m (6 ft 6 in) behind the lens and, lo and behold, there is a beautiful picture of the sun. If it is not entirely round, the lens is not at right angles to the incoming rays; turn it slightly or change its slope until the image is perfectly round. Move the paper to a distance where the sharpest image is obtained and then carefully draw the horizontal and vertical diameters. Measure the diameter, preferably the horizontal one, since the vertical one may be slightly smaller owing to refraction in the earth's atmosphere. Repeat the experiment a couple of times and take the mean of the measurements.

Repeat the measurements with the sun high in the sky. Positioning the lens will be rather more difficult, but it may be done, for instance, by nailing the cork to a tree or post driven into the ground—see Fig. 113. Note that the cork may be rotated around the nail. As before, measure the diameter of the image projected on to the paper. It will be found that, within observational tolerances, the diameter is exactly the same as that obtained from the setting sun. Even the most elaborate measurements carried out with powerful lenses do not throw up any differences.

The apparent enlargement of the sun and the moon near the horizon must, therefore, be a psychological phenomenon. But even this obeys fixed laws and may be expressed in numbers. Take a white cardboard disk of about 30 cm (1 ft) and look at it from such a distance as to make it appear the same size as the moon. Do not make

Fig. 113. Nail a cork to a tree or post driven into the ground; make sure it can be rotated around the nail.

a direct comparison because that would show immediately that the moon is always the same size, just as we have verified in the case of the sun. Therefore, look at the moon and memorize how large it looks. Turn away and compare your mental image with the cardboard disk. The test is even more interesting if you use a number of disks of increasing diameter against a dark background. Always look at them from the same distance, of course. Carry out a number of tests when the moon is high in the sky and when it is low at the horizon. The tests may also be performed with the sun, but NEVER look at the sun with the naked eye: use a darkened piece of glass. Look at the cardboard disk with the naked eye, though.

The observations are fairly difficult, because the psychological phenomenon is affected by several subtle factors and a slackening of concentration. You will note, however, that they become much easier with a little practice.

The measurements so obtained show that to most of us the sun or the moon at the horizon appears from 2.5 to 3.5 times as large as when it is high in the sky. The difference between the physical and the psychological phenomenon is thus quite large. The effect becomes even more pronounced at dusk when the sky is cloudy.

The apparent enlargement of the sun is more striking in flat countryside than in hilly or mountainous terrain, but at sea it is less marked.

When you look at the moon between your thumb and forefinger, or through a small aperture in a piece of cardboard, or through the tube formed by the rounded fingers and palm of your hand, it will appear smaller than looked at direct.

One-eyed people do not perceive an enlargement of the sun or the moon near the horizon. If you cover one of your eyes, you will initially see an enlargement, but this will gradually disappear[3].

---

[3] *Sky and Telescope*, **11**, 135, 1952

Like the sun and the moon, constellations near the horizon also appear larger: even Haidinger's brush[4] appears twice as long and wide as high in the sky.

132. The connection between the apparent enlargement of heavenly bodies at or near the horizon and the shape of the celestial sphere

Attempts have been made to connect the apparent enlargement of heavenly bodies with the apparent flattening of the celestial sphere. It is thought that we consider the sun and the moon to be as far away as the sky, that is, the sun or the moon at the horizon appears farther away than when it is high in the sky. That it subtends the same angle α at our eye we ascribe (subconsciously) to the enlargement during its descent from zenith to horizon. In other words (see Fig. 114),

$$s_1/s_2 = r_1/r_2.$$

To test the veracity of this equation, the apparent size of the sun and the moon at different altitudes above the horizon has been estimated (cf. § 131). Such tests are by no means easy. However, their results prove the assumption that the relative size of the sun and the moon is directly proportional to the distance of the vault of the sky.

The low-lying sun appears to be enlarged by adjacent clouds, but not by objects on earth that are silhouetted against the horizon. This comes about because a cloudy sky appears even flatter than a clear one and our subconscious, therefore, tells us to push the sun back, since it cannot be in front of the clouds.

In the same way, the low-lying moon looked at during a cloudy day appears larger than on a clear day. It is especially noteworthy that with clear skies the moon appears much larger at dusk than by day

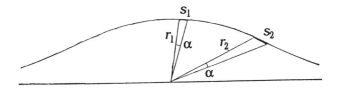

Fig. 114. The sun or the moon high in the sky appears smaller than when it is at or near the horizon.

[4] John Strong, *Concepts of Classical Optics*, Freeman, 1958.

or at night; this coincides with the more pronounced flattening of the celestial sphere apparent at dusk.

When it is misty or hazy at night, so that the moon lights up the sky around it, it appears to us as if the only slightly flattened sky is replaced by the more noticeably flattened sky observed at dusk, so that the moon appears larger than if the sky were clear.

If you think that the seemingly larger size of the moon at or near the horizon, or during hazy weather, is in some way connected with the decrease of the ambient light in those conditions, bear in mind two things: (a) the crescent of the moon does not appear larger in hazy weather, which is understandable since the crescent lights up the neighboring sky only slightly; and (b) during an eclipse of the moon, it does not appear enlarged even if it is high in the sky. These observations make it clear that what counts is the background of the sky: only this determines how large we estimate the sun or the moon to be.

Yet it must be admitted that there are objections to such a close connection between the two phenomena. Many people see the sun or the moon at or near the horizon just 'a little closer', or they are not able to say much about the distance, although they do experience the sensation of enlargement. Such objections are not necessarily conclusive, because it may well be that in some people, when asked direct questions about the distance, other psychological aspects play a role and that these affect the subconscious judgment.

133. The hollow earth

The concave earth forms a lovely contrast to the impression the sky makes on us. To air travelers, the earth seems to tilt upward toward the horizon, so that they seem to hover above a hollow dish. It appears that the horizontal plane through our eyes always remains flat, whereas the horizontal planes above and below our eyes seem to be deflected at the horizon, or at any rate at great distances, toward the one through our eyes.

Traveling a few kilometers (miles) above banks of cloud, we perceive them as curved with the convex side downward and the concave side toward us. If there is a bank of clouds below us and another one above us, it appears as if we are suspended between two gigantic convex lenses. From this, we must conclude that our brains are not easily switched off.

134. The theory of underestimation

Von Sterneck cleverly succeeded in formulating mathematically the seemingly indeterminable psychological phenomenon of the sky above us. Although he does not explain the phenomenon, he brings it down to a large set of observations with which we are confronted daily.

The farther the objects, the harder it becomes to estimate how far away they are. At night, streetlights farther away than about 150 m (500 ft) seem to be all at the same distance from us. Mountains at the horizon and constellations in the sky seem to be equally far away.

All untrained observers underestimate great distances: a fire at night; where lightning strikes; the lights of a port seen from at sea.

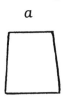

This underestimation is negligible in the case of objects that are not too far away, but it becomes more prominent the greater the distances involved. There is, however, a limit to this. Rectangular fields seen from a moving train appear to be trapezoidal, because the angle at which side *a* is seen (see illustration) matches its real but not its apparent distance.

When a car or train you are traveling in approaches a tunnel and you look at the brick wall of the tunnel entrance, the bricks appear to swell and become larger. The explanation for this is that when the real distance is halved, you will see the bricks at twice the angle, although the distance appears to be reduced by about two-thirds. This makes it appear as if the bricks become larger.

Von Sterneck related the apparent and real distances, *d* and *d'* respectively, by the simple formula

$$d' = cd/(c+d'),$$

where *c* is a constant for each special case: it is the greatest distance that in given circumstances can still be estimated fairly accurately; it varies from 200 m (220 yd) to 20 km (12.5 miles). Note that *d'* is virtually equal to *d* as long as *d* is small compared with *c*; when *d* be-

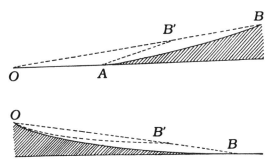

Fig. 115. Observer *O* overestimates the ascent and underestimates the descent.

comes comparable to c, increasing underestimation occurs. When d is large, the apparent distance approaches a limit. The formula is thus in good quantitative accord with experience, while many observations have shown close quantitative agreement with the computed figures.

The theory of underestimation also explains the overestimation of the steepness of mountain slopes—see Fig. 115. Observer O estimates the distance OB as if it were OB', that is, as if AB were AB'. A logical consequence of this is that the steepness of such slopes is underestimated by an observer at the top of the mountain.

We shall now see how the theory attempts to explain the apparent shape of the celestial vault and with this also the apparent increase in size of heavenly bodies near the horizon.

Let us imagine a cloud bank at a height of 2.5 km (1.5 miles) above our heads. This bank should resemble a flat plate for, owing to the curvature of the earth, our eye is at a distance of about 178 km (110 miles) from the layer of clouds at the horizon and only 2.5 km (1.5 miles) from the clouds at the zenith. The clouded sky, however, does not look at all like this! The short distance is underestimated slightly, the long distance very much. Assume that we estimate the ratio of the distances eye-to-horizon and eye-to-zenith to be about 5. This would mean that in these circumstances $c = 10.6$ km (6.6 miles): the formula for the underestimation theory furnishes the correct values (try this for yourself). It follows from this that we should see the clouded sky as a kind of vault, a hyperboloid of revolution, which does, indeed, agree with our general impression of it. Note, therefore, that we actually do not see the celestial sphere flattened, but, on the contrary, relatively higher than it is!

But what about the blue sky, and the starry sky? Von Sterneck simply takes a new value for the constant c each time and his formula describes the observation in each definite case with surprising accuracy. However, it is difficult to understand how in these cases we can speak of a certain 'distance' being underestimated. And this leads us to the more general questions: how do we get any impression at all of distance in the case of such indefinite objects as clouds? And blue sky? And a cloudless sky at night? The underestimation theory may be true as far as terrestrial objects are concerned whose dimensions and distances are known to us by every sort of experience; it is very doubtful, however, whether it can be applied to the sky above. Besides, no light has as yet been thrown on the origin of underestimation.

135. Gauss's theory of visual direction

In connection with § 134, there are a number of observations which show that the shape of the celestial vault and the apparent increase

lying down

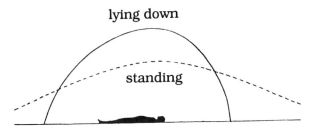

Fig. 116. The shape of the celestial vault as seen by an upright and a supine observer.

in size of the celestial bodies near the horizon depend on the direction of our gaze in relation to our body. Gauss therefore assumed that the experience of many generations has made us better adapted to the observation of those things that are in front of us than of those above us, and that this influences our estimation of distances and dimensions.

When the full moon is shining high up in the sky, sit down in an easy chair, or on the ground with your back against something sloping. If you lean right back, but hold your head in its usual position with regard to the rest of your body, and observe the moon, it seems to be appreciably larger. If you get up suddenly, so that your gaze has to be directed upward, the moon seems to be smaller again. And, vice versa, the full moon near the horizon looks much smaller when we lean forward.

Both phenomena can be seen alternately when the sun is 30° or 40° high and its light is tempered by mist or haze. Lean backward and forward and the disk appears alternately larger and smaller. Lie with your back flat on the ground; the sky appears compressed on that side toward which your head is lying now, whereas on the side opposite it seems perfectly spherical—see Fig. 116. This shows clearly that (relative to your body) looking downward and looking forward are, in the present connection, practically equivalent, whereas looking upward makes the objects seem compressed.

Hang by your knees from a horizontal bar or branch and look round you while your head is hanging down. The sky will look hemispherical.

All these observations confirm each other. In addition to this, constellations seen through a telescope, and therefore free from any external influences in the landscape, likewise seem larger when they are lying low on the horizon; the only thing that can have any influence here is the direction of our gaze.

Try to check this further by judging the apparent size of the sun and the moon in a mirror, so that in this way you see, for instance, the moon high up while your gaze is directed horizontally. If the observer is conscious of the presence of a mirror in any way, the illusion is partly lost. For this reason, this kind of experiment is very difficult to perform.

Various other theories concerning the visual impressions just mentioned are easily refuted. For example, it has been maintained that a 'physical theory' as to the shape of the celestial vault can be given, and this theory amounts to the principle, an incomprehensible one, that the brighter the sky is, the farther away it seems to be, the distance varying as the square root of the brightness. The sky when blue is darker at the zenith than along the horizon and this would make it look lower. This theory is, however, sufficiently refuted by the fact that the sky when uniformly clouded proves to be brighter at the zenith than on the horizon and yet appears flattened. Furthermore, when the sky is clouded, the clouds in front of the sun which look brighter than the rest always seem nearer to us than the surrounding parts of the sky.

136. How terrestrial objects influence our estimation of the distance to the celestial vault

If you stand in front of a long row of houses and look at those immediately facing you, the sky there will seem much nearer to you than it does above those at the end of the row.

Evidently, we estimate the distance of the sky to be about 50–60 m (55–65 yd)! But the fact that we see objects which we know to be very distant is sufficient to make their background, the sky, seem much farther away. To a certain extent, each terrestrial object has its own background in the sky. This shows how purely psychological all these phenomena must be, and how impossible it is to speak of an ideal 'surface of reference' which for us would be the celestial vault.

Looking down a long railway track or a wide road bordered by trees makes us realize the great distance: the sky seen in that direction seems much farther off than at other points of the compass. If, however, you screen off the landscape as far as the horizon with a sheet of paper, the sky there at once seems nearer.

As a counterpart to this, look upward in the same way; the sky will then seem higher. This phenomenon is particularly striking when seen from the foot of a high tower or, better still, near the tall, slender antenna towers of a broadcasting station. The sky above seems to arch until it forms a kind of cupola; between three towers, the whole sky seems to be pressed upward. Different observers draw, independently of each other, the apparent shape in the same manner—see Fig. 117.

If, when looking toward one of these towers, you divide the arc from the horizon to zenith into two parts (§ 129), the lower part will appear to be much greater than if you made your estimate with your back to the tower and at some distance from it. The angles subtended by the lower part will now seem to be greater than 45°, even as great as 56°, which means that the vault of the sky looks higher than a hemisphere!

However convincing these observations may be, remember that in themselves they can never explain the shape of the celestial vault, nor the apparent increase in size near the horizon. Even when observed through a very dark piece of glass, the sun when high will always appear small, and large when it is low, even though the landscape can then no longer be seen.

137. The apparent size of the sun and the moon in centimeters. The method of afterimages

We know that we cannot estimate the size of the sun and the moon in linear measure; we can only designate the angle subtended by them at the eye. And yet it is remarkable that a great number of people maintain that the celestial bodies are to them as large as dinner plates, while there is a minority that suggests dimensions of the order of a coin. Should you feel inclined to smile at this, remember

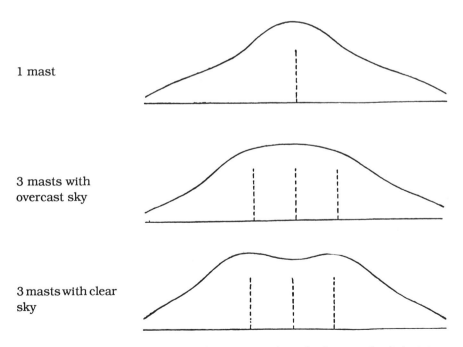

1 mast

3 masts with overcast sky

3 masts with clear sky

Fig. 117. The apparent shape of the celestial vault above radio/television antenna masts.

that even a scientifically minded man feels how perfectly impossible it would be to state that the diameter of the moon looks like 1 mm ($^{40}/_{1000}$ in) or 10 m (11 yd), whereas he knows quite well that 1 mm ($^{40}/_{1000}$ in) at a distance of 10 cm (4 in), or 10 m (11 yd) at a distance of 1000 m (1100 yd), would cover the moon exactly. The psychological factors playing a part here are as yet little understood.

Everyone knows that afterimages of the sun can be obtained by glancing swiftly at it and then blinking—see § 105. This afterimage is projected on every object we gaze at afterward. On a wall near to us, it looks very small and insignificant, on objects farther away it seems larger. (Note, however, that we do not estimate the angle it subtends but the size of 'the thing itself'.) This effect is perfectly comprehensible, for if an object at a distance is to subtend the same angle as an object near to us, it must be larger in linear measure.

When does the afterimage look as 'large' as the sun itself? According to the opinion of different observers, this occurs whenever the wall is from 50 to 60 m (55 to 65 yd) away and this applies equally to daytime and to nighttime; this therefore shows the distance which we feel to be between us and the sun or the moon. Considering that the angle subtended is $^{1}/_{108}$ rad, this would correspond to a diameter of 45–55 cm (18–22 in).

In the same way, it has been shown that the afterimage on a wall at a distance greater than 60 m (65 yd) still looks as large as that on the sky immediately above it (that is, near the horizon), while the afterimage projected high in the sky looks decidedly smaller than on a wall 60 meters away. This shows once again that to us the distance to the sky above looks less than to the horizon and that 60 m (65 yd) is about the 'limiting distance' in the theory of underestimation (§ 134).

138. The scene

By carefully measuring his early sketches, Vaughan Cornish tried to determine an important parameter: the angular size of the field that man sees as a unit, *the scene*. The general impression of a landscape is closely connected with this. The scene, measured as an angle, becomes smaller in flat countryside and larger in the mountains; it is also larger by night than by day. The more restricted the scene, the smaller the sun or the moon are drawn; however, after their size has been converted into an angular measurement, it is found to be correct.

Chapter 10

Rainbows, Halos, and Coronas

Rainbows

The following simple observations form an introduction to the study of the rainbow. What we see occurring in a single drop of water is also visible in millions of raindrops and gives rise to a glowing arc of color.

139. Interference phenomena in raindrops

Many people obliged to wear glasses out of doors complain that raindrops distort the images and make them unrecognizable. It may, perhaps, console them if we call their attention to the splendid interference phenomena visible in these same raindrops. All they need to do is to look at a source of light in the distance, a streetlight, for example. A raindrop that happens to be exactly in front of the pupil becomes strangely distorted, a spot of light with extraordinary projections and indentations, with a border of very beautiful diffraction fringes in which colors, too, are distinguishable.

One remarkable thing about it is that the spot of light remains in the same place even when the glasses are moved slightly to and fro. Another is that the general shape and protruding curves of the spot of light seem, at first, to bear no relation whatever to the shape of the raindrop. The explanation is simple. Regard the eye as a small telescope forming an image of a source of light in the distance and the drop of water as a group of small prisms held in front of the objective. It is then clear that each small prism refracts a group of rays laterally, independently of its position on the objective (provided it is still within the opening of the objective); the shape of the patch of light will depend, however, on the value of the refracting angle and on the orientation of each small prism. A drop of water extended vertically does, indeed, give a horizontal streak of light.

But now the diffraction fringes! These would not exist if the drop of water formed an accurate lens to image the source of light exactly at a point, for then all parts of the light wave front, since they left the source simultaneously, would arrive at the image together with no change of relative phase. But, since the surface of the water is curved

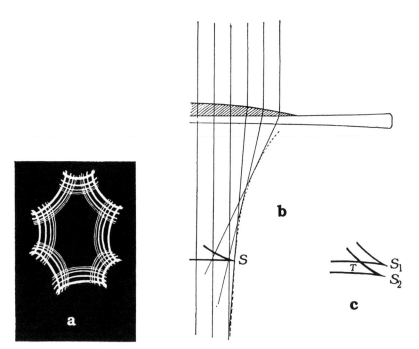

Fig. 118. Refraction of light rays by a raindrop on a spectacle lens; **(a)** interference figure; **(b)** path of the rays: the caustic curve is shown *dashed*, while the *solid line* represents the wave surface that is reversed at *S*; **(c)** two successive wavefronts, both passing through *T*.

irregularly, the refracted rays do not meet in focus, but are enveloped by a caustic (see Fig. 118b). In such a case, you will always find that through a point in the neighborhood of the caustic there pass two different rays that have traversed light paths of different lengths; interference therefore occurs. On drawing the wave surface, you will find a point of reversal giving a cusp; at any moment, therefore, there will always pass through a point *T* two wave fronts with a definite difference of phase—see Fig. 118c.

The distances of the dark fringes measured from a fixed point are given by the formula $(2m+1)^{2/3}$, where $m = 1, 3, 5, \ldots$. These distances are therefore in the ratio 2.1; 3.7; 5.0; 6.1; and so on.

Apart from the diffraction fringes surrounding the drop of water, there are weaker ones that are visible as rings round each fleck of dust contained in the drop of water on the glasses. The more carefully you clean the glasses, the fewer of those rings will be seen. It is really worthwhile studying all these peculiarities caringly.

140. How a rainbow is formed[1]

My heart leaps up when I behold
A rainbow in the sky.

William Wordsworth, *The Rainbow*

It is a summer afternoon and oppressively warm. Dark clouds appear on the western horizon: a storm is brewing. A black arch of clouds is rising rapidly, behind which the sky in the distance seems about to clear; the front edge has a light border of cirrus clouds with fine transverse stripes. It spans the entire sky and passes, awe-inspiringly, over our heads with a few claps of thunder. All at once, the rain is pelting down; it has grown cooler. The sun, already low, shines again. And in the storm, drifting eastward, appears the wide arch of a multicolored rainbow.

Whenever it occurs, the rainbow is always formed by light playing on drops of water. They are generally raindrops, occasionally the fine, tiny drops of mist. In the finest, smallest drops of all, those that make up the clouds, it can never be seen. If, therefore, you ever hear anyone say that he has seen a rainbow in falling snow or when the sky was clear, you can be certain that the snow was sleet or that one of those showers of drizzle was falling that occur sometimes without there being any clouds. Try to make more of these interesting observations yourself!

The drops in which a rainbow arises are usually not much farther than a few kilometers (1–1.5 miles) away from us. On one occasion, I saw the rainbow standing out clearly against the dark background of a wood at a distance of about 20 meters (22 yards) from me: the rainbow itself was therefore nearer still. Cases have been reported in which a rainbow was only three to four meters (10–14 ft) away.

According to an old English superstition, a crock of gold is to be found at the foot of every rainbow. There are, even today, people who imagine that they can really reach that foot, that you can cycle up to it, and that a peculiar twinkling light is to be seen there. It must be clear that a rainbow is not at one fixed point like a real thing; it is nothing but light coming from a certain direction.

Try to photograph the rainbow on a panchromatic film with a yellow filter: speed $\frac{1}{10}$ second; stop f/16.

141. Description of a rainbow

The rainbow is part of a circle; the first thing that occurs to us is to make a rough estimate as to where its center lies, that is, the direc-

---

[1] C.B. Boyer, *The Rainbow*, New York, 1959.

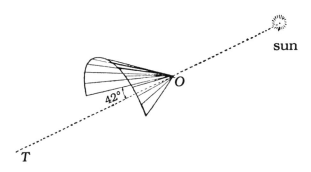

Fig. 119. The direction relative to the sun in which a rainbow is seen.

tion in which we see that central point. We notice immediately that this central point lies below the horizon and we easily find that it is the point to which the prolongation of the straight line from the sun to the observer's eye (after penetrating the earth) is directed; that is, the antisolar point. This line is the axis to which the circle of the rainbow is attached like a wheel—see Fig. 119. The rays from the rainbow to the eye form a conical surface; each of them makes an angle of 42° (= half the angle at the vertex of the cone) with the axis.

The lower the sun descends, the more the antisolar point, and therefore the whole rainbow, ascends, more and more of the circumference appearing above the horizon until it becomes a semicircle as

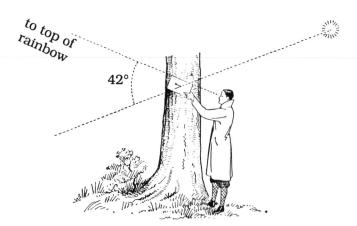

Fig. 120. Measuring the angular distance of the rainbow to the antisolar point.

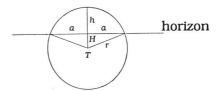

Fig. 121. Determining the antisolar point by observing a rainbow.

the sun sets. On the other hand, it disappears completely below the horizon when the sun is higher than 42°; this is why no one in our part of the world has ever seen a rainbow in the summer at about midday.

Measure half the angle at the vertex by pinning a postcard on to a tree and turning it in such a way that one of its edges points exactly to the top of the rainbow; the shadow of the pin then gives the direction of the line between sun and observer, so that the angular distance of the rainbow to the antisolar point can be read at once—see Fig. 120.

You can also apply one of the methods in Appendix A for the determination of the angular height of the top above the horizon (Fig. 121) and the angle 2α between the two ends of the arc; be sure to make a note of the time of observation. Later on you can compute the height of the sun at the time noted, which furnishes the distance H of the antisolar point T below the horizon at the same time. From these measurements, you will find three values for the angular radius, of which you can take the average value, that is,

$$r = H+h,$$

$$\cos r = \cos a \cos H,$$

$$\tan r = 1-(1-\cos a \cos h)/\cos a \sin h.$$

Properly speaking, the rainbow should not appear as an arc, but as a closed circle; you cannot follow it farther than the horizon because you can see no rain drops floating below you. In favorable conditions, the complete circle can be seen from an airplane.

A secondary rainbow round the primary rainbow is regarded by many people as exceptional. However, it is nearly always visible, though naturally much weaker than the primary rainbow. It is concentric with it, and therefore also has the antisolar point as its center, but its rays form an angle of 51° with the axis of sun and eye.

The 'seven colors of the rainbow' exist only in the imagination; it is a figure of speech that is long-lived, because we so seldom see things as they are! In reality, the colors merge gradually into one another, though the eye involuntarily sorts them into groups. It is a striking fact that different rainbows show great differences; even one and the same rainbow can change while it is being observed, and the top becomes different from the lower parts. In the first place, great differences are found when one simply measures the total breadth of the color band in angular measure—see Appendix A. Furthermore, although the order of the colors is always red, orange, yellow, green, blue, violet, the relative breadths of the different colors and their brightnesses vary in every possible manner. My impression is that different observers do not always describe the same rainbow in the same way; therefore, in order to be sure of the difference between the rainbows, either the observations of a single person should be compared or you should ascertain beforehand whether two observers generally agree on the impressions they form.

This unprejudiced description of the colors of the rainbow brings to our notice the remarkable fact that often, beyond the violet on the inside of the bow, there are several supernumerary bows as well; as a rule, they are to be seen best of all where the rainbow is at its brightest, near the highest point. Their colors are usually alternately pink and green. As a matter of fact, their name has been wrongly chosen, for although they are weaker, they form just as much part of the rainbow as the 'normal' colors do. These supernumary bows often change rather quickly in intensity and breadth, which is an indication of alterations in the size of the drops—see § 144.

The order of the colors in the secondary bow is the reverse of that in the primary rainbow: the red of bow one faces the red of the other. The secondary rainbow is very seldom so bright that its supernumerary bows become visible; they lie beyond the violet and therefore outside the outer edge of the secondary rainbow.

> E'en as, colored alike and parallel,
> two bows are drawn o'er softly clouded skies,
> the inner to the outer giving rise...

Dante, *Paradiso*

142. The rainbow in artificial clouds

The way in which a rainbow arises in a mass of drops of water is immediately visible to us when we see the sun shining on the fine spray floating above fountains and waterfalls. Along the side of a ship, where the waves break against the bow and splash into foam, rain-

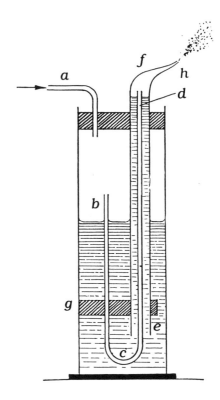

Fig. 122. Vaporizer for imitating a rainbow.

bows are sometimes seen to accompany the ship for quite a while, sometimes strong, sometimes weak, according as the cloud of fine drops is dense or thin; especially when the ship's course is in the direction of the sun is there a good chance of your being able to see this phenomenon.

Here are some simple methods for reproducing in your garden a shower of rain in which the sun will form a rainbow: (a) a garden hose with nozzle; (b) a weed sprayer; (c) a vaporizer as shown in Fig. 122; all that is required here is to blow hard with the mouth at *a*. The size of the drops can be controlled by moving the small tube *bcd* a few millimeters (fraction of an inch) up or down the wider tube *ef*, which is done by shifting the perforated cork disk *g*. The size of the aperture at end *h* is another important factor. Water can be added through the wider tube without having to open the apparatus.

The tiny drops sprayed by the vaporizers used for house plants are so fine that a real rainbow cannot be seen in them, only a white mist-bow with blue and yellow edges—cf. § 140. Only here and there, a few patches of large drops occur accidentally and the ordinary rainbow is momentarily visible.

Always look for rainbows in a direction 42° away from the anti-solar point, and preferably against a dark background.

Experiments of this kind are excellent material for observation. Rainbows can often be seen as closed circles, when there is a sufficient number of drops of water below the line of your horizon. If you move, the rainbow moves with you; it is not an object, it is not visible at a definite place, but in a definite direction; you might say that it behaves as something infinitely far off, which moves with you in the same way as the moon does. If you stand very near the cloud of drops, as, for instance, while spraying with the garden hose, two rainbows can be seen to cross. How does that come about? Shut your eyes alternately; it will appear that each eye sees its own rainbow (which follows also from the fact that the rainbow moves along with you). The secondary rainbow and the supernumerary bows can often be seen splendidly. If the direction of the jet is altered or the rainbow is seen in other places in the spray, the relative importance of colors in the bow will change: the reason for this is that the average size of the drops is different.

143. Descartes' theory of the rainbow

To investigate the path of light in a drop of water, fill a glass flask with water and hold it in the sun—see Fig. 123a. On a screen AB, provided with a round aperture (a little larger than the flask), a faint rainbow R will then appear. It has the shape of a closed circle; its angular distance is about 42°; and the color red is on the outside, just as in a real rainbow.

Hold a little screen attached to a thread in front of the flask at S and you will see a shadow on the lower part of the rainbow—see Fig. 123b. If you press a moistened finger on the flask somewhere near V, you will see a darker spot at the place corresponding to this on the lower part of the rainbow. It is evident, therefore, that the rainbow is formed by rays incident at the distance SC from the central line and reflected at V in the drop of water behind. If you hold a ring a few millimeters (about $80/1000$ of an inch) thick and in diameter 0.86 times the diameter of the flask carefully centered in the incident beam, the rainbow will disappear altogether—see Fig. 123c.

Figure 124 shows the exact course of the rays, calculated from the ordinary laws of reflection and refraction. You can see how the rays of light incident on the drop of water emerge in different directions according to the point where they strike it; one of these rays is deviated less than the others, namely through 138°, that is, it makes an angle of 180°–138° = 42° with the axis. The emergent rays are now spread out in the various directions; only those suffering minimum deviation are almost parallel to one another, and therefore reach your eye with the greatest density.

Fig. 123. Imitating a rainbow with the aid of a flask.

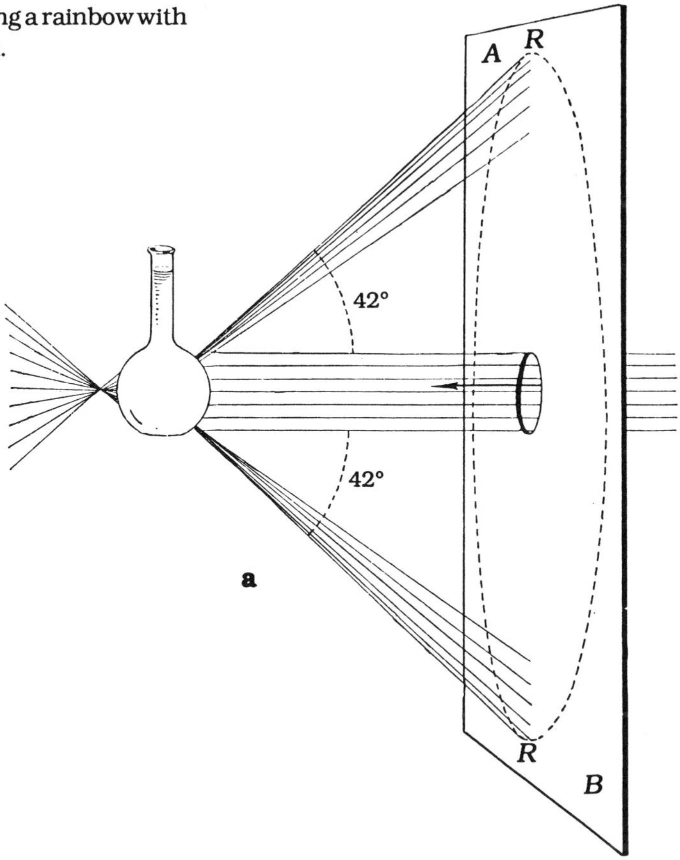

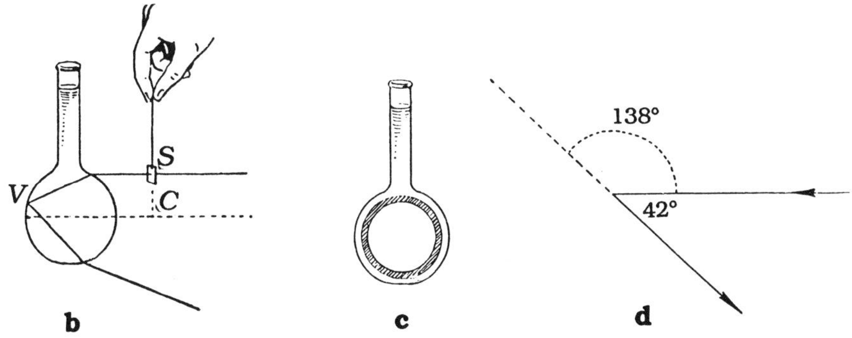

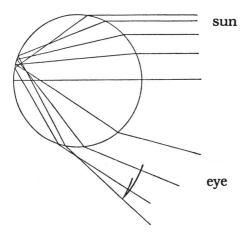

sun

eye

Fig. 124. Paths of light rays in a drop of water and the origin of a rainbow. The *bold line* shows the wave surface.

In a well-darkened room, the secondary rainbow can also be seen on the screen at an angle of 51° with the axis, or deviated through 180°+51° = 231° from the direction of the incident rays—see Fig. 125. By experiments similar to those performed with the primary bow, you can prove that the secondary bow arises from twice-reflected rays. The order of the colors is the reverse of that in the primary rainbow, exactly as in reality.

Now imagine each of the drops in a cloud reflecting, in the way described, a great deal of light into a cone of 42° and rather less into a cone of 51°. All drops seen at an angular distance of 42° from the direction of the incident ray from the sun are in such a position that they send the light of their primary rainbow toward our eye, while from those seen at an angular distance of 51° from the incident sunlight we receive the twice-reflected rays. In this way, therefore, the primary and the secondary rainbow are formed—see Fig. 126.

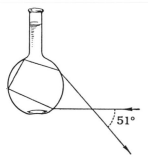

51°

Fig. 125. How a secondary rainbow arises.

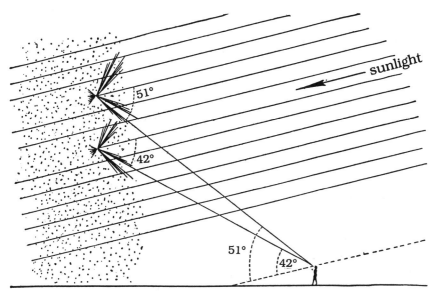

Fig. 126. Sunlight falling on to a cloud of raindrops produces a rainbow and a secondary rainbow.

The proof may also be obtained with a beaker or even a normal drinking glass, provided that this is more or less cylindrical. Work at night and use as light source a candle that has been placed at a distance of about a meter (a yard) from the water-filled beaker. The light will be too weak to be visible on a screen, but if you look at the beaker initially from a direction of 150° and reduce this to 138° (not less), you will see two lines of light that approach each other, meet, show the colors of the rainbow, and then disappear.

144. The diffraction theory of the rainbow[2]

In Descartes' theory, only the rays suffering minimum deviation were considered, as if they were the only ones. In reality, however, there are a number of rays of greater deviation, enveloped completely by a curved caustic. These are exactly the conditions under which inter- ference occurs as shown near the caustics of raindrops on one's glasses— see § 139. Particularly when dealing with tiny drops, the considera- tions of rays of light do not suffice; instead, the wavefront where it shows a cusp in the neighborhood of such a caustic must be inves- tigated—see Fig. 118.

---

[2] Buchwald, *Optik*, **3**, 4, 1948.

According to Huygens' principle, the points of the wavefront are regarded as centers of radiation and the problem is then to investigate how the vibrations reaching our eye from every part of the wavefront interfere mutually. This investigation, carried out by Airy, and completed and applied by Stokes, Möbius, and Pernter, leads to the famous rainbow integral

$$A = c \int_0^\infty \cos\frac{\pi}{2}(u^3 - zu)du$$

where A is the amplitude of the wave of light that enters our eye as a function of the angle z with the direction of the rays of minimum deviation. The integral is computed by developing it in a series, and the light intensity we see in a direction z is then given simply by A^2.

Figure 127 shows for one color how the distribution of light found with large drops (a) is altered by diffraction when the drops are small (b). The phenomenon is still, in the main, determined by the rays of minimum deviation ($z = 0$), but a number of lesser maxima have appeared besides.

Such curves must be drawn separately for a number of colors, shifted according to wavelength; for any given angle of deviation, z, a mixture is obtained and the colors of the rainbow can therefore never be truly saturated hues. Since the first and strongest maximum of each color plays the principal part and these principal maxima shift gradually with increasing wavelength, we observe the colors of the rainbow in practically the same way as we would expect from the elementary theory. The modifications caused by diffraction consist in the colors being slightly different depending on the size of the drops and the fact that inside the bow supernumerary bows appear. Finally, it must be borne in mind that the sun is not a mere point and that therefore the sunbeams are not strictly parallel (§ 1), so that, since they spread over an angle of fully half a degree, the colors of the rainbow become slightly obliterated. The diffraction theory enables us, on seeing a

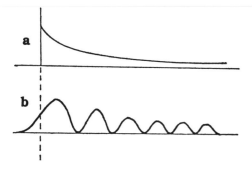

Direction of smallest deviation

Fig. 127. Distribution of light in a beam of rays emanating from a drop of water: (a) according to Descartes' theory, and (b) according to the diffraction theory.

rainbow, to state at once the approximate size of the drops causing it. The main features are as follows.

Diameter:	
1–2 mm (0.04–0.08 in)	Very bright violet and vivid green; the bow contains pure red, but scarcely any blue. Spurious bows are numerous (five, for example), violet-pink alternating with green merging without interruption into the primary bow.
0.5 mm (0.02 in)	The red is considerably weaker. Fewer supernumerary bows, violet-pink and green again alternating.
0.2–0.3 mm (0.008–0.012 in)	No more red; for the rest, the bow is broad and well developed. The supernumerary bows become more and more yellow. If a gap occurs between the supernumerary bows, the diameter of the drops is 0.2 mm (0.008 in). If there is a gap formed between the primary bow and the first supernumerary bow, the diameter of the drop is less than 0.2 mm (0.008 in).
0.08–0.1 mm (0.003–0.004 in)	The bow is broader and paler, and only the violet is vivid. The first supernumerary bow is well separated from the primary bow and clearly shows white tints.
0.06 mm (0.0024 in)	The primary rainbow contains a distinct white stripe.
<0.05 mm (<0.002 in)	Mistbow (cf. § 150)

In the main, the diameter of the drops is 0.4–1.0 mm (0.016–0.04 in). If the drops in their fall become distorted or subjected to vibrations, the rainbow becomes hazier. This seems to be associated with the fact that supernumerary bows are clearest at their highest point.

The width of the color bands is roughly proportional to $r^{-2/3}$.

145. The sky around the rainbow

An attentive observer will notice that the sky between the two rainbows is darker than the sky outside them. There is, of course, a background of clouds varying in brightness, but the effect is, nevertheless, generally distinctly visible.

The explanation is that, besides the rays of minimum deviation, every drop reflects rays in other directions that deviate more from the incident direction. These are shown faintly in Fig. 128. Note that in the secondary bow, the rays are deviated on the side opposite to that on which they are deviated in the primary bow. The observer will therefore first see faint, diffuse light from that part of the sky inside the primary rainbow caused by once-reflected rays that are deviated more than 138° and therefore make an angle of less than 42° with the axis; and then faint, diffuse light from that part of the sky outside the secondary rainbow caused by twice-reflected rays that are deviated more than 231° and therefore make an angle of more than 51° with the axis.

> It is not love that gives the clearest sight;
> It is from tears, tears as yet unshed,
> That rises high the rainbow of sadness;
> Inside its arch is the clearest light.

Fiona MacLeod, *The Divine Adventure*

Sometimes, radial streaks of light, devoid of color, are visible in the diffuse glow between primary and secondary bows[3]. These are analogous to the crepuscular rays and to rays on moving water—see §§ 217, 221, and 248). This phenomenon is explained when you imagine that somewhere between the sun and the raindrops a small cloud is floating—see Fig. 128. The drops lying inside the shadow behind the cloud cannot radiate any light toward the observer. The rainbow you see is built up of light from all the drops in your line of vision, and lacks, therefore, the contribution from the drops R; similarly, the secondary bow lacks the light from drops N, while in the diffuse light, the contributions from drops like R', R'', ... and N', N'', ... are wanting. In the plane containing your eye, the sun, and the cloud, all phenomena are weaker for that reason: a raylike shadow arises, which, prolonged, passes through the point exactly opposite the sun, that is, through the center of the rainbow.

146. Polarization of light in the rainbow

It is very interesting to try to see a rainbow reflected in a piece of glass, not in a silver-backed mirror, which would be unsuitable for this purpose, but in an ordinary piece of glass, either blackened or backed with a piece of black paper. Hold it close to your eye so that

---

[3] See the splendid photographs by G.P. Können, *Hemel en Dampkring*, Dec. 1968.

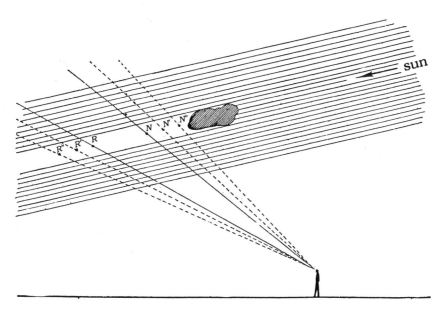

Fig. 128. Fragments of cloud between the sun and a shower of rain cause radial streaks of light.

Fig. 129. Observing polarization of the light from a rainbow.

you look into it at an angle, say at 60° to the normal. You can hold the glass horizontally or vertically as in Fig. 129. If you look at the top of the rainbow, you will see that with the glass horizontal, the reflection of the bow is very distinct and bright, whereas with it vertical, the reflection is so weak as to be almost imperceptible. This shows that the light of the rainbow has different properties in different directions perpendicular to its direction of propagation, that is, it is polarized.

There is a still easier way of making this observation, namely by studying the rainbow through a disk of Polaroid, as used for sunglasses—see § 204. If the disk is rotated slowly about the line of vision, a position will be reached where the rainbow is very bright; turning it 90° farther, the rainbow will be very weak. The light of the rainbow may be imagined as being composed of light that vibrates in a direction i and light that vibrates in a direction j at right angles to i. The theoretical ratio of their intensities, $i{:}j$, proves to be about 24:1, which indicates strong polarization. For the secondary rainbow, the ratio proves to be 9:1. Both these results agree with theory.

147. The effect of lightning on a rainbow

A striking phenomenon is the obliteration of the boundaries of the colors in a rainbow each time it thunders. The change is particularly noticeable in the spurious (or supernumerary) bow: the space between the violet and the first spurious bow often disappears entirely and the yellow grows brighter. It is as if the whole rainbow vibrates. According to the table in § 144, these alterations indicate an increase in the size of the raindrops.

The optical effect does not occur simultaneously with the lightning, but several seconds later, together with the sound of the thunder. It is also possible that, owing to the vibration of the air, the drops tend to merge into each other or that they themselves are set into vibration, which would make the bow blurred.

148. The red rainbow

During the last five or ten minutes before sunset, all the colors of the rainbow are seen to fade, except the red, until only an all-red bow is left. Within the immense semicircle, the air is salmon pink; outside it, bluish-gray—the color of the diffuse light of the sky. Sometimes, it is amazingly bright and remains visible even for ten minutes after the sun has set; the lower part of the bow is naturally screened off by that time, so that it appears to begin at some height above the horizon. Nature is here showing us the spectrum of the sunlight, and demonstrating how its composition changes during sunset. This change is caused by the scattering of the shorter light waves (see § 194).

149. Rainbows in droplets of seawater

During a sea voyage, a rainbow may be observed in the driving spray of seawater. Comparisons of this with a rainbow observed during a rain shower show that the radius of the bow in the seawater is 1° smaller, which corresponds well with the higher refractive index (1.007) of seawater.

150. The fogbow or white rainbow

When the drops are very small, the appearance of the rainbow is quite different. This can be seen very well if you stand on a hill with your back to the sun and with fog in front and below. The bow then has the appearance of a white band, as much as twice the width of an ordinary rainbow, orange on the outside, bluish on the inside. On the inside, with a space between them, one or even two supernumerary bows can be seen; strangely, the order of their colors is the reverse of those in a normal primary bow (first red, then green).

These observations are in good agreement with the theoretical calculations for drops with a radius of 0.025 mm (0.001 in) shown in § 144. With these very small drops, the radius of the rainbow is no longer 42°, but begins to diminish, and, since 'small' here means 'approaching the wavelength of light', the effect is more prominent with red rays than with blue ones. Hence the red of the supernumerary bow will be much smaller in diameter than the blue and so will lie on the inside.

Those who are so fortunate as to see this beautiful phenomenon should carry out a few measurements to determine the diameter 2θ of the bows (in degrees) (cf. Appendix A). The dark ring between the primary and the first supernumerary bow can be measured the most accurately; from the value obtained, the radius of the drops (in mm) can be computed with the formula

$$\alpha = 0.31/(41°44'-\theta)^{3/2}.$$

Alternatively, you can take the average value between the blue and the orange edges of the primary bow, but the numerator must then be altered to 0.18.

Strangely enough, the fogbow has been seen even when the temperature was –34 °C, which proves that the drops of water in the atmosphere can be very strongly supercooled. It has also been seen when the fog was so thin that the observer who saw it declared that there was no fog.

A fogbow nearly always appears when the dazzling beam of a car's headlights behind you penetrates the mist in front of you. Even ordinary streetlights frequently give rise to it, though feebly and only against a dark background. If a mist is seen backed by dark ground, the fogbow can at times be seen as a complete circle; the few meters (yards) between your eyes and the ground are then evidently enough to produce this phenomenon. On very rare occasions, a double fogbow has been observed. See also §§ 144 and 188.

151. The dewbow or horizontal rainbow

Heather, on autumn mornings, is often covered with millions of cobwebs, which, otherwise unnoticeable, are then sprinkled with dewdrops and lit up by the sunbeams. In this play of light, you can see a rainbow standing out on the ground in front of you, not as a circle, but in the shape of a wide-open hyperbola—see Fig. 130.

The explanation for this is that light reaches your eye from all directions, forming an angle of 42° with the axis through the sun and your eye. The cone so formed intersects the surface of the ground in a hyperbolic curve as long as the sun is low. In the course of the day, it would become an ellipse, but this has been seen only very seldom.

You might ask someone to help you by marking out and measuring the curve on the ground and then verify, with the help of the sun's altitude (deduced from the time of observation), that the curve is, indeed, a hyperbola corresponding to a cone with a vertical angle of 42°. Observe how the colored band increases in width the farther it is from your eye. A single instance is known of the fogbow and the supernumerary bows being observed in the dew.

The dewbow has also been observed in the following circumstances. (a) On a pond covered with duckweed. (b) On a lawn. (c) On a pond with an oily surface on which dewdrops can lie without mixing with the water; a surface of this kind may be formed, for instance, by the sooty smoke from factories. In one case, the size of the drops varied

Fig. 130. The dewbow.

from 0.1 mm to 0.5 mm (0.004–0.02 in); 20 drops per cm (50 per inch) show a very distinct dewbow. (d) On a lake or on the sea, early in the morning, when the air cool but the water is warm, so that a thin mist hangs above the surface of the water. The whole of the dewbow is not always visible, but only its two extremities. (e) On a frozen surface that can, apparently, become covered by dewdrops of suitable shape.

Volz describes how he sprayed a dark-colored car with fine drops of water, which caused innumerable globules of water of, perhaps, 1 mm diameter rolling over the layer of water, showing all colors at or near the rainbow cone and forming a dewbow[4].

This observation also has a remarkable psychological aspect. Why does a rainbow appear to us to be circular and the dewbow hyperbolic, while in both cases the light rays reach our eye from the same direction? It is a question of combining observation and expectation. When we see a dewbow we are influenced by the thought that the light phenomenon is spread out in a horizontal plane, and we subconsciously ask ourselves: what must be the true shape of the curve of light on the grass for us to see the phenomenon as we do see it? The answer is an ellipse or a hyperbola. But if, on the other hand, we ask: how do we see the dewbow?, the answer depends on the observation combined with our interpretation of it. If we saw only the light phenomenon and knew nothing about its origin, only a circular shape would occur to us. A stereoscopic estimate of the distance of individual drops and clusters of drops would certainly help us to locate the dewbow in a horizontal plane (cf. §§ 175 and 176).

For the reflected dewbow, see § 153.

152. Reflected rainbows

If you see a rainbow in the direction of a point A in a cloud (see Fig. 131) and observe the reflection of the landscape in smooth water, you will see the rainbow in the direction of point B, so that it appears lower on the reflected cloud than on the cloud viewed directly. This is because, as already stated, the rainbow does not exist as a real object in the plane of the clouds but is, as it were, at infinity. Properly speaking, therefore, it is the cloud that is displaced, whereas the reflection of the rainbow is perfectly symmetrical relative to the horizon. The shift of the cloud will be more easily observable if you are at a certain height h above the water. You are then even able to compute the distance OA of the cloud from an estimate of its displacement in angular measure, for the angular displacement is

---

[4] *Weather*, **17**, 243, 1962.

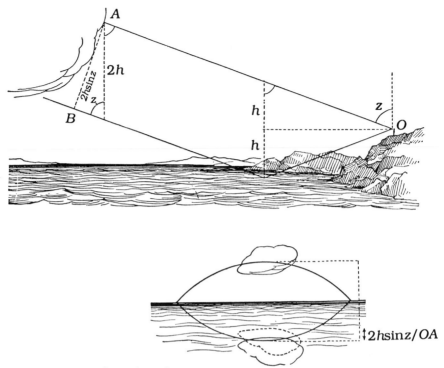

Fig. 131. The reflected rainbow.

$$2h\sin z/OA.$$

An entirely different effect occurs, however, when the sunbeams are reflected before they produce the rainbow. A shifted arc *RRS* will then appear round the center *T'*, which is the reflection of the anti-solar point *T*—see Fig. 132. This arc extends over more than a semi-circle. The distance between the tops of the two arcs is equal to that between *T* and *T'*, that is, twice the height of the sun above the horizon. In many cases, the shifted arc is only partly visible, for example, only the top or the two ends. When you observe an extraordinary rainbow, you should therefore think first of the possibility of such a reflection. Consider next where big pools can be found in the neighborhood and try to account for the incompleteness of the arc by the location of these pools. The two bows produced by reflection complement one another so as to make a closed circle—see Fig. 132. They may be distinguished by the names 'reflected rainbow' and 'rainbow with reflected sun'.

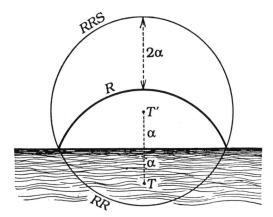

Fig. 132. (*R* = rainbow; *RR* = reflected rainbow; *RRS* = rainbow formed by reflected sun.)

153. The reflected dewbow

The dewbow can also be reflected in water and the hyperbola with its beautiful colors, formed by the drops floating on the surface, is then double. The fact that the weaker of the bows is caused by reflection becomes very clear if you happen to observe a dewbow on a frozen surface, because the second bow then disappears.

The angular distance of the bows is again twice that of the sun's height, but because the drops are this time on the surface of the water itself, it is not possible to ascertain straight away whether the reflection has taken place before or after the rays of light have passed through the drops of water. Both cases would give a hyperbola—cf. § 133; in both figures, the reflected ray rises at an angle of 42°.

However, *when the sun is fairly high* (21° to 42°), two criteria exist.

1. The part of the reflected bow near the top is absent. The explanation is that when the rays follow path II, the incident bundle of rays is partly screened off by the drop itself at *S* before it is reflected and then penetrates the drop. If the path is as in I, this characteristic peculiarity does not occur.

2. If two neighboring points of the two bows are observed with a Polaroid, it is found that the directions of the light waves differ very greatly and are as a rule not horizontal. It can be demonstrated that this will be so only if the reflection takes place before the refraction.

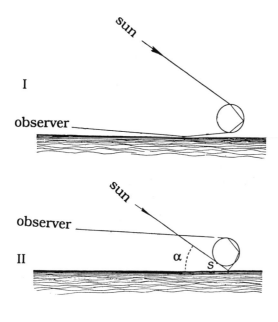

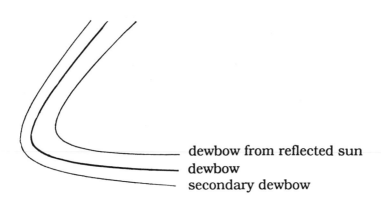

Fig. 133. Reflected dewbows. In I, the dewbow is reflected; in II, the dewbow is formed by the reflected sun.

The question remains: Why is it more usual for the rays to be reflected *first*? The answer is that the emerging rays in the case of path I run grazingly over the water and are intercepted by the neighboring drops.

Plate 1. The setting sun appears flattened and throws a narrow column of light over the water. The silhouette of a seagull is seen against the bright light. (Photo by Pekka Parviainen.) See §§ 20, 39, 262.

Plate 2. Light path and sea smoke; some fog in the cold air above the warm water. (Photo by Pekka Parviainen.) See § 20.

Plate 3. The setting sun and its mirage at the surface of the sea have fused together. (Photo by Pekka Parviainen.) See § 45, case A.

Plate 4. When the air is colder than the sea, the lower part of a distant island disappears, while the upper part is seen as a flattened mirror image. (Photo by Pekka Parviainen.) See § 42.

Plate 5. Two inversion layers have generated four additional images of the distant islands. These images are oriented alternately upside down, right-side up, upside down and finally right-side up, although this latter, topmost image is very compressed and hard to see in the photograph. This sort of observation is very sensitive to the height of the observer relative to the height of the inversion layer(s), so usually the observer has to guess whether conditions may be right for a superior image to appear and then has to start looking for it by changing his or her observing height. (Photo by Pekka Parviainen.) See §§ 43, 44.

Plate 6. The green flash. (Photo by Pekka Parviainen.) See § 47.

Plate 7. The constellation Orion rising above the eastern horizon. The colors of the brighter (overexposed) stars can be seen better in the fainter reflection. The great Orion nebula appears red in the lower part of the constellation. (Photo by Pekka Parviainen.) Cf. Fig. 72. See § 63.

Plate 8. A snowdrift colored by a red sunset and a blue sky opposite. (Photo by Pekka Parviainen.) See §§ 114, 115.

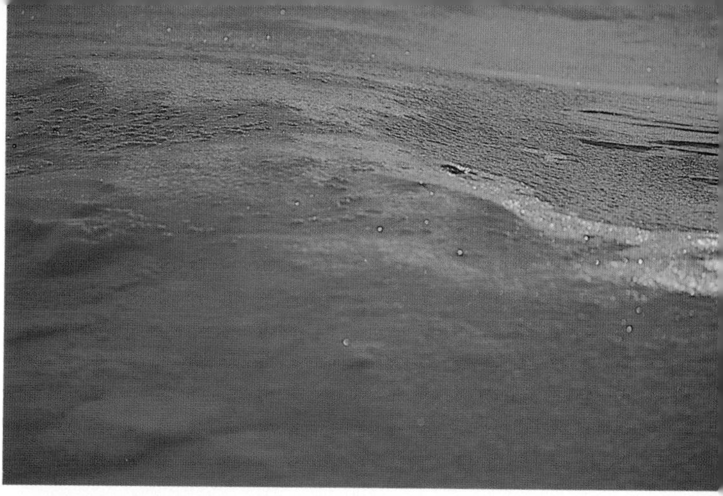

Plate 9. Primary and secondary rainbows. (Photo by Pekka Parviainen.) See § 141.

Plate 10. The fogbow appears white only and has a radius smaller than an ordinary rainbow. (Photo by Pekka Parviainen.) See § 150.

△
Plate 11. A rainbow produced by the setting sun is high and colored red. (Photo by Pekka Parviainen.) See §§ 141, 148.

Plate 12. The end of the rainbow after sunset. (Photo by Pekka Parviainen.) See § 148.

Plate 13. The end of the primary rainbow and a section of the secondary bow. The colors of the secondary bow are in opposite order to those of the primary bow. Between the bows the sky is relatively dark (Alexander's dark belt). Photo by Pekka Parviainen.) See §§ 141, 145.

Plate 14. Interference bows inside the primary rainbow. (Photo by Pekka Parviainen.) See §§ 141, 144.

Plate 15. A rainbow in a fountain. (Photo by Pentti Ramberg.) See § 142.

Plate 16. The small halo or 22° circle around the moon. Included in the display are also the tangential arcs to the 22° halo, which almost merge with the 22° circle when the moon is high. (Photo by Pekka Parviainen.) Cf. Fig. 138. See §§ 157, 159.

Plate 17. Colorful parhelion in a streak of cirrus cloud. (Photo by Pekka Parviainen.) See § 158.

Plate 18. A brilliant ice-crystal halo display on a winter morning: sections of the 22° circle, parhelia, and a sun pillar. The halos appear partly in front of the edge of the forest, showing that the ice crystals are located nearby. (Photo by Markku Pyykkönen.)

Plate 19. A halo display extending over the entire sky on 23 April 1987 in Turku, Finland: 22° circle, parhelia, 22° upper tangent arc, faint Parry arc, elongated 46° ring, faint right-hand 46° lower tangent arc, and a well-developed parhelic circle around the whole sky can be seen. (Photo by Pekka Parviainen.)

△

Plate 20. A red sun pillar after sunset. (Photo by Pekka Parviainen.) See § 168.

Plate 21. 'The queen of halos': the Kemi halo display of 19 March 1985. The circumzenithal arc dominates the upper part of the photograph. Below it are the 46° circle (or 46° upper tangent arc), Parry arc, 22° upper tangential arc, and left parhelion. (Photo by Markku Ruonala.)

Plate 22. Bright parhelic circle and 120° parhelion. (Photographed at Imatra on 20 July 1987 by Veikko Mäkelä.) See §§ 166, 170.

Plate 23. Rare halo phenomena: anthelion and faint Tricker anthelic arcs (forming a V-shape) passing across the Kuopio sky on 6 September 1985. (Photo by Marko Pekkola.) See § 170.

Plate 24. The bright sub-sun seen following an aircraft was formed on a winter's day in icy mist, visible in the photograph as a white haze. (Photo by Marko Pekkola.) See § 169.

Plate 25. A parhelion playfully appearing against a grain silo near Kuopio in the winter of 1986. (Photo by Marko Pekkola.) See § 175.

Plate 26. Interference colors in a soap bubble. The same color joins areas of equal thickness. (Photo by Pekka Parviainen.) See § 177.

Plate 27. A double ring around the sun. The innermost ring, the aureole, appears here as a bright red-edged ring. The second-order ring is multicolored. (Photo by Pekka Parviainen.) See § 183.

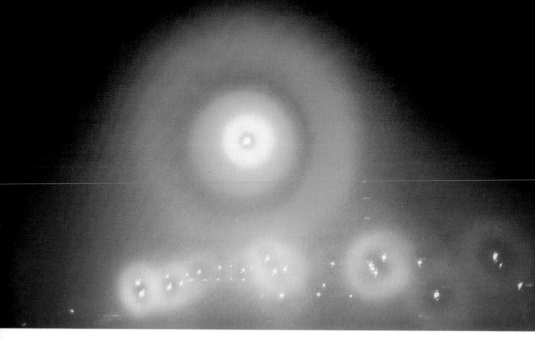

Plate 28. Coronas around the moon and streetlights in a misty window pane. (Photo by Pekka Parviainen.) See § 185.

Plate 29. A glory (to the right in the picture) and fogbow (white vertical band to the left) photographed from an airplane. At the center of the glory, the (small) shadow of the aircraft can be seen. (Photo by Marko Pekkola.). See §§ 150, 188.

Plate 30. Exceptionally bright iridescent clouds. If the cloud is thin and its droplets are of roughly the same size, the colors always appear in the same order with respect to the sun. (Photos by Pekka Parviainen.) See § 189.

Plate 31. Heiligenschein ('holy light') on a dewy lawn. The light is totally reflected from the dewdrops and appears brighter in the direction of the shadow of the viewer (that is, the camera). Photo by Veikko Mäkelä.) See § 191.

Plate 32. Heiligenschein in a forest around the shadow of an aircraft. (Photo by Marko Pekkola.) See § 193.
▽

Plate 33. Light scattered in the air covers distant objects in a hazy veil (*upper photograph*). The scattered light is polarized, however, and by twisting a polariz-

ing filter, the scattered light can be partly removed (*lower photograph*). (Photographed at the Grand Canyon, USA, by Hannu Karttunen.) See §§ 196, 205.

Plate 34. The zenith of the clear daytime sky is darker than the horizon. Seen in the photograph is the Vartiovuori Observatory in Turku, Finland. (Photo by Pekka Parviainen.) See § 200.

Plate 35. The blue color of the sky is caused by the scattering of sunlight by air ▷ molecules. The blue component of white light is scattered strongly and dispersed to form the blue of the sky, whereas the red part can penetrate the air more

easily and just reaches the ground. The light that we see at sunset in the direction of the sun has the blue component removed, so that we see a red sun. The scattered light is partly polarized. The polarization is strongest at 90° from the sun. Using a polarizing filter, the polarized light can be removed, which darkens the sky in that direction (*lower photograph*). The scattering in the much larger water droplets in clouds is different and does not give rise to polarization. (Photos by Pekka Parviainen.) See § 205.

Plate 36. The sun's rays in fog. (Photo by Pekka Parviainen.) See § 208, 217.

Plate 37. A cloud covering the sun throws dark bundles of rays across the sky. (Photo by Pekka Parviainen.) See § 209, 217.

Plate 38. Bright rays from behind the clouds. (Photo by Veikko Mäkelä.) See § 209, 217.

Plate 39. The rising sun reflected in window panes. (Photo by Pekka Parviainen.) See §§ 7, 219.

Plate 40. Crepuscular rays after sunset. (Photo by Pekka Parviainen.) See § 221.

Plate 41. Soon after sunset, the dark blue-gray shadow of the earth rises in the eastern sky. The purple glow opposite the sun is clearly visible above it. (Photo by Pekka Parviainen.) See § 219.

Plate 42. The western sky half an hour after sunset. The purple light is at its strongest, the bright glow is already sinking below the horizon. (Photo by Veikko Mäkelä.) See § 219.

Plate 43. Noctilucent clouds. (Photo by Tapani Lahdenmäki.) See § 228.

Plate 44. Noctilucent clouds. (Photo by Pekka Parviainen.) See § 228.

Plate 45. In a photograph taken from a spacecraft, the air glow is visible as a blue light in the upper atmosphere. (Photo by NASA.) See § 229.

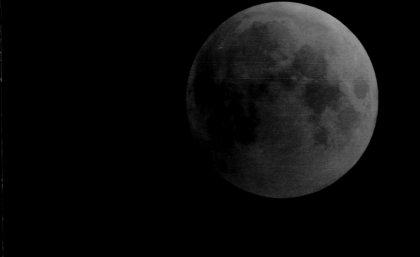

Plate 46. Because of scattering, the earth's atmosphere lets through almost only red light, so that the light refracted in the atmosphere gives a reddish color to the eclipsed moon. (Photo by Markku Pyykkönen.) See § 231.

Plate 47. The waning lunar crescent in the morning sky. The surface features on the side illuminated by the earth can be clearly distinguished. (Photo by Pekka Parviainen.) See § 232.

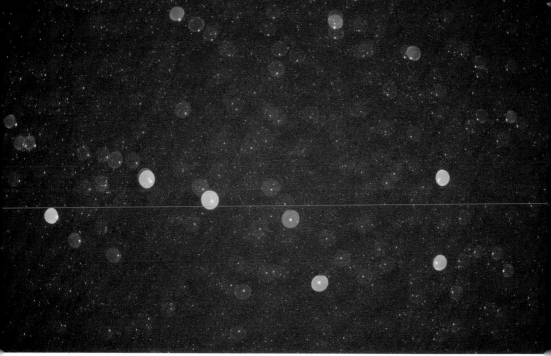

Plate 48. Poor man's spectroscopy by out-of-focus photography. Of the two right-hand stars in the Big Dipper (the Plough), the upper one (Dubhe) is clearly more yellow than the lower one (Merak). (Photo by Pekka Parviainen.) See § 234.

Plate 49. Shadows of clouds on the lower surface of a cloud after sunset. (Photo by Pekka Parviainen.) See § 234.

When the sun is low, the rays of light will first penetrate the drop and then be reflected; the top of the reflected bow is again screened off, but the amount of polarization is different. At the time of writing, no careful study has yet been made of this case.

154. Abnormal rainbow phenomena

In Fig. 134 are a few illustrations of exceptional shapes of rainbows, caused partly by reflection in surfaces of water, but for which there is no satisfactory explanation. One more reason to keep your eyes open for similar phenomena! Note especially the mutual position of the red and the violet sides of the abnormal bows.

Look for situations in which a vertical pillar of light rises from the base of the rainbow and secondary bow when these are over the surface of the sea.

155. The moonbow

> Yes, truly,
> A rainbow in the middle of the night;
> 'Tis the light of the moon by which it shines;
> 'Tis a strange and wonderful omen
> That few people have ever seen;
> 'Tis double; look: a paler one above

Schiller, William Tell

Rainbows are formed by the moon as well as by the sun, though these moonbows are naturally very weak. That is why they can be

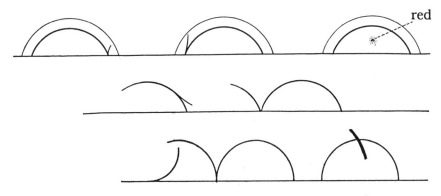

Fig. 134. Abnormal rainbow phenomena.

seen almost only when the moon is full and why they are seldom colored, just as feebly illuminated objects usually appear colorless at night—see § 92.

Do not confuse them with halos! The rainbow is only visible on the side opposite the moon!

The radius of the moonbow can be determined very accurately if there happens to be a bright star somewhere near it—cf. § 159.

Halos

156. General description of halo phenomena

After a few days of fine, bright spring weather, the barometer falls and a south wind begins to blow. High clouds, fragile and feathery, rise out of the west, the sky gradually becomes milky white, made opalescent by veils of cirrostratus. The sun seems to shine through ground glass, its outline no longer sharp but merging into its surrounding. There is a peculiar, uncertain light over the landscape; I 'sense' that there must be a halo around the sun. And often I am right.

A bright ring with a radius of rather more than 22° can be seen surrounding the sun; the best way to see it is to stand in the shade of a house or to hold your hand against the sun to prevent yourself from being dazzled—see § 183. It is a grand sight! To anyone seeing it for the first time, the ring seems enormous, and yet it is 'the small halo'; the other halo phenomena develop on a still larger scale. Put out your arm and spread your fingers wide apart; you will see that the distance between the top of your thumb and little finger is almost as wide as the radius of the halo around the sun—cf. Appendix A.

You can see a similar ring around the moon, too. I do not mean a corona a few degrees in diameter with red inside and blue outside, but the same large ring as that just described as a halo around the sun. Only once was an observer so fortunate as to see a ring around the setting sun and one around the rising full moon at the same time!

Rings of this kind are observable more often than you would think. It is fairly certain that a practiced observer in our part of the world who is on the lookout all day long will be able to see on average one halo every four days, and in April and May he may even see one every two days; the most observant see halos on 200 days a year! Does it not seem incredible, therefore, that there are still so many who have never noticed a halo around the sun?

Besides the small halo, there are still many other lightbows and concentrations of light in one spot, each with a name of its own, which combine to form the halo phenomenon; the most important are shown in Fig. 135 as if they were outlined on an imaginary celestial globe. We shall discuss these briefly in turn. It must be borne in mind, however, that as a rule only a few of them can be observed at the same time. Most of those that have been seen were caused by the sun; those belonging to the moon are much fainter and their colors are practically imperceptible (cf. §§ 92 and 155). They are generally formed in veils of cirrostratus, but seldom in cirrocumulus or altocumulus; they can be seen in thunder cirrus, but not often. All clouds giving rise to halos are composed of small ice crystals and the regularity of the shapes of these crystals is responsible for the beautiful symmetry of the light phenomena. The reason that so many ice clouds show no halo phenomena at all is that little snow stars and globular clusters of crystals are the wrong shape to refract the light in the same way as a prism does, and that with too small crystals the halo phenomena are obliterated by diffraction.

The photography of halos is of importance for scientific purposes: it is used in accurate measurements of angles and in determining light intensities. For these purposes, however, the photographic plate should be exactly perpendicular to the axis of the camera, and the distance between the plate and the objective known accurately. An objective with a large opening, a yellow filter, and panchromatic plates with an antihalation layer should be used. The exposure time with a strong yellow filter and f/12 stop is about $\frac{1}{100}$ second for the sun; for the moon 6 minutes with an f/4 stop. Try to get part of the horizon or a tree in the photograph!

157. The small ring or 22° halo (Fig. 135a)

The small ring is the most common of all halo phenomena. The ring is complete, except when the cirrostratus clouds are unevenly distributed over the sky; it is usually brightest at the top or bottom or to the left or right, rather than in the intermediate positions. The inner edge is fairly sharply defined and red in color, then follow yellow, green, and white, through to blue. The radius of the 22° halo can be measured with one of the simple devices mentioned in Appendix A, preferably from the center of the sun to the red inner edge; the best measurements give 21°50'.

The radius of the halo surrounding the moon can be determined very accurately on some nights if you happen to observe that the position of a particular star coincides with the inner edge, for example, or with the maximum of brightness of the halo. You then merely have to note the name of the star (if necessary identifying it by means of a star map) and the time. Afterward, any astronomer will be able to calculate at once how far apart the two celestial bodies were at that moment (cf. Fig. 139).

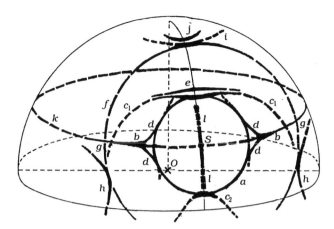

Fig. 135. Schematic representation on the celestial vault of some of the most important halo phenomena. S = sun; O = observer. *Solid lines* indicate the parts of halos that are seen most commonly, and *broken lines* those that are unusual. The altitude of the sun in the diagram is 30°, and halos are shown accordingly. The forms of many of these halos change considerably with the altitude of the sun.

a = 22° halo; b = parhelia; c = tangential arcs of the 22° halo: c_1 is the upper tangent and c_2 the lower tangent; d = Lowitz's arcs; e = Parry's arc; f = 46° halo; g = mock suns of the large halo; h = 46° lower tangential arc; i = 46° upper tangential arc; j = circumzenithal arc; k = parhelic arc; l = sun pillar.

Notice that the sky inside the small halo often seems darker than outside it; whenever this is not so, it is because the halo is superimposed on a diffuse light, decreasing gradually in brightness from the sun outward. This phenomenon reminds us very much of that observed in the rainbow (where the sky is darker between the two bows): it is caused in a similar manner.

The small halo arises from refraction of the sunlight in a cloud of small ice crystals, whose shape is known to be often that of a hexagonal prism. In every direction you look, innumerable minute prisms of this kind float about in every possible orientation—see Fig. 136. Such a six-sided prism refracts the light as if it had a refracting angle of 60°: according to its orientation with respect to the incident rays, it will deflect them to a lesser or greater extent, but if the path of the rays through the crystal is symmetrical, the deviation will have a minimum value D given by the well-known formula (given in most textbooks on physics under 'minimum deviation of a prism')

$$n = \sin\tfrac{1}{2}(A+D)/\sin\tfrac{1}{2}A,$$

The small ring or 22° halo around the sun, which is here hidden behind a lamppost. (Photo by Pekka Parviainen)

where n is the refractive index of the material of the prism and A its refracting angle. For $A = 60°$ and a refractive index $n = 1.31$, we obtain $D = 22°$: exactly the radius of the small halo!

Indeed, it is easily seen (as in the rainbow) that the rays OB, which suffer minimum deviation, will contribute by far the most to the brightness, since in that position the direction of the refracted ray changes only very slowly as the prism turns. There are, therefore, comparatively far more ice crystals sending the light to our eye in directions that lie close to this direction than lie close to other directions. Our calculations were carried out for yellow rays; for red ones, the minimum deviation is rather less; for blue ones, somewhat greater. For this reason, the inner edge of the halo is red, the outer edge blue. Since, however, the rays *EC* with a greater deviation than the minimum also contribute a certain amount of light, the green and blue 'rays of minimum deviation' will be mingled to a certain extent with yellow and red light and will therefore show a pale color. A small quantity of light will still be visible everywhere outside the ring, but not inside it, as we have observed already: the sharp inner edge as well as the hazy outer edge are thus explained. But whenever the crystals are not distributed randomly in every possible direction, but assume definite positions of preference, a differentiation in the luminosity outside the small halo takes place and certain spots of light or arcs appear: we shall examine these presently.

Let us first consider, however, whether or not the diffraction phenomena play a part here as they do in the rainbow[5]. Theoretically, they should; the ice crystal transmits only a narrow pencil of light of width h (Fig. 136) and therefore diffracts the light waves in the same manner as a slit of width h would do. Very small ice crystals would cause a white halo with a red edge just as small drops of water give rise to a fogbow—see § 150. Moreover, you can expect to see supernumerary bows appear beside the small ring (§ 144), and, indeed, these have been seen at times, but calculation shows that they must be weaker than in the rainbow and are formed on the outside as well as on the inside of the ring. Those on the inside are the easier ones to see as they are outlined against a dark background. Observations so far indicate a variation in the color and width of the small ring, but more observations are needed. Often, the best way to judge the colors is to look at them through smoked glass; estimate the width of each color separately and of the whole of them together. Name them according to your own independent opinion! Will any two observers ever call the colors of one and the same halo by the same names? Red and orange are often confused, as are blue and violet; note how seldom yellow occurs in halo phenomena.

According to the simple theory of refraction, there should be practically no blue in the small ring and absolutely no violet, and this should apply to the upper tangential arc and the mock suns as well—see § 158. However, observation sometimes shows us blue quite strongly, especially in the upper tangential arc and the mock suns, the tints of which are always vivid. The theory of diffraction explains how blue and violet can appear, if only the size of the crystals is right, and also why the tangential arc and the mock suns are more strongly colored than the small halo. Finally, the diffraction theory makes it clear why the colors are at times most vivid in the small halo and at other

---

[5] *Hemel en Dampkring*, **55**, 228, 1957.

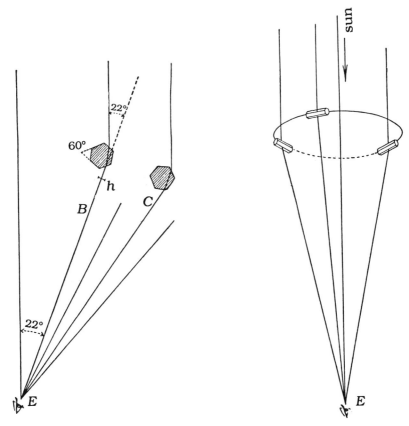

Fig. 136. How the small ring or 22° halo arises.

times in the large one: the small halo is more strongly colored when the faces of the prisms where the refraction takes place are broad, as with plate-shaped crystals; if, however, the faces are narrow, as with pillar-shaped crystals, the small halo is pale and the large one more vividly colored.

The light of the small halo is polarized to a certain degree[6]. In contradistinction to the rainbow, the vibrations in this case are stronger in directions at right angles to the ring than parallel to it. This is quite understandable since here there is no reflection at all and only two refractions. However, the effect is not nearly so pronounced as it is in the rainbow.

According to a popular belief, the small halo is a forerunner of rainy weather, and the saying 'the larger the halo, the sooner we

---

[6] Bryan O'Leary, *Astrophys. J.*, **146**, 754, 1966.

Fig. 137. Parhelia are formed by plate-shaped ice crystals. These crystals also give rise to the circumzenithal arc.

shall have rain', means that the small halo, and not the corona, predicts rain. And, indeed, cirrostratus clouds are often the forerunners of a region of depression.

158. The parhelia or mock suns (sun dogs) of the small halo (Fig. 135b)

After the small ring, mock suns or sun dogs are the most frequently encountered halo phenomenon. These mock suns are two concentrations of light on the small halo at the same altitude as the sun. It often happens that only one of the two can be seen properly and sometimes the small halo is absent, whereas the parhelia are clearly visible. The intensity of these mock suns is usually very great; they are distinctly red on the inside, then yellow, before changing into a bluish white.

On close observation, you will find that in reality the parhelia stand a little way outside the small halo, the more so as the altitude of the sun is greater; when the sun is very high, the difference may even amount to several degrees.

According to Greenler[7], the parhelia are formed when the air contains enough plate crystals floating horizontally like leaves—see Fig. 137. Through such prisms, the rays of light no longer travel along the path of minimum deviation, because they do not lie in a plane perpendicular to the axis. When the sun's altitude is h, the 'relative minimum deviation' is in this case determined by the condition

$$\sin\tfrac{1}{2}(A+D')/\sin\tfrac{1}{2}A = \sqrt{[(n^2-\sin^2 h)/(1-\sin^2 h)]},$$

so that the light behaves as if the refractive index were increased for oblique rays (cf. § 157). From this equation, the table on p. 215 has been computed. This agrees very well with the observations. For altitudes of the sun greater than 40°, we have, unfortunately, hardly any measurements, because the phenomenon is apt to become indistinct; try to fill this gap!

Mock suns have been observed in artificial clouds formed by the vapor trail of an aircraft (§ 174).

---

[7] R. Greenler, *Rainbows, Halos and Glories*, Cambridge University Press, 1980.

Altitude of sun	Distance parhelion–small halo
0°	0°
10°	0°20′
20°	1°14′
30°	2°59′
40°	5°48′
50°	10°36′

159. The circumscribed halo of the small ring (Fig. 135c)

The horizontal tangential arcs that appear as an increase of brightness at the bottom and at the top of the small halo can be seen, in favorable circumstances, to be parts of a much larger curve of light—the circumscribed halo. This very peculiar halo phenomenon is produced when the hexagonal crystals have their axis horizontal and oscillate slightly about that position; such a state of affairs will arise when the ice crystals are rod-shaped instead of plate-shaped.

The circumscribed halo depends for its shape very much on the altitude of the sun—see Fig. 138. When the sun is not high, all that can be seen is that the upper tangential bow is bent back in a downward direction on both sides; at greater altitudes, you can see an almost elliptical figure. The parts of the curves below the horizon have been found by calculation, and have been seen occasionally from a mountain, where the eye could be directed downward (presumably this would be equally possible from a tower or an aircraft).

160. Lowitz's arcs (Fig. 135d)

These are remarkable little arcs sloping downward from the mock sun and touching the small halo: a very rare phenomenon. It is pos-

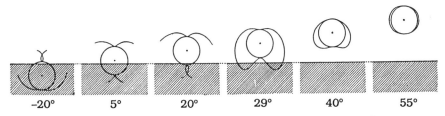

Fig. 138. Various forms of the circumscribed halo of the small ring at increasing altitude of the sun (according to computation by Pernter).

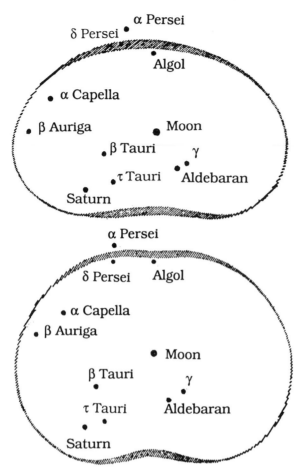

Fig. 139. The circumscribed halo relative to stars in the vicinity of the moon (at an altitude of 37°). At the top the original drawing; below it, a more exact reconstruction.

sible to see it only when the sun is high and the mock suns are consequently some distance from the small halo. The little arcs are produced when the minute vertical ice prisms, from which the mock suns arise, vibrate slightly about the vertical. Often, the only thing to be seen is an elongation of the mock sun, over 1° or 2°; the little arc is inclined at about 60° to the horizon. Only once was the arc fairly well defined and long. Therefore, it is always a good idea to observe the mock suns carefully for possible traces of this phenomenon[8].

[8] R.A.R. Tricker, *Introduction to Meteorological Optics*, Elsevier, New York.

160a. Parry's arc (Fig. 135e)

This is a small arc just above the small ring; it is always accompanied by an upper tangential arc.

161. The large ring or 46° halo (Fig. 135f)

The 46° halo appears fully twice as far from the sun as the small halo and has the same coloring, but its brightness is less and it is visible much more rarely. Accurate measurements of the radius of the inner edge are needed. This halo is produced in the same way as the 22° halo, only this time by refraction in 90° ice prisms orientated at random. As shown in Fig. 140, the same types of ice crystal can give rise to both the small and the large halo.

162. The mock suns (sun dogs) of the large halo (Fig. 135g)

These have seldom been observed, and no wonder: the refracting edges of 90° would have to be vertical in great numbers to produce it. That this should ever actually occur seems almost unthinkable, considering what the ordinary shapes of ice crystals are like.

163. The lower tangential arcs to the large halo (Fig. 135h)

Also rare! They are caused by a definite orientation in which both the axis and a side face are horizontal, while the light is refracted by

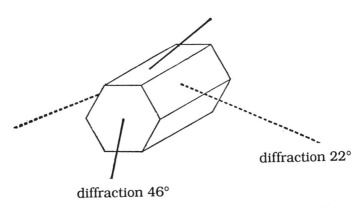

diffraction 22°

diffraction 46°

Fig. 140. In hexagonal ice crystals, light rays can exhibit a smallest diffraction of 22° or 46°.

those faces at right angles to each other. When the sun is very high, you can see the arc straighten and finally even become concave toward the sun.

164. The upper tangential arc to the large halo (Fig. 135i)

This can occur only when 90° prisms float in the air with refracting edges horizontal, the prisms oscillating round this position. Those among them that are suitably placed to give minimum deviation will then produce the tangential arc in question. Often, an arc is observed that is very like this one, but in reality has another origin; it is the circumzenithal arc of Bravais, not the true tangential arc of Galle.

165. The circumzenithal arc (Fig. 135j)

One of the most beautiful halo phenomena! Of fairly frequent occurrence, it is a vividly colored arc parallel to the horizon and showing the colors of the rainbow. It is generally a few degrees above where you would expect the upper tangential arc to the large halo to appear.

To explain it, imagine crystals in the shape of plates (see Fig. 137) floating in a stable position with axes vertical. A sunbeam will then be refracted in the 90° prism, but, generally speaking, this will not be in the position of minimum deviation. Figure 141 shows that

$$\sin i' = n\sin r' = n\cos r = n\sqrt{(1-\sin^2 i/n^2)} = \sqrt{(n^2-\sin^2 i)},$$

from which it follows at once that the angle of deviation is $i'+i-90°$. For a solar altitude $H = 10°$, this amounts to about 50°; for $H = 20°$, it has decreased to 46° (the minimum value); for $H = 30°$ it has increased again to 49.5°. This means that only when the sun is high or very low in the sky is it possible to distinguish the circumzenithal

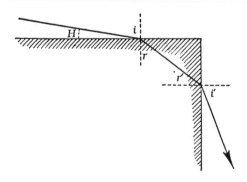

Fig. 141. Refraction of a light ray by a 90° ice prism.

arc from the upper tangential arc (with an angle of deviation of 46°) to the great circle. According to theory, you should never see more than one half of the circle; in practice, this is reduced to one-third. However, it is claimed that sometimes a complete circle (Kern's halo) has been seen.

If the tangential and the circumzenithal arcs should happen to be visible at the same time, a gap of a few degrees ought to be observed between them. And, indeed, it is on record that once a broad arc was seen, divided over its whole length by a dark band, appearing suddenly and disappearing after a short time. But observations of this kind are bound to remain rare, for, in order to be possible at all, a group of horizontally floating plates and a group of irregularly directed plates must be present simultaneously.

166. The horizontal or parhelic circle (Fig. 135k)

This is a circle running at the same height as the sun, parallel to the horizon. Though you can at times follow its course round the whole 360°, it is often difficult to see it in the neighborhood of the sun, where the sky is rather bright. The fact of its being uncolored shows clearly that it is caused by reflection, not refraction; the reflecting planes in this case are the side faces of ice prisms floating with vertical axes.

A similar band of light can be seen when you look at a source of light through a window wiped with a rather greasy cloth in one direction or reflected by finely ribbed glass. The band of light is always seen to be perpendicular to the ripples. This is a typical example of a general physical phenomenon: light reflected by a shining cylinder forms a cone, whose axis is the cylinder—see Fig. 142. Also, an observer, O surrounded by vertical cylinders receives rays of light from the cone: he or she sees a small horizontal circle in the sky with the sun, S, superposed on it.[9]

167. Light pillars or sun pillars (Fig. 135l)

A vertical pillar of light, or rather feather of light, can be observed fairly often above the rising sun or setting sun, best of all when the sun is hidden behind a house, so that the eye is not dazzled. This pillar of light is in itself uncolored, but when the sun is low and has become yellow, orange, or red, the pillar naturally assumes the same tint. It is generally only about 5° high, seldom more than 15°. When the sun is high, these pillars are rare; on the other hand, they can

---

[9] W. Maier, Z. Meteorol., **4**, 111, 1950.

often be seen very well when the sun is actually below the horizon. Pillars below the sun occur only now and then; they are shorter than those above the sun.

Imagine a cloud of ice flakes, all perfectly horizontal and falling very slowly. Under these conditions, they reflect the incident rays of the sun; these reflected rays, however, will not reach our eye. But let these same ice flakes become slightly inclined relative to their horizontal position on the compass: the reflected rays will acquire all kinds of small deviation. If the inclination remains smaller than h (sun's height), you will see a pillar below the sun, more or less the same as the paths of light formed in rippled surfaces of water (see § 20); when the inclination of the plates becomes larger than h, you will see not only a pillar below the sun, but also a fainter one above it.

This description, however, conflicts with the observations: the pillars would always have to be brighter below than above the sun.

The pillar of light has been attributed to repeated reflection, but then the light phenomenon would be much weaker and the pillar become much broader than it usually appears to be, as can be shown mathematically. Another explanation was that it arose from the curvature of the earth, which requires that in any one direction the observer should see flakes of noticeably different inclination. Finally, it was supposed to arise from ice plates rotating rapidly round a horizontal axis and for this reason assuming every possible orientation in space. This last supposition seems, indeed, to be one of the most

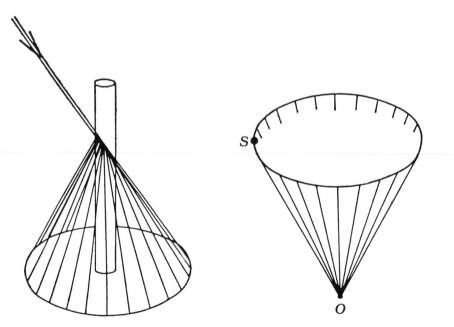

Fig. 142. Reflection of sunlight by a shiny cylinder. If there were a multitude of such cylinders, observer O would see a horizontal circle through the sun.

Light pillar in freezing fog caused by the lights of a petrol station. (Photo by Jouni Särkioja)

likely, though its calculation has never been carried out to the end—see Fig. 143b.

Current theories assume two basic forms of ice crystal: pencil and plate crystals. Both can reflect the rays to form the sun pillar as they float in the air more or less horizontally.

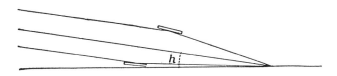

Fig. 143a. The simplest explanation for the formation of light pillars above and below the sun.

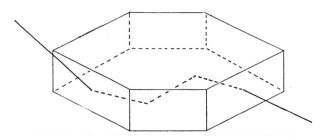

Fig. 143b. Internal reflection in a rotating ice prism is a better explanation.

168. Crosses

When a vertical pillar and a part of the horizontal circle occur at the same time, we see a cross in the sky. Needless to say, the superstitious have made the most of this!

On 14 July 1865, the alpinist Whymper and his companions were the first to reach the top of the Matterhorn, but on the way back four of the men slipped and fell headlong down a precipice. Toward the evening, Whymper saw an awe-inspiring circle of light with three crosses

Light pillar formed by ice crystals suspended in the air; the sub-sun is apparent as a brightening of the column. (Photo by Veikko Mäkelä)

in the sky: 'the ghostly apparitions of light hung motionless; it was a strange and awesome sight, unique to me and indescribably imposing at such a moment'.

169. The sub-sun

This can be seen only from a mountain top or an aircraft. It is a somewhat oblong, uncolored reflection: the sun reflected not in a surface of water but in a cloud!, a cloud of ice plates, in fact, which appear to float extremely calmly judging from the comparative sharpness of the image.

Under favorable conditions, the elliptical image is surrounded by an elliptical refractive ring with a radius of 0.5°–1°. Evidently, the ice crystals give way like pliable holes. Since they are seen at an angle, their apparent diameter in the vertical plane is smaller, and the refracted image in that direction therefore wider. This halo has sometimes been called Bottlinger's ring.

170. Very rare and doubtful halo phenomena

So far, we have treated the twelve most common forms of halo. A collection of many of the most fascinating, that is, rarest, halos still remains. Altogether there are probably more than 50 different forms of halo. The exact number is not known and there are no generally accepted lists of all halos.

One measure of the rarity of a halo is the number of times it has been observed. This, of course, means that the rarer the halo is, the less is known about it and the more uncertain it is. Thus, the last items of the following catalogue are very uncertain and should be viewed with an appropriately critical eye.

The rare halos invariably appear in connection with the most brilliant halo displays; these phenomena are like the notorious ball lightning: they do not pick the time and place to appear according to any known rules. Often, beautiful halo displays are, unfortunately, known only from amateurish reports: "I've never in my life seen anything like it ...", and "... the whole sky was filled with these strange colored arcs", and cameras always seem to have been left at home. Readers of this book will probably at least once in their life have the opportunity to witness the miracle of a sky covered in fine cirrus clouds. Active observers of the nighttime and daytime sky get these chances more often. At such times, it is to be hoped that the reader will remember this text, and calmly go inside and fetch paper, pen, and camera, and make a careful drawing of the display, taking note of the mutual distances of the halos, their directions, brightnesses, and colors, as well as taking lots of pictures. Photographic evidence becomes more important the rarer the halo. Of the rarest halos there exist no photographs whatsoever. In these cases, photographs are not only evidence, but also provide a concrete basis for computer simulations of ice-crystal models.

120° parhelia White bright patches on the parhelic circle at 120° from the sun. Still a fairly well-known sight for experienced observers, who may see a 120° parhelion even once or twice a year, often faint and diffuse, but at times quite bright. Two possible ray paths that could produce this halo are given in Greenler's book[10].

Anthelion. A white brightening opposite the sun at the same elevation as the sun. When the sun is low (0°–15° elevation), the anthelion appears as an anthelic pillar. At larger elevations, it is more point-like. Anthelia may be observed perhaps every other year.

Anthelic arcs. White faint arcs passing transversely through the anthelion, mostly visible near the anthelic point, but sometimes extending all the way to the 22° circle on the solar side of the sky. There are three main theories of the origin of the anthelic arcs: those of Hastings, Wegener, and Tricker. The halos predicted by these theories are slightly different, and at least Tricker's and Wegener's arcs seem to have been observed in nature. Wegener arcs bend away from the anthelic point at a shallow angle and may reach the 22° ring. They are more common than the Tricker arcs and might occur once every two or four years. Tricker anthelic arcs curve steeply up and down from the anthelic point. When the sun is low, only the Tricker arcs can form an X shape near the anthelion.

In 1984, two new anthelic arcs were found theoretically by Greenler and Tränkle. Recent photographic evidence from Antarctica and Finland supports the existence of these arcs. The form of the anthelic arcs of Greenler and Tränkle resembles that of Tricker's arcs, but their appearance is much more diffuse on the sky. New observations and photographs of these fascinating rare white crosses are needed to decide, for example, how rare each anthelic arc type is.

90° parhelia and 134° parhelia. In addition to the earlier mentioned 120° parhelia, brightenings of the parhelic circle can sometimes be observed at about right angles to the sun and possibly also at 134° from the sun. The existence of the former parhelia is not in doubt, but their origin and exact angle are disputed. It may be that the 90° parhelia are actually at 98° from the sun. A good way of measuring the exact angular distance in the field is to take consecutive photographs of the sun and the parhelion so that some details of the

[10] R. Greenler, *Rainbows, Halos and Glories*, Cambridge University Press,

horizon are visible in both photographs. If the exact spot of observation has been recorded, the central angle can be measured carefully afterward.

90° halo and 120° halo. Faint white arcs have sometimes been observed passing vertically through the rare parhelia. Best known of these is the 90° halo, which was first described by the astronomer Hevelius in the historical halo display of Gdansk on 20 February 1661. These halos have been explained both by means of ice-crystal models and as observational errors (confusion with portions of other rare halos).

Rare circumsolar rings. Colored rings around the sun at different radii (other than the well-known 22° and 46° circles). There are several of these, and there are numerous incompatible measurements of their exact radii. Modern theory lists the following six rings: 9° halo; 18° halo; 20° halo; 23° halo; 24° halo; and 35° halo. In addition, there is possibly one at 27–28°, the so-called Scheiner halo, but this very uncertain phenomenon has not yet been photographed. These circles are quite rare, probably caused by pyramid-shaped ice crystals of different sizes, and several appear together. The existence of these halos was in doubt for a long time until the magnificent halo display in southern England and Holland on Easter Day 14 April 1974, when up to six different solar rings including the usual 22° circle were reported from several places. Observations were made by 12 independent observers and the display was also photographed.

Helic (or *heliac*) *arc.* An arc passing obliquely through the sun forming a loop above it. When the sun is low, the loop of the helic arc is large, extending slightly past zenith on the side of the sky opposite the sun. As the height of the sun increases, the size of the helic arc decreases and the loop is pulled in, first inside the 46° circle and then inside the 22° circle. The helic arc has been observed some ten times.

Subhelic arc. Observed a couple of times as a companion to the helic arc going in the same direction as the helic arc several degrees outside it. According to American simulations, the intersection point of the loop formed by this white arc is located at the subsolar point.

Subanthelic arc. An arc forming a loop round the anthelic point. Very rare; about five known observations, among them the Kuusankoski display on 10 March 1920.

Vertical elliptical halos. These are little vertically elliptical rings that are sometimes seen for only a few seconds or minutes, surrounding more often the moon than the sun. Not much is known about these strange rings and their theory remains unsolved as yet. Until recently,

Historical halo displays

Gdansk, 20 February 1661. Observed by the astronomer Hevelius. One of the earliest well-observed halo displays. There is only one major rarity in the picture: the 90° halo, which need not have been centered on the sun, although Hevelius has drawn it like that. The display and the one observed by Tobias Lowitz in St. Petersburg in 1790 are among the most famous halo displays.

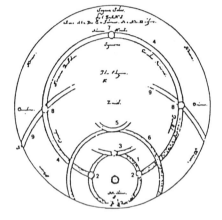

1 = 22° halo
2 = parhelia
3 = 22° upper tangential arc
4 = parhelic circle
5 = circumzenithal circle
6 = 46° halo
7 = anthelion
8 = 90° parhelia
9 = 90° halo

Dorpat (Tartu) halo display of 5 June 1849, observed by Mädler and Clausen. The zenith is at the center of the figure and S = sun. The observers have included in their drawing lines of constant altitude at 10° intervals from horizon to zenith.

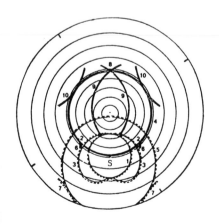

1 = 22° halo
2 = parhelia
3 = 22° tangential arcs (complete)
4 = parhelic circle
5 = 46° halo
6 = Lowitz arc: small fragments beneath the parhelia
7 = 46° lower tangential arcs
8 = anthelion
9 = Wegener anthelic arcs
10 = Arctowski arcs

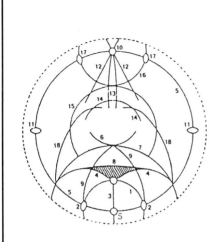

	1 = 22° halo
	2 = parhelia
	3 = sun pillar
	4 = 22° upper tangential arc
	5 = parhelic circle
	6 = circumzenithal arc
	7 = 46° halo
	8 = upper Parry arc (typical bright region between it and the upper tangential arc)
	9 = upper Lowitz arc
	10 = anthelion
	11 = 90° parhelia
	12 = Wegener anthelic arcs
	13 = Tricker anthelic arcs
	14 = helic arc
	15 = subhelic arc
	16 = subanthelic arc
The great halo display of Kuusankosi, Finland, on 10 March 1920. The display features many rare phenomena. About ten observations were made, the best by E.A. Biese, shown adjacent. The zenith is at the center of the figure and S = sun.	17 = either a brightening caused by the intersection of two halos or previously unknown parhelia
	18 = unknown pair of arcs that could be badly drawn 46° supralateral arcs (bending upward because the sun is low)

these phenomena were considered uncertain, but in December 1987 and February 1988 two of these rings (Hissink's elliptical halo: vertical axis 10–11° and Schlesinger's elliptical halo: vertical axis 7°) were photographed by Finnish amateur astronomers and pictures were published in the December 1989 issue of *Weather* magazine.

Bouguer's arc. A white arc situated like a rainbow in the sky opposite the sun. Either an independent form of halo or confused with a fogbow, which under some conditions might be visible at the same time as a halo display.

Arctowski's arc. Possibly related to the Bouguer arc. White arcs curving like rainbows on the sides of the sun and the anthelion. All known observations were made before 1921.

8° parhelic circle. A white, faint ring 8° below the parhelic circle and parallel to it. Three possible observations are known (in all cases, only parts of this hypothetical circle were seen: Java, Indonesia 1933, the Netherlands 1950, and Antarctica 1951). There is no generally agreed name for this doubtful, strange form of halo.

171. Oblique and distorted halo phenomena

Pillars of light have sometimes been observed that were not vertical, but inclined as much as 20° with respect to the vertical. The oblique pillarlike patches on undulating water were explained by the dominating direction of the wavelets; here we can obviously assume that the ice crystals do not float horizontally, but are wafted in a slanting direction by certain air currents; exactly how is not easy to explain. Another possibility is reflection by prism faces at the end of the ice crystals.

In the same way, upper tangential arcs are known which touch the small circle at 10° to 12° from the top. The horizontal circle has occasionally been seen inclined. Once, when the sun was 50° high, it appeared to be curved toward the horizon on both sides, and at 90° from the sun, it was only 25° above the horizon. On another occasion, this circle ran 1° to 2° below the sun. The mock sun of the small circle was once observed to be 40' too high; this was seen particularly clearly because the sun was about to set.

The circumscribed halo has been seen distorted; at the lower edge, it did not come to 22° but to 28° from the sun[11].

More observations are needed, and special care should be taken to avoid all personal errors of judgment; make use of a plummet; take photos with a plummet held at some distance in front of the camera, so that it appears (somewhat blurred) on the film.

172. The degree of development of halo phenomena

The regularity of natural phenomena is always exaggerated by inexperienced observers: they draw snow crystals perfectly symmetrical, count seven colors in the rainbow, and see lightning as a zigzag. Similarly, there is a tendency to describe halo phenomena as being more complete than they actually are. Yet there is a vast difference between seeing half the circumference of the small halo and seeing all of it. The 'imperfection' of natural phenomena is also governed by fixed laws and is in its way only another irregularity.

This is why it is important to note the degree of development of each halo phenomenon by making an estimate of its light intensity as well as the extent of the part visible. By averaging the observations, the influence of any haphazard irregularity in the distribution of clouds can for the most part be eliminated. It is found as a rule that those parts whose intensity is greatest are also developed the most frequently. A halo of particularly strong brightness is on average also

---

[11] *Sky and Telescope*, **21**, 14, 1961.

particularly extensive. A moderately thin layer of clouds is the most favorable for the development of halos; very thin layers contain too few crystals, and very thick ones either do not transmit enough light or scatter it in all directions.

A very interesting fact is that the top part of the small circle is seen on average about three times as often as the lower part. As a reason for this it has been suggested that the path of the rays through the layer of clouds is much longer for the lower part, but this may be an advantage as much as a disadvantage.

173. Families of halos

Halo phenomena like the small and the large halo appear to point to pillar-shaped crystals, twisting and turning in turbulent air; mock suns and circumzenithal arcs appear to be caused by quietly floating crystal disks. That explains why during the thundery summer months halo phenomena usually concern the small halo, whereas this halo hardly ever occurs during autumn and winter. It is clear that certain parts of the halo phenomena will occur simultaneously, that is, there are families of halos.

As far as the shapes of the crystals are concerned, these depend on the circumstances in which the crystals have grown. Pillars come about in the higher atmosphere, whereas disks are formed at lower altitudes where it is less cold.

174. Halo phenomena in aircraft trails

Halo phenomena, more particularly mock suns, but also small halos, circumzenithal arcs, and paranthelia, have often been observed in the cirruslike vapor trails of aircraft. From these observations, it is clear that the ice crystals in these trails lie predominantly in a vertical position.

During wartime, the shock wave of antiaircraft grenades could often be seen as a fast moving wavefront against the wispy cloud (§ 145). Exceptionally, these dark waves moved along the horizontal circle. It must be assumed that in this case the ice crystals oscillated with respect to their vertical position every time a wave passed.

175. Halo phenomena close to the eye

Walking down a narrow street, an observer saw a halo round the moon, but noticed that part of it was projected onto a dark wall, and formed a whole with the remainder projected onto the sky. Even when

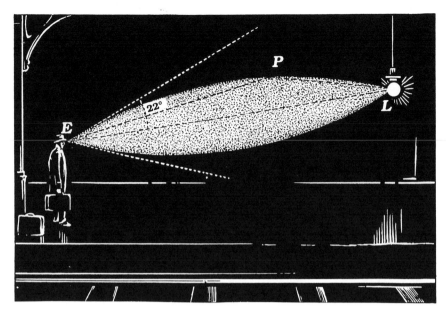

Fig. 144. Small ring, observed very close to the eye.

he screened off the moon with his hand, he could still see the halo: it could not therefore be a phenomenon in the eye itself, but evidently there were ice crystals floating between his eye and the wall, only a few meters (yards) from the ground.

One very cold evening (10 °C or 17 °F) beautiful halo phenomena could be seen in the steam from a train in a railway station. Near one of the lights, where the cloud of steam was blown in every direction, a cigar-shaped surface of light could be seen, with one end near the eye and the other near the light—see Fig. 144; all little crystals traversing this surface were lit up, but the space inside was quite dark; the cone tangential to the surface had an angle at the vertex of about 44°. It is clear that the cigar-shaped surface is simply the locus of all those points P such that the sum of the angles subtended by EP and PL at L and E respectively is 22°.

The remarkable part of this observation is its three-dimensional nature; this is only possible because the source of light is so near and the eyes, working together, see the individual points of light and estimate their distance stereoscopically.

That same evening, in a quieter part of the station, it was observed that the lamps there produced light crosses. This phenomenon is not new: in Russia and Canada in the winter, pillars of light can often be seen above distant lamps, which proves the presence of a floating mist of ice crystals in the air.

The small halo, the mock suns, the upper tangential arc, and the large halo have been seen at times in masses of whirling snow. It is interesting that mock suns in these conditions are often seen as almost vertical light pillars in the colors of the rainbow; sometimes they reach a height of 15°! Even more surprising is that in one case the sub-sun could also be seen, circumscribed by a sub-sun ring of 22°. It was rather more hazy than usual, and its colors were fainter. The sun was 11° above the horizon and parts of the phenomenon were seen against the background of distant mountains[12].

176. Halo phenomena on the ground

We have seen the rainbow projected on a horizontal plane as a dew-bow; in the same way you can sometimes see, on freshly fallen snow, the small and the large circle in the shape of hyperbolic arcs (see Fig. 145) especially when the temperature is below 12 °C (15 °F), more often when there is hoarfrost. To observe it, you should try to see it about half an hour, or at the most an hour, after sunrise or before sunset. The streak of light consists of a number of tiny separate crystals scintillating with the most wonderful colors; these are mostly red and gold-brown, but the tints are evidently not very saturated. When you move, the light phenomenon moves with you.

The angle contained by lines from the sun and eye to the crystal can be determined by simple measurements, and you can show that the light rays are refracted through an angle of 22° or 46° respect-

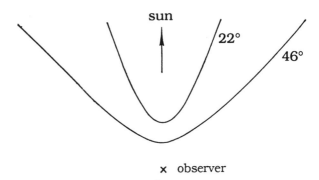

x   observer

Fig. 145. The small ring and the 46° halo portrayed as hyperbolas in fresh snow on the ground.

---

[12] Gäbler, *Z. Meteorolog.*, **8**, 127, 1954.

ively. Examine the shapes of the crystals through a magnifying glass and then draw and measure them. Also, take photos of the phenomenon!

Coronas

177. Interference colors in oil spots

When the ground is wet after a shower of rain, you can often see colored patches on the dark Tarmac of roads, patches sometimes as large as 50 cm (2 ft) in diameter and made up of concentric colored circles. On certain days and on certain roads, these patches can be very beautiful, though as a rule they are merely blue-gray spots. They are evidently formed by drops of oil from passing cars; each drop spreads out into a very thin film and the combination of light reflected from the upper and the lower surfaces of the film produces interference colors, in other words, the famous Newton's rings, identical to those in the lovely hues of soap bubbles. Their explanation can be found in ordinary textbooks on science, but it should be pointed out that what you have here is proof that light is a wave phenomenon.

In the table below, the colors are enumerated, beginning at the outside of the spot and gradually approaching the center; the thickness of the oil film is in micrometers (μm).

I	black	0	III	violet	0.385
	light gray	0.080		green	0.455
	yellowish brown	0.115		yellow	0.505
	red	0.170		flesh-colored	0.525
II	violet	0.190	IV	blue-gray	0.595
	blue	0.210		green	0.655
	green	0.270		flesh-colored	0.695
	yellow	0.305			
	red	0.340	V	blue-green	0.820

The layers of oil are thus thinnest at the edges and grow thicker toward the center. Sometimes, they reach no further, even in the center, than the first steps of the color scale; at other times, they are so thick that, after the colors mentioned in our table, pink and green alternate with one another several times, growing steadily paler and turning into an almost pure white so that no more rings can be seen in the middle.

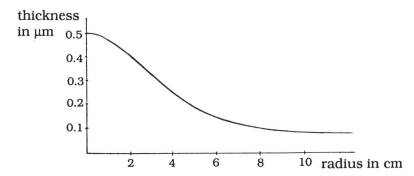

Fig. 146. Cross section, to scale, of a drop of oil on wet Tarmac; measured with the aid of the interference colors.

Measure the diameter of a regularly shaped spot across the different colors and then draw to scale the transverse section of the layer of oil—see Fig. 146. If you repeat this after ten minutes, you will see that the mound of oil has flattened out. Follow one definite color as a function of time and you will notice that the ring first expands and then contracts. Why? In the end, all you see is a gray spot whose origin would never have occurred to you if you had not observed its formation. The best way is to stand and watch a single spot and measure every change in it. It will not require all that much patience; perhaps not more than half an hour. Protect it from cyclists and pedestrians and pray that it may reach the end of its life before a car runs over it!

Observe the oil spot obliquely; the colors become displaced as if the layer had become thinner. For, if you look at it more slantingly, the colored rings seem to contract so that at any particular point the color is replaced by the color that belonged originally to a thinner ring. Try to account for this by calculating the difference in phase of the two interfering rays.

Stroke it with your finger: the colors begin to change, but resume their positions with surprising rapidity; the rings have grown smaller, as a little of the oil has been taken away.

Sometimes, you will see finely shaped double spots that apparently belong together. There is nothing mysterious in this: they are simply a normal spot after a car tyre has passed over it.

Do not be satisfied until you have made colored rings yourself. A drop of paraffin or turpentine poured on to a pond produces indescribably lovely colors. But if you use oil for this experiment, there is a surprise in store for you! The oil does not spread out into a film and you will see nothing. The same thing happens on a wet road or on a surface of water. Are the spots in the road caused by petrol, perhaps, and not oil? Again, you will be disappointed, for petrol produces only grayish white spots, apparently extremely thin and bearing no resemblance whatever to the magnificent rings of color. Closer investigation has shown that only the used, oxidized oil dripping from a car engine is capable of spreading on a wet surface. The more complete the oxidation of the oil, the thinner the layer becomes.

Most oil spots show radial bands. Each colored ring merges into the next with fringes, as it were, and the outermost, white-gray ring likewise ends in fringes. By pouring some petrol on to a wet road, you will see how the spot it forms spreads and branches out on all sides, causing radial bands and fringes while you watch. The same phenomenon can frequently be seen in colored films floating on dirty water. It may be that complicated molecular forces are at work here.

Interference colors are present wherever a thin film is formed; for instance, on the thin layers of tar and paraffin floating on water; lines of constant color are lines of constant thickness, and their distortions betray to us all the currents and eddies of the liquid.

If by chance a fairly thick layer of oil floats on the water, and the wind blows over it obliquely, you will observe beautiful interference colors in equidistant bands, proving that the layer gets thicker toward its source. It is interesting to note how the ripples of the surface of the water are damped down by the layer of oil and have disappeared completely before the first visible gray begins. A layer of not more than 0.08 µm thick is sufficient to cause this damping.

178. Interference in the fabric of an umbrella

When you look through a dry umbrella at a light that is sufficiently far away to form a point source, you will notice a beautiful pattern of diffraction and interference. If the weave of the fabric is horizontal and vertical, the diffracted images are arranged in horizontal and vertical rows. What you see is not the fabric itself, because when the umbrella is moved the pattern stays in place. Moreover, the threads of the fabric are much closer together than the diffracted images. Your umbrella behaves as an optical filter.

The underlying theory may be found in physics textbooks. It explains how the distance between the diffracted images is determined. In our observation we are concerned with both vertical and horizontal threads; the diffraction maxima that occur at the vertical threads and which form a horizontal row are themselves converted to a set of vertical dots of light by the horizontal threads. The dots farthest away from the source of light show some color: they are, in fact, minute spectra.

When looking through your umbrella, you will probably see a number of lights at various distances. The most distant show a distinct diffraction pattern, whereas of the nearer ones, which you see at a relatively large angle, the dots fuse into a hazy blot. (This phe-

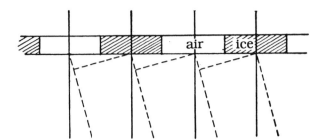

Fig. 147. Colors of mixed plates.

nomenon is used in interferometers to determine the diameter of stars—
speckle interferometry.)

179. Magnificent colors on a freezing window

This as yet little-studied phenomenon may be observed regularly
during cold winter evenings when the temperature has dropped to
below 10 °C (14 °F) in a train or bus. The breath of the passengers
freezes on the windows. When the vehicle passes a streetlight, you
will notice that the light gives rise to a wonderful display of color:
certain parts of the thin frozen layer are tinted sky blue, others red
or green. These colors remain more or less the same over an area of
about 1 cm² and all of them are visible only in transmitted and not
in reflected light. The tints are so lovely and saturated that you will
realize at once that this is something very remarkable. The phenomenon
normally lasts only for a few minutes, after which the layer of ice becomes thicker and the colors disappear.

The phenomenon may, however, be repeated as often as you like in
the right conditions. If you breathe on a very cold window (temperature below 5 °C or 22 °F), it seems (a) that your breath is frozen first
into small hemispherical lumps of ice; (b) after about half a minute,
cracks are formed in the layer of ice and the ice particles gather into
small groups, until (c) they form long needles between which you can
see the transparent ice. It is only in stage (b) that the colors appear,
and this explains their short duration.

Another typical peculiarity is that the observed lamp or source of
light itself becomes colored and, when you go on breathing on to the
windowpane, becomes brown-yellow, purple, blue, green, and yellow: the order of Newton's colors. A bright corona with complementary color appears around the light source; it has a radius of about
1°, which appears to increase gradually. This is best observed by
stopping breathing for a moment and keeping your eye *very close to
the glass.* By day, for example, bright snow-covered roofs may look

pinkish red and the surrounding dark parts, green. Extensive bright areas, like the sky, do not change color, because in all directions you see simultaneously the colored light source and the complementary scattered colored light of adjacent areas. *When you look at the glass at an angle, the colors change* as if the layer had become thicker.

One explanation for the colors is refraction by tiny droplets or grains. When these have a diameter of not more than a few μm, the elementary theory of coronas no longer holds, because, apart from the light that is refracted *around* the droplets, light that *penetrates* the droplets also plays a role. The light source itself now exhibits a color, with around it a complementary color that changes little with the angle of refraction—see § 187.

Another explanation, not very different from the first one, considers the layers to be composed of bordering areas of different materials, here ice and air—see Fig. 147. Some of the rays from the light source have traveled through air, others, through ice, before reaching our eyes. This causes a phase difference between them, which results in one color becoming extinguished and the light source becoming colored. However, light is refracted at the boundaries of the areas and at a given angle of refraction and given dimension of the interstices, the path difference will just compensate for the phase delay, whereupon the color that had been extinguished reappears in the refracted light. A layer composed of ice and air would have to be about 1 μm thick, while the interstices between the grains would have to be about 0.1 mm ($^4/_{1000}$ in). When the grains are equispaced, the corona will be well defined and separated from the light source by a dark border; when they are not, the source is evenly surrounded by light. Some parts of a window behave in the first manner and others in the second.

If you hold your eye a little distance from the glass, you will see that each distinct point of it lights up, in a color specific to that area, only when it is seen at a certain angle relative to the light source. This will be clear from the explanations given earlier.

It is noteworthy that around the aureole of a very bright light source there are faint coronas of different colors (eyes close to the glass).

The icing of window may assume different forms, for example, when the temperature is not very low. Typical coronas with abnormal color order will then arise, just as are found on windows on which large drops of water have condensed—see § 185.

180. Interference colors in ferruginous water

The brown water of ditches running across heathland, where the soil is ferruginous (rich in iron), is sometimes covered with a thin iridescent layer, in which the pale colors resemble mother-of-pearl. These colors are caused by the colloidal solution of iron oxide present in the water arranging itself in small parallel plates, about 0.25 μm apart, and this laminated membrane acts more or less like a Lippmann color photograph.

181. Diffraction of light

When, at night, a car travels toward you with its headlights casting a fierce glare on the road and a cyclist chances to cross on front of the dazzling light, so that for a moment you stand in his shadow, then suddenly the cyclist's silhouette is outlined by a strangely beautiful light apparently radiating from its edge. The same effect may be observed around pedestrians and trees. It is a diffraction effect. Diffraction is the name given to the slight bending that a ray of light undergoes at the edge of an opaque screen, when part of the wavefront penetrates the region where, according to geometrical optics, shadow would be expected. The light so deflected is fairly intense if the angle of deviation is small, but diminishes rapidly at larger angles, which accounts for the beauty of the effect when the cyclist is far away and the car far beyond that.

A similar phenomenon, on a larger scale, can be seen in mountainous country where the air is pure, when, standing in the shadow of a hill, you see its treeclad upper part as a dark outline against the morning sky. When the sun is about to rise, those trees situated where the light is at its brightest are surrounded by a brilliant silvery white radiance.

It is said that gorse bushes in particular, seen against the sun, can produce this kind of effect.

182. Diffraction of light by small scratches

If you look at the sun through the window of a train or car, you will see thousands of very fine scratches on the glass, all arranged concentrically round the sun. Through whatever part of the window you look, what you see is always the same, from which it may be concluded that the glass is covered all over with small scratches in all directions, although you notice only those that are at right angles to the plane of incidence of the rays of light (cf. § 29). The reason is that every scratch spreads the light in a plane at right angles to its own direction and is therefore only visible to the observer in this plane.

Where such fine scratches are concerned, we can no longer speak of reflection or refraction, and it is better in this case to regard the deviation of the light rays as diffraction. If you look carefully at one of these scratches, you will see that, in certain definite directions, it

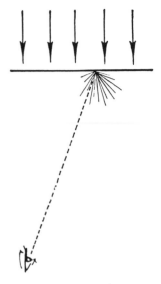

Fig. 148. Diffraction of light by small scratches.

shows the most magnificent colors in every possible sequence; if you use a Polaroid, you will find that the light is strongly polarized when the direction of incidence and observation is oblique. All these phenomena are very complicated and can be explained only partly by theoretical optics.

Diffraction can also be observed on the threads of cobwebs that glitter in the same color along their entire length, proving that they are the same thickness all over. There are threads of different colors.

183. Coronas

> A great, still softening
> Descends from the sky;
> The clouds are colored
> In iris tints around the moon
>
> P. Verlaine, *La Bonne Chanson*

When thin, white, fleecy clouds glide slowly past the moon, our eye is unconsciously attracted to this illuminated part of the sky, the center of the nocturnal landscape. And each time another cloud appears, we see beautifully variegated rings of light around the softly

Coronas around streetlights in fog. (Photo by Veikko Mäkelä)

radiant moon, rings with a diameter of only a few times that of the moon itself.

If we investigate the sequence of these colors, we will see that next to the moon is a bluish border, merging into yellowish-white, and this in turn has a brownish outermost edge. This aureole is the corona phenomenon in its simplest form, and by far the most frequent form of all. It becomes really remarkable only when it is surrounded by larger and more beautifully colored rings. The sequence of these rings can be seen from the table below, which agrees almost exactly with the scale of Newton's interference colors, except that meteorologists have decided on the limits between the various 'orders'

I	aureole	(bluish)	III	blue
		white		green
		(yellowish)		red
		yellowish-brown		
II		blue	IV	blue
		green		green
		(yellow)		red
		red		

in a way slightly different from that of physicists, namely, so that each group ends with red. On very rare occasions, three groups have been observed outside the aureole ('fourfold corona').

It seems almost certain that the color gradations vary occasionally; those colors between brackets in the table are present at certain times and absent at others. When we investigate this changeability of the coronas, the phases of the moon should be borne in mind, for they cause the diffraction pattern to be more blurred at some times than at others.

The best way to estimate the radius of the coronas is to take as starting point the red border with which every order ends, because that color stands out most sharply, and then to compare the size of the corona with the diameter of the moon (32'). The size of the coronas is found to vary considerably; the brown border of the aureole, for instance, can have a radius of barely 1°, whereas at other times it is as much as 5°. Extreme values that have been recorded are 10' and 13°.

Coronas round the sun can be seen very often, at least as often as round the moon, but they are not noticed so frequently because everyone naturally avoids looking into the dazzling light. And yet, owing to the intense luminosity of the sun, the coronas around it are usually the finest of all.

Observations can be facilitated by making use of one of the following suggestions.

1. Observe the sun's reflection in calm water; this was how Newton made his famous observation of a corona around the sun.

2. As a mirror, use a piece of black polished marble glass, or goggles worn by welders, or an ordinary piece of glass blackened by black varnish. You should hold these close to the eye to be able to survey a large field.

3. Use marble glass or welder's goggles that are sufficiently transparent to allow you to observe the sun without being dazzled.

4. See that the sun is screened off by the edge of a roof.

5. Look into a spherical mirror a few meters (yards) away, and intercept the sun's image with your head.

The aureole is visible faintly in almost every type of cloud. It is, however, much stronger in altocumulus or stratocumulus, which usually also show a faint indication of the second colored ring. The most beautiful coronas of all, with delightfully pure tints, occur in thin cirrocumulus and, evidently, in cirrus.

At times, faintly luminous coronas can be seen even around Venus, Jupiter, and the brighter stars.

184. The explanation of the corona phenomena[13]

The coronas we see in the clouds are formed by diffraction of light by the drops of water in the clouds. The smaller the drops, the larger the coronas. In clouds where the drops are all of equal size, the coronas are well developed and their colors pure; in those clouds, however, in which drops of all sizes are mixed together, coronas of different sizes occur simultaneously, the one overlapping the other. This is why finely developed corona phenomena occur only in very definite kinds of cloud, where circumstances causing the condensation of the water vapor are sufficiently uniform; and for the same reason, a finer distinction in the sequence of the tints will depend on the number of drops of various sizes, on the thickness of the clouds, and so on.

The general line of argument in the theory is this:
(a) the diffraction by a moderately dense cloud of water drops, all of the same size, is essentially the same as that by one drop, only the intensity of the diffracted light is greater;
(b) the diffraction produced by a drop is the same as that produced by a small aperture in a screen (Babinet's principle);
(c) the diffraction by an aperture is calculated by taking the aperture as the starting point of vibrations (Huygens' principle), and by ascertaining how the waves from all parts of the opening enter the eye and interfere.

It is quite an easy matter to observe the resemblance between the corona and the diffraction image of a circular hole. In front of a window on which the sun is shining, hang a piece of cardboard perforated in the middle, but with the perforation covered by a piece of silver paper pasted on to the cardboard. Prick a hole in the silver paper with a needle and look at this brilliant point of light in the direction of the sun at a distance of about a meter (3 ft), holding before your eye a second piece of silver paper, also provided with a fine needle hole. The holes should be made with the finest of needles, which should be rolled to and fro between the fingers while the hole is being made; the holes themselves should be not more then 0.5 mm ($^{20}/_{000}$ in) in diameter. The small hole at which you look will appear broadened into a disk, which is a miniature aureole, and surrounding this disk you will see a system of rings corresponding to the successive orders of the corona. The finer the hole in front of your eye, the larger the diffraction pattern.

The successive maxima and minima can be compared in every respect to the diffraction fringes occurring at a parallel slit, although their distances are somewhat different. The outermost red borders of the aureole and of the first order lie at $\delta = 0.00070/a$ and $0.00127/a$,

[13] Reesinck, *Hemel en Dampkring*, **44**, 127, 1946.

where a is the diameter of the hole in mm, and δ is the angular distance reckoned from the center.

We are able, therefore, to calculate from the coronas how large the drops are that form the clouds. If the radius δ of an aureole around the moon is four times the diameter of the moon itself, that is, $4/108$ radians, the clouds are formed of drops with a diameter of $108/4 \times 0.00070 = 0.076/4 = 19$ μm. This calculation is not quite exact, because the sun or the moon are not mere points, but have a radius of 16'. The outermost border, therefore, clearly becomes too large, and these 16' are, for this reason, often subtracted from the observed angle before applying the formula, but it is very doubtful whether we are justified in doing this[14]. Generally, you will find that the size of the drops in the clouds is 10–20 μm.

It is almost certain that coronas can also be caused by clouds of ice needles of equal thickness that diffract the light in the same way as a slit does. For coronas with the finest coloring and the best development are observed now and then in the thin, high cirrus clouds, which consist of ice needles.

The thickness of the ice needles can be calculated just as simply as the size of the water drops: in the case of the corona mentioned above, where the brown border had a radius of four lunar diameters, the thickness of the ice needles would be $0.062/4 = 15$ μm.

It is very difficult when observing a corona to say whether it is caused by drops of water or by needles of ice. With ice needles, the distances between the successive dark minima are all exactly the same and equal to the distance between the center and the first dark minimum, whereas with water drops, the radius of the aureole is 20 percent larger than the widths of the orders following. Moreover, the light intensity of the successive orders diminishes much more slowly with ice needles than with water drops. But these distinctions are not easy to observe. The best measurements favor at one time one order of formation, at another time the other, in both cases agreeing with what you might expect judging from the kinds of cloud.

For the physicist, the presence of a beautiful corona is not only an indication of the great uniformity of the water drops or the ice needles in the cloud. He or she also concludes from it that the cloud was probably formed fairly recently: it is 'a young cloud'. For swarms of drops show a continual tendency to become of unequal size; those that happen to be a little smaller evaporate the quickest, whereas the larger ones grow the fastest at the expense of the small ones.

When cirrocumulus or altocumulus (fleecy clouds) pass before the moon, you can sometimes see very well how the coronas extend

---

[14] *Hemel en Dampkring*, **44**, 131, 1946.

Fig. 149. Asymmetrical corona near
the boundary of a cloud.

asymmetrically toward the edge of the cloud each time a new one
drifts before the moon—see Fig. 149. The drops are evidently smaller
in the outer parts of these clouds than in the inner parts. It is, indeed, quite obvious that they have already begun to evaporate in
these outer parts.

Although the coronas described arise in clouds, they do appear
from time to time with a clear sky. Beware, however, of confusing
them with phenomena in your eyes—see § 186. It appears that in
quiet areas, particularly when there is a temperature inversion, the
dust particles in the atmosphere float down, so that when many of
them of the same size have come together coronas can occur.

185. Coronas on window panes

If you walk on a winter's evening past well-lit restaurants, you can
often see that the lights are surrounded by colored rings, caused by
moisture on the windows. They are larger on some parts of the window than on others. Often, you will see only the aureole; sometimes,
however, the colored rings are surprisingly beautiful: it is as if some
panes always show better ones than others do. The explanation is
that the coronas are caused by diffraction of the light by the minute
drops of water on the window, and the more equal the drops are in
size, the more lovely the coronas are. It is not unlikely that drops
condense more evenly on some kinds of glass than on others.

These coronas bear a strong resemblance to the cloud coronas. In
the one case, the diffracting drops are on the window, in the other,
they float as particles of a cloud high up in the air. And yet there is
a difference between the coronas on the panes and those in the air:
the source of light of the former is surrounded by a dark field instead
of by a luminous aureole. This is caused by the uniform arrange-

ment of the drops that are formed at equal distances from each other, whereas the drops in a cloud are distributed irregularly. The formation of coronas by misted-up windows is therefore a rather complicated phenomenon: the one or two inner rings arise mainly because of mutual interference of the drops that act as light sources, and are at more or less equal distances from each other. The outer rings, however, are caused by each separate drop and their position is determined by the more or less equal dimension of the droplets.

If you look through a window slantwise, you can see the shape of the corona become first elliptical, then parabolic, and finally even hyperbolic. If the conditions were the same as in the case of the dew-bow (§ 151), you would understand by this that the coronas, as they are delineated on the window pane, are elliptical, and so on; but, seen from my eye, they lie on perfectly conical surfaces round the axis of the eye and lamp and they project themselves as circles. Here, however, the conditions are different. In projection, the coronas have actually become ellipses; they have undergone a further extension in a horizontal direction, evidently because every drop seen in that direction is foreshortened, that is, elliptical. At the same time, this proves that the diffracting particles are not spherical, but hemispherical or segments of a sphere. For that direction in which the projection of the drops is the smallest, the corona will be widest.

On misted windows, the coronas round the reflection of the sun can also be seen; strictly speaking, this phenomenon cannot be seen in the sky, but it differs only very slightly from a real corona.

Sprinkle a thin layer of lycopodium powder (used by chemists to cover pills) on a small piece of glass. Look through the glass at an electric lamp at least 10 m (11 yd) away. You will see it surrounded by magnificent coronas. This powder is the only one that will produce this phenomenon, because the lycopodium spores, which are all of about the same size, behave alike, whereas with irregular particles of matter larger and smaller coronas become confused. If you hold the glass in an inclined position, the coronas undergo no changes in projection, by which they differ from those in a misted window. The field surrounding the source of light is luminous and not dark, which is to be expected from the irregular separations between the lycopodium spores.

If you breathe on a window pane from a distance of 30–60 cm (1–2 ft), and then examine and measure the coronas formed, you will observe that they do not increase in size as the condensed moisture evaporates; this shows that the drops become less convex, but are not reduced in circumference.

Often you will see in misted-up windows coronas of a completely different color order, starting at the light source: dark green – pale green – red – yellow – green – dark purple – brownish – white. This is so if the drops are fairly large, because they then do not act as transparent disks: the passed rays also contribute to the interference phenomenon. These abnormal coronas are, of course, not found in the reflected light.

On windows covered in hoarfrost, you can sometimes see a large corona with a radius of about 8°, which is, however, probably a halo. This is so because it has red inside and blue outside, that is, the ice crystals act as prisms, as we have seen in § 157, but they have a smaller angle of refraction. Often the halo appears double, as if double refraction had occurred!

Watch the coronas in the clouds formed in the air by your own breath on winter days: the brown edge has a radius of 7–9°.

Lovely corona phenomena can be observed above a cup of tea or water at a temperature of 40–65 °C (104–150 °F), when the sun is low. Look at a small angle through the cloud of vapor above the cup, when you will see beautifully colored fragments of vapor, particularly purple or green. You can bring your eye fairly close to the vapor cloud to prevent the colors mixing. In favorable conditions, it is possible to see the colors at angles of up to 60° relative to the source of light.

186. Coronas originating in the eye

Whatever light source you look at: a distant streetlight, the headlights of a car approaching in the distance, or the image of the sun reflected by the bodywork of a car, you will notice that the brightness reduces away from the center of the source and that the aureole consists of thousands of dots of light that form part of a network of fine radial lines. If you move your eyes slightly, the dots begin to wander; if you then keep your eyes fixed again, the dots become still after a few seconds.

This very important phenomenon is caused by diffraction by small grains in the liquid of the eyes. No corona is formed since the grains are of different sizes. The dottiness is the result of the irregular spread of the density of the grains, whose dispersed rays therefore interfere with each other. Recent research seems to indicate that the radial network comes about because the observation is made in white light; if the color (wavelength) changes, the rays are diffracted more or less by the same swarm of grains. Indeed, there is no such network if the light source is a sodium lamp. If you stand so far from such a light that it has become a point source, you will see the dots but no radial lines. If you then get closer to the light, other properties of the lamp begin to play a part, causing each diffraction dot to be stretched to a line parallel with the light source.

A completely different phenomenon is the faint, colored corona that I have seen for years around bright sources of light, but which is now gradually becoming less clear. This corona is seen around all bright sources of light against a dark background, and also around the moon when the sky is clear, and around the blazing sun as it pierces the dense foliage of a tree. The radius of the circle of light is about 6°. It is colored blue inside, red on the outside; it must, therefore, be attributed to diffraction and not to refraction. The resemblance to the coronas in the clouds is striking, but there is a decided difference. If I stand where the moon is just screened off by the corner of a house, a 'cloud corona' remains visible, whereas an 'eye corona' disappears entirely as soon as I screen off the source of light. Evidently, it arises in the eye itself (it is said to be entoptic).

The fact that I can see, sometimes for weeks at a stretch, certain sectors of this corona with extraordinary clarity cannot be explained by diffraction by small particles. Take a piece of paper with a hole of 2 mm ($^{80}/_{1000}$ in) diameter in it and hold it before the pupil of your eye, first in the very center and then more and more toward the edge of the pupil until only two parts of the corona remain. If the hole is to the left or right of the pupil, only the parts below and above the source can be seen; if the hole is below or above the pupil, only the parts to the left and right of the source can be seen. From this we conclude that the corona in question is due to diffraction by radially arranged filaments, since that would explain all the details of the experiment. The use of the small hole is a reliable method for distinguishing this sort of entoptic corona. After all, if the diffracting centers were grains and not filaments, the screening off would only make the corona feebler, but to the same extent along its entire circumference.

There are times when I can hardly see the corona, unless I look upward or sideways, or unless I am tired. At other times I can see it continually.

Experiences of this kind help us to decide with greater accuracy in what part of the eye the corona is formed. It appears at night the moment I look at a streetlight, but disappears in a few seconds. I have noticed that this is connected with the contraction of the pupils when the eye, after its adaptation to the darkness, suddenly encounters a strong light. This is why anyone waking up in the middle of the night and becoming suddenly aware of a light sees a bright corona around it. It seems probable that the corona is formed in the outermost parts of the crystalline lens and therefore disappears immediately the pupil contracts.

In some people, the lens has become clouded and real coronas are formed by the small grains in the eye, all about the same size.

Quite a few observers see smaller coronas whose first bright ring has a radius of only 1°30'. These are caused by diffraction by the nuclei of the cells of the cornea and the membranes enveloping the lens. Here there is no diffraction by individual grains but because of the acting in unison of a large number of equidistant (about 30 μm) grains.

Finally, there are also the slightly larger coronas that seem to grow stronger and clearer when the eye is very carefully exposed to vapors of osmic acid. In these cases, the cells of the cornea protrude like so many lumps, sufficiently uniform in size to cause a corona by diffraction.

187. Green and blue sun

One observer has stated that when he was looking at the sun through a column of steam issuing from the funnel of an engine, the sun appeared bright green during three definite puffs, though all the other puffs had no particular effect at all. I, too, once noticed a similar effect during the departure of a local train. The engine (a fairly old-fashioned one) emitted clouds of steam, which again and again darkened the low-lying sun for a moment as they rose into the air. As one such cloud gradually dispersed and disappeared, there came a moment when the sun could be seen again; its color was sometimes light green, sometimes pale blue and even light green merging into pale blue or vice versa. After a fraction of a second, the light was so fierce and the cloud so thin that nothing more was to be seen.

Phenomena like these occur when the drops of water of which the steam consists are very small, that is, 1–5 μm. It is then no longer correct to describe the way in which they affect the light by imagining the water drops to be replaced by small apertures or opaque disks that diffract the light (cf. § 184). An approximate idea of the phenomena can be obtained by examining the united effect of diffracted light, light reflected on the surface, and directly transmitted light[15].

Green, pale blue, and azure blue colors of the sun and moon have been observed repeatedly to last for hours at a time without the presence of steam and were seen best of all during the years following the eruption of Krakatau in 1883. At that time, tremendous quantities of extremely fine volcanic dust were hurled into the highest layers of the atmosphere; it took years for the dust to settle, by which time it had spread all over the world and caused the most magnificent sunrises and sunsets everywhere. You can imagine the passing dust clouds on certain days to consist of very fine grains all of the same size; this would explain the very striking colors of the sun (cf. § 234). Blue coloration of the sun has been observed during sand storms.

The blue sun of 26–28 September 1951 drew attention over the whole of central and western Europe[16]. The light of the sun was subdued,

---

[15] Van de Hulst, *Light Scattering*, 1957.
[16] W. Gelbke, *Z. Meteorol.*, **5**, 82, 1951. P. Wellmann, *Z. Astrophys.*, **28**, 310, 1951. Wilson, *Mon. Not. R. Astron. Soc.*, **111**, 478, 1951. *Mar. Obs.*, **21**, 167, 1951.

the moon and even the stars were indigo blue, and Bishop's ring was visible. It soon became apparent that the cause lay in the gigantic clouds of fine, oily droplets, not larger than 0.5 μm, probably mixed with soot, that were the result of large forest fires in Alberta, Canada. They had reached Europe in four days, transported on an air current some 5–7 km (3–4 miles) high. Reports from aircraft said that the clouds reached a height of up to 13 km (8 miles).

Under the same group of phenomena can be included an abnormal corona that was once observed in the mist: a vivid yellow-green aureole was encircled by a broad red ring, which in its turn was surrounded by a blue one, while green rings were also present. The explanation lies almost certainly in the smallness of the fogdrops.

188. The glory[17]

If you happen to be on the top of a hill when the sun is low, you can sometimes see your own shadow outlined against a layer of mist, in which case the head of your shadow will be surrounded by a glory that has the same vivid colors as those shown by coronas round the sun and moon. On one occasion, a fivefold glory was observed. Note, however, that although everyone sees his own shadow and also the shadow of those around him if they are near enough to him and if the mist is far enough away, the glory can be seen by each person around his or her own head only!

The glory has been seen by the light of a standard lamppost, but only against a very dark background.

When you are flying above stratocumulus, you may see the shadow of the aircraft silhouetted against the clouds, surrounded by colored rings. Sometimes, these rings expand and then contract again, according to the size of the cloud drops. From the position of the shadow of the plane relative to the glory, it is immediately evident whether you are at the front or toward the tail of the aircraft, since the center of the glory indicates the antisolar point—see Fig. 150.

Often, a much larger, nearly white, fogbow edged by faintly colored borders can be seen around everything—see § 150.

In a rare case, the glory of an aircraft was seen against the background of a desert sandstorm[18].

A good explanation of the glory was not given until the earlier part of this century. Its similarity to a corona made many observers believe that the cloud of water drops reflects the sunlight in some man-

---

[17] Van de Hulst, *J. Opt. Soc. Am.*, **37**, 16, 1947; *Light Scattering*, 1957. Also, Naik and Noshi, *J. Opt. Soc. Am.*, **45**, 733, 1954.

[18] *La Météorologie*, **34**, 171, 1954.

Fig. 150. Glory observed from a position near the tail of the aircraft.

ner into the same direction from which it arrives and that these reflected rays are refracted by other droplets in their path, just as the *direct* rays are in coronas. It is now known that the glory is formed during the back-scattering of the light.

The radius of the glory often changes continually: some parts of the fog appear to be formed by large drops and others by smaller ones. When the fog has just arisen, the glory is very large: it has been calculated that the associated droplets are normally not larger than about 6 μm, whereas their usual size is 15–25 μm.

Often, the glory is surrounded by a fogbow: this is always so when the distance between our eye and the mist is greater than 50 m (55 yd) or so. It is remarkable that the fogbow appears much farther away than the glory: no doubt psychological factors must be at play here.

From the simultaneous observation of the two phenomena, it follows that the glory is formed by water drops and *not* by ice crystals. Of the two ways in which we have seen coronas can be formed, we find only one here. Since we are now certain that a glory is formed by drops of water, it is interesting that the temperature of the layers in which the phenomenon is observed is usually a few degrees below zero. It follows that the water drops in many instances are supercooled.

Although, at first sight, the glory bears a strong resemblance to the corona, there are some typical differences between them. For instance, the first dark ring of a glory is hazier than that of a corona; the outer rings are relatively bright. The most important difference, however, is the strong polarization in a glory, which is readily determined with the aid of a Polaroid.

> And art thou nothing?
> Such thou art, as when
> The woodman, winding westward up the glen
> At wintry dawn, where o'er the sheep-tracks' maze
> The viewless snow-mist weaves a glist'ning haze,
> Sees full before him, gliding without tread,
> An image with a glory around its head.

> The enamoured rustic worships its fair hues,
> Nor knows he makes the shadow, he pursues!

S.T. Coleridge, Constancy to an Ideal Object

189. Iridescent clouds

Those not accustomed to studying the heavens will be surprised to learn that clouds can often show the most glorious and the purest colors, such as green, purple-red, blue ... . These colors are in no way related to twilight phenomena and appear both when the sun is low and when it is high. They are distributed irregularly over the clouds in the form of colored edges, spots, and bands; some observers maintain that they have a 'metallic' luster; what do they mean? Our feelings at the sight of such lovely clouds are of intense delight, which is difficult to describe, but which is certainly caused, to no small extent, by the purity of the colors, their delicate intermingling, and their radiant light. It is difficult to take your eyes off this exquisite sight.

Iridescent clouds like these appear at all seasons of the year, but especially in the autumn. They appear close to the sun, and within distances of 2° from the sun they are mostly dazzlingly white. If you use a piece of dark glass, they can be seen, most frequently of all, from 10° to 30°; purple and red are the colors that occur the most, growing paler as the distance increases. Iridescent clouds have been seen by a few observers at still greater distances (up to 50°) and even near the antisolar point.

The intensity of the light is often so fierce as to be almost intolerable for many observers. Always stand in the shade of a house or a tree, or use one of the protective measures given in § 183.

After staring at the iridescent clouds for a long time, without applying one of these methods, I occasionally found that afterward the colors purple and green danced before my eyes: these are the colors that remain as an afterimage of all such fierce impressions of light (cf. § 107). And, as it happens, these are the most predominant colors of the iridescent clouds, so that I almost wondered whether the whole phenomenon was not a consequence of tired eyes. However, this is most certainly not so, for two different observers see the colors in the same way, which remain visible when the light is tempered in one of the ways indicated above; and, finally, the iridescence is often seen on clouds of comparatively faint luminosity.

Tints in the clouds can nearly always be seen if the clouding of the sky is fragmentary, and are absent only when the sun is very low, or when the sky is absolutely white instead of blue. Three groups may be distinguished.

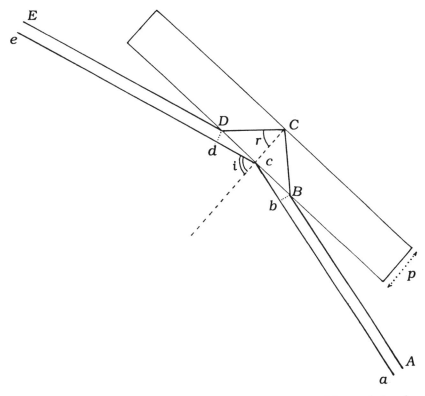

Fig. 151. How colors are thought to arise in iridescent clouds.

1. Those with the loveliest iridescence of all are the brilliant white altostratus clouds, which look almost like cirrus clouds, only they are more flaky and float at a lower level; that they are not very high is seen when the shadows of high cumulus are cast on them at times when the sun 'draws water' or when, at sunset, they are not illuminated for as long as the real cirrus.

2. Cirrocumulus and altocumulus also show lovely iridescent hues; in both these groups, the colors are arranged in stripes, bands, and 'eyes'. Iridescence is seen particularly when the clouds change shape rapidly, shortly before and after a storm.

3. Cumulus, cumulonimbus, and cumulostratus show iridescence only at the edges, but the light there is so blinding that it is hardly possible to observe it without using a black mirror or something of that kind; a cumulus on the point of dissolving as it passes across the sun is a grand sight!

For the rest, the question remains whether the colors in the third group can be considered 'genuinely' iridescent and whether they can be counted as belonging to the same phenomenon as groups 1 and 2.

The arrangement of the colors should give us valuable indications as to the way in which they arise. At first sight, the distribution of the colors seems very irregular, but after a time we begin to discover some kind of law. The distribution of the colors in clouds at some distance from the sun is evidently determined by the structure of the cloud: certain streaks show the same color all over or a purple-red edge is seen round the cloud, and so on. If the clouds are nearer the sun, the main factor is the distance. You will notice, for example, that the clouds begin to show iridescent colors each time they reach a certain part of the sky; or that the colors are arranged in more or less irregular rings around the sun.

We are probably justified in assuming that iridescent clouds are nothing but parts of coronas. Which color appears at a given point depends on the product (cf. § 184)

$$\text{size of the particles} \times \text{angular distance to the sun.}$$

It then becomes quite clear that, when the angular distance is great, the dimensions of the cloud are negligible and that all parts can be considered as being equally far from the sun; the color is then determined by the size of the particles, which can differ noticeably between the edges of a cloud and the center—see § 184. With small angular distance, however, the variation of this factor will play the main part. According to this supposition, iridescent clouds are characterized by drops of uniform size in each definite part of the cloud, but not of the same (uniform) size in all parts. Not everyone agrees with this theory, but, in my opinion, there is no better one.

The iridescent clouds at distances greater than 30° from the sun are very interesting. What is frequently taken for iridescence is often simply a fragment of a halo. But there are certain instances where the observation is indisputable, as I know from my own experience. In such instances, you would have to imagine extremely minute particles (2 µm) or little feathery ice crystals forming a kind of diffraction grating.

A completely different explanation of iridescent clouds has been argued convincingly[19]. Imagine a cloud of ice crystals of thickness p and refractive index n spiralled up by air currents. In only one particular position will they reflect the light of the sun into our eyes. Since one ray is reflected by the front of the disk and another by the back, interference as in soap bubbles arises. In Fig. 151, it is seen that the difference in paths is given by

---

[19] H. Dessens, *Ann. Geophys.*, **5**, 264, 1949.

$$BCD-bcd = 2[(nP/\cos r - P\tan r \sin i)]$$

$$= 2P/\cos r(n-\sin i \sin r)$$

$$= 2Pn(1-\sin^2 r)/\cos r$$

$$= 2Pn\cos r.$$

Iridescent clouds are normally seen close to the sun; the angle i is about 70–80°, the difference in paths is rather more than P. The colors we see are hardly saturated, probably because the path difference corresponds to some 45 times the wavelength: the disks are thus only a few µm thick. The distribution over the cloud is dependent mainly on the various thicknesses of the disks. The reason that so few clouds are iridescent would be explained by the fact that the disks rarely are of equal thickness.

The light of iridescent clouds is not polarized.

Though less frequently than around the sun, iridescent clouds have been observed around the moon, and are then paler in color, evidently because of the very faint luminosity.

Iridescence has on a single occasion been observed on the vapor trail of an aircraft.

190. Mother-of-pearl clouds[20]

These are very rare and remarkable kinds of iridescent cloud, on a much larger scale than the usual forms; whole banks of clouds are sometimes as iridescent as the scales of fishes, and sometimes full of pure tints and lovely colors. They are particularly beautiful just before sunset at distances of 10–20° from the sun. Their salient feature is that they remain visible for as long as two hours after the sun has set, a fact that points to their great height. This was determined to be 22–29 km (13–18 miles), while ordinary clouds are never higher than 12 km (8 miles). When the mother-of-pearl clouds grow dark, they do so fairly suddenly, in about four minutes, the space of time needed for the sun's disk to sink below the horizon, so that it seems very likely that their illumination is caused not by the twilight but directly by the sun.

The arrangement of the colors depends almost entirely on the part of the cloud. Sometimes, these clouds are striped, undulating, cirruslike; at other times, the entire cloud bank is almost one color, with spectral colors along the edges or in oblong horizontal rows, between which the sky can be seen: a strange, opal-colored back-

---

[20] J. Hallett and R.E.J. Lewis, *Weather*, **32**, 56, 1967.

ground. The colors sometimes remain constant, at other times they change gradually; they disappear as soon as the distance from the sun to the cloud exceeds 40°. The whole scene is indescribably lovely and majestic.

The colors are explained by diffraction at very small droplets (about 1 μm), which do not obey elementary theory (see §§ 179 and 187). It is also possible that diffraction is caused by tiny slivers of ice as in irisating clouds.

If the clouds are examined through a Polaroid filter, the colors will be seen to change on rotating the Polaroid. On one occasion, a halo was observed in these mother-of-pearl clouds, which indicates that they probably consist of ice crystals (cf. § 156). They are formed most often just after a depression has passed when the sky is clear. They are usually visible in southern Norway in winter, when a deep depression lies to the north or east, or while a storm is raging over the Atlantic Ocean and a relatively warm, dry wind (föhn) is blowing; for the sky is very clear at such times and the highest layers are observable.

Presumably, the water vapor condenses at great heights owing to the lifting of the air flowing across the Scandinavian mountains. The droplets form around dust particles that float in these air layers (cf. § 222).

An exceptionally lovely development of mother-of-pearl clouds was observed on 19 May 1910, the day when the earth passed through the tail of Halley's comet. It would seem as if there were some connection between these two phenomena: the penetration of cosmic dust into our atmosphere?

191. The heiligenschein on bedewed grass

In the early morning, when the sun is still low and casts your long shadow on the dewy grass, you may perceive a remarkable aureole of uncolored light, lying near and above the shadow of your head, called heiligenschein (holy glory). It is neither an optical illusion nor a contrast phenomenon, for when the shadow falls on a gravel path, you no longer see this aureole of light.

This phenomenon is at its best when the length of the shadow is at least 15 m (yd), and when it falls on short grass or clover, grayish white from the heavy dew. In such circumstances, the heiligenschein is very pronounced. It is less distinct in the middle of the day after a shower, or at night in the light of strong lamps. If there is any doubt about this phenomenon, the best way to make certain is: (i) survey the whole lawn, and note how the light increases near your shadow; (ii) take a few steps: you will see the glow of light go with you, and places where the grass was not particularly bright become illuminated as your shadow approaches; (iii) compare your shadow with those

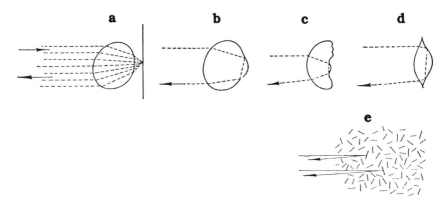

Fig. 152. The forming of the heiligenschein on bedewed grass.

of other people: you will see the heiligenschein surrounding only your own head. This may lead you to philosophize! When Benvenuto Cellini, the famous Italian artist of the sixteenth century, noticed it, he thought that the shimmer of light was a sign of his own genius!

What is the explanation of this curious phenomenon? The dew-drops are certainly essential, for when the dew has evaporated the heiligenschein practically vanishes; it can be brought about once more by sprinkling water on the grass. Drops of water sprinkled on a white sheet or a piece of white paper sparkle clearly when the shadow of your head falls close to them.

Fill a spherical glass flask with water and hold it in the sun's rays; this represents a drop of dew on a large scale. Hold a sheet of paper behind it to represent the blade of grass on which the dewdrop is formed. If you observe this flask from a direction forming only a small angle with the direction of incidence, you will see that it is brightly illuminated, provided the paper is held a short distance away from it, more or less at the focus.

This leads us to assume that each of the dewdrops forms an image of the sun on the blade of grass supporting it, and that rays are emitted from the image along almost the same path as the path of the incident rays, that is, in the general direction of the sun—see Fig. 152a. This would explain why the drops seem to emit light from within, in the same way as the eyes of a cat. It is also a good explanation of why you can see so much light coming from the grass in directions close to that of the antisolar point, and why the intensity of the light diminishes rapidly when you look away from it. But why, then, is this light not green?

There must be other factors at work. If you look at your flask again, you will see that the front of it reflects as well as the back. A simple calculation shows that the brightness of the reflection from the back is about half that of the light re-emitted by the blades, and that of the reflection from the front, about an eighth.

But a much stronger light comes from the neck and the flat base of the flask: light that has undergone total reflection. And in the dewdrops, this is very likely to be the most important factor, since the drops are distorted irregularly (see Fig. 152b, c, d) especially on hairy, white woolly plants, and the light, being totally reflected at various points, is as fierce and white as when it arrived from the sun. This second group of reflected rays shows no decided preference for reflection in the direction of incidence. But the following ingenious observation has been made: only those blades of grass on which the sun's light actually falls re-emit light, and these are naturally unscreened in the direction of the sun by other blades, whereas in most of the other directions there is no clear opening in front of them—see Fig. 152e. This explains why an observer always sees more light when looking more or less in the direction of incidence. This curiously simple principle, put forward by Seeliger and Richarz, has already been applied in astronomy to explain the distribution of light in the rings of Saturn, which are known to be composed of small stones*.

The combination of the different light effects just mentioned appears to be a sufficient explanation of the whiteness, as well as of the direction, of the light of the heiligenschein.

192. The heiligenschein on surfaces without dew

This phenomenon is much more difficult to observe, and the methods described in § 191 will come in very useful. It has been seen on fields of stubble, on short grass and, even on rough soil; I have seen it clearly and unmistakably, when the sun was low, on a well-kept lawn, where all the blades of the grass were upright and of equal length, and still more clearly on clumps of the grass Molinia coerulea.

If the observer is standing at some distance from the lawn, say, a few hundred meters (yards), his shadow is so hazy as to be almost indistinguishable (cf. § 2) and all that strikes you is the heiligenschein itself, as a patch about 2° in diameter (that is, about four times the diameter of the moon), somewhat elongated in the direction toward you.

The explanation is the same as the one given by Winterfeld for the heiligenschein on dewy grass (cf. § 191) and which we may formulate as follows. The sun illuminates most of the stalks through the spaces between the foremost rows; anyone looking more or less in the direction

---

* It is now (1993) thought that the rings of Saturn are composed mainly of particles of water ice, and possibly ice-covered rocky particles—Translator.

of the sun's rays will see all the small illuminated surfaces; if he looks more sideways, he will see many blades in the shade: the average brightness, therefore, is less.

A strong heiligenschein can often be seen on the white chenopodium. This plant is covered with a farinaceous coating of globular cells, which evidently act in the same way as the dewdrops and are very strongly developed on certain varieties of this species.

193. Heiligenschein round the shadow of an airplane or balloon[21]

Whenever you are flying in an aircraft, or enjoying a flight in a balloon, watch the shadow of the plane or of the basket passing over the countryside below. It is surrounded by a light aureole which, at greater heights, transforms into a bright spot of light, about 2° wide. The phenomenon may be seen above all kinds of terrain, even barren ground, but is at its most beautiful above woods in autumn colors. It becomes more pronounced on fields and meadows covered with dew; on cornfields it changes into a vertical pillar of light, parallel to the direction of the stalks of corn. Above stretches of water, however, it becomes faint or reverts to the normal dark shadow.

This is a particularly beautiful form of heiligenschein for, owing to the great distance from the airplane or balloon to the earth, you can see everything beneath you at a very small angle with the incident rays of the sun. If the shadow floats over banks of clouds, there is a chance of seeing a magnificent shadow phenomenon with colored glory rings—see § 188.

---

[21] First observations date from the era of balloon travel. Butler, *J. Opt. Soc. Am.*, **45**, 328, 1955.

(Photo by Veikko Mäkelä)

Chapter 11
Light and Color of the Sky

194. Scattering of light by smoke

Let us begin our observations concerning the scattering of light by taking a walk beside a busy canal or river. Many of the passing boats have oil or petrol engines that emit fine smoke which looks blue against a dark background. If, however, the smoke is seen against the light background of the sky, it does not appear to be blue at all, but yellow. It is clear then that the blueness is not an inherent property of the smoke in the way that the blue of blue glass is, but results from the smoke dispersing the blue rays more than the yellow or red ones.

Against a dark background, the smoke is illuminated by rays from the sun falling on it obliquely from all directions except from behind; these rays are scattered by the smoke in every direction and some of the scattered rays enter our eyes and make the smoke visible. The particles which make up the smoke scatter blue light much more than red or yellow: therefore we see the smoke as blue. On the other hand, when the background is bright, we see the smoke by transmitted light and it appears yellow because the blue in the incident white light has been scattered in all directions, very little can reach our eyes, and only the yellow and red remain to be transmitted and give color to the smoke.

> Years gone by, I used to see something similar to this in Killarney, when on windless days the columns of smoke rose above the roofs of the cottages. The lower part of each column was shown up by a dark background of pines, the top part by the light background of clouds. The former was blue because it was mainly seen through dispersed light, the latter was reddish because it was seen through transmitted light.
>
> J. Tyndall

This same phenomenon of blue in scattered light and of yellow in transmitted light can be seen very clearly in the smoke issuing from the exhaust of diesel engines at the moment when they are being accelerated. Or, again, in the smoke of dry leaves, weeds, and rubbish of bonfires in the autumn, and in the smoke from chimneys when there is a wood fire.

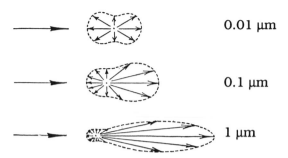

0.01 μm

0.1 μm

1 μm

Fig. 153. Scattering of light in all directions by particles of increasing size.

In all these cases, the smoke consists of extraordinarily tiny drops of tarlike moisture, whereas the combustion of ordinary oil produces much coarser flakes of soot. It is the size of the scattering particles in comparison with the wavelength (λ) of the light (0.0006 mm) that decides the color of the smoke. When the particles are not larger than one-tenth or two-tenths of a wavelength, the scattering is proportional to $1/\lambda^4$, and it therefore increases rapidly toward the violet end of the spectrum; the scattering by such small particles, whatever they may consist of, always shows a beautiful blue-violet light. But with larger particles, this increase of the scattering toward the violet is much less pronounced, and the scattering is then proportional to $1/\lambda^2$. When the particles are very large, the dependence of the scattering on the wavelength is no longer noticeable and the scattered light is white. By 'very large', we mean very large in comparison with the wavelength: for example, 10 μm!

This explains why the smoke of a cigar or cigarette is blue when blown immediately into the air, but becomes white if it has been kept in the mouth first. The particles of smoke in the latter case are covered by a coat of water and become much larger.

The steam of an engine is bluish close to the exhaust opening of the safety valve, and white higher up, owing to the increased condensation and the larger drops. Notice the difference between the smoke and the steam of an engine, in incident as well as in transmitted light, and take care never to confuse them.

We have so far considered scattering in comparatively rarefied clouds of smoke, but in very dense smoke, the phenomena are more complicated, for then the light undergoes repeated scattering from one particle to another. Watch the smoke rising from dry leaves on a bonfire and you will see that the edges of the smoke column are a lovely blue, like that in the smoke of all wood fires, but the parts toward the center, where the smoke is thickest, are almost white. It is easy to prove that the light which reaches our eyes after being scattered by layers of sufficient thickness will always be white, however blue the scattering by each particle may be. This is because all the light falling on the cloud of smoke must ultimately leave it if there is scattering only and no absorption—see § 200.

Our chimney smoke and the smoke from factories is generally black in incident light, however thick and opaque the column of smoke, which shows that the soot flakes not only scatter light, but also strongly absorb it. Thin layers of smoke of this kind make the sky seem brown when you look through them and yet the color of the smoke in scattered light can hardly be called bluish. The brown color must, therefore, be attributed to absorption by the smoke particles. This agrees with the fact that the absorption of carbon increases rapidly from the red to the violet of the spectrum; this characteristic is exemplified in the blood-red color of the sun when seen through the smoke of a house on fire.

195. The blue sky

> Above the clouds the sky is always blue!
>
> H. Drachmann

In unending beauty, the blue sky spans the earth. It is as if this blue were fathomless, as if its very depth were palpable. The variety of its tints is infinite; it changes from day to day, from one point of the sky to the other.

> Something into which you can see, transversely through those parts that are close to you, but which are in reality far away; something that has no surface and into which we can submerge, deeper and deeper, without limit into the depths of space.
>
> Ruskin, *Modern Painters*

What can be the cause of this wonderful blue? Not light emitted by the atmosphere itself, for then it would shine at night, too. Not a source of blue light somewhere behind it, for at night we can see the beauty of the dark background against which the atmosphere is visible to us. It must, therefore, be inherent in the atmosphere itself. And yet it is no ordinary absorption color, since the sun and the moon are by no means blue, but yellow rather. It must then, surely, be a case similar to that of very fine smoke. This leads us to assume that the light of the sky is simply scattered sunlight. We know that the scattering by small particles is greater the nearer we are to the violet end of the spectrum. The color of the sky is, indeed, largely composed of violet (to which our eye is not very sensitive) and further of a fair amount of blue, a little green, and very little yellow and red; the sum of all these colors is sky blue.

What are those particles of matter that scatter light in the atmosphere? In the summer, after a long period of drought, the air is filled with innumerable particles of sand and clay borne by the wind and clouding our view of the distant landscape, and it is at times like these that the sky seems less blue and more whitish. But, after a few heavy showers, when the rain has washed away the dust, the air becomes clear and transparent, the sky a deep and saturated blue. Whenever high cirrus clouds appear, filling the air with ice crystals, the lovely blue disappears and changes into a much whiter color. Therefore, it can be neither the actual grains of dust nor the small particles of water and ice that cause the blue scattering that colors the heavenly vault. The only possibility is that the molecules of air themselves act as scattering centers, very weak ones, certainly, but strong enough to cause a noticeable brightness in a layer many miles deep, and with a decided preference for the violet and the blue rays (the $1/\lambda^4$ law of Rayleigh).

Sunlight, as we see it, lacks the blue and violet rays that the air has scattered. The sun, therefore, takes on a pale yellow hue, which becomes more pronounced the lower it is, for its rays then have to traverse a longer path through the air. This color changes gradually into orange and then into red: the red is peculiar to the setting sun.

When the sky is generally cloudy, the sky no longer appears blue, although the scattering continues undiminished. This is because the illuminating air then has a background that is much brighter and very extensive.

Rayleigh's famous law of scattering for particles smaller than one tenth of the wavelength of light is expressed by

$$s = k\,N(n-1)^2/\lambda^4,$$

where s denotes the scattering per unit volume, N the number of particles per cm^3, and n the refractive index.

196. Aerial perspective

The woods are blue,
Far against the gray ...

J. Reddingius, *Johanneskind*

Distant hills disappearing in a brightening veil of mist. (Photo by Pekka Parviainen)

A distant wood forms an excellent background against which to observe atmospheric scattering, and the more distant it is, the hazier and bluer it seems. The thick layer of air between us and the wood, illuminated laterally by the sun's rays, scatters light that is superimposed on the background, just as the light of a veil covers the object behind it. In this way, the contrasts between the light and dark parts are softened, making the background more uniform and also more blue. Our estimate of the distance of groups of trees is involuntarily influenced by the extent of this aerial perspective. A tree standing 100 m (110 yd) away has a more bluish tint than one close to us. The green of meadows is made blue-green (and afterward blue) by the distance amazingly quickly. Distant hills are often a lovely blue, like that so much used by 16th-century painters, such as van Eyck and Memling, in their background landscapes. Dunes along coasts with their luxuriant vegetation, undulating like waves, crest after crest, farther and farther away, also show these 'blue' horizons beautifully. Owing to this aerial perspective, every tint approaches the same blueness, and merges harmoniously into the others; only the red of houses and the green of meadows quite near to us are conspicuous and break the color harmony. Observe this for yourself in the landscape.

On the other hand, you can try to find complementary changes of color in a bright background. In mountainous country, choose the snowclad mountains; in flat country, look at the rows of cumulus clouds, dazzling white when close by, and becoming gradually yellowish farther back in the landscape.

Yet the scattered blue light on a dark background is much more distinct than the yellow coloring of the bright parts. In the former case, darkness is replaced by a small quantity of light; and in the latter case, there is only a small change in an already considerable brightness; the *relative* difference is much smaller—see § 77.

> The sky was that pure Our Lady blue,
> And over the earth floated high, fat, yellow clouds,
> Lit from above like snow.
>
> Timmermans, *Pallieter*

In 1960, F.W. Went showed convincingly that the peculiar bluish haziness that is so pronounced on warm summer days against a background of dark woods and mountains cannot be explained by dispersing air molecules or the smoke of our cities. He argued that coniferous woods, areas of heathland, and fallen leaves emanate a cloud of organic vapors (terpenes and others), which are partly oxidized by sunlight and ozone and then transformed into macromolecules. These, according to Went, contribute greatly to the distant blue of the landscape[1].

In the wide open spaces of flat countryside, aerial perspective develops in all its glory, and, owing to the constant changes in the degree of moisture, the blue scattering of air molecules and the stronger but grayer light of the hazy sky predominate in turn.

Sometimes, between two showers of rain, a wedge of high pressure passes over us, and the air is very transparent and pure. Shadows and colors in the foreground become distinct and the dark parts of the background change to purplish-blue.

On a hazy day, the foreground is less richly colored, verging more on gray. The undulations in the ground in the middle distance stand out more because the hollows are seen through a thicker curtain of mist than the heights (see, however, § 110).

In beautiful summer weather, when the barometer is high, there are many particles of dust in the air, the sky is very bright but not very blue, so that the contrasts of light and shade are less pronounced, and, moreover, the observer is continually blinded by the brightness of the sky.

Moonlit scenery is at its best when there is absolutely no mistiness, for this makes the light weaker, the contrasts less striking, and the scene is likely to turn into a monotonous gray.

---

[1] *Nature*, **187**, 641, 1960

It is because of aerial perspective that the sailor sees the coast loom blue and ethereal in the distance, a contrast to the darker blue of the waves, whose more powerful shapes develop in the foreground of the scene. The distant land seems to him a place of peace, an enchanted kingdom ...

197. The hand held above the eyes[2]

Where does the habit come from of holding a hand above our eyes when we look at a distant object? The hand shields the eyes from sideways-incident light. Such light would be dispersed in the eye and cause the image of the landscape to be veiled in white light. The shielding becomes even more effective when the fingers are bent to form a funnel and we look through the small aperture at the end of it. It is very odd that this causes a change in the tints of the landscape.

When you look first of all at nearby objects you will notice that all colors are saturated and pleasant: a fir tree becomes greener. When you slightly open the aperture through which you are looking, the colors begin to blanch noticeably. Even a slight widening makes quite a difference, which shows that the dispersion happens primarily at small angles. Saturated colors also make objects easier to distinguish: this explains the habit of putting one's hand above one's eyes.

Now look at the distant landscape. It appears to be covered by a light haze, mostly bluish in hue, which is caused by dispersion in the air and dust particles. It is peculiar that we hardly noticed the haze when we looked at the landscape as a whole. In the mountains we often see a slope as grayish or brownish, covered here and there by a patch of green trees. Looking through the funnel, however, we notice that the entire slope is really blue, as are the trees, although the slope is slightly darker and grayish blue, whereas the trees are greenish blue. It seems as if we are subconsciously trying to remove a homogeneous veil from the whole landscape. Even in flat countryside it is surprising how strong and bluish that veil of air is.

Such experiences are gained when we look at the landscape through windows; as soon as we use a cylinder, we notice how dusty the window panes are, something we had not noticed before.

We can make similar observations from an aircraft. The shadows of clouds, ponds, and lakes appear noticeably bluer when seen through a cylinder than in the general landscape. The entire landscape is covered by a haze, which gets denser near the horizon.

The observations discussed here may be made more precisely and interestingly with the aid of a simple tool that will be described in the next section.

---

[2] M. Minnaert, *Proc. Acad. Amsterdam, B* **56**, 148, 1953.

198. Experiments performed with a nigrometer

A nigrometer is essentially a very simple instrument. It consists of a cardboard cylinder of the kind used for sending drawings by post, 50 cm (20 in) long, with a diameter of, say, 25 mm (1 in), which is provided with a lid at both ends. In one of these lids, a hole is cut with a diameter of 6 mm (¼ in), and in the other lid one of 3 mm (⅛ in). A cap of black paper is then fitted round both ends of the cylinder and the apparatus is ready for use.

When you look through this apparatus, hold the smaller of the two apertures before one eye, which then sees the other aperture illuminated against an almost completely dark background. You can now repeat all the observations described in § 197. The apparatus is, however, particularly suitable for observing the scattering of small quantities of air, because it is so sensitive.

Direct the cylinder toward a window some distance away and you will see the dark window opening look distinctly bluish in color, which is the scattered light of the sunlit air between you and the window opening. Go closer to the window: the nearer you get, the weaker the bluish light becomes, the shorter the scattering column of air. For short distances, it is better to direct the nigrometer toward a box, black inside, with a small opening, which forms an almost perfect 'black body'.

We will now determine what size a column of air must be to scatter to the same extent as the entire depth of the atmosphere. Hold a piece of glass, blackened at the back, in front of half of the aperture, at an angle of 45° with the axis of the cylinder. If you can, choose your direction of observation in such a way that the reflected light comes from a part of the sky about 60° away from the sun—see Fig. 154. Through the uncovered half of the aperture, the dark window opening is visible. Now, how far back must you go to see both halves of the aperture equally strongly illuminated? When the weather is sunny and bright, you will find the required distance to be about 330 meters (350 yards); when it is sunny, but slightly hazy, you may find the distance to be, perhaps, only 130 m (140 yd).

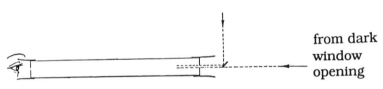

Fig. 154. Measuring atmospheric scattering with the nigrometer.

By the reflection, the piece of glass reduces the light to 5% of its original intensity—see § 63. The amount of scattering by the sky at 60° from the sun is therefore roughly equal to that of a column of air of 20×330 m = 6.6 km (20×350 yd = 4 miles). If we were able to compress the atmosphere so as to make its density over its entire height equal to the density at the earth's surface, its 'equivalent height' would be 8.8 km (5.5 miles). Since the total weight of the atmosphere is 1.033 kg cm^{-2}, and 1 cm^3 of air weighs 0.001 293 g, the 'equivalent height' is 1 033/0.001 293 = 800 000 cm or 8 km (5 miles).

The agreement with our optical determination turns out to be not at all bad! We may consider it proof that the scattering particles, by which the aerial perspective at the earth's surface is caused, are of the same nature as those responsible for the blue color of the sky. The fact that our result, 6.6 km, falls somewhat short of 8 km may be taken to prove that, owing to their higher content of dust, the lower layers of air scatter more strongly than the upper layers. Besides, our computation is in all respects a very rough one: you can hardly expect it to yield more than the right order of magnitude.

199. Measuring the blueness of the sky (the cyanometer)

Mix zinc white and bister with prussian blue or cobalt blue in different proportions. Since these mixtures do not fade, painted on strips of cardboard and numbered they form an excellent means for measuring the color of the sky. The method is particularly suitable when you are traveling, and the composition of the light of the different numbers on the scale can be examined colorimetrically later on. Similar scales (cyanometers) can be bought ready made. Take care when you use them to stand with your back to the sun and let it shine on the scales.

200. Distribution of light over the sky

On a bright day, study the distribution of light over the sky with a cyanometer or nigrometer. Above all, study your surroundings intently. Use a small mirror to compare one part of the sky with another and draw lines of constant brightness (isophotes) and blueness in a diagram like that in Fig. 155. Repeat this for different altitudes of the sun.

According to the physicist C. Dorno, 'In time, the practiced eye sees the course of the isophotes as if they were painted in blue on the background of the sky'.

The theory of light and color distribution in the sky is complex, because each volume of air is lit not only by the sun, but also by the

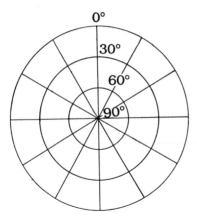

Fig. 155. Diagram for drawing
the lines of constant brightness
and blueness of the sky.

blue sky. Moreover, the exact effect of particles and droplets of water
is difficult to ascertain[3].

The darkest point always lies in the vertical circle through the sun
at a distance of about 95° from the sun when it is low, and at a distance of about 65° when it is high. Through this point passes the
'line of darkness' that divides the sky into two: a bright region surrounding the sun, and another bright region opposite it. The shape
and size of these regions vary according to the altitude of the sun.
This distribution of light may be considered to be caused by the following three phenomena.

1. The brightness increases rapidly close to the sun and even becomes dazzling, its color approaching white more and more (you should
stand in the shadow of a building near the edge of the shadow).

2. At a distance of 90° from the sun, the sky tends to become darkest and bluest, but ...

3. ...there is another effect. The light intensity increases from the
zenith to the horizon, while at the same time the color changes to white.
This effect combines with the two just given.

You can measure the first phenomenon very well with the nigrometer. Cover one half of the field with a piece of blackened glass, which
will reflect that part of the sky close to the sun, and turn the other

---

[3] Chandrasekhar and Albert, *Trans. Am. Philos. Soc.*, **44**, 643, 1954.

half in a direction 40–50° from the sun. By varying the direction a few degrees one way or the other, you can easily find a direction in which both halves of the field are equally bright; the change in brightness produced by such a movement is particularly marked in the half of the field illuminated by the reflection of the bright part of the sky. The fact that such an adjustment is possible leads us to the conclusion that at this point close to the sun the brightness must be at least twenty times stronger than at a distance of 45° from the sun. This exceedingly strong scattering at small angles with the incident light must be ascribed to coarser particles, both dust and drops, floating in the air. This agrees with the fact that the color near the sun is less blue, but whiter and even yellowish like the sun itself, for these large particles scatter all colors to about the same extent—see § 193.

The second effect is a consequence of the law of scattering itself. At an angle of 90°, the scattering must be almost twice as weak as at the antisolar point; moreover, the coarser particles hardly, if at all, scatter the light at such a large angle. What you see is therefore only the saturated deep blue scattered by the molecules of the air themselves.

The third effect arises chiefly from the great thickness of the layer of air between your eye and the horizon. Although every particle of the air scatters the violet and blue rays preferentially, these, in their turn, are weakened most in their long path from the scattering particle to your eye. When there is a very thick stratum of air, these two effects just counteract one another.

Suppose an element of volume at a distance x from your eye scatters the fraction $s\,dx$. This amount of light is weakened by a factor e^{-sx} before reaching your eye. The light received from an infinitely thick layer would therefore consist of the sum of similar contributions arriving from all the elements dx, that is,

$$\int_0^\infty se^{-sx}dx = 1$$

This is evidently independent of s, that is, of the color. The sky close to the horizon must therefore show the same brightness and color as a white screen illuminated by the sun.

It is also quite possible that the layers close to the ground contain more floating particles of dust, which make the scattering of light more intense and color whiter, even when the layer of air cannot be considered to be of infinite thickness.

It has been found[4] that the color of the sky is also influenced by

---

[4] E.O. Hulburt, *J. Opt. Soc. Am.*, **43**, 113, 1953.

ozone, a special form of oxygen, O_3, that occurs in the higher layers of the atmosphere. Ozone has a true blue color, caused by absorption, not by scattering. This faint color of ozone becomes more noticeable when the sun sets. If only scattering were involved, the sky around the zenith would become gray or even yellowish. That the sky at the zenith remains blue at sunset and even afterward is a consequence of ozone absorption.

The darkest parts of the sky are always the most blue and the color there is the most saturated. This means that no clouds occur that have particles smaller than 0.1 μm, for these would increase the light intensity locally but leave the blue unchanged.

Ruskin mentions the blue sky as being the finest example of a uniform gradation of color. He advises us to study a part of the sky after sunset, mirrored in a window pane, or in its natural frame of trees and houses. Try to imagine that you are looking at a painting and admire the evenness and the delicacy of the transitions.

Observe the blue sky through a piece of red glass, large enough to cover both eyes. The zenith looks menacingly dark compared with the horizon; the blue is hardly transmitted through the glass, whereas the whitish color of the horizon is. This also explains why the thin haze of cirrus seen through red glass exhibits such a wonderfully delicate structure.

201. The variability of the color of the blue sky[5]

The color of the blue sky changes daily in proportion to the quantities of dust and waterdrops present in the air; the cyanometer is indispensable for comparisons of this kind. The yardstick is the color of the bluest and darkest parts of the sky—see § 199.

The deepest blue is seen during the temporary clearing up of the weather between two showers of rain, in the wedges of high pressure, when the air is pure, fresh, and polar-continental. Then, the sky becomes gradually whiter toward the sun, which is surrounded by an even, white disk with a diameter of about eight degrees (type A). On the other hand, when an area of low pressure approaches and maritime-tropical air masses bring cloud and murkiness, or in the dust-laden air of summer, the white disk around the sun expands to some 25° (type B). There are all kinds of transition—cf. §§ 200 and 227.

Compare the blue of the sky with the skies of more southern areas during your holidays. Compare the blue of the tropical skies with the blue sky in England or the Midwest of the USA.

---

[5] F. Volz, *Ber. Dtsch. Wett.*, **2**, No. 13, 1954

Compare the blue at different times of the day. The sky is at its bluest during sunrise and sunset, which is readily understood, since a point near the zenith is then 90° from the sun and 90° from the horizon—cf. § 200.

> Above all, lo, the sky so calm, so transparent after the rain, and with wondrous clouds.
>
> Walt Whitman, *Come Up from the Fields Father*

202. When is the color of the distant sky orange and when is it green?

We have seen that when the sky is cloudless, the horizon has the same color as a sheet of white paper illuminated directly by the sun. It is clear, therefore, that toward sunset, when everything is flushed by the sun's warm orange glow, the same color must appear all along the horizon, too.

There are times, however, when the distant horizon becomes orange long before the moment of sunset. A heavy, dark bank of clouds stretches across the whole landscape and there remains, far away near the horizon, only one low patch where the sun is shining—see Fig. 156. At such times, this small portion of the heavens has a surprisingly warm orange color, throwing up the dark, black silhouettes of distant farms, and made all the more impressive by the darkness of the rest of the landscape. It is interesting that Ruskin, without any theoretical bias, noticed this phenomenon in all its essential aspects: 'The horizon may be yellow when the sky is covered with dark clouds, except for one open stretch in the distance from where all the light comes.'

The explanation is as follows. Consider a volume of air at a distance x illuminated by sunlight that has traveled over a path of

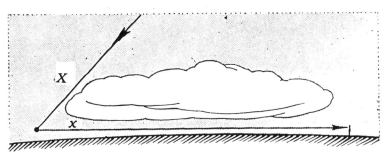

Fig. 156. When a large part of the landscape is covered by a heavy bank of clouds, the horizon sometimes shows a warm orange color.

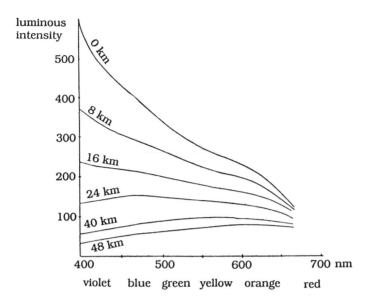

Fig. 157. Composition of light coming from a small volume of air lying at various distances from our eye. For calculating this figure, use was made of the coefficients of scattering that have been observed for the atmosphere as a whole. Strictly speaking, those belonging to its lowest layer should have been used.

length X in the atmosphere. Assuming that a small fraction, s, of light is scattered per kilometer of path traversed, the intensity at x will be proportional to e^{-sX}. The molecules of air at x scatter toward our eye a fraction of the incident light proportional to s, so that, if the intensity at x were unity, the fraction reaching our eye would be se^{-sx}. But the intensity at x is proportional to e^{-sX}; hence, the amount of light actually entering our eye is proportional to $se^{-(X+x)s}$. This expression yields a maximum for moderate values of s, but, for small and large values of s, it becomes practically zero. In other words, light of longer wavelengths is not scattered to a great extent by the air through which it passes; light of shorter wavelengths, on the other hand, is weakened considerably while traveling over the long distance through the atmosphere. The graphs in Fig. 157 show the composition of the light that reaches our eye from volume elements of air for which $X+x$ equals 0, 8, 16, ..., 48 km (0, 5, 10, ..., 30 miles). The color in the light reaching us with maximum intensity moves more and more from blue toward red, according as the illuminated part of the air is farther away from us. When $X+x = 35$ km (22 miles), the color is almost green and at 45 km (30 miles) it has changed into orange.

This also explains the origin of the lovely green seen in the color of the sky at times, for instance, after a fall of snow. It follows from Fig. 157 that in that tint the green predominates only slightly over the other colors, so that the green color will be saturated only slightly, as is in fact observed.

The green and yellow components in the light from the horizon are in reality always there, but, when the air is cloudless, they mix with the blue of the nearer particles to produce white. The exceptional color effects appear as soon as a shadow falls on part of the light path; and whenever different openings occur in the clouds covering the sky, very different shades of color become possible.

203. Color of the sky during eclipses of the sun

A partial eclipse of the sun provides us with an opportunity of seeing how the color of the sky is changed by the shadow of the moon and how the color on the side from which the shadow comes differs from that on the side toward which the shadow moves.

A total eclipse of the sun, occurring, alas, far too seldom, shows much more magnificent colors. The side of the sky from which the shadow approaches is dark purple, as if a thunderstorm were gathering. During totality, the sky in the distance is a warm orange color because the parts of the atmosphere there, being outside the zone of totality, are still illuminated by the rays of the sun and are now seen straight across an unilluminated part of the atmosphere—cf. § 202.

204. Observing polarization

When light falls obliquely on to a sheet of glass or a surface of water and is reflected, something in the reflected rays has changed: their light is polarized. The same thing happens after refraction or in dispersion by small particles (blue sky). Those changes are most easily detected with the aid of two pieces of Polaroid, as used in sunglasses. Even the cheapest Polaroid glasses are good enough for our purpose.

When you hold one piece behind the other and rotate it, you will notice that the field becomes alternately light and dark. Or take one piece and look through it at a steeply sloping (angle of incidence about 60°) piece of, preferably dark, glass—see Fig. 158. Rotate the Polaroid in its own plane and again the field will be alternately light and dark. The explanation of this phenomenon is that the glass reflects primarily the oscillations that are perpendicular to the plane of incidence V; the Polaroid passes the oscillations mainly in one direction. Each time this direction coincides with that of the reflected beam of light, the field becomes brighter; when the two directions are per-

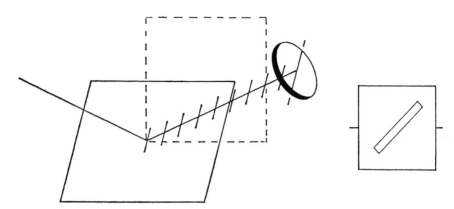

Fig. 158. When the light is reflected obliquely by glass, it becomes polarized. It vibrates predominantly in a direction at right angles to the plane of incidence, which is readily shown with a piece of Polaroid. *At the right:* a simple polariscope made from a strip of cellophane or similar thermoplastic fixed on a piece of Polaroid.

pendicular to one another, the field is dark. Mark the edge of the Polaroid to show which direction of oscillation is passed. Note, however, that it is always easier to find the position in which the Polaroid quenches than that in which it passes optimally (the two directions are, of course, at right angles to one another).

Let us now make a polariscope, for which we need a strip of thin cellophane, cut, for instance, from the wrapping of a packet of cigarettes. Combine the inclined sheet of glass and the Polaroid as in Fig. 158 and quench the light that is passed. Then, insert the strip of cellophane between the two and note that this is doubly refractive, so that it lights up. Leave the Polaroid unchanged, but turn the strip until it is as bright as possible and then glue it on to the Polaroid. The Polaroid and the strip of cellophane now form a very sensitive detector for polarized light. Rotate the combination in its own plane. As soon as the strip becomes darker or brighter than the surrounding Polaroid, you know that the incident light is polarized. When the strip is dark, the direction of oscillation of the light coincides with the marker you made earlier, whereas if the strip is as bright as possible, the incident light oscillates in the direction perpendicular to the marker. Note that the strip must always be at the side of the Polaroid away from you.

205. Polarization of the light from the blue sky

We will now investigate whether the light from the blue sky is polarized. First look in a direction R, about 90° away from the sun, which should be not too high, and turn the Polaroid in its own plane: it will become alternately light and dark. The light from the sky is therefore polarized. The light vibrates at right angles to the plane of incidence, that is, at right angles to the plane sun–R–eye.

Now turn in other directions and conduct the same test; the general rule is normally confirmed. Polarization is strongest at 90° from the sun. Clouds are only slightly polarized, as are mist and haze. It is the tiniest particles, that is, air molecules, that polarize strongest.

It is for this reason that the Polaroid enhances the visibility of distant objects by day, provided it is held such that the scattered light is blocked. White pillars in the distance, lighthouses, seagulls, and so on, become much clearer compared with the background. However, this observation is successful only on bright days, because when there is a mist, the light of the gray sky is not noticeably polarized.

In countries like Canada and the USA, Polaroids are used to detect forest fires, because smoke does not polarize the light and is therefore quite distinct from the background of the sky.

Faintly visible clouds can be made much more distinct when you look at the sky through a Polaroid. Find such a cloud at a southerly or northerly latitude of 20–40°, when the sun is low in the east or west. Turn the Polaroid till the sky grows dark and the cloud does not change. In a similar manner, it is possible to improve the visibility of a faint star at dusk[6].

In some cases, nature herself arranges tests of this kind for us: a surface of water may be used as well as a piece of Polaroid to detect polarization, particularly when the angle of incidence is greater than 50°. When you are surrounded by a smooth surface of water and look around you when the sun is low, provided the angle of incidence remains greater than 50°, the water on the north and south sides should appear noticeably darker than on the east and west sides. My own experience is that this experiment is sometimes a success, but not often; the sky is usually not sufficiently uniform in brightness or the water not sufficiently smooth. More convincing is that, sometimes, small clouds, hardly visible in the air, can be seen more clearly in the reflection in the water in the same way as when they are looked at through a Polaroid.

The proper instrument for examining the polarization of the sky is Savart's polariscope, a simple, yet very sensitive, little apparatus. Unfortunately, however, very few nature-lovers possess one. For

---

[6] *J. Opt. Soc. Am.*, **43**, 177, 1953.

those who are sufficiently interested to make a series of systematic observations, this is a fascinating and many-sided field of meteorological optics[7].

Above the sun and the antisolar point, there are areas of abnormal polarization. Is it possible to detect these with your Polaroid?

206. Haidinger's brush

Many a laboratory physicist is astonished and inclined to disbelieve us when we tell him that we are able to see with our naked eye, unaided by any instrument, that the light from the sky is polarized! It does, however, require a certain amount of practice. If you have a piece of Polaroid, look through it at a white cloud or other evenly illuminated plane, turn the Polaroid and try to recognize that remarkable pattern known as 'Haidinger's brush' (see Fig. 159) from the fact that it, too, has turned. It is also possible to look at the reflection of the sky in a sheet of glass at the angle of polarization (§ 204) to get practice with fully polarized light. After you have observed the reflection of the uniformly blue sky for a minute or two, a kind of marble effect will begin to appear. This is followed shortly by Haidinger's brush,

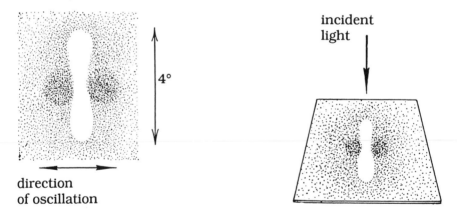

Fig. 159. Haidinger's brush, a remarkable pattern that can be seen in the blue sky and is an indication of the polarization. The light brush is yellowish, the clouds at either side are blue.

---

[7] R.A.R. Tricker, *Introduction to Meteorological Optics*, Elsevier. New York; Mills & Boon, London, 1970.

a yellowish brush with a small blue cloud on either side. The yellow brush lies in the plane of incidence of the light reflected in the glass, in other words, since physics teaches us that the reflected light vibrates mainly at right angles to the plane of incidence, the yellowish brush is always at right angles to the direction of the light vibrations.

It disappears in a few seconds, but if you fix your eyes on a point close to it on the glass surface, you will see it again. The pattern is not easily distinguished from its surroundings and the task consists in learning to pick out this faint contrast from among the unavoidable irregularities of the background. Practice a few times daily for a few minutes at a time. After a day or two, you will be able to distinguish Haidinger's brush fairly easily when you look at the blue sky, although the light emitted by it is only partly polarized. I can see it particularly clearly in the twilight when I stare at the zenith; the whole sky seems to be covered by a network, as it were, and everywhere I look I see this characteristic pattern. It is very pleasing to be able to determine the direction of polarization without an instrument in this way, and even to obtain an estimate of its degree. The yellow brush is generally found to be pointing toward the sun if you extend it as the arc of a great circle, which shows that the scattered light vibrates, in general, perpendicularly to the plane containing the sun, the molecule of air, and the eye.

Haidinger's brush can be seen still more clearly in the reflection of the sky in a spherical mirror when your head screens off the image of the sun (cf. § 15).

In this case, a small region can also be seen near the sun in which the yellow brush does not point in the direction of the sun, but at right angles to it; the boundary between the normal and region of deviation can be seen as a kind of shadow.

Haiginger's brush is caused by the dichroism of the yellow spot of our retina. That all observers apparently do not see this remarkable pattern in the same way no doubt depends on the difference in shape and structure of this yellow spot[8]. For instance, some cannot see the

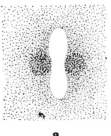 

Fig. 160. We do not always see Haidinger's brush in the same way: in (**a**) yellow is continuous, while in (**b**) blue is.

a   b

[8] Hl. de Vries and A. Spoor, *Physica, Utrecht*, **19**, 419, 1953.

blue part of the pattern; some see the yellow region continuous; others, the blue—see Fig. 160. The following assertions are opposed to one another.

1. Your first impression is that yellow is continuous; when the eye is fatigued from gazing too long at it, the image changes and blue is seen to be continuous.

2. The continuous color is always the one perpendicular to the line joining the eyes. If, therefore, you look at a fixed point of the blue sky and turn your head through 90°, you will see first the one and then the other color to be continuous. The transitory nature of the pattern makes it difficult to form an opinion about this.

Some observers see the typical pattern best by vigorously bending the head alternately to the left and the right.

Haidinger's brush can be seen with much greater clearness if you hold a green or blue glass in front of your eyes, whereas it disappears when a red or yellow glass is used. It is remarkable that it appears about twice as large near the horizon as near the zenith, just like the sun, the moon, and the stars—see § 131.

207. Double refraction in windows

Looking, from the outside, at windows of trains and cars, you often see a wonderful pattern of more or less regular bluish flecks when those windows reflect the blue sky, preferably at right angles to the low sun (Fig. 161a). This effect is more clearly observed when the train has tables with a glass surface (Fig. 161c), which reflect the blue sky from within, while the pattern of flecks is white or light blue. The phenomenon may also be seen when you look through a window at a small angle to the blue sky (Fig. 161b). It is a wonderful sight: the window and the sky are totally clear, but together they produce the pattern.

The explanation for this phenomenon is that the windows are made from safety glass. This type of glass is cooled very rapidly after heating by a number of jets of cold air that are placed in a chessboard pattern, which causes tension in the glass: it becomes double refractive like crystal. Because of this internal tension, this glass does not shatter into sharp splinters during a collision, but rather breaks into a number of lumps that are far less dangerous.

When such a safety window is illuminated by polarized light from the blue sky and we place an analyzer behind it (either a reflecting surface, a, c, or a refracting glass surface, b), we see all double refracting parts portrayed bright or dark, just as when we insert a

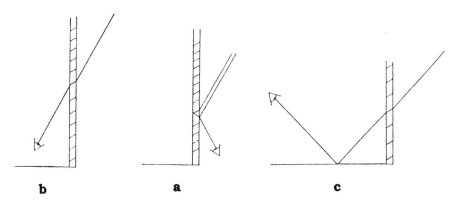

Fig. 161. Observing double refraction in windows in various circumstances.

crystal disk or a strip of cellophane between two crossways or parallel pieces of Polaroid.

The phenomenon is particularly visible when, traveling in a car, you look through the windscreen when you are wearing Polaroid sunglasses; when the sky is blue, you see a very bright, almost disturbing, pattern of bluish flecks.

> Sometimes, when I sit reading by myself in the living room, I let my book rest and look through the open door of the balcony at the graceful drooping branches of the high birches that are already in the shadow of dusk, and at the clear sky, which, if you stare at it intently, suddenly shows a yellowish hazy fleck that disappears quite quickly again.
>
> L.N. Tolstoy, *Childhood*

208. Scattering of light by fog and mist

In meteorology, there is fog when visibility is reduced to below 1 km (1100 yards), mist when visibility is reduced but not below 1 km, and haze when visibility is reduced but not below 2 km.

A thin early morning mist, with the sun shining through it, is delightfully exhilarating and lends a poetic touch to the most prosaic scenery. Fog obstructs the view in the distance, but covers the trees and houses near to us with a haze such as we are accustomed to seeing only on objects far away; at the same time, we are struck by the large angle subtended by them, which in its turn conveys to us the impression of their being extraordinarily high. By the combination of these impressions, which often is quite subconscious, fog

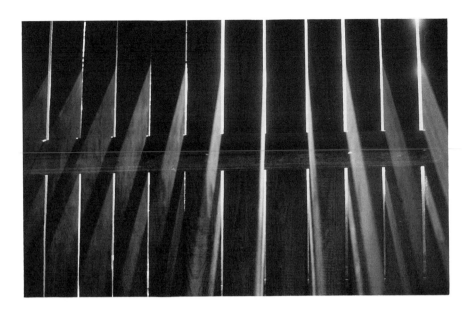

Scattered sunlight in the front room of a sauna. (Photo by Hannu Karttunen)

gives a palatial stateliness to large buildings, and elevates the tops of towers into the clouds.

The colors of objects seen through fog are generally unchanged. The sun, though much less bright, is still white, and there is no noticeable difference in color between the streetlights in the distance and those close by. Yet there are other cases as well, for instance, when the sun, at a considerable height above the horizon, shines red through the fog. Everything depends, of course, on the size of the drops in the mist; the source of light appears reddish when the drops are so small as to approach the wavelength of light and therefore scatter chiefly the blue and violet rays, while the yellow and red rays are scattered to a much smaller degree—see § 194.

> It smothers, stifles; it's smugglers' paradise;
> ...
> Clearing a spot here and there,
> The sun hangs over the gloomy field;
> Red, like an old, worn-out,
> No longer current copper coin.
>
> G. Gezelle, *Fiat Lux*

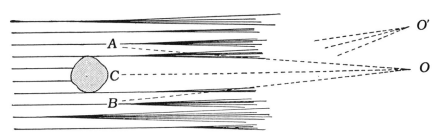

Fig. 162. How shadows arise behind an object in fog.

The fog itself is white at such times, decidedly whiter than the faded orange sun, for it is illuminated by both the scattered and the transmitted rays. Fog like this is not bluish: the scattered light amounts to perhaps 99 percent of the incident light, and is therefore bound to be almost as white as a whole, even though each element of volume may show a preference for scattering blue.

Notice that *fog leaves the silhouettes of objects as sharp as they were.* Everything is covered in a veil of general light, so that contrasts become less marked, but there are no diffuse transitions from light to dark objects.

Comparatively large drops scatter most of the light forward at small angles into the original direction of incidence—see § 194. This explains why a thin mist can be seen so much more clearly roughly in the direction of the sun. The splendid photographs of sunny mist in a wood are taken against the light with the camera pointing a little away from the sun.

The most striking thing about fog is the 'solidity' of shadows—see Fig. 162. On approaching a tree whose trunk is illuminated by the sun, you will see a great deal of light in the directions AO and BO, because in those directions there lie a number of drops of fog that by scattering light make the air appear self-luminous. Along CO, you see much less light because you are looking through air that is not illuminated. If you move your eye a little to one side, as far as O', the light and the dark regions of the fog overlap, and the shadow becomes indistinct; moreover, you will see hardly any light arriving from the directions AO' and BO', because at such fairly large angles the scattering has become negligible.

In this way, a shadow hangs in space behind each branch and behind each post, and you see nothing of these shadows until you are almost in them. Still stranger is this scene at night, when every streetlight and the headlights of every car cause the fog to become luminous and to cast shadows behind every object, which, however, are visible only from behind. A walk through the fog is a real pleasure, optically speaking!

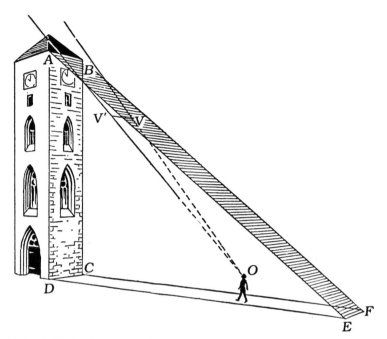

Fig. 163. In fog, a shadow seems to rise above towers that are situated in the direction of the sun.

Especially striking is the shadow that is seen rising in such misty weather above a tower in the direction of the sun or above a post that just covers a streetlight. This wonderful phenomenon is explained when you realize that there is a sheet of air, *ABCDEF*, behind the tower that screens the fog from the sun—see Fig. 163.

Sometimes, you can see the streaks of shadow when looking across them, for instance, when the sun's rays shine obliquely over the roofs of the houses and you look more or less along the line of the shadow, traced faintly in the air.

Backward scattering by fog is far more difficult to observe. The fog must be formed of very fine drops and yet be dense; there must be a dazzling source of light behind us, and a dark background in front of us. Sometimes, you can see your shadow projected on the fog simply by standing before an open window on a foggy night with a strong light behind you. Note that the shadow is not cast on the ground, for it remains even if the lamp is a little lower than your head. Let your eyes grow accustomed to the darkness outside and protect them with your hands from light from the side—see Fig. 164. The shadow of your arms on the fog is very elongated and that of your body conical and huge. All the shadow streaks converge toward the shadow of

Fig. 164. The specter of the Brocken.

your head, which is also the antipoint of the lamp. A glow of light surrounds this point, most noticeably when you move slightly to and fro. This wonderful picture is nothing less than the 'specter of the Brocken', which is so impressive when seen with fog and sun on a high mountain top. The great size of this phenomenon is caused by the shadow not lying in one plane but extending over a depth of perhaps tens of meters (yards).

A cyclist with the glaring headlights of a car shining on him from behind sometimes sees his own shadow in the fog magnified to an enormous size. The light from the lamp of another cyclist, if directed toward the head of the first, produces the same phenomenon.

The glow of light and the shadows traced on it arise from the backward scattering of a small fraction of the light by the drops of fog; all those beams that appear to converge toward the shadow of our eye are, in reality, parallel, or nearly so—cf. §§ 217, 221, and 248.

209. Scattering of light by clouds

It is remarkable how certain kinds of cloud obscure the sharp outline of the sun until only a round mass of light remains that grows fainter toward its periphery. An example is altostratus through which the sun shines as if through frosted glass. On the other hand, some other forms of cloud reduce the brightness of the sun and form a general haziness, but leave the edge of the solar disk sharply outlined.

How to explain the scattering of light in the first case has yet to be investigated. It may be caused by irregular curving of the rays in air layers that are locally warmer or colder, drier or more humid.

210. Visibility of drops of rain and water

During a shower, it is worth while observing in which direction the falling rain is seen most easily. The drops are not visible against the bright sky or against the ground, but they are against houses and trees. Evidently, they can be seen only when they deflect the light from its path and bring brightness where formerly it was dark. Apparently, then, the light rays are deflected chiefly through fairly small angles between 0° and 45°. The more the brightness of the background changes for a given small deflection of the light, the more clearly the drops will be seen. If the sun is shining while it rains, the drops in the vicinity of the sun are seen to sparkle brighter than ever; this is caused by the enormous difference between the brightness of the sun and of the sky, so that every refracting drop is conspicuous.

You can nearly always see them shining like pearls against a dark background; against a light sky, they seldom appear dark. This is an application of the general principle that the eye is sensitive to the

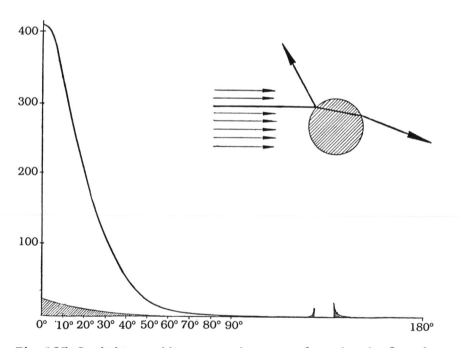

Fig. 165. Sunlight, sparkling in raindrops, is refracted and reflected in every direction. The graph shows the distribution of light at various angles of deflection. The *shaded area* indicates the share of the reflected rays; at 129° and 138°, the secondary rainbow and primary rainbow respectively.

ratio of light intensities, not their difference—see § 77. If light of intensity 100 falls on a drop and the intensity scattered by the drop is 10, it will show up very well against a dark background of intensity 5, since the ratio of intensities is 2:1. On the other hand, the diminution in intensity of the transmitted light from 100 to 90 means that the intensity ratio of the drops seen against the sky is only 10:9, which is scarcely perceptible. But if they are close to us, for instance, large drops off our umbrellas, they look dark as they fall, and during a heavy shower we can see dark parallel streaks against the light background of a gap in the somber rain clouds. Similar phenomena can be observed in fountains and in the jet of water from a fountain.

By applying the ordinary laws of optics, it is easy to calculate the contributions to the resulting distribution of light caused by the rays reflected at the surface of the drop and the rays that have passed through the drops, after refraction, respectively—see Fig. 165. It appears that the latter play by far the larger part and that they do, indeed, cause the light to deviate only through fairly small angles, just as direct observation had led us to conclude.

211. Dispersion of light by a dewy meadow

When you travel by train or car in the early morning sun and look over the heavily dewed fields or meadows alongside the road or track, you will notice that they disperse a remarkable amount of light into the distance, toward the sun. The color of the grass there can hardly be seen, it is much whiter than near to you. It is, of course, the dewdrops that reflect light; in the parts of the field nearest to you, only separate dots of light can be seen here and there, but farther away, there seem to be many more and brighter dots.

The explanation for this is that in the distance the angle between the incident and reflected ray is largest, while the angle of deflection is smallest. It is clear from the previous paragraph that the dispersed light must be strongest there; furthermore, the phenomenon is particularly perceptible when the sun is low.

212. Dispersion of light by steamed-up windows

When you look through the steamed-up windows of a train or car you see streetlights as spots of light, some small, some large, depending on how densely the window is steamed up. It is fairly easy to estimate the radius r of such a spot and determine the distance A to your eyes (Fig. 166). You will find that dispersion stops when angle $\alpha = r/A = 0.05$–0.1 radians, that is, 3–6°.

Note that the dispersing droplets are not little spheres but sphere segments of small height. The rays that enter a droplet near its edge

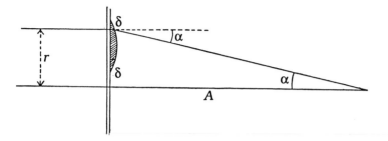

Fig. 166. Refraction of light in water drops on a window pane.

are deflected most. They are refracted as in a prism at an angle $\alpha = (n-1)\delta$, where δ is the angle of refraction and n is the refractive index (1.33). Since $\alpha = 3\text{--}6°$, $\delta = 10\text{--}20°$.

213. Visibility of particles floating in the air

The foregoing description of the visibility of water drops can be applied more or less to everything floating in the air. Clouds of dust are seen much better in the direction toward the sun than away from it. When the weather is sunny, a slight haziness along the horizon, to a height of about 3° above it, can often be seen when you look toward the sun; at a distance of not more than about 1 km (1100 yd), colors in the scenery are no longer clearly distinguishable, and the spires of distant churches cannot be seen. If you look away from the sun, the same haziness along the horizon is seen to be darker. The difference between the light hazy band near the sun and the dark one opposite can be seen particularly clearly when, in an aircraft or climbing a mountain, you reach the top surface of the haze. The point of transition lies about 80° from the sun, where the brightness of the layer is practically equal to that of the sky.

When night begins to fall, the rising moon is colored a deep red, but changes with surprising rapidity into yellow-white.

If, while there is some mist about, you stand in the shadow of a chimney, you can see the sun surrounded by an aureole of light that was not perceptible as long as you were dazzled by the sun's glare. At times, there is a red edge to the aureole. A similar, though feebler, light effect, caused by dust and tiny drops of water, can also be seen even when there is no mist—see § 227.

Swarms of insects resemble dancing sparks of light when they are on the same side of the observer, whereas on the opposite side they are barely visible. The beards on ears of rye waving high in the air shine with a lovely golden purple when seen against the rays of the setting sun. Dry leaves, stones and twigs all shine whenever they are seen toward the sun, but hardly or not at all in the opposite direction.

These observations confirm that light is diffracted only through small angles at the edges of a screen. The same is true of the reflection, refraction, or diffraction by small globes if they are not too small—see §§ 181, 194, and 210. Objects of irregular shape act in much the same way as small screens and spheres of about the same size.

214. Searchlights

The beam of a searchlight provides scope for various interesting observations. Remember first of all that the beam would not be visible at all but for the particles of dust and drops of water in the air that are illuminated by it. The brightness of the beam is therefore a criterion of the purity of the air.

It seems strange that the beam ends as suddenly as it does, even when the sky is very clear and there is no cloud to act as a 'screen'. The explanation is that an observer at O (see Fig. 167) sees light arriving along AO, BO, CO, and so on, from all the points along the beam. But however long the beam, he can never see any point on it in a direction beyond OD parallel to LC. This direction represents the 'end' of the beam for the observer and therefore fixes accurately its direction in space. The fact that he receives an appreciable amount of light from the remote parts of the beam must be attributed to the obliquity with which at those distances his line of vision traverses the beam, and therefore the thick layer of scattering particles along that line; on the other hand, in the direction OA he looks through the illuminated air for a short distance only.

Go and stand close to the beam and compare the light intensity in directions of 45° and 135°. You will find that the forward scattering along $A'O$ is much stronger than the backward scattering along AO. Yet the amount of scattering material in the line of vision is the same

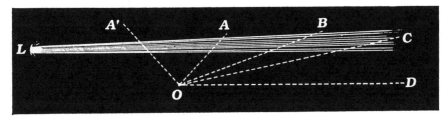

Fig. 167. The track of a beam from a searchlight appears to end suddenly in a very definite direction.

in both cases and we may take it that the diameter of the beam in the direction of A differs so slightly from that of A' that the difference can be safely neglected. Obviously, the explanation is to be found in the unsymmetrical scattering of the dust particles, for these are fairly large and therefore scatter most in a forward direction—see § 194. A more reliable way of carrying out this experiment is to stand near a lighthouse and compare intensities of the beam when it shines obliquely away from you.

A few experiments of this kind can be carried out with the beam of a really good electric torch, provided the night is dark enough. You can even point out to other people some particular star, so clearly defined is the 'end' of the beam.

215. The effect of haze on visibility[9]

A simple test shows how the visibility of distant objects is reduced by haze caused by dispersed light.

Look at a dark object near the horizon through a thin sheet of glass. When you incline the glass, the contrast of the object is reduced considerably. Roughly, this reduction is given by

$$\text{contrast in haze} = \text{normal contrast} \times (1-R),$$

where R is the reflecting power of the glass (see § 63).

Polarization will spoil the quantitative measurement, but qualitatively the test is striking. The test will be even more telling if you use field glasses and cover half of the objective lens with a mirror that reflects the sky into the glasses (see Fig. 168).

216. Visibility[10]

Visibility is measured in a stretch of open country in which a series of well-known landmarks can be chosen at increasing distances from the observer; suitable landmarks are factory chimneys or church spires in far-off villages, of which the distance can be obtained from a good map. Then, each day, determine that point which is only just visible: the distance of that point is defined as the 'visibility'[11]. If the number of points at your disposal is insufficient, estimate the visibility according to your general impression on a scale from 0 to 10. Obviously, the result is an extremely intricate combination

---

[9] J.E. McDonald, *J. Atmos. Sci.*, **19**, 114, 1962.
[10] W.E. Knowles, *Vision through the Atmosphere*, Toronto, 1952.
[11] L. Faitnik, *Z. Meteorol.*, **5**, 1, 1951.

Fig. 168. Imitating haziness of the air.

of several factors, in particular of the drops of water and particles of dust in the air by which a false light is spread over the darker parts. Suppose that an object reflects an amount of light A; the air in front it, an amount B; and the air behind it, an amount C. Moreover, suppose that after being diminished by their passage through the atmosphere, amounts a, b, and c of A, B, and C enter your eye. The visibility of the distant object is then determined by $(a+b)/(b+c)$, which is also the fraction on which the 'visibility', as defined by the distance measured above, depends. This explains why the visibility is not governed by atmospheric conditions only, but also depends to a certain extent on the position of the sun. To reduce the effect of the sun to a minimum, it has been agreed that the landmarks or reference points should preferably be objects seen at an angle of >0.5° and <5° against the background of the sky. It is interesting that, when these requirements are met, the visibility is virtually independent of the sun and of the kind of landmark chosen. Even their color is not important, since distant objects always turn gray before they disappear altogether owing to the haze of scattered light.

The visibility of objects is much less at night than by day, because the threshold for observing brightness ratios is then much higher—see § 79. By the light of the full moon, visibility is about $\frac{1}{5}$ of that by day.

Many observations have been made and their results worked out statistically by innumerable observers. The main factor determining the visibility is undoubtedly the quantity of dust carried by the wind; moisture condenses round the dust nuclei and the drops thus formed scatter the light. From this it is clear that both the amount of dust and the humidity of the air have a great influence.

Well away from cities and factories, large dust particles seem to consist primarily of salt crystals originating from the millions of drops of sea water thrown into the air by surf. Over land areas, they tend to be ammonium sulfate crystals, $(NH_4)SO_4$. Industry emits vast volumes of combustion gases into the atmosphere that contain ammonia, NH_3, as well as sulfur trioxide. These gases combine into crystals or dissolve in the tiniest drops. To these are added soot and other smoke particles. Polar air is particularly devoid of dust and will therefore afford the best visibility.

For visibility over short distances (<1 km), it is important that water vapor condenses round the dust nuclei: the droplets so formed scatter the light. It is understandable, therefore, that, apart from the amount of dust, moisture in the air also has a large influence: the higher the humidity, the poorer the visibility. This influence is particularly important when the humidity rises above 70% and the air particles consist of salt crystals.

In a small town in Scotland, the visibility was found to be 6–9 times greater when the wind blew from the mountains than when it had passed over a densely populated region.

The influence of moisture is evident from the fact that the visibility was four times as great when the psychometric difference was 8° as when it was 2°. You can picture this very clearly for yourself by drawing lines on a map in the direction from which the wind comes, and making the length of the lines proportional to the visibility distance. This should be done for various degrees of humidity. In this way, a set of curves will be obtained that show the average transparency of the air from different sources.

When a mass of air is stationary for a long time, dust gradually sinks down to the lower layers of the air: visibility will then gradually become worse. Rising air currents during windy, sunny weather take dust particles up into the atmosphere and so improve visibility. Rain and snow showers drag dust particles with them and thus clean the air in a different way. Therefore, visibility is generally better in windy weather; in summer (March–October) rather than in winter; in the afternoon rather than during the morning. After a prolonged period of rain or snow, virtually all the dust has been removed from the air: the visibility is then excellent.

All droplets, ice needles, dust and smoke particles, and salt crystals floating in the air are jointly called aerosols.

Study visibility also with the aid of a piece of red glass, particularly when a blue haze covers the distances. Is it true that in that way you can discover details that you did not perceive in white light? Cf. § 200.

It is remarkable that the same quantity of water per cubic meter in the atmosphere can cause different transparencies, depending on the size of the drops. If V is the volume of water present per unit volume of air, and is divided into drops with a diameter d and therefore with a volume of about d^3, the number of drops will be V/d^3 and, since each drop screens off an area of (about) d^2, the whole area, blocked by the drops, will be $Vd^2/d^3 = V/d$. Therefore, the smaller the drops, the less transparent their aggregate. There is a limit to this, however:

when d becomes smaller than the wavelength of the light, the light will diffract around the droplets.

In reality, the quantity of water per cubic meter will depend on the type of rain and each kind of rain has its own size of drops. There are, however, cases in which visibility low to the ground reduces appreciably during a heavy shower, namely when the drops hitting the ground splash up in much smaller ones.

217. How the sun 'draws' water

> And so the two of them walked in the direction of the setting sun,
> The sun that hid behind dark clouds which threatened thunder,
> And, urgently, here and there through the haze, in fiery darts,
> She threw her rays over the landscape.

Goethe, Hermann und Dorothea

When, on a lovely fresh autumn morning, the bright sunshine penetrates the foliage of the trees, you can see how beautifully parallel the pencils of rays seem in the misty air. On drawing nearer, it seems, however, as if they are no longer parallel, but radiate from a single point: the sun.

The same phenomenon on a large scale is also familiar to us. When the sun is hidden behind loose and heavy clouds, and the air is filled with a fine mist, groups of these sunbeams can often be seen darting from the sun through the openings in the clouds, showing a path of light through the mist, thanks to the scattering by the drops of which it is constituted. All these beams are in reality parallel (their extensions pass through the sun, but this is so far away that I am quite justified in saying 'parallel'). Their perspective gives us the impression that they diverge from one point, their 'vanishing point' being the sun, in the same way that railway lines appear to run toward each other in the distance.

Depending on the shifting of the clouds, some of these beams become stronger or weaker, or move from one place to another, and so on. Sometimes, the whole landscape is filled with them; or, again, the sun is hidden by a solitary cloud casting a dark shadow. Shadow beams of this kind are often seen in mountainous regions, cast by ridges and peaks of mountains in front of the low-lying sun.

Light beams can also arise from the moon, but with such feeble intensity that they are only visible when the scattering in the atmosphere is strong. This very rare phenomenon conveys an impression of ominous gloom.

Why are bundles of rays visible only at relatively small distances from the sun, seldom as far as 90°, for instance? Cf. § 208.

218. The sun below the horizon

The table given here is intended as a tool for observing phenomena associated with twilight. The first column gives the true altitude of the sun under the horizon, not taking into account effects caused by the curvature of the earth. On the same line is found how many minutes after sunset this altitude is reached. Strictly speaking, the table is intended for latitudes of about 50°.

declination δ =	−20°	−10°	0°	+10°	+16°	+20°	+24°
	21 Jan	23 Feb	21 Mar	16 Apr	5 May	21 May	21 June
	22 Nov	20 Oct	21 Sep	28 Aug	9 Aug	24 July	
sunset at	17^h07	18^h09	18^h54	19^h38	20^h08	20^h35	21^h03
	16 41	17 37	18 41	19 37	20 17	20 44	

altitude	Time after sunset in minutes						
0°	0	0	0	0	0	0	0
−2°	15	14	14	13	15	16	18
−4°	28	28	26	28	30	33	37
−6°	45	40	39	42	46	50	58
−8°	59	53	52	56	62	69	80
−10°	73	65	66	71	79	89	107
−12°	87	79	87	98	113	113	137
−14°	100	92	92	103	118	137	221
−16°	114	105	106	119	139	171	

219. Twilight colors[12]

To most of us, the ideal sunset is draped in purple golden clouds, glowing with an inner glow of a deep warm color. With childlike delight, we try to find a camel or lion depicted in it, or a flaming palace and a fantastic sea of fire. The physicist, however, tries to begin his observations with the sunset in its simplest form and prefers a perfectly cloudless and bright sky. He studies the fine ranges of color, evanescent, tender tints, transitions from the blue of day into the dark depths of night, which are perceptible only after a certain amount of practice, but return ever and again in more or less the same order, their development forming a grand drama of nature: the drama of the departing sun.

[12] G.V. Rozenberg, *Sumerki*, Moscow, 1963; English translation, New York, 1966.

The sun's rays traced out in hazy air. (Photo by Pekka Parviainen)

What causes this sense of infinite calm emanating from these light phenomena? Compare them with the rainbow, arousing feelings of cheerfulness and joy. This twilight atmosphere is surely caused by the broad arches of interflowing color, lying so flat across the sky as to be almost horizontal. The horizontal line, wherever it may be in the architecture of the landscape, brings rest and peace.

A serious study of the colors of twilight will provide you with information concerning the condition of the highest layers of the atmosphere far above the regions where the clouds are formed, layers of which we know hardly anything, except what we gather from their scattering effect on the light. The best months for beginning this study are October and November. The distinctness of the phenomena varies from day to day, their colors often being robbed of their glory by dust and haze, and more especially by the smoke of our towns. For this reason, the studies should be repeated again and again.

To see the fine twilight colors properly, your eyes must be perfectly rested. However brief your glance may be of the sun before it sets, you will be too dazzled for some time to be able to continue your observations satisfactorily. If you intend to observe the eastern sky, do not look too long at the very bright sky in the west. Each time you have rested your eyes for a moment by going indoors, or by glancing at a book, you will realize how much richer the colors of the twilight phenomena are, and how much farther they reach than you first thought. My advice is, therefore: begin by following the development of the twilight in general and, after that, study the peculiar beauty of each part of the sky.

After sunset the shadow of the earth rises as a dark band above the opposite horizon. The shadow boundary is rarely as sharp as seen from the ground as from the air. (Photo by Marko Pekkola)

Compare different parts of the sky with each other frequently with the aid of a small mirror held at arm's length, in this way projecting on that part of the sky at which you are looking a part from a quite different direction.

You may experience some difficulty in seeing any shape at all in color phenomena merging so completely into one another. Yet the secret is quite simple. You draw imaginary lines of equal brightness or equal hue along the sky; these are the lines mentioned again and again in descriptions, as, for instance, when it is said that twilight phenomena develop usually in the shape of colored arcs

The following is a description of a typical sunset in medium northerly or southerly latitudes on a clear evening—see Fig. 169. The minus sign given with the sun's altitude denotes its depth below the horizon.

Sun's altitude 5°; half an hour before sunset. The color of the sky near the horizon changes into warm yellow or yellow-red, a color entirely different from the usual whitish-blue seen there by day. The horizontal stripes below the sun become faintly visible as a long, yellowish band of color. (By 'stripes' is meant that the lines of equal hue run horizontally, and not that there are sharp boundary lines.) Above them, concentrically around the sun, is a large, very luminous,

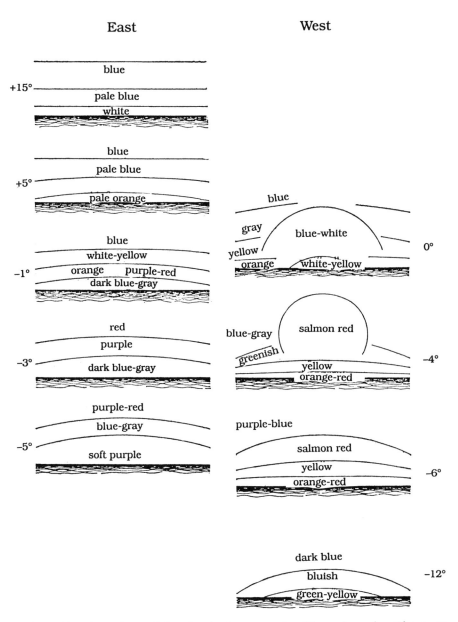

Fig. 169. The colors of the sky during sunset, with a clear sky. The numbers give the height of the sun above and below the horizon.

whitish patch of light, the bright glow, often bordered by a faintly indicated brown ring.

If there are white clouds near the eastern horizon, they assume a soft red hue, and the sky above shows the upper part of the countertwilight, a colored border of 6° to 12° in height, showing transitions to orange, yellow, green, and blue.

Sun's altitude 0°; sunset. Here is where the interesting part begins. In the west: along the horizon lies the color bank of horizontal stripes, the colors from below upward are white-yellow, yellow, and green. Above it stretches the magnificent bright glow, transparent and white, encircled by the brown ring, its height reaching as far as 50°. In the east: the earth's shadow begins to rise almost at the same moment as the sun begins to set. It is a very striking bluish-gray segment, shifting gradually across the purple layer, which, as a rule, cannot be followed farther than about 6° above the horizon. Occasionally, it seems as if a trace of the earth's shadow is visible a long time before the sun begins to set, but this is simply a layer of dust or mist. Above the earth's shadow, the countertwilight is visible in all its glory. Higher, the bright reflection of the light in the west, a widespread diffuse illumination, appears.

Sun's altitude –1° to –2°; 10 minutes after sunset. In the west: the horizontal stripes (from below upward) become brown, orange, and yellow. The bright glow with its brown ring still reaches a height of 40°. In the east: the earth's shadow rises higher and higher, and everything within it is now of a dull, uniform hue, more or less green-blue (a subjective contrast color! Cf. § 114). The countertwilight develops its border of colors, from below upward, violet, crimson, orange, yellow, green. and blue, and above it the bright reflection.

Sun's altitude –2° to –3°; 15 to 20 minutes after sunset. In the west begins the most interesting of all twilight phenomena. At the top of the bright glow of light at about 25° above the horizon, a pink-red spot appears. It gets quickly larger and larger, but, at the same time, its imaginary center slides downward so that it develops into a segment that becomes flatter and flatter. This purple light radiates colors of a wonderful soft transparency, more pink and salmon-colored than true 'purple'. The color of the horizontal stripes has grown more dim. In the east, the earth's shadow is higher still. The upper countertwilight reaches its strongest development. Above it is the bright reflection.

Sun's altitude –3° to –4°; 20 to 30 minutes after sunset. In the west: the bright glow of light is still 5°–10° above the horizon. There is strong development of purple light; the brightest light is 15°–20° above the horizon—its upper limit is at about 40°.

Sun's altitude –4° to –5°; 30 to 35 minutes after sunset. In the west: the strongest development of the purple light. Buildings facing west are flooded with a purple glow; the soil has a warm tint, as have the trunks of trees (birch trees especially). In the heart of the city, in narrow streets from where no western horizon can be seen, the general illumination of the buildings shows clearly that the purple light is shining. Be careful not to gaze at the sky in the west too long and stay as much as possible indoors, only going out occasionally for observations. In the east: in the earth's shadow, a pale meat-red-colored border sometimes appears, the lowest countertwilight; it is caused by the east being illuminated by the purple light instead of by the sun itself. It is seldom seen in moderate, maritime climates. The stars of the first magnitude have become visible.

Sun's altitude –5° to –6°; 35 to 40 minutes after sunset. In the west: the bright glow has disappeared. The purple light begins to fade away, apparently mingling with the horizontal stripes, for these are getting brighter and orange-colored. In the east: the boundary line of the earth's shadow has faded altogether. If there is a lower countertwilight, a second faint earth shadow can be seen at the moment the purple light disappears.

Sun's altitude –6° to –7°; 45 to 60 minutes after sunset. In the west: the purple light disappears, leaving a bluish-white glow, the twilight glow, reaching a height of 15° to 20°. The horizontal stripes become orange, yellow, and greenish in that order. The disappearance of the purple light gives us the impression that the illumination of the landscape is decreasing rapidly; reading becomes difficult, the 'civil twilight' is over.

Sun's altitude –9°. In the west: the twilight glow still reaches 7° to 10°. In the east: the lower countertwilight has vanished; only one last, very feeble reflection remains. The darkest point of the sky is now near the zenith, a little toward the west.

Sun's altitude –12°. In the west: the horizontal stripes are considerably weakened and are now a faded green. The green-blue twilight glow is still 6° high.

Sun's altitude –15°. In the west: the twilight glow is still 3° to 4° high.

Sun's altitude –17°. In the west: the twilight glow has disappeared. Stars of the fifth magnitude are becoming visible. This moment can be determined fairly precisely and changes according to the season of the year and from day to day. The 'astronomical twilight' is over.

Remarks on the purple light. The intensity of the purple light varies very much from one day to the next. The presence of very thin veils of clouds, floating high up in the air, can intensify it to a great extent, and its development is often strikingly beautiful when the weather has cleared up again after several rainy days. It is, on average, stronger in late summer or in the autumn than in spring or early summer. It is polarized to a small extent only, whereas in the surrounding parts of the sky, polarization is particularly strong. The experiment with Haidinger's brush is sufficient to prove this difference—see § 206.

Its development during the course of the twilight is not always as has been outlined. It may arise in one of the following ways: (i) from the brown border encircling the bright glow; (ii) from the bright glow itself, which passes from yellow to pink and purple; (iii) from the countertwilight, which spreads more or less invisibly over the zenith and on reaching the west becomes visible there; (iv) from delicate cirrus clouds, illuminated by the sun after it has set; (v) from a purple patch formed at the top of the bright glow and spreading from there: this is the type described earlier, but it does not occur often.

> I would ask each pupil who wants to develop his sense of colours to reserve each morning a quarter of an hour to observe the sunrise. He will find that this will render his thoughts during the rest of day purer and calmer.
>
> Ruskin, *The Ruskin Art Collection*

> Never, if you can help it, miss seeing the sunset and the dawn.
>
> Ruskin, *The Laws of Fesole*

220. Measurement of twilight phenomena

The earth's shadow is quite easy to measure (see Appendix A). Make a graph in which its height is plotted against time. At first, the earth's shadow rises at about the same rate as the sun sinks, later, twice or even three times as fast[13]. The height above the horizon at which the earth's shadow vanishes gives you an idea of the purity of the air. It is very sensitive to the slightest trace of turbidity: the more particles of dust in the atmosphere, the sooner the shadow becomes invisible.

---

[13] A theoretical explanation of the velocity at which the earth's shadow rises was given by Fensenkov, *Astron. J. (Russia)*, **23**, 171, 1946; **26**, 233, 1949. V. Leftus, *Bull. Astron. Inst. Czech.*, **1**, 102, 1949.

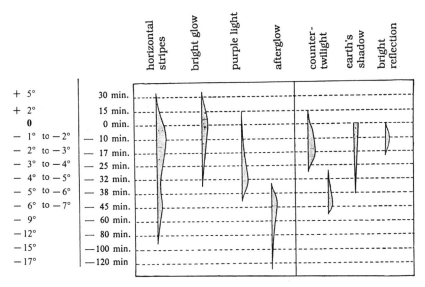

Fig. 170. Concise table showing the development of the different twilight phenomena.

The earth's shadow can be photographed using panchromatic film and a yellow filter; exposure time is about 1 s. The resulting photographs enable a number of interesting measurements and observations to be made.

Measurements of the bright glow and the purple light are more difficult. Apart from its being desirable to rest the eye from time to time, it should be borne in mind that every dark silhouette against the background of the sky is bound to show a contrast effect, and is for this reason to be avoided. It is quite surprising how the line that we had estimated to be the boundary of the purple light can be influenced simply by holding out a pencil or a flat strip of wood. The best method is to compare its height with trees or towers in the landscape.

Measurements in different colors have shown that the general lighting around sunset shows a peak of blueness for some minutes; only afterward does the sky begin to take on a reddish color. It also appears that the purple light does not arise because of an increase in brightness, but rather through a slower decrease in brightness of a certain part of the sky compared with parts around it. In this way, a maximum of relative brightness is produced, and this leads to the visual impression of fresh radiation being developed there.

The modified color must be ascribed to a slower decrease of the intensity of certain wavelengths than that of others.

After the purple light has faded away, the movement of the afterglow becomes interesting. Its topmost boundary is, in reality, the last stage of the earth's shadow, which has passed the zenith and now appears on the western side. It descends rapidly at first, and then more and more slowly.

221. Crepuscular rays

Twilight phenomena are remarkably beautiful when clouds, hidden by the western horizon, spread their strips of shadow over the evening sky like a huge fan. They radiate from the imaginary point below the horizon where the sun is, exactly in the same way as the sunbeams 'drawing water' (§ 217); only this time, the sky is very clear and you can see how the dark beams are outlined especially in the purple light, their blue-green color forming a particularly good contrast, the more so because there is also a subjective color contrast contributed by the eye. The crepuscular rays show how the sky would appear if the purple scattering were absent, and you will notice now, for the first time, exactly how far the purple light extends. They can be observed not only in the west, where the sun is setting, but also, occasionally, in the eastern sky against the purple background of the countertwilight, where they converge toward the antisolar point.

Therefore, whenever crepuscular rays are observed, the eastern sky should be included in the observations. Accurate observation teaches us that the crepuscular rays in the east and in the west correspond exactly in pairs, and are apparently the same rays, which in reality run around the entire celestial vault, but of which the ends are the parts we see best. It is even possible at times to follow these stripes all the way round, like huge arcs converging at their extremities. These familiar stripes we know, however, to be really parallel: their arched shape is caused by optical illusion (§ 128).

Crepuscular rays are visible only where scattering particles float in the air. With the sunbeams 'drawing water', they are outlined against the light mist; with the purple light, against the far finer particles of dust, causing this twilight phenomenon. In twilights without the purple light, the crepuscular rays are absent, and they never appear outlined against the greenish parts of the sky. On the other hand, they can remain visible long after the purple light has melted away into the horizontal stripes; this is, indeed, a proof that the former of these light phenomena is always present, contributing appreciably to the light of the western sky.

Crepuscular rays can more readily be seen near their vanishing point than in directions at right angles to this, in the same way that twilight phenomena in general are more pronounced in the eastern and

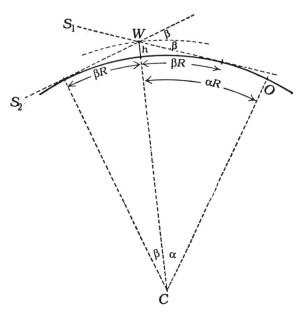

Fig. 171. How to estimate the distance of the clouds causing the crepuscular rays.

western sky than in between. And this, again, follows from the law of scattering (cf. § 208).

We can estimate how far the shadow-casting cloud is from us. If the cloud rested on the earth, it would produce crepuscular rays the moment the rays of the sun became tangential to the earth. Then, if the crepuscular ray became visible the instant the sun is at an angle α below the horizon, we would know that the distance between the cloud and our eye is αR, where R is the radius of the earth. If, however, the cloud were to occupy the position W, at a height h, its distance to the observer, as shown in Fig. 171, could have any value between $R(\alpha-\beta)$ and $R(\alpha+\beta)$, depending on the sun's position in directions between S_1 and S_2. Here, $\cos\beta = R/(R+h)$, or, approximately, $\beta = \sqrt{(2h/R)}$.

Suppose now a crepuscular ray is observed half an hour after sunset, that is, when $\alpha = 4°$. The kinds of cloud that cause this phenomenon can safely be assumed never to be at a greater height than five kilometers (three miles), that is, β can, at the most, be equal to $\sqrt{(2\times3/4000)} = \frac{1}{25}$ rad (roughly), or 2.3°. For this value of β, $\alpha-\beta$ and $\alpha+\beta$ will amount to 1.7° = 0.03 rad and 6.3° = 0.11 rad respectively, and the distance of the cloud can therefore have any value between 190 and 700 km (120 and 450 miles). This result makes it clear why crepuscular rays sometimes are visible when, to all appearances, the sky is perfectly cloudless.

222. The explanation of twilight phenomena (Fig. 172)

Follow in your imagination the course of the sun's rays when it is close to the horizon. They travel a long distance through the atmosphere and their color becomes more and more red as the molecules of air scatter the violet, blue, and green rays. In this way, the setting sun acquires its copper-red color. Once hidden below the horizon, its rays continue to illuminate the layers of air above our heads. The lower layers are the denser and they scatter most, whereas the upper layers become increasingly more rarefied, thus scattering less and less. If you are at O_1 and look upward along O_1A, the layer of air is not very deep and, moreover, the molecules do not scatter much at an angle of 90°. Close to the zenith, therefore, the sky will be dark. Looking along O_1B and O_1C, on the other hand, your eye will receive a considerable amount of scattered light, because your gaze now travels a long way through the illuminated layer. The light arriving from B will be stronger because, apart from the scattering effect of the air, you also receive the rays scattered over small angles by little drops and the coarser particles of dust. Here you find the explanation of the origin of the horizontal bands, of which the direction corresponds with the layerlike grouping of the larger particles. At the same time, this furnishes the explanation of the countertwilight in the direction O_1C and why its color changes from blue through green and yellow into red: because, as you lower your gaze, it travels through layers that are so dense and extended that finally the only light by which they are illuminated is red. Still lower, along O_1D, your gaze meets the earth's shadow, so that you should receive no light at all from D but for the fact that objects lying in that direction are illuminated by a faint diffuse light from all parts of the sky, making all contrasts vanish. After some time, you are at O_2, where you can no longer see the red border of the countertwilight, for you are now looking in a direction making a larger angle with the rays of the sun and your gaze no longer grazes the plane separating the illuminated and the nonillu-

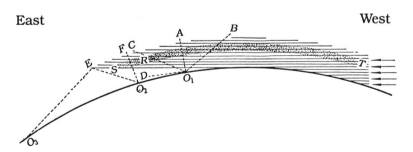

Fig. 172. Explanation of the twilight colors.

minated parts of the air. The amount of light arriving along the ray from E is insufficient, while the steeper ray from F conveys equal amounts of blue, yellow, and red. The boundary of the illuminated part of the atmosphere in this way becomes increasingly indistinct and dull.

Still later, the slope of the illuminated twilight layers has become so much steeper that you no longer see any red coloring in the western sky. Next, imagine being at O_3. The boundary, E, of the illuminated atmosphere, which had at first climbed the eastern sky as the boundary of the earth's shadow, has risen higher and higher and then passed the zenith (without your seeing it do so) to appear again in the western sky; for the direction of your gaze toward E once more makes a small angle with the separating plane between the illuminated and nonilluminated parts. Moreover, the scattering through small angles by the larger particles comes into play again, and the general illumination of the scenery is so much weaker now that you are struck even by a fairly faint brightness. That is why E is found as the upper limit of the twilight glow.

Finally, it remains to explain the purple light, which can only be done on the assumption that there exists a layer ST of extremely fine particles of dust between 10 and 25 km (6 and 15 miles) up in the air where the stratosphere begins[14]. The beam of light by which we see this layer illuminated arrives from the sun when it is already below the horizon. The color of the lower parts of this beam will be an intense red, since these rays have traversed the longer and denser layers of air. The part SR of the layer will therefore contribute the greater part of the purple light. The striking feature here is that the scattering by SR is seen only at O_2 and not at O_1 (where it ought to be visible in the eastern sky). From this, it may be concluded that the scattering particles are considerably larger than the molecules of air and scatter chiefly in a forward direction (cf. § 194); they have dimensions of 0.1–1.0 µm. Whenever in the evening you see the purple light appear, take it as an indication that you have entered the cone of forward scattering of the dust layer.

223. Are there any differences between dawn and dusk?

If any, they are so small that it is not possible to mention any really typical differences. One important thing, however, is that the eye is completely rested in the morning and sees the light intensity increase continuously, so that it is more sensitive to dawn phenomena than to dusk phenomena. The latter have generally a greater richness of color on account of the greater humidity of the air, and be-

---

[14] C. E. Junge, *J. Meteorol.*, **18**, 81, 1961.

cause the air is a little more turbulent and contains more particles of dust than in the morning.

224. 'It is darkest before the dawn'

Many observers believe in the literal truth of this English proverb. Just before day begins to dawn, they feel slightly nervous and some feel that things which they are sure they could see before perfectly well then seem to disappear.

The measurements of the illumination do, indeed, show irregular fluctuations at times, but they are too variable and too small to have any real meaning. The first brightness of dawn possibly disturbs the adaptation of the eye, though it still too feeble and too limited in extent to illuminate the surroundings perceptibly (cf. § 85).

> The mist had not risen to the higher grounds so that for some time they had the advantage of star-light. But this was lost as the stars faded before the approaching day.
>
> Sir Walter Scott, *Waverley*

225. Morning and evening red sky as weather forecasts[15]

> When it is evening, ye say, it will be fair weather for the sky is red.
> And in the morning, it will be foul weather today, for the sky is red and lowring.
> O, ye hypocrites, ye can discern the face of the sky; but can ye not discern the signs of the times?
>
> Matthew

This ancient and universal rule, as modern statistics prove, is in the majority of cases actually fulfilled. Each case has its own individual explanation. The horizontal stripes are red only when the air contains dust or water droplets; in the morning there is not much dust and the red color must then be caused by water. With high pressure and fine weather in the evening, the sky is clear and the purple light visible.

A pale yellow, dull, and drizzling sky in the west when the sun is setting is looked upon as a forerunner of storm and rain.

---

[15] D.J. Schove, *Weather*, **4**, 274, 1949.

The sun sets weeping in the lowly west,
Witnessing storms to come, woe and unrest.

Shakespeare, *Richard II*

226. Disturbances in the normal course of twilight

The twilight phenomena are an extremely fine reagent for testing the purity of the high layers of air. The abnormally colorful sunrises and sunsets in the years 1883–86 were a direct consequence of the presence of finely distributed volcanic ash, ejected high into the air during the eruption of the volcano Krakatau in the Dutch East Indies (now Indonesia) and spread in the course of a few months all over the world. But before that time, and afterward too, small optical disturbances have taken place repeatedly which could usually be traced to volcanic eruptions: 1831, Pantellaria, near Sicily; 1902–04, Mont Pelée, Martinique; 1907–09, Sjadutka, Kamchatka; 1912–14, Katmai, Alaska; and 1963, Agung, Bali[16] *. After every violent eruption of Vesuvius or Etna, we may expect abnormal twilights, though it usually takes more than a week for the finely divided ashes to reach central and northern Europe.

It seems very probable that a strong development of spots and prominences on the sun causes disturbances in the twilight phenomena, because the electrons, ions, and atoms ejected by the sun may be the cause of ionization in our atmosphere.

A third cause of disturbance was discovered when the earth passed through the tail of Halley's Comet on 18 and 19 May 1910. The magnificent twilight phenomena seemed to be an indication that particles of dust from the comet had entered our atmosphere (§ 194). Equally striking phenomena were seen in 1908 when the earth was struck by a huge meteorite landing in the desert wastes of northern Siberia†.

The chief optical phenomena indicating the occurrence of a period of disturbance are given below.

---

[16] After the eruption of Agung, there were innumerable occasions of purple golden skies in central Europe during 1964–65. See *Meteorol. Geophys.*, Berlin, Meteor. Abt., **53**, No. 11, 1965.

* And, among others, 1986, Mt. St. Helens, Washington State, USA, and 1991–92, Mt. Pinatubo, the Phillipines—Translator.

† Known as the Tunguska event; it is now thought that this was (part of) a disintegrating comet rather than a solid body that crashed into the earth—Translator.

1. Bishop's ring. For the whole day, the sun is in the center of a shining, bluish-white disk, encircled by a red-brown ring. The brightest part of the ring has a radius of about 15°. When the sun is very low, this 'Bishop's ring' becomes a kind of triangle with a horizontal base. The fact that cirrus clouds can be seen passing in front of the ring proves that it occurs very high in the atmosphere.

2. A similar copper-red ring with a radius of about 25° can also be seen at times round the antisolar point.

3. The blue of the sky is turbid and whitish; when the sun is low, it is a dull red, owing to the layer of haze it has to shine though. Stars of the sixth and even of the fifth magnitude are no longer visible.

4. Abnormally few halos.

5. Abnormally clear nights.

6. Abnormally strong, fiery, purple light.

7. Second purple light. This is a change in the course of the twilight. When the purple light has declined and the sun is 7° to 8° below the horizon, a faint red-violet glow appears where the purple light had risen, develops in a similar manner, and declines when the sun is 10° to 11° below the horizon[17].

8. Luminous night clouds.

9. The moon has a greenish hue.

Even the uninitiated are struck by the more pronounced of these phenomena. But it requires a great deal of practice to be able to observe the fine distinctions, which prevent the possibility of there ever being two sunsets alike, and which are, at the same time, a very sensitive means of identifying the slightest disturbance in the optical phenomena.

227. The glow of light around the sun

If you stand facing the sun in such a way that the sun itself is screened off by the edge of a roof, you will see a radiance spreading out on all sides round the sun, and diminishing gradually as the dis-

---

[17] *Nature*, **178**, 688, 1956.

tance from the sun increases. As mentioned in § 201, two types of light distribution with many gradations can be distinguished. Some observers speak of a silver-white disk, others of a yellowish-white aureole, of varying and changeable size.

An accurate photometric investigation of the light around the sun has seldom been carried out. In all probability, what appears to be a ring is simply a rather slower decrease of the light intensity, which otherwise diminishes gradually as the distance from the sun increases. This scattered light is no doubt caused by diffraction of the sunlight by particles of dust, drops of water, or grains of ice, all of which scatter mainly through small angles—see § 184. Owing to their being of every size, these aureoles and coronas are superposed on one another, so that we can hardly speak of colors. The varying brightness and distribution of light in this glow are a criterion of the purity of the air, and it is certainly very well worth our while to continue to observe them. They at once betray the occurrence of optical disturbances in the atmosphere and are closely related to the twilight phenomena.

Whenever there are volcanic ashes floating in the air, an indistinct brown-red ring appears as the circumference of the glow of light: 'Bishop's ring' (§ 226).

228. Noctilucent clouds[18]

These are very thin clouds, much higher than all other kinds, but they have also been observed under normal atmospheric conditions. Strangely enough, they have been seen only between latitudes 45° and 60° north, and the same south, especially from the middle of May to the middle of August.

As long as the sun has not yet set, the sky seems perfectly clear. About a quarter of an hour after sunset, noctilucent clouds begin to appear in the shape of either delicate feathers or ribbing or bands; they are clearest of all an hour or more after sunset. They stand out bright against the background of the afterglow (§ 219), whereas ordinary cirrus clouds are dark. It is evident, therefore, that they are still bathed in sunlight, and so must be high in the stratosphere; properly speaking, they do not emit light themselves. Their bluish-white light can be observed for hours, but the later it gets, the smaller the illuminated surface of the layer and the lower it is above the horizon; at midnight, it reaches a minimum, after which it becomes brighter

---

[18] See the overview by B. Zwart, *Hemel en Dampkring*, **65**, 195, 1967, with references. *Scientific American*, **208**, 128, 1963. B. Fogle, *Geophys. Inst. Alaska*, May 1966. B. Fogle and B. Haurwitz, *Space Sci. Rev.*, **6**, 27, 1966.

Noctilucent clouds. (Photo by Pekka Perviainen)

than before. These clouds are seldom seen higher than 10° above the horizon.

Their mysterious silver-white splendor is very imposing. They appear to reflect the sunlight unchanged: the fact that their color appears to be bluish* must therefore be ascribed to the contrast with the orange-yellow twilight border along the horizon. Their light is polarized, with the electric field at right angles to the plane sun–cloud–earth, that is, the same as in the blue sky and in various scattering processes. The polarization increases rapidly with the distance to the sun and can be as high as 50°.

Their height can be determined from observations of the upper limit of the illuminated part, preferably carried out for different positions of the sun below the horizon. In one instance, it was found that the upper limit and the horizon made angles η of 10°, 5°, and 3°, when the sun was at angles α of 12°, 13°, and 14° respectively below the horizon.

Taking the radius of the earth, R, as 6370 km (3960 miles), the height, h, in km of the noctilucent clouds can be calculated from

$$h = (R/2)\{[\cos\eta - \cos(\eta + \alpha)]/\sin(\eta + \alpha)\}^2$$

---

* But see Plate 44. Translator.

$$\approx 800\alpha^2[(2\eta+\alpha)/(\eta+\alpha)]^2,$$

if η and α are small angles, expressed in radians. The height so found must be increased somewhat, because the sun's rays nearly tangential to the earth are not scattered.

A more accurate method is photographing them from two positions: the height so found is normally 75–90 km (45–55 miles). When the height is known, the true size of the ribbing delineated in these clouds can be found; the distance between successive ribbings is variable: on average, it is 10 km (6 miles).

The importance of the noctilucent clouds lies in the fact that they are the only source of information concerning the currents in the uppermost layers of our atmosphere. If no photographs can be taken, the velocity of the clouds can be determined with the aid of a cloud mirror. Normally, they arrive from the northeast at a velocity of 40 m s^{-1} (44 yd s^{-1}). On occasions, velocities of up to 300 m s^{-1} (330 yd s^{-1}) have been measured.

The nature of the scattered particles and their origin was found only in 1962 after rockets had been launched to take samples of the particles. It was discovered that these consist primarily of nickel and iron, that is, they must originate in the dust of meteorites like those particles that enter our atmosphere and thereby vaporize, shown by the light trails in the night sky (falling—or shooting—stars). The size of the largest of these particles is 0.2–1.0 μm; they are enveloped in a coat of ice. Evidently, water vapor is taken up to these great heights by air currents and then deposited on to the particles, which serve as nucleus, at temperatures of 95 °C (203 °F). In summer, the amount of water vapor in the stratosphere is at its highest, while the temperature there is at its lowest.

For photographing these clouds, a camera with a large-aperture lens is necessary. With a lens of f/3, the exposure times were 16 s, 35 s, 72 s, and 122 s, when the sun was 9°, 12°, 14°, and 15°, respectively, below the horizon.

229. Nocturnal twilight and nocturnal light phenomena

By the dark light that descended from the stars ...

Corneille, *Le Cid*

If you wish to study the faintest forms of twilight phenomena, begin at night, and, while your eyes are well rested, observe the first stages of dawn. Choose a moonless night with a cloudless sky in May or August to September, and a spot as far as possible from human habitation.

It will not be easy to break your usual daily routine and begin at midnight with a few hours of observation out of doors. But once this difficulty is overcome, you will be abundantly rewarded by the sight of the magnificent scene unfolded before you. The glory of a starlit sky is beyond the imagination of the ordinary town dweller. The extent to which your eyes are capable of adapting themselves to the dark is quite astonishing, and it is also remarkable how many more stars you will be able to see after waiting for an hour than when you first got outside. You might almost think that the whole sky is luminiferous. This is a suitable time for observing very faint light phenomena, some of which can be seen fairly clearly, while others are more often invisible.

First of all, you will probably see here and there a faint glow low down on the horizon. This is the reflection of the lights from distant towns and villages. It is clearer on some nights than on others, according to the cloudiness, mistiness, or clearness of the sky. These factors can easily be taken into account if the observations are always carried out from the same place.

Right across the sky, like a ribbon, runs the Milky Way, consisting of large and small clouds of light interspersed with dark spaces. Those who have never observed a starlit sky before will be surprised at the brightness of some of its parts.

Sometimes, broad, bright stripes[19] can be seen. These occur particularly in December, and are supposed to be caused by swarms of cosmic dust particles penetrating our atmosphere. It has been found that these float at heights of about 120 km (72 miles). Occasionally, these stripes or bands of irregular light phenomena change completely within about half an hour. Sometimes, the whole sky is covered with such parallel stripes that move very slowly: about 1° per minute, which is evidently caused by their great height. At other times, the only thing that is noticeable is that the border of the earthlight along the horizon is more pronounced than usual.

A few times a year, the Northern Lights (aurora borealis) or, in southern latitudes, the aurora australis, can be seen in latitudes down to 45–50°, at least in years of great sunspot activity. They appear in the sky to the north (or south, as the case may be) as arcs, bundles of rays, and so on; the rays more often than not move very rapidly, increasing and decreasing in length.

All along the zodiac, there is an increased brightness in the sky from the zodiacal light, which becomes remarkably strong close to the sun, and diminishes rapidly toward the antisolar point. It resembles an oblique pyramid of light rising from the horizon, in the

---

[19] C. Hoffmeister, *Ergeb. Exakten Naturwiss.*, **24**, 1, 1951.

spring in the west after sunset, in the autumn in the east before sunrise (cf. § 230)

Independently of all these phenomena, the sky, as a background, possesses a positive brightness: your outstretched hand, the silhouettes of trees and buildings, stand out darkly against it. Fifty percent of this brightness is caused by the millions of invisible weak stars; five percent by the scattering of starlight by the atmosphere of the earth; and the rest by earthlight. The background of the sky becomes clearer as your gaze approaches the horizon, where the earthlight (ionospheric light) forms a band that is brightest at about 15°. This phenomenon is a steady, faint luminescence of the ionosphere, which has been illuminated all day by the sun and slowly reradiates this energy at night. Its spectrum contains highly interesting lines that are radiated at heights of 85–165 km (50–100 miles). Some observers claim that this light is slightly irregular and clouded. The more obliquely you look, the further you gaze through the luminescent layer and the brighter the light. The reason that it gets dimmer again nearer the horizon is attenuation by the air.

Photometry shows that the color is decidedly red, but, since the cones in our eyes cannot perceive this, the night sky looks blue to us.

The brightness of the night sky does not change much from one night to another: only during exceptionally clear nights does it increase to up to four times its normal value, even when there is no moon. Then, you can see the hands on your watch and distinguish large letters. Such exceptions are to be ascribed to strong currents of rarefied gases shot at our atmosphere by the sun.

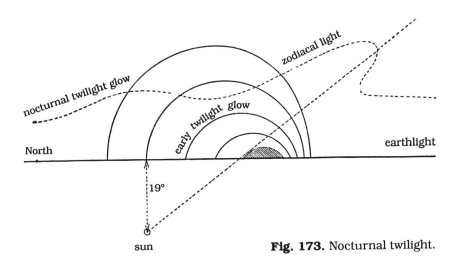

Fig. 173. Nocturnal twilight.

Finally, we turn to the observation of the nocturnal twilight phenomena. Examine the border of earthlight along the north side of the sky. Here, the border rises by about 10° in a gradual slope: the maximum lies somewhere above the point at which the sun, now, of course, invisible, lies below the horizon. This is the nocturnal twilight glow. It can always be recognized by the fact that it invariably moves eastward with the sun as the night advances. Its altitude above the sun is about 40°; in the most favorable circumstances (in Greenland), it is observable to a height of 55° above the sun. It is clear, therefore, that at our latitudes the nights are never completely dark in the summer; the twilight lasts in reality the whole night long. Only in the winter is our sky perfectly dark. You can also understand why the tropical starlit sky is such a dense black, since the sun at those latitudes descends so steeply and so far below the horizon. There are occasions when the nocturnal twilight is abnormally strong.

Two-and-a-half or three hours before sunrise, the twilight glow becomes asymmetrical, rising in the east and descending from there more steeply to assume after a while the shape of a cone of light sloping upward: the *zodiacal light* with its axis having practically the same inclination as the ecliptic (§ 230).

About two-and-a-half hours before sunrise, while the sun is still 20° below the horizon, a very faint bluish light appears at the base of the zodiacal light, a little to the right of the sun. It is observable only with difficulty, and rises slowly upward at the same time, spreading toward the left, that is, toward the sun (see Fig. 173). This is the early twilight glow, which reaches the zenith in half an hour's time. The twilight arcs usually lie vertically above the sun. If the early twilight glow seems to have shifted to the right, it is because its brightness is added to the brightness of the zodiacal light on the right. However, the stronger it becomes, the more it predominates, until it has regained its normal position above the sun. For the rest, it continues to accompany the sun in its daily motion, moving, therefore, slowly more and more toward the right.

The fainter stars (fifth magnitude) have now faded, but the stronger ones are still perceptible: the main features of the countryside can already be discerned. In the western sky, the counterglow has grown very pronounced. The yellow twilight now begins to make its appearance, fading away at the top into a green-blue tint. The twilight proper has begun: the sun's altitude is 17° to 16° (see also § 219).

In other seasons of the year, the course of the phenomena is the same, but the sun's altitude is different. In the middle of June, for instance, the sun descends no farther than 10–15° below the horizon, so that all kinds of phenomenon that occur only when the sun's position is much lower are not seen.

230. The zodiacal light[20]

When the evening twilight has drawn to a close, or when the morning dusk is about to begin, you can see, in some months of the year, the softly radiant zodiacal light rising obliquely in a rounded pyramid. The steeper it rises, the better you can observe it. The most favorable times are in January, February, and March in the evening in the western sky, and in October, November, and December during the evening in the eastern sky (rather less so in the early morning).

In June and July, nothing of it is to be seen in our latitudes (40–60°), because then the sun does not descend far enough below the horizon, and the zodiacal light cannot be distinguished from the lingering twilight phenomena.

To determine its position, we must begin by finding the zodiac itself, that is, the great circle running through the constellations of Aries (the Ram), Taurus (the Bull), Gemini (the Twins), Cancer (the Crab), Leo (the Lion), Virgo (the Virgin), Libra (the Balance or Scales), Scorpio (the Scorpion), Sagittarius (the Archer), Capricornus (the Sea Goat), Aquarius (the Water Bearer), and Pisces (the Fish).

This is the path we 'see' the sun cover in the course of the year. We cannot, of course, see the constellations at the actual moment the sun is in them, but as soon as it has declined and darkness has set in, the remaining part of the zodiac becomes visible. A kind of luminous mist extends along that circle, at its brightest and broadest near the sun, growing narrower as it runs out in both directions. On the one side of the sun is the part of the zodiacal light that we see in the early morning; on the other side, that observed in the evening. During the winter, an experienced observer can see the zodiacal light in the evening as well as in the morning for six consecutive months.

The light itself is faint, of the same order as the Milky Way, but not so 'granular', and milkier. Practice is needed to see it. There must, of course, be no moon, and every light, even in the distance, is a hindrance, while luminous planets, like Venus and Jupiter, can also be troublesome. The vicinity of large towns should always be avoided; the best place from which to observe is an elevated spot with an open view in all directions.

You should begin by drawing on a star chart the outline of the zodiacal light relative to stars that are easily recognized, and afterward to trace lines of equal luminosity. The part in the middle is the brightest; the brightness diminishes gradually toward the top and the edges, but more abruptly on the south than on the north side, so

---

[20] 'Les particules solides dans les astres', Int. Colloq., Liège, 1954. D.E. Blackwell et al., *Astron. Astrophys.*, **5**, 1967.

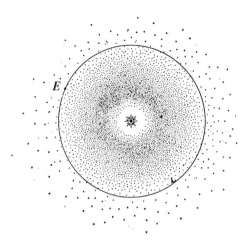

Fig. 174. How the zodiacal light arises.

that the greatest brightness is shifted toward the south relative to the axis of symmetry of the weaker parts. With the aid of this kind of rough drawing, you will be able to estimate the breadth of the light phenomenon, which, measured at right angles to its axis, amounts to about 40°, 20°, and 10° at distances of 30°, 90°, and 150°, respectively, from the sun.

You will be well repaid if you take the trouble to devote a whole night to observing the zodiacal light and admiring the beautiful variations of the changing scene. About two hours after sunset, when the sun's position is –17°, a very faint, wedge-shaped cone of light becomes visible, rising obliquely, toward the southwest. When the sun's position is –20°, the sky has become so much darker that an enormous pyramid of light is observable. This western zodiacal light becomes, in the course of the night, more upright and spreads wider and wider; its position relative to the stars remains on the whole the same. A slight shifting is just perceptible, the stars that were a little to the south shift their positions later on more to the north of the zodiacal light. The best time for observing this curious phenomenon is in the first half of winter.

Gradually, the western zodiacal light begins to decline and the eastern zodiacal light appears in the east. It is now nearly midnight, the best time for finding the famous gegenschein or 'counterglow', one of the most difficult phenomena to observe, which you can hope to see only on clear winter nights, when the sky is very dark. At the antisolar point (see § 141) that is, almost in the south, an extremely faint bridge of light is observed, connecting the tops of the eastern and western zodiacal lights. Later on in the course of the night, the eastern zodiacal light can be seen moving with the stars, but at the same time shifting slightly; the stars seem to move from the north to the south side of the pyramid. Once more it is as if the zodiacal light accompanies the daily rotation of the sky, but falls behind very slightly relative to the stars.

Day approaches; when the sun's position is $-20°$ or $-19°$, it seems as if the base of the pyramid of the east zodiacal light has become broader and brighter. When it reaches $-19°$ to $-17°$, the early twilight glow appears—see Fig. 173.

The zodiacal light arises from the tremendous disk or ring of cosmic dust surrounding the sun and scattering its light—see Fig. 174. How the density of the dust in that lens is distributed and how far past the orbit of the earth, E, it stretches is not accurately known, but investigations are being carried out with the aid of space probes. Close to the sun, there is an empty space, where, owing to the great heat, dust cannot exist. The brightness of the cloud of dust can be seen to increase gradually the more our line of sight approaches the sun. The distribution of the light cannot be observed accurately because neighboring parts of the sky are illuminated at the same time by the nocturnal twilight (see § 229), which can be regarded as the very faint light scattered by the highest layers of the atmosphere, and as such constitutes the last stage of the evening twilight. It is possible that to this must be added the emission of self-generated light when these strongly ionized atmospheric layers come within the shadow of the earth and the ions are able to recombine. The brightness of this light also increases nearer the sun, but this increase is much quicker than that of the cosmic constituent of the light; its lines of constant brightness span the sun like arches, as do all real twilight phenomena; the zodiac has no effect on them—see Fig. 173.

The combination of these phenomena forms the typical light pyramid of the zodiacal light, and from the changing position of the horizon and zodiac you can understand why this light phenomenon shifts to a certain extent in the course of the night and of the year, although the shift also depends on the geographical position of the place of observation. To this must also be added the glow known as 'earthlight', which shows its maximum light intensity at about $15°$ above the horizon. Finally, there is the extinction of light by the atmosphere of the earth, which causes the glow near the horizon to be weakened increasingly.

It is seen, therefore, that twilight phenomena prevent us seeing the zodiacal light closer to the sun than $30°$. The farther from the sun, the less hindrance these phenomena cause, but, of course, also the weaker the zodiacal light gets, partly because of the dependence of the scattering on the angle and partly because of the increasing rarefaction of the cloud. In the gegenschein you can see the light scattered back at $180°$ by the outer parts of the cloud of dust.

It has been maintained that the zodiacal light grows periodically brighter and weaker every two or three minutes and that these changes coincide with disturbances of the magnetic compass needle. It is also said that the light is particularly strong during magnetic storms. Before accepting these observations, you would do well to determine their reality by letting at least two persons carry out observations simultaneously and independently, and also to make quite sure that they are not caused by veils of clouds, shadows of clouds, or polar light.

There seems to be such a thing as lunar zodiacal light, too, which appears just before the moon rises and after it has set. However, this light is at least as difficult to observe as the gegenschein.

231. Eclipses of the moon and dust in the atmosphere[21]

Eclipses of the moon are caused by the shadow of the earth falling upon the moon. Wouldn't it be worth while seeing what this shadow looks like? Viewing it in this way, a lunar eclipse is really a means of learning something about our own earth.

No two lunar eclipses look the same. It very seldom occurs that the moon is so completely eclipsed as not to be visible at all in the night sky. The coloring in the center of the shadow is generally a faded copper red, surrounded by a grayish edge.

These colors, and the way they change, lead us to suppose that we are not dealing with an ordinary shadow. Indeed, closer investigation shows that it is quite impossible for the shadow of the earth's globe to cause an eclipse of the moon, because the curvature of the rays in our atmosphere makes the rays bend more or less round the earth! This curvature causes the attenuation of the light at the gray edge. The central shadow of the earth is illuminated faintly by the beam of light that has traversed the lower layers of the atmosphere up to a height of about eight kilometers (five miles) and has become dark red in color on the way. This takes place in the same way as the change in color of the sun's rays that reach us during twilight through a dense atmospheric layer; however, the color is even duller owing to the fact that the distance traveled by the rays of light is now twice as long. The color of the central parts of the shadow of the earth is therefore an indication of the degree of transparency of our atmosphere. It is not a mere coincidence that the moon, when eclipsed, should seem extremely dark at times when our atmosphere contains great quantities of dust from volcanic eruptions. The lunar eclipses are

---

[21] F. Link, *Die Mondfinsternisse*, Leipzig, 1956. General overview by F. Link in *Physics and Astronomy of the Moon*, ed. by Z. Kopal, New York, London, 1961.

also, on average, darker when the moon is in the northern part of the shadow of the earth than when in the southern part, so that there is evidently more volcanic and desert dust in our northern than in our southern hemisphere. In winter, these eclipses are clearer; in spring, darker. But they are also darker or grayer, or clearer and more orange, depending on the phase of the sunspot cycle. This would be associated with the changes in ultraviolet radiation and the streams of ions, emanating from the sun's corona, that can reach the moon also during an eclipse and so make its surface fluoresce and light up.

A simple way of indicating the brightness of a lunar eclipse is dividing it into the following classes:

0	very dark, moon almost invisible;
1	dark, gray, hardly any details visible;
2	dark red, border edge fairly bright;
3	brick red, bright or yellowish border edge;
4	orange-red, border edge bluish.

A systematic comparison of notes made on these lines over a number of years will provide material for numerous remarkable conclusions.

232. The ash-gray light[22]

When the moon is almost new, or has just been new, you can see at the side of her slender crescent the rest of the moon's surface, faintly illuminated—see Fig. 92. This ash-gray light comes from the earth, which shines like a large, bright source of light on to the moon. The remarkable thing is that the ash-gray light is not always equally strong. At times, it is almost invisible; at others, almost milk white and so bright that the darker spots usually visible on the moon's surface can be distinguished. The changes in the strength of the ash-gray light are attributed to the fact that the half of the earth facing the moon contains at times many oceans, and at other times many continents, and is at times more clouded, and at other times clearer. In this way, a glance at the ash-gray light will give you a comprehensive impression of the conditions on one hemisphere of the earth. But here, also, the influence of the solar activity is noticeable.

Estimate the strength of the ash-gray light on a scale from 1 to 10 on a number of days (1 = invisible; 5 = fairly visible; 10 = exceptionally bright). You will very soon notice that the visibility is highly dependent on the phases of the moon, because its bright crescent blinds

---

[22] F. Link, *Die Mondfinsternisse*, Leipzig, 1956, p. 221.

you as it gets broader. A comparison of the visibility of the ash-gray light on various days, therefore, has meaning only when it is made for equal phases. On the other hand, the moon's height above the horizon appears to influence the visibility only to a very slight degree.

233. Unidentified flying objects (UFOs)[23]

In 1947, an American businessman flying over the Rocky Mountains noticed a row of peculiar planes that seemed to move at an incredible speed and which he compared with 'flying saucers'. His story caught the public eye and soon there were hundreds of such sightings every year, not only in the United States, but also in Europe and other parts of the world. Normally, what is seen are spots of light moving in irregular orbits that sometimes come to a standstill before assuming great speeds again. At the time some people even claimed to have contacted these travelers from Mars.

Long before 1947 there were reports of such sightings, particularly in 1882 and 1897, although 1863, 1894, 1896, and 1908 also had their 'flying saucers'. They are also reported in ancient times, in the middle ages and in the Bible.

Interest in these stories has long since waned*, since analysis has shown that the vast majority of the sightings are explained simply by one of the following.

1. The planet Venus when very bright or another low, bright star; its apparent movement is caused by scintillation (see §120).

2. A bright meteor or bolide (fireball): its trail may show irregular distortions. A comet. A mock moon, which may be seen quite often. The moon behind a veil of cloud.

3. One of the thousands of balloons released by meteorological services all over the world.

4. A normal aircraft, seen in unusual light.

5. Halo phenomena, particularly a mock sun or sub-sun.

6. A mirage.

---

[23] D.H. Menzel, *Flying Saucers*, Cambridge, 1953. D.H. Menzel and L.G. Boyd, *The World of Flying Saucers*, New York, 1963.
* Although since Minnaert wrote this, it seems to be on the increase again—Translator.

Many rare atmospheric phenomena have been thought to be UFOs, for example, the almond clouds seen here. (Photo by Kalervo Kuronen)

7. Banks of mist or cloud seen in unusual light.

8. A variety of things, too many to mention, but including a parachute, a kite, a cobweb, an afterimage in the eye, and polar light.

9. Intentional deceit or a joke.

Never believe that photographs are proof; the most wonderful effects may be obtained on film by bad focusing, air haze, reflections in the lens, movement of the camera, errors during developing and printing, and so on.

It is interesting and telling that not one sighting has ever been reported by an astronomical observatory.

Chapter 12

Light and Color in the Landscape

234. The colors of the sun, moon, and stars

It is difficult to judge the color of the sun, owing to its dazzling brightness. Personally, however, I would say that it is decidedly yellow and this, combined with the light from the blue sky, forms the mixture that we call 'white', the color of a sheet of paper when the sun is shining and the sky is clear. Estimates of this kind give rise to difficulties, owing to a certain vagueness in the notion 'white'. Generally speaking, we are inclined to call the predominating color in our surroundings white or nearly white—cf. § 114.

On a cloudy or misty day, the rays from sun and sky are already intermingled owing to innumerable reflections and refractions by drops of water, and the color of the sky is therefore a compound white. If we consider that the blue light from the sky is in reality scattered light that was first contained in the light from the sun, we must conclude that the sun, seen outside the atmosphere, would also be almost white.

We know already that the orange or red colors of the setting sun are accounted for by the rapidly increasing length of the path traversed by its rays before they reach our eye; gradually, the more refrangible rays become almost completely scattered and only the dark red ones remain—see §§ 47 and 195.

In a few rare cases, the sun, when high, shines copper red through mist, that is, when the mistdrops are very small and therefore scatter the shorter waves preferentially—see § 208.

In other cases, it is bluish and this is said to occur most commonly when the clouds have an orange-colored edge. It is possible that color contrasts play a part here or that inexperienced observers confuse the colors of clouds in the immediate neighborhood of the sun with the color of the sun's disk itself. Entirely different is the phenomenon of the blue sun when seen through a dense cloud consisting of drops very uniform in size—see §187.

The moon by day is a striking pure white, because then the intense blue scattered by the sky is added to the moon's own yellowish light. Also, when it rises and sets by day it is practically colorless, dull and only slightly yellowish. It grows gradually a deeper yellow as the sun sets and the blue light of the sky disappears; at a certain moment it becomes a beautiful pure yellow, though the color probably seems stronger to us because of the psychological contrast with the still faintly blue background. As twilight draws to its close, the color returns to yellow-white; very likely because the surroundings become darker, so that the moonlight appears very bright to us and so, owing to a curious peculiarity of our eye, tends to white like all other very bright sources of light—see § 93.

The moon remains for the rest of the night a light yellowish color, exactly like the sun by day. The color becomes most nearly white on very clear winter nights when the moon is very high; but near the horizon, it shows the same orange and red colors as the setting sun; that the impression made on our eye by the colors of the moon is rather different is caused by the much lower intensity of the light.

The full moon in the middle of the blue earth shadow has a lovely bronze-yellow color, no doubt caused by complementary contrast with its surroundings. When encircled by small clouds of a vivid purple-red, its tint becomes almost green-yellow; if these clouds become salmon pink, it changes almost to blue-green. These contrast colors are still clearer in the moon's crescent than in the full moon.

The planet Venus, seen against the purple twilight sky, can also appear emerald green[1].

Not to be confused with the color of the moon is the color of the landscape by moonlight, which is commonly considered to be blue or green-blue. The rods in our eye that at night assume the function of seeing appear to cause a peculiar impression of gray-blue, 'rod blue'. This effect is amplified greatly by the contrast with our orange-colored artificial light, which makes the blue of the sky, illuminated by the moon, all the more striking.

To obtain a preliminary idea of the differences in color shown by the stars, look closely at the large square of the constellation Orion. You will notice that the color of Betelgeuse, the bright star α at the top to the left, is a striking yellow, or even orange, compared with the three other stars—see Fig. 72. Close to this constellation you can see another orange-colored star, Aldebaran, in the Bull.

The next important thing is not to be satisfied with this first and very easy distinction of color, but to try to trace finer differences of tint. This is a severe test for our sense of color, but a great deal can be done by practice. Since the differences in the colors of the stars are caused by their different temperatures, you will understand their showing the same succession of colors as a glowing body cooling down gradually, that is, from white, via yellow and orange, to red. It has not been definitely settled whether the hottest stars should be described as blue or as white, since different observers are not of the same opinion as to what 'white' really is. Some are influenced more

---

[1] B.N. Himmelfarb, *Priroda*, **8**, 1964, p. 80.

than others by the faintly illuminated background of the sky, which seems bluish to us and which we are accustomed to considering colorless simply because it is the average color of the scenery at night.

The following scale gives an idea of the different colors occurring among the stars, together with the numbers by which they are usually denoted and a few examples. Color estimates made independently by skilled observers often turn out to be a whole class above or below the average given. The estimates in the examples given here were made by observers who did not see blue as such and therefore gave no stars negative values.

-2	blue	2	whitish-yellow	6	orange-yellow
-1	bluish-white	3	primrose yellow	7	orange
0	white	4	pure yellow	8	yellowish-red
1	yellowish-white	5	deep yellow	9	red

Sirius = α CMa	0.8	Kochab = β UMi	5.8
Vega = α Lyr	0.8	Arcturus = α Boö	4.5
Regulus = α Leo	2.1	Antares = α Sco	7.5
Procyon = α CMi	2.4	Venus	3.5
Altair = α Aql	2.6	Mars	7.6
Dubhe = α UMa	4.9	Jupiter	3.6
Merak = β UMa	2.3	Saturn	4.8
Polaris = α YMι	3.8		

The stars, too, naturally become more reddish the nearer they approach the horizon, but their scintillation then usually prevents us from judging their color correctly. It is a remarkable fact that on earth we designate a glowing body at 2500 °C as white hot, whereas a star of the same temperature appears to us orange-red! It is probable that this physiological phenomenon must be ascribed to the star being so much less bright, so that the red component of the light impression on the eye is perceptible, whereas the green and blue components fall short of their threshold values. Another explanation can be found in § 93.

235. The color of the clouds

It is a pleasure to watch the beautiful summery cumulus clouds drifting past and to try to account for the fact that certain parts are light and others dark. Where the sun illuminates these clouds, they

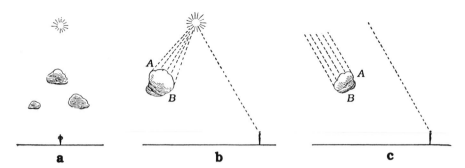

Fig. 175. Light and shadow on cumulus clouds. (**a**) The landscape and the observer seen from north to south. (**b**) Erroneous subjective conception and expectation. (**c**) True positions. In (b) and (c), the landscape is seen from east to west.

are a dazzling white, but they become gray or dark gray underneath as we watch them pass overhead. The drops of water are so closely packed that the light hardly enters the cloud, but is reflected back from the greater part by the numerous drops; the cloud resembles an almost opaque white body. If the sun is covered by cumulus, they appear dark, but their edges are light: 'every cloud has a silver lining'! Thus, the distribution of light and shade provides us with interesting information concerning the various parts of the clouds, above, below, in front, behind, and the actual shapes in space of these huge masses. It is not always easy to form a correct idea of these proportions or to realize the position of the cloud in relation to the sun. If, for instance, there are clouds in front of you, and the sun is some distance above them, you will be quite surprised at seeing almost only shadow—see Fig. 175a. You do not realize sufficiently the enormous distance of the sun and unconsciously you imagine it to be fairly near and expect light on *AB*—see Fig. 175b, instead of remembering that the sun's rays illuminating the cloud run parallel to the line from the sun to your eye—Fig. 175c.

However capricious the play of light and shade may be on the dark clouds, however complicated the shadows they throw on one another, it seems impossible to explain all the differences in color of the cumulus clouds by these alone. If, when the weather is clearing up after a storm, only a few small cumulus are left, brilliantly illuminated by the sun, with no possibility of one casting its shadow on another, they grow darker and darker and are finally blue-black when they are about to disappear. The impression is generally that thin parts of cumulus seen against the blue sky do not show a color consisting of blue + white (as might be expected), but of blue + black!

At other times, a cumulus cloud is gray when seen against the background formed by another big cloud that is completely white, so that there can be no question of the brightness increasing simply with the total thickness of the layers. The optics of these phenomena, though we see them day after day, has not yet been sufficiently investigated. You have to be careful, of course, before accepting the idea that clouds really can absorb light; you should first try to explain everything as if they were solid white objects, and then remember that they are really scattering mists, and, finally, consider the possibility of their containing dark dust particles as well.

It is interesting to compare them with the white steam (not the smoke) from a locomotive. In some cases, the latter appeared whiter when observed at a large angle with the incident light, and less bright when observed from the direction of the sun, so that the eye received the light rays reflected more or less in the direction of incidence. In other cases, the steam seen from all directions was much brighter than the brightest part of the cumulus clouds, which was probably because of the great distance of the latter, and the weakening of the light by scattering in the air.

Dark cumulus clouds seen from a great distance often look bluish. This is not the color of the cloud itself, but the scattered light reaching us from the atmosphere between the cloud and our eye. The farther away such a dark cloud is from us, the more its color is bound to approach that of its background, the sky. On the other hand, bright clouds close to the horizon become yellowish in color—see § 196).

We ought to extend our investigations to the other types of cloud as well, and try to explain why rain clouds, for example, are so gray; why in thunder clouds a peculiar leaden color can be seen side by side with a faded orange. Is it dust? Our knowledge, however, of all these things is so incomplete that we prefer to spur the reader on to begin investigations of his or her own.

The distribution of light over the celestial vault, when it is entirely and evenly overcast, is very characteristic and forms a counterpart of the distribution of light when the sky is bright blue. Compare, for instance, by means of a small mirror, the zenith and the horizon: the latter is always the brighter of the two with the ratio varying between 3 and 5[2].

---

[2] Fritz, *J. Opt. Soc. Am.*, **45**, 820, 1955.

236. The color of clouds during sunrise and sunset

If we had always lived in a land where there are no clouds, only low mist or haze, what would we have thought if a stranger had come to tell us that in his country these layers of mist rise high in the sky and become purple, crimson, scarlet and gold?

Ruskin, *Modern Painters*

In our description of a sunset, we began by ignoring the clouds. But now, we will discuss for a moment the origin of these wonderful cloud scenes, with their infinite wealth of color and variety of shape and their apparent absence of all regularity. Let me begin by stating that what now follows concerns chiefly what we see before the sun sets, whereas the real 'twilight phenomena' themselves have been discussed in § 219. As soon as the sun has gone down, the magnificence of the clouds has gone, too.

Shortly before sunset, the clouds are illuminated by:

(a) direct sunlight, becoming gradually yellow, orange, and red colored in succession, the lower the sun declines;

(b) light from the sky, orange-red toward the sun, blue elsewhere; this orange-red light must be attributed to the strong scattering by the large particles of dust and waterdrops, which causes only a slight deviation of the rays—see §§ 208 and 222; the blue light arises from backward scattering by the air molecules.

Now, imagine a cloud in the neighborhood of the sun, at first very thin, and becoming gradually denser. Its drops scatter light over small angles, so that thin veils of clouds will certainly send a great quantity of light toward us from the sun lying obliquely behind them, and the more scattering particles there, the stronger the warm orange-pink light. But there comes an optimum when the layers become either too dense or too thick to permit light to traverse them easily. Heavy clouds transmit practically no light at all and only reflect toward us the light of the part of the sky that is still blue, which illuminates them from our side—see Fig. 176. This shows that the finest sunsets are to be expected when the clouds are thin or when the covering of the sky is fragmentary. On the side the sun is setting, we see thin clouds, illuminated from behind, thicker or denser clouds from the front: the former are orange-red, the latter a darker gray-blue. This contrast in color, which often goes with differences in shape and structure, is one of the most delightful features of these cloud scenes.

The edges of heavy blue-gray clouds are often a wonderful gold. Note that the edge *A* (Fig. 176), clearly nearest the sun, gives a stronger light than edge *B*, because (a) there, the angle of deviation of the light rays is smaller; (b) if we imagine the cloud to be perfectly

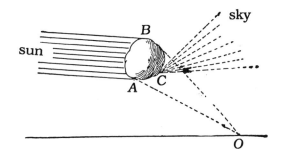

Fig. 176. Illumination of a cloud just before sunset.

round and full, it follows that on the side nearest the sun we must be able to see a little strip illuminated directly by the sun.

This beautiful scattering is not shown along the edges of clouds much farther away from the sun: they are illuminated directly on one side, and on the other by blue light from the sky, so that, here too, a play of colors arises of orange and blue. As the sun sinks lower, the colors become warmer until the clouds opposite, in the east, begin to show the purple of the counterglow.

When the sun sets completely, its glow withdraws gradually from the various parts of the sky, the high clouds remaining illuminated longest of all. This develops into another lovely contrast: behind, clouds still illuminated by the sun and, in front of them, clouds illuminated only by light from the sky.

The apparent clearing of the sky at twilight is often nothing but an optical illusion[3]. When the clouds are no longer illuminated by the sun, but only by the scattered light from all parts of the sky, the contrast in brightness, just like the contrast in color, between the clouds and the background of the sky is reduced considerably; moreover, these contrasts cannot be perceived too well owing to the faint illumination.

237. Illumination of clouds by terrestrial sources of light

When you walk through the open countryside in the evening and the sky is uniformly cloudy, you can see here and there in the distance a faint glow, low in the sky. This glow comes from a town or large village, which you can identify by the direction in which it lies. Estimate the angle α of the glow above the horizon in radians and read the distance A of the town or village from the map; the height, h, of the

[3] Atkins, *Nature*, **155**, 110, 1945.

clouds is then $h = \alpha A$. In 1884, the glow above London could be seen up to distances of about 60 km (40 miles). How far would it be visible today?

A closer study of this glow of light above a large town will repay you for the trouble. You will very soon notice that it differs from day to day: its variability is almost as great as that of the aurora borealis. You will discover two component parts in this light phenomenon:

(a) a hazy mist of light caused by the general illumination of the air with its particles of dust and water, which is strongest near the horizon;

(b) a patch of light on the layer of cloud, the circumference of which is almost an exact replica of that of the town (that is, more or less circular), but, when seen from a distance, appears foreshortened more or less to an ellipse with fairly sharp edges, especially when the cloud layer is smooth. If the sky is bright and cloudless, or else very misty, no light is to be seen above the town. If the sky is hazy, a mist of light is developed that is not very sharply defined. If the sky is covered by a layer of clouds, the patch of light becomes clearly visible.

Every sort of combination is possible and sometimes shadows are formed by isolated low-lying clouds, or irregular masses of light separate themselves from the main mass of light. The altitude of the clouds can, of course, be determined by measurements on the patch of light: the most exact values are given by the height of its boundaries. Carried out by a skilled observer, this method is so precise that it enables one to ascertain whether the cloud layer follows the unevenness of the ground.

La Cour succeeded in carrying out observations of this kind by day also. Once, after a fall of snow, he observed that the cloud layer was darker above the sea than above the snow-covered country: the line of demarcation became surprisingly distinct when he moved so far away that it was not higher than 20° above the horizon. Afterward, he discovered that darker regions became marked out on the clouds above woods as well; even the town of Copenhagen, where the snow had already thawed on the roofs, showed a darker region of this kind. From all these gradations of light, the altitude of the cloud layer could be determined, and a set of consistent values obtained.

Of all these phenomena, the easiest to observe is the difference between snow-covered country and sea and is therefore the best one to begin with. It is nothing but the famous ice blink and water-sky of Arctic explorers, by which they are warned of the approach of pack ice.

> And in the evening, I saw a remarkable glow of light over the sky to the north, strongest near the horizon, though it could be followed all along the vault of the heavens, right up to the zenith: a wonderful, mysterious half-light, like the reflection of

a huge fire a long way off, but in the land of ghosts, for the light
was a ghostly white.

Fr. Nansen, *Boken om Norge*

It is not generally known that the sand of the Egyptian desert also
colors the clouds with a glow that is distinctly recognizable from a
distance. A shallow place in the Indian Ocean, where the green of the
sea was very pronounced, threw a pale green light on to clouds
300–400 m (350–450 yd) high. And even above heathland when the
heather is in bloom and lit by the sun, the loose, drifting clouds are
colored a lovely purple underneath. Herring fishermen notice the approach of shoals of herring by their reflection in the clouds (herring
blink).

238. Factors determining the color of water[4]

Infinitely changeable, full of evanescent marble-patterned gradations, varying in every ripple, the fineness of its composition and ev-
erlasting joy to the eye ...
  Let us try to analyze this.

1. Part of the light received by us from water is reflected by the surface; so long as this is smooth, it acts like a mirror, and the color of
the water is blue, gray, or green, according to whether the sky is
clear or heavily clouded or the gently sloping banks are covered with
grass. But if the surface of the water becomes rippled, the colors of
sky and banks intermingle, sparkles of the one flashing across the
other. When it is very rippled, the water simply reflects a mixture of
color.

> What we commonly suppose to be a surface of uniform colour
> is, indeed, affected more or less by an infinite variety of hues,
> prolonged, like the sun image, from a great distance, and our
> apprehension of its lustre, purity, and even of its surface, is in
> no small degree dependent on our feeling of these multitudi-
> nous hues, which the continual motion of that surface pre-
> vents us from analysing, or understanding for what they are.
>
> Ruskin, *Modern Painters*

2. Another part of the light has penetrated the water and is there
scattered by particles of dust and by the general turbidity. These

---

[4] See, for instance, Hulburt, *J. Opt. Soc. Am.*, **35**, 698, 1945

particles are as a rule so large that they scatter all rays to the same extent: the emergent light then has the same color as the incident light; if they are particles of sand or clay, the emergent light may be of a brownish color. In very deep, pure water, however, an appreciable part of the light is scattered by the water molecules themselves, and has the same lovely blue color as the sky or a thick block of glacier ice.

3. Finally, in shallow water, part of the light always reaches the bottom and suffers diffuse reflection; at the same time, it assumes the color of the bottom of the water.

4. On their way through the water, rays of light undergo continual changes:
(a) owing to scattering, they lose part of their intensity; in pure water, violet and blue rays in particular are weakened—see § 194;
(b) owing to the true absorption of the water, which is already quite noticeable in layers a few meters (yards) deep, they lose their yellow, orange, and red rays, exactly in the same way as the light transmitted through colored glass.

Scattering is invariably present, even in the purest water, for the molecules are not uniformly distributed in the water, and this causes an irregularity and a certain 'granularity'; each molecule, moreover, deviates from the spherical shape. This scattering can be compared in every respect to the scattering in the air: it also increases proportionally to $1/\lambda^4$, and is therefore greatest for blue and violet rays. In less pure water, there are floating particles; if they are extremely small, their effect is added to that of the molecules and causes a blue-violet scattering. If they are larger than, say, 1.0 µm, they scatter all colors equally and mostly in a forward direction—see § 194.

Ordinary soapy water is a good example of a liquid containing very minute scattering particles. Illuminated from the front, and seen against a dark background, it appears bluish; illuminated from behind, it appears orange.

The absorption by the water of lakes and rivers must be ascribed chiefly to the presence of chemical compounds of iron (Fe^{+++} ion) and of humic acids. For iron concentrations of 1 part in 20 million and humic acid concentrations of 1 part in 10 million (such as occur in practice), the water ought to show a much stronger color than it actually does. Evidently, the Fe^{+++} compounds oxidize the humic acids under the influence of the light, while they themselves are changed into Fe^{++} compounds. The latter combine again with oxygen to once more become Fe^{+++} compounds, and so on.

We shall now give some examples to show how these various factors combine in bringing about the color of the water.

239. The color of puddles along the road

A simple case is that of puddles made in the road by rain. If the angle at which you look at them is large, the reflection on the surface seems almost perfect and the objects reflected are rich in contrasts, the black branches of trees are very black indeed. If you draw nearer, so that you look more and more steeply, the reflection becomes much weaker (§ 63), and it seems as if it were covered all over by a sort of uniform haze; all the colors are paler, and what is most striking is that the dark parts are no longer really dark, but gray. The haze is caused by light falling from all sides on to the puddle, penetrating the water and scattering in all directions. If the water is not clear, but milky, the scattering is caused by floating particles of dust; if it is colored with, for example, washing blue, the scattered light will have become blue, and this color combines with the images reflected; if the water is clear, but the bottom of it light, as in pools of sea water on the beach, all the reflected images become tinged with a sandy color, and, when seen nearly perpendicularly, the bottom is visible, but only a few of the brightest reflections can be seen. When the water is clear, however, and the bottom is dark, the reflected images remain, when seen nearly perpendicularly, pure and rich in contrast, albeit less luminous. In dark, quiet pools, the reflected foliage of trees shows at times a purity of color and a distinctness greater than that of the actual objects reflected. This is a psychological effect mainly caused by the fact that the surrounding scenery is less dazzling—see § 9.

Ask someone to help you by standing at different distances from the pool and watch how his or her reflection changes. This experiment will prove especially striking on the seashore.

You see here demonstrated on a small scale the reason that objects below sea level (such as rocks, submarines, and so on) can be seen more easily from an aircraft than from a ship.

> Now, the fact is that there is hardly a roadside pond or pool that has not as much landscape in it as above it. It is not the brown, muddy, dull thing we suppose it to be; it has a heart like ourselves, and in the bottom of that there are the boughs of the tall trees and the blades of the shaking grass, and all manner of hues of variable pleasant light out of the sky.
>
> Ruskin, *Modern Painters*

240. The color of inland waterways and canals

Ripples on a surface cause an ever-changing variety of light and color on every canal and every ditch—see §§ 20 and 24. To find out whether any definite part of the surface is rippled, you should look at it from different directions. Slight ripples become visible only along the boundary lines of bright and dark reflections; in the reflection of the uniformly blue sky, they cannot be seen, nor in that of the dark masses of dense woods. Large ripples, however, produce a shading of shadow and light, even in fairly large uniform regions, either because they make the rays deviate so greatly or because the coefficient of reflection at the front and that at the back of the wavelets become appreciably different—see Fig. 179.

Observations like these teach us that boundary lines between the rippled and the smooth parts of a surface of water are nearly always delineated with amazing sharpness.

Undulations on a surface of water are visible only near the boundary of dark and light reflections.

This is not to be attributed to irregular distribution of the currents of wind, as is shown especially clearly by the fact that when it is raining and the whole surface of the water is set into uniform vibration, the boundary lines are still absolutely clear. The real cause is nothing but the presence of an extremely thin film of oil, not even a millionth of a millimeter (2 molecules of oil!) thick, and yet quite thick enough to dampen the ripples caused by wind or rain. This film is formed by the remains of animal and vegetable matter, used oil left in the wake of passing boats, or refuse in drain water. The wind blows this greasy layer along and gathers it together at one side of the canal. You will always notice that water is rippled at the side where the wind comes from, and calm along the opposite bank. In this smooth part, a lot of twigs and leaves are floating, but they barely move relative to one another, because they are kept in their places by the very thin film of oil.

In this way, the striking difference between the lively, sparkling surface of the water of a brook in a wood, and the leaden-colored, syrupy waterways in the poorer districts of a big town is satisfactorily explained.

We will follow up these observations of light phenomena on the surface by studying the way in which this reflection continually competes with the light coming from below. Stand under the trees at the water's edge. Here and there, you can see the reflections of dark treetops and between them bright patches of blue sky. In places where the clear sky is reflected, you cannot see the bottom of the water, as the light coming from below is too weak. In places where the dark trees are reflected, you can see a dark mixture formed by the color of their leaves, the color of the bottom of the water, and the diffuse light scattered by the particles of dust in the water. Notice that you can see the bottom of the water only close to the bank. The reflection of the dark keel of a boat shows a greenish watery color, whereas a bright white band running along the boat remains white.

Notice that you can see the bottom of the water only close to the bank. Looking from any distance at all across the water, it is no longer possible to see the bottom, even if the water is not any deeper, for the reflected light becomes much stronger when the angle of incidence is large and predominates over the light coming from below.

The higher the sun, the less light is reflected from the surface and the more penetrates into the water, so that the amount of scattered light increases. It is often striking to see, when the sun is high and bright, how an entire pond lights up with an internal glow.

> Under sunlight, the local colour of water is commonly vigorous and active, and forcibly affects, as we have seen, all the dark reflections, commonly diminishing their depth. Under shade,

the reflective power is in a high degree increased[5], and it will be found most frequently that the forms of shadows are expressed on the surface of water not by actual shade, but by more genuine reflection of objects above.

A very muddy river is seen during sunshine of its own yellow colour, rendering all reflections discoloured and feeble. At twilight, it recovers its reflective powers to the fullest extent and mountains are seen reflected in it as clearly as if it were a crystalline lake[6].

Ruskin, *Modern Painters*

Here are a few simple means of eliminating the reflection on the surface.

1. Hold a black umbrella above your head.

2. Find a place where you can get under a bridge. In sunny weather you will see the beautiful yellow-green color scattered by the water. The ripples on the surface can only be seen by the refraction they cause; below the water surface, it seems as if objects move gently to and fro · as if the water were gelatine.

3. Hold a small mirror under water at different angles and judge in this way the color of the light that has penetrated the water from above after it has traversed the water for a certain distance. If this experiment is made in the water of an ordinary ditch, you will be able to observe the yellow color of the light caused by true absorption. Where the water is very shallow, a piece of broken white china, dropped on to the bed of the ditch, or a piece of white paper held under water, will serve the same purpose. At sea, a white disk, let down to a certain depth, is used, but this cannot really be considered a simple experiment.

4. Use a water telescope, which is simply a thin metal tube, if possible with a piece of glass stuck to one end—see Fig. 177. With this, you will be able to judge the color of the light coming from below, caused by scattering from the bottom or by floating particles of dust.

---

[5] The physical explanation is that the reflective power is precisely the same in the shadow as in the sun, but the ratio reflected light/scattered light from the depth is smaller in the sun and greater in the shade.

[6] Our explanation is that at twilight the light comes from one definite direction, and the general illumination has disappeared, which during the day produces the scattered light from below and is superposed on all the reflected images.

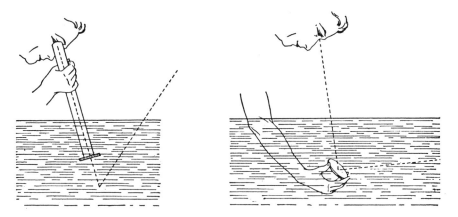

Fig. 177. Observing the color of water without letting its reflection on the surface interfere.

5. Look though a Polaroid (sunglasses) held in such a way as to extinguish the reflected light—see § 245.

241. The color of the sea

Reflection is the great factor determining the color of the sea. It takes place, however, in an endless variety of ways because the surface of the sea is a moving, living thing, rippling and undulating according to the way of the wind and the formation of the shore. The principal rule is that all far-off reflections are shifted toward the horizon, owing to the fact that our gaze falls on the slopes of the distant wavelets—see § 23. The color of the sea in the distance is therefore about the same as that of the sky at a height of 20–30° and therefore darker than the sky immediately above the horizon (§ 200), and all the more so because only part of the light is reflected.

Apart from this, the sea has a 'color of its own', the color of the light scattered back from below. From an optical point of view, an important characteristic of the sea is its depth, a depth so great that practically no light returns from the bottom of it. This 'color of its own' is to be attributed to the combined effects of scattering and absorption in the masses of water. A sea that only scatters light would, apart from its reflection, be milky white, for all rays entering it are bound to come out again in the end. A sea that only absorbs would be as black as ink, for then the rays would return only after having reached the bottom, and the slightest absorption on this very long passage through the water would be sufficient to extinguish them. However, as already stated, the color arises from the combined effects of scattering and absorption: the kinds of light only slightly subject to scattering penetrate the water farthest before they are scattered back, and during this long journey they suffer the most weakening by absorption.

Broadly speaking, you could say that the quantity of light returning from below will be greater the larger the ratio *coefficient of scattering/coefficient of absorption*. The complete theory, however, is by no means simple.

A simple test will show how the color of the sea comes about. Let a bluish liquid in a black container represent the sea, so deep that you cannot see its bottom: it looks jet black. Into this, pour a murky liquid such as watered-down milk: you will suddenly see the light blue color becoming visible. This experiment can also be done by placing a piece of blue glass first on black paper and then on white paper.

The floating particles that cause the scattering by sea water have been investigated thoroughly in the English Channel[7]. Their average number decreases with increasing depth: each cubic meter (10 cubic feet) of the upper layers contains, on average, 0.3 cm³ of microscopic plants and animals, and almost as many mineral particles, such as clay, wood and rope fiber, pieces of shell, and grains of soot. There are no particles smaller than 0.1 μm. The existing particles are counted under an ultramicroscope.

The direct influence of the bottom of the sea on the color of its expanse of water cannot be observed in seas that exceed a meter (yard) in depth. Ruskin, in *Modern Painters*, maintained that even at a depth of 100 m (110 yd), the bottom contributes considerably to the color of the sea, and further assertions of this kind may be heard from seafaring people. The truth is that a local elevation at the bottom of the sea alters the swell of the waves and the rippling of the water above it and, correspondingly, more solid particles are stirred up there than where it is deeper, causing an increase in the scattering. So the bottom of the sea has, indeed, some effect but not a direct one.

Near coasts where the sea is a beautiful green, from well below the surface dark rocks and seaweed often shine through surprisingly purple-colored, which is undoubtedly caused by the contrast with the surrounding green. Our eye becomes particularly sensitive to this contrast because of the hazy veil which the light-scattering layer of water spreads over everything (cf. § 250).

---

[7] Atkins, Jenkins, and Warren, *J. Mar. Biol.* (UK), **33**, 497, 1954. Atkins and Poole, *Proc. R. Soc., Dublin*, **26**, 313, 1954. *Bull. Am. Meteorol. Soc.*, **28**, 125, 1947.

242. Light and color at the North Sea

The following observations were carried out during a holiday on the flat, sandy coast of Holland, which runs virtually due north and south, and from where magnificent sunsets can be seen over the sea. The phenomena are, of course, differently distributed over the day for differently oriented coasts; the essential point is the position of the sun relative to the surface of the sea.

No wind, blue sky. The sea, in the calm of early morning, smooth as a mirror. The sky, blue everywhere, but hazy. A tiny wave at our feet curls on to the beach, leaving a narrow line of foam that whispers and dies away. A hush follows ...

Standing on a dune, we see the surface of the sea spread out in front of us like a map. One part of it is so smooth that it reflects the blue-gray sky above perfectly, without any distortion, as a lake does. Other parts are blue-gray, too, but darker in tone. Their boundaries are clearly marked, and their distribution is so distinct that one can hardly refrain from sketching them. However, after a comparatively short time, they appear to have altered their position completely. For this reason, the lighter colored parts cannot be 'sandbanks' as seaside visitors usually call them; they are caused by an imperceptible, extremely thin oily film spread over the surface of the sea, similar to that on canals and ditches (see § 240) and sufficient to damp any ruffling of the water. These oily films probably arise from refuse in the wake of ships or from their used fuel oil. Where there is no film, the water is slightly ruffled, as will be seen later on in the day when the sun shines above the sea, making the rippled parts sparkle like a sea of light. The color shown by these parts is now darker, because (1) the front of each ripple reflects a higher and therefore darker blue part of the sky; and (2) the reflection is less grazing and therefore less luminous. Using a Polaroid with a vertical direction of polarization, the darker parts are seen to be much darker, and the difference between them and the lighter parts becomes more pronounced. The fact that the lines of demarcation between the various regions appear to run parallel to the coast almost everywhere is caused by perspective shortening, for, in reality, the regions covered by oil may have all kinds of shape—see Fig. 178. A few real sandbanks are conspicuous by their rather deeper yellow color, but only where the sea is very shallow, for instance, 10–20 cm (4–8 in).

Bathing in the afternoon, we are struck by the unusual clearness of the water when the sea is calm. As far as one meter (one yard) down, we can see every detail at the bottom and even minute swimming creatures. There is no sand in the water, or very little, and that only where a wavelet is about to break and tiny clouds of sand are whirled upward behind it. When we look down at the water close to us, the reflection of the sky hardly interferes and the yellow color of the sand at the bottom dominates up to a depth of about 20 cm (8 in). At a depth of 11.5 m (12.5 yd), the color changes into a lovely green and now we have to form a kind of water telescope with our hands to avoid the reflection of the sky—see § 240. This green is the color of the light that has penetrated the water and has been scattered back. However, as soon as we look at the surface of the sea a little farther off, reflection predominates and the blue sky is mirrored everywhere. A wonderful interchange of sea green and sky blue!

In the evening, the sun goes down behind a blue-gray bank of clouds a few degrees in height. Above that, there is a shimmer of twilight orange and gold, merging gradually into the darker blue of the evening higher up in the sky. The sea is as calm as ever, reflecting, without distortion, the whole scene. But, as we look toward the west, we begin to see very small ripples (§ 24) and in the distant parts of the sea, where the blue-gray bank of clouds is reflected, every ripple forms a little orange-yellow line (the slanting wave reflecting a higher part of the sky). Nearer to us, where the sea is orange-yellow, the wavelets produce a darker hatching by reflection of the still higher, bluer sky. Toward the northwest and southwest, where the twilight colors are disappearing and where our gaze no longer falls at right angles on the slopes of the waves, the sea is a pure reflection of the uniform bank of clouds, unchanged in color and brightness, so that the line of the horizon vanishes and sea and sky merge into one, while the sailing ships in the distance seem to drift in a blue-gray infinity.

A few days later, with the weather about the same but the wind perhaps slightly weaker, the parts of the sea covered by the thin film of oil were also visible in the evening, reflecting the blue-gray bank of clouds, whereas the ruffled parts, by the displacement of the images, reflected the orange-yellow sky.

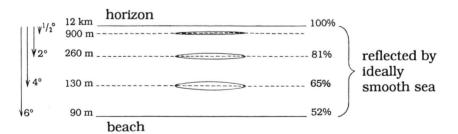

Fig. 178. The sea, seen from a dune 9 m (30 ft) high. The ellipses show the perspective shortening of a circle at different points on the surface of the sea.

Slight wind, clear blue sky with a few isolated clouds. Before even reaching the top of the dune, we are struck by the strong contrast between the blue-black sea and the light sky near the horizon. Visibility is exceptionally good, horizon and distant objects stand out with clear-cut distinctness: a condition that lasts all day. There is a slight west wind blowing; breakers extend along the coast in two or three lines of foam, though in the open sea no foam is to be seen. We take up our post on the dune.

The separate breakers along the shore (see Fig. 179) are dark, yellow-green in front, for our gaze strikes the front slope of each wave nearly at right angles and therefore only a little reflected light reaches us and that, moreover, from a dark part of the sky. We do, however, see yellow-green light that either has been scattered back from the depths of the sea or has penetrated the back of a wave and emerges at the front; but, since this is after all very feeble, the fronts of the waves are dark. On the other hand, the backs of the waves reflect the light blue sky along the horizon. In this way, each wave shows a lovely contrast between its dark yellow-green front and its light-blue back. These light-blue backs develop between the breakers into wide, flat troughs, slightly rippled and good reflectors, and likewise blue. The few rows of sandbanks running along the coast are easily distinguishable by the waves breaking on them, while the spaces in between are smoother and calmer. Farther away from the beach, the shading of the waves becomes finer and finer. There are no more breakers, but the contrast between the front and back slopes re-

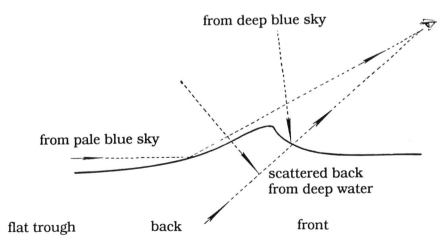

Fig. 179. How different colors arise in a wave of the sea.

mains. As we look more and more grazingly across the water, we can no longer see the troughs between the waves, and finally their back slopes disappear entirely. The fronts are now much less steep and reflect chiefly the sky at a height of about 25°. This 'displacement of reflected images' (see § 23) accounts for the dark blue color of the sea and for the contrasts between sea and sky at the horizon. This contrast is at present so strong because the sky actually at the horizon is so light and yet, at only a short distance above it, such a deep blue. Check this by projecting the reflection of the higher parts of the sky in a small mirror on to the neighborhood of the horizon: it is amazing! Notice, at the same time, that the sea in the distance is markedly darker than the darkest parts of the sky: the reflecting power of the sea's surface is far from 100%. The contrast between sea and sky is strongest in the west and becomes less to the north and the south, because the vast majority of the waves come from the west, whereas when we look northward or southward, our gaze is more nearly parallel to the crests of the waves so that their effect is less—see § 24.

We might perhaps doubt whether the strong contrast shown between sea and sky has no other reason than the rapid increase in brightness of the blue sky near the horizon. Nature will convince us. For a moment, part of the western sky is covered by veils of cirrus, so that the sky up to 30° from the horizon is practically uniformly white; the strong contrast between sea and sky in that direction disappears immediately and the sea becomes much greener and lighter. As soon as the cirrus disappear, the contrast returns.

The extent to which reflection influences the color of the sea must not lead us to neglect other factors altogether. Here and there, the shadow of an isolated cloud can be seen. There, the sea is darker; in sunlit parts, it looks more sand-colored. This is partly a contrast phenomenon, however, for when you look through the hole of your half-clenched fist or through the hole in the nigrometer (see § 197) you see that in reality it is blue there, too, albeit less than in the shadowy parts[8]. In any case, these shadows prove clearly that the color of the sea is not determined entirely by reflection, but that part of the light is scattered back from below. The shadow becomes visible because the light scattered back is weaker there than elsewhere, whereas the reflected light is not weakened—see § 241.

Does the sand at the bottom shine directly through the water and can the sandbanks be recognized as such from a distance? Not according to my own experience; certainly not to anyone observing them from a dune or from the beach. The sand is visible only where

---

[8] The sea shows the loveliest blue when it is quite smooth, the sky bright blue, and the sun screened by a cloud so that the sea is in a shadow.

the water is very shallow, perhaps 10–20 cm (4–8 in). The position of sandbanks is revealed by formation of surf just there and because the spaces in between are smoother—see § 241.

A striking fact is that the sea near the horizon often has a border of gray running to blue (or blue running to darker blue); the breadth of the border does not exceed half a degree. It begins to disappear as soon as we leave the dune to look at it from the beach and disappears completely when we bend down on the beach. This shows that it is no contrast border—see § 110. It is probably caused by the fact that the sea is comparatively dark, becoming bluish in the distance owing to scattering by the air[9] (see § 196). We can also imagine the sea to be less turbid at such a long distance from the coast: this would make the clearer water in the distance recognizable at once, if only we are standing high enough to see so far.

Rossmann[10] has observed this phenomenon at the coast of Florida and gave as an explanation the reflection of the blue sky at the zenith by the sloping edges of the breakers. Diffraction sometimes causes a widening of the border. Questions: (1) is the blue border strongly polarized?; (2) is the breadth largest at right angles to the coast?

Later in the day, the sun has moved and in the afternoon we can see thousands of scintillations in the direction from which it shines. We cannot see the reflected image of the sun itself as we are looking much too closely along the surface of the water; we see only part of the immense path of light cast by it on the irregularly undulating surface. The sea in that direction becomes light gray, almost white.

After sunset, the sea in the west reflects the bright glow and the gold-colored cirrus veils; its undulating surface and shifting reflections show us the average color of the western part of the sky. Toward the north and the south, the sky is less colored and the tints of the sea are less bright. Our gaze is attracted again and again by the glory of color in the west. Between the gold-yellow of the clouds there appears here and there a patch of blue sky, the blue wonderfully saturated by the contrast. The colors in the sky become gradually orange and the sea follows them, while the foam of the breakers seems violet by contrast. Right in the foreground there is a streak of wet sand, in which reflections of certain parts of the sky are smooth and perfect (without being shifted): first a lovely clear blue, and later a tender green. Finally, the cirrus clouds in the west are no longer illuminated, their color becomes dark violet in tone and, in the same way, the colors of the sea are subdued; but, among these peaceful evening hues, the wet sand of the beach traces a warm orange-colored stripe.

---

[9] This border is also clearly visible on days when the sky is a featureless gray, but the wind moderate and the sea rather dark.

[10] Rossmann, *Meteorol. Rundsch.*, **13**, 1, 1960.

Strong wind rising, gray sky. All over the sea, the gathering waves are crested with foam, four or five fringes of froth run along the coast; from the southwest the wind comes up, chasing the waves before it. The sea is gray like the clouds, a slightly greenish-gray. Close to the coast, we see the waves separately and discover that the greenish component arises from their front slopes, which reflect little light, but emit gray-green light scattered from within. The water seems very turbid; stirred as it is, there will be a lot of sand floating in it. The sea is darkest toward the southwest where the wind is coming from; toward the south, and especially toward the north, its color becomes lighter, approaching that of the gray sky, although still remaining a little darker, since we are now looking parallel to the waves. Near the horizon, the sea is more bluish, the color of the dark low clouds, which owe their bluishness to scattering over these long distances, whereas, above our heads, they are normally bright or dark gray; moreover, the phenomenon of the blue rim on the horizon makes the contrast still stronger—see previous page. Wherever a stray dark cloud hangs aloof in the gray sky, an indistinct, shifted dark blue-gray reflection is recognizable on the surface of the sea. The horizon is nowhere sharply defined; especially to the south and north, a mist of waterdrops is splashed into the air by the foam of the breakers, reducing our range of vision to only a few kilometers (a mile or so) and causing sea and air to intermingle in the distance.

With weather clearing and wind from the northwest, the state of affairs resembles, more or less, the one just described, but the sky is a confusion of blue patches, white clouds dazzlingly illuminated by the sun (tinged with light yellow by aerial perspective—see § 196), and dark bluish masses. At all points of the compass, the sea reflects an average of the color of the sky at a height of 20–30°. Only the large masses are discernible in this reflection, while the sunlit clouds are the most prominent feature, throwing a shining light over the dark, restless sea.

Storm. I am still behind the dune and the houses, but I can already hear the raging of the sea. From the promenade, I have a full view of the foam from the breakers, more than two-thirds of the sea covered with boiling froth, white at the crests, dirty white and frayed out to a network in the troughs between the waves. As usual, the front of the waves is darker to the west than to the south or north and this makes the scene to the west seem wilder and richer in contrasts. In a high sea, separate crests of froth rise on all sides out of the dark water. A sunlit streak far to the south stands out sharply, a dazzling white on the foaming surface, appearing at first very narrow and long and then, as it approaches, extending over a wide area. The color of the sand appears very distinctly in those parts where there is no foam and the sunlit sea reflects darker clouds. The light scattered back from the depths is, during such illuminations as this, as strong as possible, the more so because the raging waves stir up and keep floating great quantities of sand. The sky is very dark in some parts, lighter again in others, and there are a few patches of blue. The shifted reflections are still discernible, though only very indistinctly, in the general color of the sea. The predominant impression is the foam.

Examine light and color over the sea under every possible condition of wind and cloud.

Compare the tints on rocky and sandy coasts.

Examine also the color of the sea while you are bathing; look at the waves not only seaward, but also landward; find the shadow of other bathers and your own. Use the water telescope.

If you have the opportunity to walk on one of the piers of a harbor, go and compare the calm sea between the two piers with the sea outside. The condition of the sky is the same; differences arise from differences in the undulating of the sea's surface or in its turbidity.

Examine the general brightness of the sea's surface late in the evening and at night: these are good times because things are not complicated by differences of color and the smaller details will not divert your attention.

Investigate every day the clearness of the horizon and ask yourself on what this depends; look at the horizon in various directions. Normally, the sea is darker than the sky, but when the clouds are evenly gray up to a height of about 40°, the horizon becomes practically invisible.

Beware of contrast phenomena! To compare different parts of the sky and the sea, you can benefit from the use of a small mirror—see § 200. Hold your hand, or any dark object, between the two fields A and B to be compared; in this way, both A and B will be seen bordering the same field. Use the nigrometer!

Never confuse shadows and reflections of clouds; they fall in entirely different places. When there are separate clouds in the sky, the whole of the light distribution over the sea is dependent on the combination of reflections and shadows.

243. The color of the sea seen from a ship

Compared with the scene from the beach, there is one great difference: the absence of surf. This makes the whole picture around the observer much more symmetrical. This symmetry is broken, however, by the wind, which gives a definite direction to the waves, by the smoke from the ship, which has the effect of a dark cloud, by the foam in the wake of the keel, and by the sun.

Close to and behind the ship, the color of the light returning from the depths can be judged best of all, because there clouds of air bubbles are being continually chased through the water and then rise slowly to the top. In these places, a lovely green-blue tint is clearly visible, the same tint as that seen reflected by the white bellies of porpoises frolicking around the ship, or by a white stone as it falls into the water. This tint is to be seen in every ocean, whether the sea there as a whole is indigo blue or green. It is caused by true absorption in the water, whereby the yellow, orange, and red constituents are removed from the light; the violet rays are scattered away from the observer and so only the green is left to give the characteristic color. The parts where there is only a little froth among the foaming masses of green are mostly a kind of purple color, that is, the complementary color to green, and one which we must consider a physiological contrast color—see §§ 114, 241, and 250.

In the shallow seas in the vicinity of ports or mouths of large rivers, the sea water is very muddy. This causes a comparatively large quantity of light to be scattered back from below, so that the conditions there are, to a certain extent, the same as those seen when the swarms of air bubbles in the wake of a ship are observed. The green color predominates, probably because the water of the river brings into the sea humic acids and ferric compounds—see § 238: their yellowish absorption is superposed on the blue-green color of the water. This is the kind of shallow green sea on which shadows of clouds stand out magnificently purple-violet on calm days—see § 247.

The 'water color' shown by white objects at small depths is not as a rule the same as the 'proper color' of the deep sea. Whereas this water color is green, the color of the sea can, for instance, become blue or indigo when the scattering particles are very fine and reflect back the blue-violet rays.

To investigate the color of the sea, the reflected light must be avoided by looking, for instance, at the front of a wave or by using one of the methods mentioned in § 240. The color of the sea depends clearly on which sea is being crossed: this can be observed splendidly during a sea voyage from England or the USA to Australia. Generally speaking, the color distribution is[11]:

olive green	north of 40° North;
indigo	between 30° and 40° North;
ultramarine	south of 30° North.

The splendid turquoise blue of tropical seas results from the purity of the water. It is well known that sea water at higher latitudes contains much more floating microscopically small plant and animal life than tropical waters: it is quite possible that their scattering and brownish or greenish color alter the hue of the sea.

---

[11] Hulburt, *J. Opt. Soc. Am.*, **35**, 698, 1945

It sometimes happens that olive green regions move in patches down to lower latitudes. It might be worth while trying to ascertain whether or not this green color changes with the seasons at a particular place, as there are already some indications in this direction.

The origin of the green color of certain deep seas has not yet been explained satisfactorily. Observations have shown that the water of these seas contains great quantities of floating particles, but although, as shown by calculation, the ordinary absorption by water, combined with scattering by large particles, can cause every kind of transition from dark blue to light blue or gray, it can never account for the green. This has led some to ascribe it to diatoms and to the feces of birds that feed on diatoms, and others to the yellow color of the scattering particles that might, for instance, consist of yellow sand.

There are a few rare cases where sea water looks milky white: evidently, there must then be large numbers of floating particles near the surface that scatter light in the topmost layers; this scattering predominates entirely over absorption.

244. The color of lakes

The color of lakes is a source of great beauty in mountain scenery. Their depth is usually sufficient to minimize any effect arising from the color of the ground at the bottom, in which respect, therefore, they resemble seas. But they differ from these in their much greater smoothness, a result in its turn of the water's surface being so much smaller and of the mountains along their banks sheltering them from the wind. For this reason, the regular reflection from their surfaces plays a much more prominent part than in the case of the sea; the colors at sunset are nowhere so beautifully mirrored as in a lake, and the varying tints of mountain lakes are certainly to be attributed partly to the reflection of their shores. However, should these be high and dark, reflection on the surface is eliminated and, instead, large areas of the lake show the color of the light that has penetrated the water nearly perpendicularly and is scattered back from it again. By applying the methods mentioned in § 240, some idea can be obtained of these 'individual colors'. They differ from lake to lake and can be classified as (1) pure blue; (2) green; (3) yellow-green; (4) yellow-brown.

Closer examination in laboratories has shown that the water of blue lakes is almost absolutely pure and that the color is caused by absorption by the water in the orange and red parts of the spectrum. To account for colors (2), (3), and (4), there is a constantly increasing proportion of iron-salt and humic acids and also scattering by brown-colored particles in these waters.

Very often, the green color of smaller lakes is caused by microscopic green algae growing there in vast quantities; often, they are still a distinct green in winter when the trees are bare and everything is covered by snow.

Red coloring can be brought about by other microscopic organisms, such as Beggiatoales, Oscillaria rubescens, Stentor igneus, Daphnia pulex, Euglena sanguinea, or Peridinia.

For polarization, see § 245.

245. Observations of the color of water with a Polaroid filter

A Polaroid filter, as you may remember, transmits only those rays that vibrate parallel to its 'marker'—see § 204. Since light reflected by water vibrates chiefly in a horizontal direction, the reflected light can be virtually extinguished by holding the Polaroid with its marker vertical; this extinction is complete when the angle of incidence is 53° to the vertical (angle of polarization). Try this with a small pool of water in the road after a shower. Stand about 5 m (5 yd) away from it and hold the marker vertical: the effect is amazing, for you can see the bottom of the pool nearly as well as if there were no pool at all. Rotate the Polaroid alternately into a horizontal and vertical position and you will see that the pool seems to become smaller and larger.

As a rule, the Polaroid heightens the color of a wet beach, seaweed, granite blocks, a wet road, painted surfaces; everything, in short, that shines in a landscape. The reason is that it invariably takes away part of the surface reflection, which had mixed white with the color of the object itself.

The contrast on a calm sea between the sunny parts and the shadows of the clouds is accentuated by a Polaroid with a vertical marker. The rays reflected at the surface are extinguished, causing the differences in the scattered light to appear more clearly.

It also intensifies the contrast between those parts of the sea covered by a layer of oil and the remaining parts (see § 242), perhaps because the reflection in the ripples takes place at an angle different from the one in the smooth parts, or else because the polarization by reflection is disturbed by the layer of oil.

The effect of the Polaroid is striking when there is a wind blowing. Look at the raging waves with the marker vertical: the sea now seems much rougher than when observed with the marker horizontal. In the former case, the Polaroid extinguishes the light reflected, thus making the surface of the sea darker, whereas the foam, retaining its brightness, is more striking.

Often, provided the Polaroid is adjusted properly, the horizon becomes more distinct. Looking in a direction at right angles to the sun, you see the sea become decidedly darker and the blue sky relatively brighter when the light vibrations are vertical—see § 242. For this reason, Polaroids are routinely mounted in sextants.

The following experiments concern the polarization of light scattered in deep tropical seas, the water of which is pure. Let us assume that you can carry out the experiment when the sun is fairly high and the surface of the water smooth. Stand with your back to the sun, look at the water more or less at the angle of polarization and hold the marker of the Polaroid vertical. The light reflected is extinguished and you can see the lovely blue glow of the light that comes from below after scattering. Turn the Polaroid so that the marker is horizontal: the sea will then appear less blue than without the Polaroid.

Carry out this experiment also when the sun is moderately high, holding the marker vertical again, and vary the azimuth. A comparison between the color on the side toward the sun and away from the sun is particularly interesting. On the side toward the sun, you see a dark indigo color, because, looking in a direction at right angles to the sun's rays, you have not only extinguished the light reflected, but also the light scattered from the depths of the water. On the side away from the sun, the color is bright blue, because you are looking pretty well in the direction of the sun's rays that penetrate the water and the light scattered back in your direction is almost unpolarized. These experiments prove that the light scattered by the sea is to a great extent polarized like that in the air, and the scattering is therefore by very small particles, probably the water molecules themselves.

With the use of a Polaroid, a characteristic difference has been discovered between the radiation scattered back in blue lakes and in dark-brown lakes. To see this, look in the direction of the sun, avoiding reflection by using a water telescope—see § 240. The Polaroid shows that in blue lakes the light scattered back vibrates horizontally, as is to be expected when the scattering particles are very small, whereas the larger particles in brown lakes scatter practically unpolarized light, in which the vertical component, on emerging from the water, predominates slightly (provided the water telescope has no glass at the end).

246. Scales for judging the color of water

The scale generally used is that of Forel. First make a blue solution of crystals of copper sulfate and a yellow one of potassium chromate: 0.5 g $CuSO_4$ Aq in 5 cm^3 ammonia made up with water to 100 cm^3; 0.5 g K_2CrO_4 in 100 cm^3 water.

Make the following mixtures:

(1)   100 blue + 0 yellow
(2)   98 blue + 2 yellow
(3)   95 blue + 5 yellow
(4)   91 blue + 9 yellow
(5)   86 blue + 14 yellow
(6)   80 blue + 20 yellow
(7)   73 blue + 27 yellow
(8)   65 blue + 35 yellow
(9)   56 blue + 44 yellow
(10)   46 blue + 54 yellow
(11)   35 blue + 65 yellow
(12)   23 blue + 77 yellow
(13)   10 blue + 90 yellow

Browner colors are often required, especially when judging the color of lakes. To meet this requirement, a brown solution can be made as follows:

0.5 g cobalt sulfate + 5 cm^3 ammonia + water up to 100 cm^3.

Mix this solution with Forel's green solution (strength 11) in the following proportions:

(11-1)   100 green + 0 brown
(11-2)   98 green + 2 brown
(11-3)   95 green + 5 brown
(11-4)   91 green + 9 brown
(11-5)   86 green + 14 brown
(11-6)   80 green + 20 brown
(11-7)   73 green + 27 brown
(11-8)   65 green + 35 brown
(11-9)   56 green + 44 brown
(11-10) 46 green + 56 brown
(11-11) 35 green + 65 brown

These different mixtures can be kept in test tubes of, say, 1 cm ($^1/_2$ in) in diameter.

The chief difficulty when applying this scale is to know which point of the water's surface should be taken as a norm of comparison. It is usual to try to judge the 'proper color' of the water itself.

Neither of the scales is wholly satisfactory. Another way would be to try to reproduce the color in paint and keep this for future comparisons.

247. Shadows on water

> ...whenever shadow is seen on clear water and in a measure, even on foul water, it is not, as on land, a dark shade subduing the sunny general hue to a lower tone, but it is a space of an entirely different colour, subject itself, by its susceptibility of reflection, to infinite varieties of depth and hue, and liable, under certain circumstances, to disappear altogether.
>
> Ruskin, *Modern Painters*

Light sent to us from the surface of the water derives partly from that surface and partly from below, so that, if we intercept the incident rays, both parts can be changed.

The influence of shadow on reflected light

> When a surface is rippled, every ripple, up to a certain variable distance on each side of the spectator, and at a certain angle between him and the sun, varying with the size and shape of the ripples, reflects to him a small image of the sun (cf. § 20). Hence, those dazzling fields of expanding light so often seen upon the sea. Any object that comes between the sun and these ripples takes from them the power of reflecting the sun and, in consequence, all their light; hence, any intervening objects cast upon such spaces seeming shadows of intense force, and of the exact shape, and in the exact place, of real shadows.
>
> Ruskin, *Modern Painters*

The truth of Ruskin's words can be judged best of all when, on a windy night, the water of a canal, for instance, is very ruffled. As you walk along, look at the reflection of a streetlight spreading out into an irregularly flickering patch of light over which there is a continual gliding of shadows, for example, from the trees between the lights and the canal. Not until you have reached the most favorable viewpoint will you notice the presence of these shadows on the water, which are visible only within a small solid angle. Ruskin had long discussions with critics and other interested persons as to whether one might speak of 'shadows' at all in this sense. It is, of course, a question of words!

A rather different effect is brought about when the moon is reflected as a long path of light and you suddenly see the dark, black silhouette of a sailing boat glide in front of this shining streak of luminosity. The boat itself is now a dark object on a background of light, but it also throws its shadow in your direction across the rippling water, and here the above considerations apply, too.

The influence of shadow on light that is scattered back. Shadows are marked clearly on turbid water; the degree of distinctness of the shadow is a direct indication of the turbidity or purity of the water. Notice the shadows of bridges and trees on waterways. When you are crossing the sea, try to find your shadow on the water. You will only see it on that side where the ship has stirred the water and mixed it with air bubbles, and not where the sea is clear and deep blue. Observe the shadows of clouds on the sea's surface.

The shadow becomes visible because the light that penetrates the water and is returned after being scattered is less in those parts of the surface than elsewhere. On the other hand, light reflected at the surface is not weakened and therefore becomes relatively more important. This explains why, when the sky is blue, the shadow of a cloud on the sea is often bluish, though, owing to the contrast with the surrounding green, the color may shift a little toward purple.

Apart from the clearness of the water, the direction of observation is important, too. When bathing in very clear water, you will see no shadows; when bathing in slightly muddy water, you will see only your own shadow and not those of other bathers, but in very muddy water you will see those of all the bathers. Observe that a shadow cast by a post across the rather turbid water of a canal can be seen properly only if you go and stand in the plane containing the sun and the post: therefore, look toward that part of the sky where the sun is. You will then see the shadow loom up on the water rather suddenly. This is the same phenomenon as that described in connection with

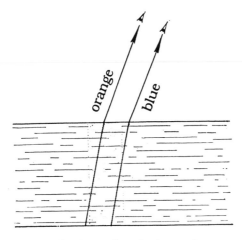

Fig. 180. How colored edges arise on shadows on turbid water.

mist: you have to look over a fairly long distance either through the water in the shadow or through the illuminated water.

Shadows on slightly muddy water show still another phenomenon: their edges are colored: the one toward you is bluish, the one away from you is orange. This phenomenon can be observed in the shadow of every post or bridge or ship. It is caused by scattering by innumerable particles of dust floating in the water; many of these are so small that they show a preference for scattering blue rays. It can be seen in Fig. 180 that the particles on your side are luminous on a dark background so that they send a bluish light to your eye, whereas on the side of the shadow away from you, you can see light from the bottom of the water (or from the scattering water in the neighborhood), deprived of its blue rays and colored orange by the nonilluminated particles in the shadow. This shows that the phenomenon is the same as that of the blue sky and the yellow setting sun—see § 195. Our eye is made particularly sensitive to it by the two contrasting colors along the edges.

The color dispersion that occurs together with the refraction also causes edges of shadow that happen to have the same colors as the scattering edges. The relative importance of these factors will depend on the numbers of floating particles.

Examine the color of the edges from every viewpoint for different directions of incidence of light and shadow. Note also the distinct bluish color of nar-

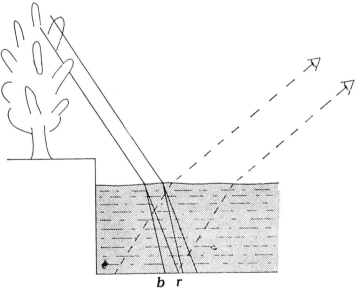

Fig. 181. How colored edges arise on shadows on turbid water.

row pencil beams of light that penetrate the foliage in a wood and fall on the water of a clear stream, forming an orange patch of light on the bottom.

248. The aureole of light about our shadow on the water

> Look'd at the fine centrifugal spokes
>> round the shape of my head in the sunlit water ...
> Diverge, fine spokes of light, from the shape of my head,
>> or any one's head, in the sunlit water!

Walt Whitman, 'Crossing Brooklyn Ferry' (*Leaves of Grass*)

This lovely phenomenon can be seen best of all when looking from a bridge or deck of a ship at your shadow falling on the restlessly dashing waves. Thousands of light and dark lines diverge in all directions from the shadow of your head. This aureole can be seen only around your own head (cf. §§ 188 and 191). The rays do not converge precisely at one and the same point but only approximately. Another remarkable thing is the increase in the general brightness in the surroundings of the shadow.

Nothing of it can be seen on calm water or on water with even waves; it can be seen only well when irregular little mounds of water rise from the surface. The water must be rather turbid: the farther you are from the coast and on the open sea, the weaker the aureole becomes.

The explanation is that each unevenness in the water's surface casts a streak of light or shade behind it; all these streaks run parallel to the line from the sun to the eye so that you can see them meet perspectively at the antisolar point, that is, in the shadow image of your head—see § 221.

The streaks are at times so clear that they can be followed even at a fairly large angular distance from the antisolar point. Usually, however, they are clearest of all near the antisolar point, because in that direction our gaze traverses a long path, through either clearly illuminated or shaded water. The increase in the general intensity of light in the vicinity of the antisolar point is, perhaps, to be attributed to the fact that the scattering of particles is stronger backward than across the beam—see § 194.

Another aureole of this kind can be observed when you stand in the shade of a solitary tree whose spreading branches cast patches of light and shade on to the water beneath. The rays of light penetrating the liquid give the same optical effect as those caused by unevenness on a surface.

It is interesting to realize that actually the rays of light do not run at all parallel with the line connecting sun and eye, for, as a conse-

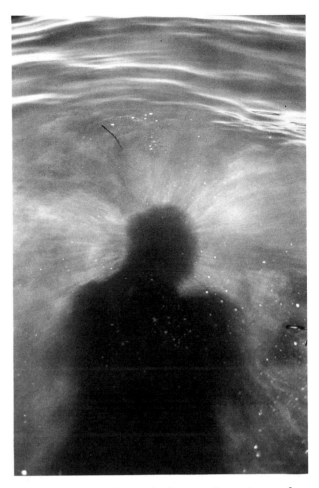

This photograph of the shadow on the water surface was taken holding the camera in front of the eye: bright rays appear to radiate outward from the head. (Photo by Hannu Karttunen)

quence of refraction, they are deflected through a certain angle. But, on the other hand, our eye sees the traces of those pencil beams in their turn on the water, altered by refraction, so that, after all, the part of the pencil beam traveling in the water is seen as the prolongation of the part traveling through the air.

249. The water line along the sides of a ship

> Three circumstances contribute to disguise the water-line upon
> the wood: where a wave is thin, the colour of the wood is shown
> a little through it; when a wave is smooth, the colour of the
> wood is a little reflected upon it; and when a wave is broken, its
> foam more or less obscures and modifies the line of junction.
>
> Ruskin, *Modern Painters*

You might, however, be equally justified in stating that the water line
is made visible by these very same factors! Observe, in the case of ships,
sailing or lying still, what the optical phenomena are by which we
judge where the water begins, that is, the position of the water line.

250. The color of waterfalls

When the light is favorable, the green color of water falling over rocks
can often be seen very well. It is a remarkable fact that rocks emerging here and there from the water, in reality black or gray, appear to
have a reddish tinge: this must obviously be explained as a contrast
color—see § 114.

This phenomenon can be seen most distinctly where the water foams
and splashes. It is known that, in a laboratory, contrast colors occur
with greater intensity if the boundaries between the fields are made
indistinct. To reproduce the case in question, lay a strip of gray
paper on a green background, with a small sheet of tissue paper over
it, and then observe how beautifully the reddish contrast color of the
gray can be seen through it. It seems not at all improbable that a
similar part is played in nature by the translucent watery mist. Cf.
§§ 241 and 243.

251. The color of solids. Variability of shadows

We have studied the way light is reflected by lakes, rivers, and seas,
either directly by the surface or by particles below the surface. At the
same time, we have obtained a model of the way in which a solid is
illuminated and reflects light. In rocks, stones, earth, and tree
trunks, which are considered opaque, we find that what happens in
a layer of several meters of water occurs in less than a millimeter in
solids: dispersion and absorption are much greater, but the optical
phenomena are actually the same. The typical character of a solid is
expressed in its degree of smoothness, roughness, or lack of luster.
We speak of regular or irregular reflection, or dispersion of light.

Solids that display regular reflection of light are rare in the outdoors, but there are glass, ice, and metals. Also, glazed roofing tiles and slates sometimes reflect the sunlight strongly, and windows of buildings in the distance reflect the light of the setting or rising sun. The crystals of freshly fallen snow can reflect the sun in the most bizarre and unexpected way.

An example of irregularly reflecting surfaces is a wet road, which gives rise to light columns, similar to those caused by a rippling water surface. A peculiarity of objects whose surface reflects and disperses light internally is that they give an image and a shadow simultaneously. We have already seen this phenomenon with clouds over the sea (§ 235, Fig. 175); on a smaller scale it is caused by birds hopping on moist sand in the sunshine.

Most solids out of doors, however, are matt, that is, they are covered in minute lumps and bumps that do not reflect but disperse light. Sunlight falling on to a field or other stretch of land illuminates it in such a way that it is equally visible from all directions. However, on close inspection, it appears that the dispersion of light by such a solid varies in different directions. For example, at night the ground in front of a streetlight is illuminated quite well, but that behind it appears pitch dark. In such a situation, estimate from a distance where the brightest circle of light is; when you then walk toward the lamppost you will notice that it is not directly beneath the lamp but somewhere closer to you. In other words, the light is not dispersed equally in all directions; the surface displays a transition from regular reflection to general dispersion. The asymmetry of light dispersion may also be studied by a comparison of the landscape away from the sun and toward it.

Shadows on the road surface may appear or disappear according to the direction of observation. When at night you observe shadows caused by posts and trees illuminated by a street light, you will notice that when you look in a direction at right angles to the incident light, the shadow is hardly perceptible, but when you look in the direction of the light, the shadow is very clear. The explanation of this is that it is not the shadow that changes but the brightness of the surroundings: the road surface disperses light mainly in a forward direction, seen from the side it is almost as dark as the shadow itself.

The phenomenon of appearing and disappearing shadows is even more clearly perceptible when observed in the light from two streetlamps—see also § 257.

It is because of the numerousness of the light-dispersing surfaces that the landscape shows the gradual transition from light to dark, from one color to another. Reflections from water or smooth solids add bright stretches of light here and there that give life and sparkle to the landscape.

252. Light dispersion by a rimed surface

When, after a period of frost, thaw sets in, trees and walls get covered in myriads of tiny ice crystals: hoarfrost. These crystals disperse light in a special, almost unique, way: when you look at right angles at the layer of ice, it is hardly perceptible; when you look more and more obliquely, the brighter the layer becomes, until, at very small angles, it is almost silvery white.

Evidently, each crystal disperses the light in all directions like a miniature lamp. The more obliquely we look, the more of these sources of light come into our field of vision. That is, the normally observed surface brightness at angle θ increases in direct proportion to $\sec\theta$, until we look at such a small angle that the crystals cover each other. The peculiarity of this kind of dispersion lies in the fact that the distances between the individual crystals are relatively large, so that the limit of brightness is reached only at very acute angles. A similar phenomenon may sometimes be observed when a bright white surface is covered in droplets of water.

253. The color of green leaves

Trees, meadows, fields, as well as separate leaves, show us a wealth of green in infinite variety. To discover some kind of regularity in this abundance of phenomena, we will begin by examining one leaf of any 'ordinary' tree (oak, elm, or beech), so as to gain an insight into the formation of groups of color in a landscape.

A leaf on a tree is usually much more strongly illuminated on one side than on the other, and the color is essentially determined by whether you are looking at the side that is directly illuminated or the other side. In the former case, the light sent to us from the leaf is partly reflected at its surface, so that the color becomes lighter but grayer. Moreover, when the leaf is illuminated from the front (relative to the observer), a bluish hue mingles with the green, and when from the back, a yellow hue. This reminds us of our observations concerning the scattering of light—see § 196. And, indeed, in a leaf, though much less than 1 mm ($^{40}/_{1000}$) thick, all the processes of reflection, absorption, and scattering take place in the same way as in an ocean tens or hundreds of meters (yards) deep. Absorption is caused here by the chlorophyll grains; scattering is probably brought about by innumerable grains of all kinds in which the contents of cells are so rich, or perhaps by the unevenness of the leaf's surface.

From an optical point of view, a leaf is much more complex than a lake or a sea; indeed, a more complex object is difficult to imagine! It is illuminated not on one, but on two sides; moreover, one side is matt and the other is shiny, while the intensity and color of the inci-

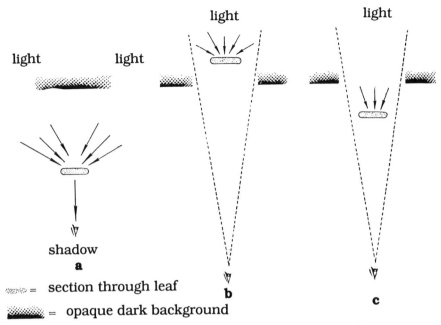

light   light   light   light

shadow

a

≈ = section through leaf

b

= opaque dark background

c

Fig. 182. Green leaves under different conditions of illumination.

dent light are usually different at the two sides. The possible combinations of optical phenomena are astronomical!

The emerald green of grass in a bright light is particularly lovely seen from a shady spot against a dark background—see Fig. 182a. It seems as if each little blade were literally burning with a green inward glow. The incident light pouring on it laterally is scattered by the millions of minute grains, so that each blade casts a stream of light sideways toward your eye.

The difference in color between grass illuminated from the front and from the back can be seen at once by standing in a meadow and looking alternately toward and away from the sun. This difference corresponds to the difference, familiar to painters, between the green of Willem Maris in his landscapes, painted against the light, and the green of Mauve, who shows a preference for working with his back to the light.

Illumination by the sun and that by the blue sky differ in that the light of the sun is stronger, but is reflected more locally, so that a leaf seems patchy. Should the leaf reflect the sun's rays more or less at the regular angle of reflection, its color more nearly approaches light gray or white. If the sun is very low, flooding the landscape with a deep red light, the foliage of the trees loses its fresh green tint and becomes faded-looking: there are hardly any green rays left in the light source to be scattered back by the leaves.

The upper sides and undersides of leaves differ in tint even if the illumination is the same. The upper side is smooth, therefore reflects better, and so is also more patchy. The underside is duller and paler and shows more pores; the cells lie much farther apart, and there are spaces filled with air that reflect the light before it penetrates the inside of the leaf—see § 258. The upper side as a rule is at the same time the illuminated side. Note the differences in color when you turn the leaf of a tree by 180° while the illumination, and so on, remains the same. Whenever the wind is rather strong, all the trees look patchy on the lighted side and the general color becomes paler than usual; the leaves are turned about in every direction so that their upper sides are seen quite as often as their undersides.

Young leaves are fresher, of a lighter color than old ones; this difference becomes less noticeable in the course of the summer.

The leaves on the outside of the crown of the tree differ from those inside; they differ not only in size, thickness, and hairiness, but also in color. The color of the shoots at the foot of the tree, and on the trunk, is usually very light.

Finally, an important part is played by the background. Stand under a tree and study its crown. The same leaves, first a fresh green against the background formed by other trees, change into black silhouettes as soon as you look at them against the sky—see § 109. The effect depends on the ratio of the brightness of the leaf to the brightness of the sky as a background. It is therefore weak if the leaf is illuminated from all sides, especially if the sun shines on it (Fig. 182b) and strongest if the leaf receives light from a limited part of the sky only, as generally occurs when a tree is surrounded by others (Fig. 182c), or during the one-sided illumination of twilight. The difference between the ordinary green and the black silhouette is then so great that you can hardly believe it to be merely an optical illusion! And yet it is nothing but a matter of contrasts; the bright sky is so enormously brighter than terrestrial objects.

254. The direct influence of light on the color of green leaves

Apart from the effects discussed in the preceding section, which are purely optical, light causes certain direct changes in plants, which result in their changing color within a few minutes.

In the shade, the leaf-green grains in the leaf arrange themselves at the upper and lower edges of the epidermal cells, which gives the leaf a fresh green appearance. In bright sunlight, however, the grains shift to the sides of the cells, which gives the leaf a yellowish appearance. This effect is particularly noticeable in duckweed.

Under the influence of sun or wind, a number of plants, such as aconite (monk's hood), shine as if they were lacquered. This is caused by the swelling of the epidermal cells, which stretches the surface of the leaf until it is perfectly smooth.

255. Light and shade in the crown of a tree

The foliage around the crown of a tree becomes a fine fabric, a myriad of dots and dashes between you and the sky. If you look more closely into the crown, you will see that it becomes ever denser, but never opaque; it is always transparent, with openings of light that give you a through-view to the sky. Then you see, heavier and heavier, a mass of lighted foliage, blinding and inextricable, except here and there where a single leaf is visible. Then, under this mass, deep through-views of broken, irregular darkness that gradually turns into a series of transparent, green-lit, hazy hollows; and numerous intertwined branches. The beams of sunlight that rain down from above and briefly stroke the shining leaves lose themselves and then become visible again on an emerald sod or knurled roots. Then they are dispersed upward to the whitish undersides of vague clumps of foliage. The shadows of the higher branches form a gray pattern on the velvet trunk and rest as checkered shading on the glistening earth. But everything is penetrable and transparent, and yet inextricable and incomprehensible; except where, close to you, two or three unmoving large leaves, standing out right across this maze and mystery of blinding light and dreamlike shade, make us think of the realization of what we feel and imagine, but can never distinguish individually.

> The trees were broad and full; and the light that hung around their trunks was green like moonlight.
>
> Timmermans, *Pallieter*

256. Vegetation in the landscape

Separate trees. Trees, among all the elements that go to form a landscape, are virtually the only ones to show, when illuminated laterally, the wonderful beauty of contrast between their sunlit and their shaded sides. For this reason, they give us the impression of being solid things, 'showing again and again that space with its three dimensions is a visible reality'. This contrast is toned down by the roundness of the treetops, but accentuated again by the contrast in color.

Trees seen against the light stand out darkly against the distant background and make us feel their distance, their remoteness, more sharply; this is caused by the stereoscopic effect quite as much as by the difference in the shade of color. This explains why a tree is so often depicted in the foreground of stereoscopic prints and of landscape paintings. The effect is to a certain extent comparable to that of a landscape seen through an open window or from under the vault of an archway. Seen from under the high trees of our avenues, the buildings of a town seem larger and more stately.

The most striking contrast with its background is shown by a tree delineated against the orange glow of an evening sky. The silhouette of the fantastically distorted juniper on a solitary sandhill, or of the solemn firs with their dense growth of needles, is black, its outline very sharp. Other trees are more open: the thinnest is the birch, with its graceful arabesques, its color forming, especially against the light, a lovely contrast to the color of the sky.

> On a sunny morning at the end of February, I will show you the color of the birch twigs against the azure vault. All their slender sprays seem to glow with a purple fire, while, across that delicate glow, the sky looks down on you with wonderful tenderness. Wait, watch attentively, and do not depart before you have understood. Such a store of happiness is to be gained that you can wait patiently until the winter for this wonderful light to appear again.
>
> Duhamel, *La Possession du Monde*

Woods. The silhouette of a wood seen close to you and against the light is certainly very irregular, but the wood itself is too transparent, and its light effects too varied, to give an impression of strength and massiveness. The effect of unity is more pronounced at a greater distance, when the tops of trees shine gold and green against the deepening blue of the hills behind, or when the sunlit foliage of groups of leafy trees stands out against the tall dark fir trees. A distant wood in flat countryside can actually be compared to rows of hills: its shade is at least as dark, its color, owing to scattering in the atmosphere, is just such a lovely misty blue; it is arranged in successive rows made individually distinct by aerial perspective—see § 110.

The scenery in the interior of the wood is unique of its sort, showing, as it does, neither horizon nor a definite outline. In the spring, you can see above your head young green leaves everywhere, glistening in the yellow-green transmitted light. In summertime, after the tiring glare of the white sky, so trying to look at, your eyes can rest here, once more free to look about in every direction.

The wood is illuminated most of all at midday when the sun shines from such a height as to penetrate the tops of the trees. The play of light and shade differs in every plane; its charm disappears as soon as you focus your eyes at a certain distance, but it reappears when you no longer consciously try to find it, but surrender spontaneously and naturally to the influence of your surroundings. On autumn mornings, the sun's rays strike here and there between the trunks and their path can be followed through the slightly hazy air, especially when you look in a direction near the sun (§ 217); in this way, the fascination of aerial perspective is brought very close.

Flowers. Heather is about the only one of our flowers (in Holland) to cover extensive surfaces of land. In August, when it is in full bloom, a curious harmony of color arises, of purple country and dark-blue sky, which some do not admire, but which to others, in the abundant light and freedom of nature, is exceptionally impressive. Gray clouds covering the sky soften the harmony of colors, but at the same time weaken the contrast between light and shade.

Fruit trees in blossom owe their splendor largely to the meager development of foliage at that time of the year. The white and the pale soft pink against the blue sky are at their very best only when the sun shines on them, or when seen from the top of a dyke or hill with meadows in the background.

Meadows. One level expanse of a single color gives an impression of smoothness and open space and yet, thanks to its many details, it is sufficiently varied to suggest buoyancy and softness. Why else should its aspect be so different from that of an expanse of sand? Seen at a distance, the green runs to blue-green and, farther off, it approaches more and more the atmospheric blue of the sky.

257. Illumination of a landscape toward and away from the sun

There is a remarkable difference in color and structure to be seen in almost any landscape, depending on whether you look at it toward the sun or away from it. The entire aspect of the scenery changes. Use a mirror to view the scene in two directions simultaneously.

1. A field of young corn, a meadow, a field of lupins, is yellow-green toward the sun, but away from the sun, it is bluish. The reason? Look very closely at one little leaf in particular. Pick it and hold it toward the sun and then away from the sun. In the former case, you will mainly see light falling through the leaf, in the latter case, light reflected by its surface—see § 253. The colors and light are sometimes influenced by the direction of the wind.

2. The waves in a field of ripe rye are caused primarily by the changing aspects of the ears. Suppose that the wind is blowing toward the sun: facing the sun, you will see virtually only bright light waves, which arise when the ears incline toward the sun to such an extent

as to reflect the sunlight toward your eyes; looking away from the sun, you will see a few bright but more dark waves. The latter arise when the ears bend in such a way as to cast shadows on those near to them.

These phenomena change with every direction of wind, and of gaze, and with the altitude of the sun.

3. A lawn mown with a lawnmower looks much lighter in color when the direction of mowing is away from you than when is toward you; in the former direction you see much more reflected light. The contrast on a field of stubble is very strong; there, the successive rows are alternately light and dark because the mowing machine has passed alternately up and down. If you turn around, you will see the shades the other way about. Freshly plowed land glistens if you look at right angles to the direction of the still damp furrows.

4. Duckweed on the water of a ditch behaves in exactly the opposite way to grass. Away from the sun, it is yellow-green, but toward it, pale gray-green. Very close observation shows that in the latter case irregular reflection on the surface is much stronger. You do not see through the leaves of this plant.

5. Heathland, when the heather has stopped flowering, is darker seen toward the sun; away from the sun, more glistening, silky, light brown-gray, evidently owing to reflections.

6. Fruit trees in full bloom are white only when seen away from the sun. Seen toward the sun, the blossoms stand out black against the sky.

7. Similarly, the branches and twigs of trees are gray and brown seen away from the sun; black, without detail, toward the sun.

8. A brick-paved road is brown-red toward the sun, white-gray away from the sun.

9. A gravel road is white-gray toward the sun, brown-gray away from the sun.

10. Sea foam is a pure white away from the sun; toward the sun, however, it is rather darker than its surroundings among the myriads of reflections and flickerings of the playful water.

11. An uneven road, covered with snow, seen toward the sun, looks, as a whole, darker than the smooth snow at the side; away from the sun, it is the other way round.

A lawn, showing the tracks made by a lawnmower. The alternate bright and dark strips disappear when you look at them at right angles.

12. Consider waves on a lake, the wind blowing toward the sun: if you look away from the sun, the water appears a somber blue, with here and there blue-black streaks radiating from the point of observation, corresponding to the blue parts of the sky; each one of the many waves stands out separately. When you look toward the sun, everything is a laughing bright blue, waves can be seen only in the distance, in endless numbers.

13. Notice that when you look toward the sun all objects having their shaded side toward you appear dark, but with lovely light edges. This is the charm of photos taken against the light.

These and many other instances give altogether an inexhaustible opportunity for observation. Always try to find the explanation by first observing things as a whole and then individually. Also, compare §§ 213 and 259.

258. How colors are affected by humidity

Humidity alone is not sufficient to explain this enlivening of color. You must also take into account that as soon as objects are covered by a thin film of water, their surface becomes smoother; they no longer scatter white light on all sides, and therefore their own color predominates and becomes more saturated.

Rain alters the color of the ground altogether. Street cobbles reflect more strongly the farther away they are from you and the more steeply your gaze falls on them. It is surprising how splendidly not only Tarmac, but also very uneven paved roads can reflect at large angles. The color of roads of sand, soil, and gravel grows darker and warmer; the first drops of rain stand out as dark spots[12]. Why? The water penetrates every gap between the grains of sand. A ray of light, which otherwise would have been scattered by the topmost layers, can now penetrate much deeper before it is sent back to your eye, and is almost entirely absorbed over this longer path.

A pool of water on a Tarmac road reveals in beautiful shades of color:

(a) the surface of the water reflecting the blue sky;
(b) a black edge where the ground is still damp;
(c) the gray surroundings.

Algae in a ditch form a dark-green, fibrous mass; a portion protruding from the water looks a much paler green because of the air between the fibers. But hold those paler parts under water, shake them, and press them together, and air bubbles will issue from them, while at the same time they become darker.

> It is true that the dusky atmosphere 'obscures all objects', but it is also true that nature, never intending the eye of man to be without delight, has provided a rich compensation for this shading of the tints with darkness, in their brightening by moisture. Every colour, wet, is twice as brilliant as it is when dry; and when distances are obscured by mist, and bright colours vanish from the sky, and gleams of sunshine from the earth, the foreground assumes all its loveliest hues, the grass and foliage revive into their perfect green, and every sunburnt rock glows into an agate.
>
> Ruskin, *Modern Painters*

259. Light accentuation in the landscape after rain

After it has rained, the landscape changes; it shows all the signs of the shower. Not only the heavy, moving clouds and the clearing sky

---

[12] Dry soil reflects about 4% of the light; wet soil, 8–9%. Dry sand reflects about 37%; wet sand, about 24%.

with its stark contrasts, but also the shining light that is spread all over the landscape, contribute to this very special atmosphere.

It is especially the wet leaves that cause the bright spots of light: the leaves of the turnips, the crowns of the oak trees, the rushes along ditches and ponds. But all this glitter can only be observed at the side facing the sun at relatively small angles with the incident rays.

With this illumination, we are struck by the bright lighting, in the direction of the sun, of wet, dead leaves that lie here and there on the grass. This effect is used effectively by archeologists to trace flint-stone weapons: walk into the direction of the low-lying sun and note the fragments that glitter brightly in the distance. In other words, use is made of the reflective properties of the flint stone which deflects the rays of light less than its surrounding.

260. Human figures in the landscape

From my window, I see a man stripped to the waist, working at the floor of the gallery. When I compare the color of his skin with that of the wall outside, I notice how colored the half-tints of the flesh are compared with those of the inanimate material. I noticed the same yesterday in the Place St. Sulpice, where a young urchin had clambered on to one of the statues of a fountain, standing in the sun. Dull orange was his flesh, bright violet the gradations of the shadows and golden the reflections in shaded parts turned toward the ground. Orange and violet predominated in turn or became intermingled. The golden color was slightly tinged with green. The true color of the flesh can be seen only in the sun and in the open air. If a man puts his head out of a window, its coloring is quite different from what it is indoors, which shows the absurdity of studies done in a studio where each does his best to reproduce the wrong color.

Delacroix, *Journal*

When, in the open, you see a girl in a white dress, the side of hers that is turned toward the sun will be blindingly bright. The other side, however, will appear bluish. If the girl stands between a green, sun-drenched lawn and the sun, the folds of her dress on the side of the lawn will appear green.

Leonardo da Vinci, *Trattato*

261. Shadows and dark patches

Look around and see where there are dark patches in the scenery: (a) in woods and shrubberies: between the trunks and stems; (b) in the town: open windows in the distance and gateways. These are excellent examples of the 'black body' as it is termed by physicists. They are spaces in which you can look only through a narrow aperture; the light rays that enter it can emerge only after being reflected a number of times, becoming considerably fainter each time. A body of this kind absorbs nearly all the rays: dark woods re-emit only 4% of the incident light and dark gate openings sometimes less than $\frac{1}{1000}$th On the other hand, you must bear in mind that the darkness of a wood is only relative, and if you draw near and your eye has adapted itself to the light, you will see that everything in it shows light and color. Similarly, every detail in a room, seen from inside, can be distinguished, whereas the same room seen from outside through the open window looks pitch dark.

Delicate objects outlined against the bright sky usually look black, but this is only because of the contrast. This is so, for example, for foliage—see § 253.

Examine systematically the colors of shadows!

> All ordinary shadows must be coloured somehow, never black or nearly black. They are evidently of a luminous nature ... It is a fact that shadows are colours just as much as light parts are.
>
> Ruskin, *Modern Painters*

Where the sun shines, its brilliant yellowish rays predominate over the light radiated from the sky, but in the shade, light falls only from the blue or gray sky. Shadows are, therefore, generally bluer than their surroundings and this difference becomes accentuated by contrast.

> From my window, I see the shadows of people walking along the shore; the sand in itself is violet, but the sun makes it golden; the shadows of those people are so violet that the ground seems yellow.
>
> Delacroix, *Journal*

262. Silhouettes

We speak of silhouettes when objects are portrayed against a light background as dark shadow outlines filled in with black. They may be brought about in various ways, of which a number have already been discussed. Others are:

1. When buildings and trees are portrayed against a brilliant golden twilight sky, while they are only faintly illuminated by the darkening evening sky at the side from which we are looking. The one-sided-ness of the illumination at this hour of the day is the prime cause (see § 253). Silhouetting may come about in the middle of the day when there is heavy cloud, except for a light band near the horizon that glows in a yellowish orange color (see § 202).

2. At night, when a light brightly illuminates the road surface and somebody moves between the spot of light and our eyes. Also, when the sun or moon makes the sea glitter like a stream of light, against which a sailing boat is portrayed as a black object.

3. When drizzle or mist spreads a haze that erases all small differences in brightness, while large objects remain recognizable: their outline sharp. Trees, churches, houses, and other buildings, are silhouetted dark gray against a light gray background.

4. At night, when large objects are portrayed against a starry sky.

263. Unidirectional and omnidirectional illumination

The impression of a landscape is determined to a large degree by the light in which it is seen: this determines the mood and creates the atmosphere. We shall first consider point-source or unidirectional lighting, then multidirectional or general lighting, and finally diffused lighting.

At night, the light of an arc lamp casts sharp, dark shadows, because it is virtually a point source that dominates all other sources of light near it. Faces in this sort of light look old because the lines are starkly accentuated.

When the sun shines and the sky is clear, shadows are also sharp and dark, but they are softened slightly by the diffuse light from the blue sky. When the sun is half hidden by clouds, shadows become blurred; when it has disappeared completely behind the clouds, no well-defined shadows are cast, but instead there are dark and bright areas. The transition may also happen in a different way: if an open patch in the woods is lit by a small part of the sky, which may be smaller or larger than the open patch and that may therefore bring about other effects as well.

When the sun is high in the sky, shadows do not play an important part in the landscape: all things are tiringly bright; only when the sun sinks lower do the rich alternations between light and shadow come about.

In flat or gently undulating countryside, shadows exaggerate the relief when the sun is very low; its rays then fall almost tangentially across the land and cause very special alternations of light and shadow. On a small scale, this may be perceived around sunset on a sandy plain: every stone, every unevenness casts a long shadow; the entire plain resembles a moonscape and gives an impression of unreality. A similar effect may be seen when the sun is high in the sky and throws its rays almost in parallel with a plastered wall: every unevenness is highly accentuated and clearly visible.

Another, very interesting impression is obtained when the sun is low in the sky and there is a bright light behind us: we then see objects silhouetted against the bright sky around the sun with each object surrounded by a golden edge of light.

Finally, we must say something of the peace, harmony, and tranquility that descend over the landscape when, after days of sunshine and blue skies, the sky becomes overcast. All brightnesses are less clear and more equal to each other; shadows have become almost extinct; and local reflections have disappeared. Free and without being blinded, our eyes can roam in all directions again. Someone once remarked: 'Note how the faces of people at twilight when the sky is overcast look softer and show more tenderness.' That remark has reconciled me with yet another gray day on more than one occasion.

A very special effect arises when the sky is overcast and the gently rolling landscape is covered in freshly fallen snow. In the faint light, the snowy land looks so even that it is impossible to say where a hill begins or ends. When you walk across such a field, only your sense of balance tells you when you are going up a hill and when you are going down it.

Compare the lack of structure in such a landscape with the sharply defined bluish shadows of ski tracks in the sunshine. Notice how the glittering of a rippling water surface disappears when the sky becomes overcast. Every time, you will get a strong impression of the significance of the sun and shadows for our versatile sight as well as for the creation of differences in brightness in the landscape.

> The moving, waving and radiating of a directed beam of light; not the dull, general light from the sky that falls on to the landscape without life, direction or meaning, and treats everything the same; but the breathing, living, jubilant light that has feeling and enjoys itself, that accepts one and rejects the other, that seeks and finds and loses again, darting from rock to rock, from leaf to leaf, or sparkles, depending on what it strikes; or, in more sober mood, enveloping and devouring everything in the deep fullness of its rest, and then again losing itself in con-

fusion, doubt, haziness or passing by and disappearing, caught in melting mist or united with the melancholy of the air. But always, blazing or dying down, sparkling or shining quietly, the living light breathes even in its deepest rest; it may sleep, but will never die.

Ruskin, *Modern Painters*

Chapter 13

Luminous Plants, Animals, and Stones

264. Glowworms

> Tell B that I have crossed the Alps and the Apennines, that I have visited the 'Jardin des Plantes', the museum arranged by Buffon, the Louvre with its masterpieces of sculpture and painting, The Luxembourg with the works of Rubens, and that I have seen a glow worm!!!

Letter from Faraday to his mother, *Life and Letters*

As a matter of fact, glowworms are not worms at all, but beetles. The female glowworms are wingless and creep about, the males fly. The common glowworm (Lampyris noctiluca) is abundant in some of the southern counties of England and is found in Scotland south of the Tay, but not in Ireland. The luminous organs occupy the last two segments of the hinder abdomen and contain a substance which, when oxidized, becomes luminous by chemiluminescence. The color of the rays emitted is precisely the one to which our eyes are most sensitive and contains infrared, so that this beetle might be called a really ideal source of light, if only it would shine somewhat brighter!

The female emits the brightest light, and remains still, while the male flies about humming softly. Even the eggs and pupa are luminescent. It appears that occasionally you can find a luminescent snail shell: it is not the snail that emits light, but the glowworm that attacks the snail, eats it, and penetrates the shell.

There is a delightful charm in such a feebly shining yellow-green point of light in the grass: it looks just like a starlet. And this gives us the idea of estimating its luminous intensity by comparison with a real star, say, Vega, which in summer is high in the sky. Such a comparison is not all that simple, but by getting closer to the insect and then moving away from it again, then getting closer again, and so on, I estimate that the glowworm at a distance of 13 m (45 ft) is about as bright as Vega. Now, it is known that that star appears as bright to us as 1.4 candles at a distance of 1000 m (1100 yards). It follows that the luminous intensity, i, of the glowworm is $i/13^2 = 1.4/1000 \times 1000$, from which $i = 0.0002$ candela.

265. Luminescence[1] of the sea

Luminescence of the sea is caused mainly, at least in our latitudes (40–60°), by millions of microscopic marine animals of the species Noctiluca miliaris. These are protozoa belonging to the group known as 'flaggellates', about 0.2 mm ($\frac{8}{1000}$ in) in size, that is, just large enough to be seen with the naked eye as tiny, separate dots. They emit light only when oxygen is dissolved in the water, as by stirring or by the breaking of the waves. This causes a certain substance to become oxidized, but not noticeably heated; nor does its light show the same composition as that of a glowing body; it is not a case of heat radiation but of chemiluminescence: it contains neither ultraviolet nor infrared rays, but only those colors that convey a strong impression of light to our eye, such as, in particular, yellow and green.

If you immerse your fingers into the sea when luminescent organisms are present in great numbers, you may feel a slight pricking. By this you can foretell by day whether the beautiful luminescence will be visible that night.

Luminescence of the sea can often be seen splendidly on thundery evenings in summer after a hot day. The glow of lights along a promenade or from hotels can always make you doubt whether what you see is really luminescence or the white foam on the crests of waves (see § 81); for this reason, the beauty of this phenomenon is only perfect on an absolutely dark night. If, however, the conditions for observing are not so ideal, the next best thing is to take off your shoes and socks or stockings, go into the water and stir it with your hand below the surface.

If luminescence cannot be seen clearly, you will nevertheless see, while stirring, many a small stray spark here and there emitting light for a second and then going out. Fill a small bucket with sea water and put it somewhere where it is absolutely dark. Even on less favorable days, you will see signs of luminescence by pouring the water into a bin, or by exciting the microscopic beings by adding alcohol, formol or some acid to the water. Pour the luminescent water into a glass and the little animals collect on its surface. Tap the glass: the mechanical vibration will cause them to emit light, and if you do this repeatedly, the emission of light becomes gradually feebler.

Occasionally, sea water is luminescent without your being able to distinguish the sparks. This is accounted for by the presence of bacteria (Micrococcus phosphoreus).

---

[1] The word 'phosphorescence', often used in this context, has a quite different meaning and should never be used in connection with the luminescence of the sea.

Draw up a scale for the luminescence of the sea. Practice on cold evenings when luminescence is certain not to be present and examine the appearance of foaming crest; on favorable evenings, you will then be able to observe the difference.

If you are on a trip across the sea, especially in the tropics, go and stand on a dark night on the bow or stern of the ship out of the way of lamplight. You will see an almost continual display of sparks of light shooting past; this is made up of all kinds of luminous marine animal.

In the Indian Ocean, the entire sea seems at times to be luminous, while a system of enormous bands of light seems to rotate like the spokes of a wheel over its surface; these are wind waves and bow waves of the ship, which, as they pass along, make the water turbulent and therefore luminous[2].

266. Luminous fish and potatoes

It is because of luminous bacteria and not protozoa that fish in darkness sometimes seem to emanate a pale greenish light. The same effect may be noticed in potatoes, particularly during warm, humid weather.

267. Luminous wood and leaves

Sometimes on warm summer nights in a damp wood, you can see how decaying wood emits a faint light. This is caused by the fibers of the honey fungus (Armillaria mellea), which lies embedded in it everywhere.

Owls that live in hollow trees can get fibers of the fungus in their feathers and become luminous[3].

In spring or winter, try to find tree trunks from which the bark can easily be peeled and on which are dark, bifurcated fibers. Lay pieces of these trunks in damp moss and take them home. Keep them in a shady place under a bell-jar. In a few days' time, the fibers of the fungus covering the wood will begin to give out light. Occasionally, decaying branches, too, emit light: this is caused by bacteria.

The dry leaves of the beech and oak, gathered together in thick layers and half-decomposed, clearly emit light at a certain stage of decay. Try to find layers 10–30 cm (4–12 in) deep; do not take the loose leaves at the very top, but those lying underneath, close to-

---

[2] *Mar. Obs.*, 1954 and 1955

[3] D.H. Menzel and L.G. Boyd, *The World of Flying Saucers*, New York, 1963, p. 118.

gether, with yellow-white spots, and carry a handful of them into a perfectly dark room. The luminosity in this case is ascribed to fungus fibers of a species not yet determined.

268. Cats' eyes at night

We all know the fierce light cats' eyes seem to radiate. Yet, in reality, this light is only reflected, but directed reflected light, like that of a reflector on a bicycle or of the heiligenschein on dewy grass (see § 191). The rays penetrating the cornea form a very clear image on the background of the eye and this image reflects its rays through the same cornea: the pencil of light returns along practically the same path as that along which it entered. To see the phenomenon most clearly, the light, the eye of the cat, and the eye of the observer must lie in a straight line. This can be achieved by holding an electric torch level with your eyes; the shining of the cat's eyes will still be visible at a distance of some 80 m (90 yd). You will be astonished how many cats are looking at you!

The light reflected by dog's eyes is reddish. Sheep, rabbits, and horses also have luminous eyes, but human beings have not. These animals have directly behind the retina, between the retina and the choroid, a layer of strongly reflecting fibers, the tapetum. This enhances night vision: the light passes through the retina twice.

269. Reflection of light on mosses

On a beautiful clear morning, with dew everywhere on the grass, luxuriant clumps of moss of the kind Mnium that grow in fairly dark ditches, and which have two rows of leaflets on their delicate little stems, give the impression of being strewn with little shining stars. Each star radiates a goldish-green light, much steadier than the light of a sparkling dewdrop. On closer inspection, you will discover that there are little drops hanging everywhere under the leaflets. From this, it may be concluded that sunlight penetrates the edges of a leaf, whereupon it suffers total reflection in the drop and emerges after passing once more through the leaf: the gold-green color arises during this process.

Schistostega osmundacea, the famous luminous moss in the caverns and crevices of the Fichtel mountains in Bavaria, shows light reflections that are still more beautiful. In this moss, the spherical cells themselves play the part of reflecting drops.

270. Fluorescence of plant juices

In the spring, cut some pieces of the bark or leaves of the widely cultivated manna ash tree (Fraxinus ornus) and put them in a glass of water. The plant juice mixes with the water and this mixture begins to exhibit a peculiar blue luminescence that can be seen best if you cast a cone of the sun's rays through the fluid with a convex lens (magnifying glass). The phenomenon is accounted for by the liquid absorbing the violet and the, to us invisible, ultraviolet rays of the sun and emitting blue rays in their stead. A transformation of this kind is called 'fluorescence'.

The bark of the horse chestnut shows this phenomenon, too.

271. Luminescent ice and snow

An old legend relates that ice fields, after being illuminated for a long time by the sun, give a faint light at night. Snow, several degrees below freezing point, is also said to give light when brought into a dark room after the sun has cast its rays on it. Hailstones, especially those that fall first in a hailstorm, are said to show a kind of electric luminescence.

It is most likely that these observations are optical delusions, but experiments with careful precautions would be very interesting.

272. Scintillation from stones

Occasionally, you can see how the hooves of a horse strike the cobbles of a street with such force as to cause sparks.

Look for flints or quartzites, that is, ordinary pebbles, along the roadside. The latter are brownish stones slightly transparent along the edges, usually softly rounded without a crystalline structure. Knock two stones of this kind together in as dark a place as possible: sparks will arise and there will be a peculiar smell. This can be observed with other stones as well. The sparks are caused by particles being knocked off and becoming heated by the collision so that they glow. Certain gases are set free and these cause the peculiar odour.

273. Will-o'-the-wisps

Folklore tells us of will-o'-the-wisps dancing like tiny flames over a churchyard or enticing travelers into the morass. Their existence, however, is by no means a fairy tale. They have been seen and described by the famous astronomer Bessel and other excellent observers: the difficulty is that this phenomenon can occur in many different shapes.

Will-o'-the-wisps are found in bogs or places where peat is dug and along dykes: they have been seen occasionally on the damp, freshly manured ground of a nursery garden whenever someone stamped on the soil, and in muddy ditches or in drains when the water in them was stirred. They occur more during summer and on rainy, warm autumn nights than during cold seasons. They resemble tiny flames, about 1–11 cm (0.5–5 in) high and not more than 4 cm (2 in) broad. Sometimes, they are right on the ground, at other times they float about 10 cm (4 in) above it. That they dance about is apparently not true. What really happens is that they go out suddenly while another flame arises quite nearby and this probably accounts for the impression of rapid movement. Occasionally, they are blown along by the wind about half a meter (a few feet) before they become extinguished. Many other cases have been observed where a will-o'-the-wisp has burnt steadily for hours on end, a whole night long, and even in the daytime.

When a new flame arises, at times you hear the pop of a little explosion. The colors are said to be sometimes yellow, sometimes red or blue. In many cases, when an observer put his hand in the little flame, no heat was felt; a walking stick with a copper ferrule, held in the flame for a quarter of an hour, was almost at the same temperature as before; even dry reeds did not catch fire. In other cases, paper and cotton waste could be lighted by the flame. Generally, there is no smell, occasionally a faint smell of sulfur.

What do these mysterious flames consist of? Most observers now assume that it is a form of chemiluminescence probably caused by the combustion of methane.

Appendix A
Measuring Angles out of Doors

1. Try to estimate, without any auxiliary means, the altitude of stars. To this end, try to fix the position of the zenith first, then turn around and judge whether you would again locate it at the same place. After this, try to determine an altitude of 45°, then of 22.5°, and of 67.5°. You will find that you have a tendency not to bend your head sufficiently backward—cf. § 129. The errors made by a good observer never exceed 3°.

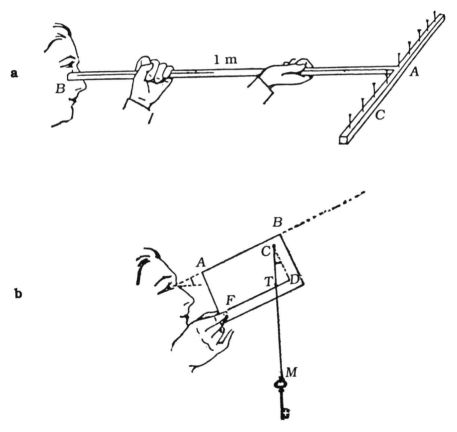

Fig. 183. Simple aids for estimating angles.

2. Stick three pins, *A*, *B*, and *C* in a piece of wood or a postcard in such a way that the angle to be measured is included exactly between the sighting direction *BA* and *BC*. The piece of wood must be properly fixed, either flat on a table or nailed to a tree. Then draw the lines *BA* and *BC* and read the required angle on a protractor (see also Fig. 106).

3. Fasten the middle of a lath (strip of wood), into which you have set nails or pins at equal distances from each other, to the end of another lath, 1 m (3 ft) long, and at right angles to it—see Fig. 183a. Hold the end of the rake thus produced with its stick *B* pressed against your cheekbone: when the nails *A* and *C* appear to cover the points in question, *AC/BA* will be equal to the required angle expressed in radians (one radian is 57°). If, for example, *AC* = 7 cm (3 in), *AC/BA* = 0.08 rad = 4.7°. For angles exceeding 20°, the calculation is not quite so simple.

4. Stretch your arm right in front of you and spread your fingers as wide apart as possible. The angle subtended by the tops of thumb and little finger will be about 20°. Or, again, with your arm outstretched, hold a short lath at right angles to the direction in which you are looking and measure in centimeters the apparent distance α between the two points under observation. The angle will then be about α degrees. This method can be made more accurate by measuring the precise distance from the lath to your eye.

5. There is a simple apparatus for measuring angles above the horizon that gives results correct to 0.5°. Take a rectangle of cardboard pierced at *C* and hang a thread *CM* through *C*, carrying a weight to make it serve as a plumbline—see Fig. 183b. Sight, say, a treetop whose height you want to measure accurately along *AB*, turn the cardboard ever so slightly out of the vertical plane, so that the thread hangs free, and then turn it slowly back so that the thread presses gently against it. The lines *CD*, perpendicular to *AB*, and *DT*, parallel to *AB*, must be drawn on the cardboard. The length of *CD* should preferably be 10 cm (4 in). The angle *DCM* will then be equal to the angle between *AB* and the horizontal plane and can be measured with a protractor or computed as $\tan^{-1}(TD/CD)$; for small angles, *TD* (in cm)/10 or *TD* (in inches)/4 is equal to the angle in radians.

Cf. §§ 1 and 141.

Appendix B
Photographing Natural Phenomena

Most celestial light and color phenomena can be photographed with any type of camera whose exposure is determined automatically or by an exposure meter. However, the large selection of lenses available for system cameras (such as 35 mm SLR cameras) clearly offers the best opportunities for capturing all types of phenomenon. The following suggestions are intended for users of system cameras.

The basic equipment of the photographer might be, for instance, 28 mm, 50 mm, and 135 mm objectives, a teleconverter doubling the focal length, a tripod, and a cable release. A zoom objective covering the corresponding range of focal lengths is also suitable. The speed of zoom lenses is usually one or two aperture stops lower than that of corresponding fixed-focal-length lenses, and this limits the pos-

Pekka Parviainen waiting for the sun to rise—with camera, of course!

sibilities of photographing auroras and noctilucent clouds, and also photographing by moonlight. For stellar photography, fixed-focal-length objectives are the only reasonable choice. For winter and stellar photography, it is also essential that the time exposures (B) of the camera work mechanically and do not consume battery power (this can be easily checked by removing the batteries from the camera and trying whether the exposure works regardless.)

If you can afford to further extend the selection of focal lengths for photographing light and color phenomena in the atmosphere, it is worth while getting an 18 mm or 20 mm superwide-angle objective. Another excellent selection of lenses would be: 18 mm, 24 mm, 35 mm, 85 mm, 200 mm, and a teleconverter doubling the focal length. The quality of the objectives should be as high as possible, provided the weight and price of the lenses do not become prohibitive.

Celestial light and color phenomena are often rather faint, so one should use a high contrast positive film. Different objects require films of different sensitivities. Color negative film is only suitable if you develop the prints yourself. If you use black and white film, much of the beauty of the phenomena is lost, but it is possible to bring out special effects in the darkroom by choosing high contrast papers and suitable exposures during the enlargement process.

Photographing in cold climates puts great demands on the camera and its batteries. Even a new button battery freezes rapidly at –15 °C (5 °F). To prepare for cold weather, you can connect the camera to an external battery that is kept in your pocket. Completely mechanical camera bodies also work in freezing conditions. In rare and rapidly changing situations, it is worth while squandering film. Several different exposures should always be made over a certain range, since the subjects under discussion are exceptionally difficult to capture without a small overexposure or underexposure. In the rush to get out, you should take along enough film. For night filming, a torch is essential. More than anything, getting the right pictures requires that the photographer is prepared to forgo his warm room and brave the cold to watch the sky.

Ordinary clouds can be photographed according to the exposure meter. With a zoom lens, the field of view can be controlled, making it far superior to fixed-focal-length lenses. The effect of the pictures is enhanced enormously if in clear weather you use a polarization filter to separate cumulus and cirrus clouds from the blue sky. Using this filter in sunny weather, you also get more saturated colors in ordinary landscape pictures. Using a teleobjective, interesting cloud details can be picked out.

Halo phenomena require for their general appearance that as large a field of view as possible is included in the same picture. At least a

28 mm wide-angle objective is needed (the 22° halo can then be included in its entirety in one picture). For successful halo photographs, a film with as high a contrast as is available should be used. In halo displays, the sun usually also has to be included in the picture. You then have to try to hide it behind a treetop, a streetlight, or a house. If hiding it is impossible, you should place the sun as near the center of the picture as possible to minimize internal reflections in the lens. These troublesome reflections are also visible in the viewfinder: the best way of avoiding them is to seek a suitable position for the sun with the aid of the viewfinder. If the sun is included in a halo picture, you should make sure that the fastest shutter speeds of the camera are sufficient for correct exposures. The exposure time should be increased toward overexposure, especially if the unshielded sun is included in the picture. Halo displays normally last tens of minutes or even hours, so there is usually enough time to plan the picture and find a suitable background. These suggestions apply also to photographing lunar halos.

Iridescent clouds and colored arcs are usually visible in small parts of clouds near the sun, and you should therefore use a short telephoto lens. The sun must not be included in the picture, nor should you try to get too near to it, so as to avoid reflections inside the lens. (All types of picture always turn out better if direct sunlight cannot get into the lens, even from farther outside the picture.) In photographing halos close to the sun, the sun itself should always be hidden behind, for instance, a treetop. For photographing iridescent clouds, all slide films are suitable and the exposure can be automatic or left to the exposure meter.

The rainbow appears larger when the sun is lower. The primary rainbow can be included in its entirety (180°) in the picture with an 18 mm superwide-angle lens. However, this type of lens distorts the corners of the picture, so it does not look entirely natural. The rainbow seen during summer afternoon showers is often so small that it can be photographed with an ordinary wide-angle lens. Beautiful pictures of the ends of the rainbow and of the interference bows can be obtained also with 35–135 mm lenses. The exposure may be determined with the exposure meter; some compensation toward underexposure is recommended. The rainbow is at its best only for a brief moment, so there is not much time to plan the picture. On the other hand, there is always time to get away from disturbing electricity and telephone wires. The formation of the rainbow can be predicted from the motions of the clouds. In this way, you gain some time to prepare for the rush.

Mirages normally appear very 'small'. Thus, a fairly long-focus tele-photo lens (focal length of at least 300 mm) is needed. The likelihood of mirages can be predicted, for instance, by watching the variations in air and water temperatures. Mirages usually last a long time, so there is time for planning the pictures. It is worth noting that near the open sea distant clouds can also appear as mirages.

Lightning cannot really be properly photographed except at night during strong lightning activity. The idea is to choose a suitable aperture and to take repeated pictures with a suitable exposure time in the direction of the lightning. This always uses up a lot of film and the results may still be disappointing.

It is impossible to guess the exact location of the next lightning strike, so a 28 mm wide-angle lens should be used in these attempts. If a distant thunderstorm remains stationary for some time, try 50 mm or 85 mm objectives to get good pictures. For lightning photography at night, time exposures (B) can be used. A suitable aperture for streak lightning is f/5.6–f/8 if the sensitivity of the film is 400 ASA. With this combination, you can use exposures of about 20 seconds, even if there are streetlight or advertizing signs in the picture, provided these are at least 100 m (110 yd) away. In darker surroundings, you can increase the exposure times to tens of minutes. Sheet lightning and lightning above the clouds can be photographed with 400 ASA film and apertures f/2.8 or f/2. Of course, the pictures will then show only the contours of clouds and possible glimpses of the surrounding landscape.

As already mentioned, lightning photography consumes a lot of film. For this reason, it is a good idea always to keep at hand inexpensive experimental film that you can use for this purpose without too much worry about the cost. Sometimes, the intervals between lightning flashes are quite constant. By observing the lightning activity, these intervals can be estimated and the exposure centered at the expected times in order to save film. Once there has been a lightning flash, the exposure should be stopped immediately; trying to get several lightning flashes in the same photograph can easily lead to over-exposed pictures. The worst problem in taking the photographs is the rain that comes with thunderstorms and which will soak the equipment. The camera can always be wrapped in a plastic bag, but the front lens of the objective will almost always get wet. It is best to keep the wind in your back; in light rain, the hood of the lens will give some protection.

Photographing lightning in the daytime is difficult. The only way is to watch the front of the storm and to release the camera every time there is a flash. The idea behind this strategy is that lightning strokes have a tendency to occur in pairs close to one another in time and space.

Auroras may vary quite a lot in brightness. For bright displays, you can rely on an automatic camera, which you should adjust slightly toward underexposure. If the exposures given by an automatic camera turn out wrong, you can use the rule of thumb that for bright auroras in latitudes around 60° you should use aperture f/2 and an exposure time of 10 seconds if 400 ASA film is used. Fainter auroras demand exposure times twice as long; bright auroras at higher latitudes may be successfully photographed with exposures of about 5 seconds. Because of the extent of auroras, a 28 mm wide-angle lens is required. For some storms covering the whole sky, a fish-eye lens is needed.

An auroral display usually starts to develop slowly, so there is time to prepare and seek out a suitable spot in the vicinity. The strongest auroral outbreak then starts quite rapidly and lasts for a few minutes only. The preparations should then be finished, the camera ready on its tripod, and the cable release attached to the camera. Strong auroral outbursts may be repeated several times during one night. If some quiescent auroral activity continues after the burst and you have the time, it is worth waiting in the hope of renewed outbreaks.

Noctilucent clouds visible at latitudes of around 60° in early summer are very slight and faint. They are also very extended and are best photographed with a superwide-angle or fish-eye lens. The pictures often look very dull, so it is better to concentrate observations and photography at the end of July and August. The clouds are then much brighter relative to the background sky and they also extend to the northern horizon, where they can be photographed with an ordinary wide-angle lens. The best results will probably be obtained with a 35 mm lens. For film, use a high-contrast, slow slide film (50 ASA will be enough even for the darker northern sky of early August). If the noctilucent clouds are at the center of the viewfinder, the exposure can be determined automatically or with the exposure meter. Aesthetically more pleasing pictures are obtained with a slight underexposure.

Photographs of noctilucent clouds do not always give the impression of night pictures, because the stars mostly appear faint. To make the pictures more informative, you can place in the foreground distant streetlights, buildings with illuminated windows, and so on. Ordinary dark clouds silhouetted in front of the noctilucent clouds also create a nightlike atmosphere. To some extent, the chances of noctilucent clouds in July–August can be judged during the day. Also, since the displays last for hours, there is time to prepare and plan the pictures.

Photographing by moonlight is possible only during full moon in snowy conditions or near water. A fast film and a high-speed lens are essential. The light and shadow give rise to a very high contrast image. Exposures can be determined automatically or with an exposure meter. Exposure times are roughly the same as for auroral displays. The slowness of films for long exposure times (the so-called reciprocity effect) takes care of a suitable underexposure and creates a romantic atmosphere.

Appendix C
Further Notes and References

For this new edition, it was felt desirable to omit the older and less accessible footnote references from the main body of the book. However, for completeness, these, mainly pre-1945, references are listed here in order of the sections or chapters to which they belong. In addition to what follows, good standard works quoted by Minnaert include Perntner-Exner, *Meteorologische Optik*, Vienna, Leipzig, 1922; F. Linke, *Handbuch der Geophysik*, **VIII**, Berlin, 1942–1961; and S. W. Visser, *Optische Verschijnselen aan den Hemel*, Gorinchem, 1957; to which may now be added R. A. R. Tricker, *Introduction to Meteorological Optics*, Elsevier, New York, 1970; and R. Greenler, *Rainbows, Halos, and Glories*, Cambridge University Press, 1980.

Chapter 1

§ 2   Goethe, *Farbenlehre*, **I**, 1, 394–395.

§ 3.   A. Wigand and E. Everling, *Verh. Dtsch. Phys. Ges.*, **14**, 748, 1912. *Dtsch. Luftf. Z.*, **16**, 298, 1912. *Science*, about 1930.

Chapter 2

        M. Pollock, *Light and Water*, London, 1903.

§ 9   H. R. Mill, *Geogr. J.*, **56**, 526, 1926. Vaughan Cornish, ibid., p. 518. *J. Opt. Soc. Am.* **10**, 141, 1925.

§ 10   Based on notes from G. J. F. Becker and R. J. van der Linde.

§ 13   Ramsauer, *Ann. Phys.*, **84**, 730, 1927.

§ 15   A. Hoffman, *Das Wetter* **34**, 133, 1917. F. Volz, *Handb. Geophys.*, **VIII**, 878–882, Figs. 278–280.

§ 16   Boys, *Soap Bubbles*.

§ 17   F. A. Forel, *Le Léman*, **II**, Lausanne, 1895.

§ 20   J. Piccard, *Arch. Sci. Phys. Nat.*, **21**, 481, 1889. J. Spooner, *Correspondance Astronomique*, 1 May 1822, p. 331. G. Galle, *Ann. Phys.*, **49**, 255,

1840. C. Schoute, *Hemel en Dampkring*, **7**, 1, 1909. A. Wigand and E. Everling, *Verh. Dtsch. Phys. Ges.*, **15**, 237 and 1117, 1913; *Phys. Z.*, **14**, 1156, 1913; *Meteorol. Z.*, **31**, 150, 1914. K. Stuchtey, *Ann. Phys.*, **59**, 33, 1919. W. Shoulejkin, *Nature*, **114**, 498, 1924. E. O. Hulburt, *J. Opt. Soc. Am.*, **24**, 35, 1934. *Scripps Inst. Oceanogr.*, nos. 731 and 737. Ruskin, *Modern Painters*, **III**, 511.

§ 22   Minnaert, *Physica*, **9**, 925, 1942. With information from E. W. M Blokhuis.

§ 23   E. O. Hulburt, *J. Opt. Soc. Am.*, **24**, 35, 1934. Shoulejkin, *Fizika Morja*, Moscow, 1941. A. Ricco, V. Cerulli, and A. Venturi, *Mem. Spettr. Ital.*, **17**, 203, 1888; **18**, 23, 45, and 57, 1889. J. Spooner, *Correspondance Astronomique*, 1 May 1822, p. 337.

§ 28   F. A. Forel, *Le Léman*, Lausanne, 1895, **II**, 507. Minnaert, *Physica*, **9**, 1942.

§ 29   Fokker, *Physica*, **2**, 238, 1922. Neuberger, *Meteorol. Z.*, **55**, 68, 1938.

Chapter 3

§ 30   F. A. Forel, *Le Léman*, Lausanne, 1895, **II**, 454 and 456. L. Boltzman, *Populäre Schriften*, p. 59.

§ 31   Kerner von Maurilaun, *Pflanzenleben*.

§ 32   With information from K. Braak.

§ 33   *Z. Phys. Chem. Unterricht*, **4**, 86, 1891; **37**, 90, 1924. E. Barthel, *Arch. Syst. Philos.*, **19**, 355, 1913.

§ 34   H. M. Reese, *J. Opt. Soc. Am.*, **21**, 282, 1931.

§ 36   Based on information from Prof. D. Tinbergen.

§ 38   Based on information from Prof. H. C. Burger

§ 40   Forel, *C. R. Acad. Sci.*, **153**, 1054, 1911; *Proc. R. Soc. Edinburgh*, **32**, 175, 1912. *Onweders en Optische Verschijnselen in Nederland*, **42**, 37, 1921.; **47**, 52, 1926. Drachten, *Hemel en Dampkring*, **13**, 70, 1915.

§ 41   W. Hiller, *Phys. Z.*, **14**, 718, 1913; **15**, 303, 1914. Ball, *Philos. Mag.*, **35**, 404, 1868. *Ann. Phys. (Pogg.)*, **134**, 336, 1868.

§ 42   H. Futi, *Geophys. Mag.*, **4**, 387, 1931. L. A. Ramdas and S. L. Malurkar, *Nature*, **129**, 6, 1932. W. E. Schiele, *Veröff. Geophys. Inst. Leipzig*, **7**, 144, 1935. K. Braak, *Tijdschr. Kon. Ned. Aardr. Genootschap*, **39**, 587, 1922. L. G. Vedy, *Meteorol. Mag.*, **63**, 249, 1928; *Hemel en Dampkring*, **15**, 71, 1917.

§ 43   *Onweders en Optische Verschijnselen in Nederland*, **14**, 63, 1893.

§ 44   F. A. Forel, *Proc. R. Soc. Edinburgh*, **32**, 175, 1912. *Arch. Sci. Phys. Nat.*, **3**, 545, 1897. *C. R. Acad. Sci.*, **153**, 1054, 1911. *Onweders en Optische Verschijnselen in Nederland*, **40**, 46, 1919; **54**, 40, 1933. J. Pinkhof, *Hemel en Dampkring*, **31**, 252, 1933.

§ 45   A. L. Colton, *Contrib. Lick. Obs.*, **1**, 1895. A. Ricco, *Mem. Spettr. Ital.*, **30**, 96, 1901. Prinz, ibid., **31**, 36, 1902. Arctowski, ibid., **31**, 190, 1902. Wegener, *Beitr. Phys. Atmos.*, **4**, 26, 1912. A. Bracke, *Déformations du Soleil*, Mons, 1907; *Publ. Astron. Soc. Pacif.*, **45**, 270, 1933. Havinga, *Hemel en Dampkring*, **19**, 161, 1922.

§ 46   Reimann, *Meteorol. Z.*, **4**, 144, 1887; *Onweders en Optische Verschijnselen in Nederland*, **21**, 51, 1900. J. Cassini, *Mem. Acad. Paris*, **10**, 234, 1693. *Edinburgh Philos. J.*, **10**, 362, 1824.

§ 47   Fisher, *Pop. Astron.*, **29**, 1921. Mulder, *The Green Ray or Green Flash*, The Hague, 1922. Feenstra Kuiper, 'De Groene Straal', dissertation, Utrecht, 1926. *Ann. Hydr.*, **63**, 336, 1935; **65**, 489, 1937. *Mem. Spettr. Ital.*, **31**, 36, 1902. *Nature*, **156**, 146, 1945. *Hemel en Dampkring*, **33**, 219, 1935. *Onweders en Optische Verschijnselen in Nederland*, **48**, 81, 1927. *Hemel en Dampkring*, **19**, 83, 1921. N. Dijkwel, *Hemel en Dampkring*, **34**, 261, 1936. *Nature*, **111**, 13, 1923. *Meteorol. Z.*, **49**, 271, 1932. S.W. Visser and J. T. Verstelle, *Hemel en Dampkring*, **32**, 81, 1934. *Proc. R. Soc.*, **126**, 311, 1930. P. Moureau, *La Nature*, 294, 1929.

§ 48   S. W. Visser, *Hemel en Dampkring*, **19**, 83, 1921.

§ 49   *Nature*, **94**, 61, 1914. *Q. J. Theor. Appl. Meteorol.*, **62**, 128, 1936. *Ann. Soc. Meteorol. France*, **47**, 1899. W. M. Lindley, *J. Brit. Astron. Assoc.*, **47**, 298, 1937.

§ 50   *Hemel en Dampkring*, **20**, 130, 1932.

§ 51   *Handb. Geophys.*, **VIII**. *Philos. Mag.*, **13**, 301, 1857.

§ 53   Dufour, *Philos. Mag.*, **19**, 216, 1860. *Arch. Sci. Phys. Nat.*, **29**, 545, 1893. Bigourdan, *C. R. Acad. Sci.*, **160**, 579, 1915. J. N. Dörr,

Meteorol. Z., **32**, 153, 1915.

§ 55   C. Rozet, *C. R. Acad. Sci.*, **142**, 913, 1906; **146**, 325, 1906. *Nature*, **37**, 224, 1888. S. A. Mitchell, *Handb. Astrophys.*, **IV**, 353, 1929.

§ 65   H. Bock, *Z. Phys. Chem. Unterricht*, **53**, 139, 1940.

§ 66   Niederhoff, *Z. Sinnesphysiol.*, **65**, 27 and 232, 1934; **66**, 213, 1936.

Chapter 6

Helmholtz, *Physiologische Optik*, 3rd edn. W. St. Duke-Elder, *Textbook of Ophthalmology*, 1938.

§ 68   O. von Aufsess, *Das Sehen unter Wasser*, 1912. A. Bierman, *Reflex*, **7**, 39, 1936.

§ 69   Helmholtz, *Physiologische Optik*, 3rd edn., **2**, 217 and 255.

§ 73   H. Meyer, *Ann. Phys. (Pogg.)*, **89**, 429, 1853.

§ 75   M. N. Stoddard, **13**, 156, 1852. Ahmed, *Natuurk. Tijdschr. Ned. Ind.*, **98**, 48, 1938. *Hemel en Dampkring*, **41**, 17, 1943. Ruskin, *Modern Painters*, **III**, 327 and 442.

§ 76   *Ann. Hydr.*, **37**, 1909. *Hemel en Dampkring*, **14**, 60 and 180; **17**, 68, 1919. *Die Himmelswelt*, **44**, 70, 1934.

§ 79   Helmholtz, *Optisches über Malerei*, Pop. Wiss. Vorträge, 1871–1873, p. 71.

§ 80   Helmholtz, *Optisches über Malerei*, Pop. Wiss. Vorträge, 1871–1873, p. 71.

§ 84   Parenago, *Astron. J. (Russ.)*, **7**, 203, 1930. Smosarski, *Ann. Inst. Phys. du Globe, Paris*, **22**, 70, 1945.

§ 85   W. van der Elst, *Hemel en Dampkring*, **21**, 2, 1923. *Die Sterne*, **20**, 51, 1940. Ellison, *J. Brit. Astron. Assoc.*, **26**, 227, 1916.

§ 86   Goethe, *Farbenlehre*, **I**, 1, § 17. Leonardo da Vinci, *Trattato*, 1804 edn., pp. 308–315.

Chapter 7

§ 90   Faraday, *Experimental Research in Chemical Physics*, p. 142.

§ 92   O. Lummer, *Grundlagen, Ziele und Grenzen der Leuchttechnik*, Munich, 1918, p. 70.

§ 98   P. M. Roget, *Philos. Trans.*, **115**, 131, 1825. Plateau, *Ann. Phys. (Pogg.)*, **20**, 319, 1830. L. Burmester, *Ber. Akad. München*, 142, 1914. Bouasse, *Formes et Couleurs*, Paris, 1917, p. 236 . W. A. Gardner, *J. Opt. Soc. Am.*, **31**, 94, 1941. Pohl, *Mechanik*, p. 187 (gives incorrect explanation). *J. R Inst.*, **1**, 205, 1831.

§ 100 Woog, *C. R. Acad. Sci.*, **168**, 1222; **169**, 93, 1919.

§ 102 *Z. Phys. Chem. Unterricht*, **42**, 252, 1929. W. A. Gardner, *J. Opt. Soc. Am.*, **31**, 94, 1941.

§ 103 H. S. Gradle, *Science*, **68**, 404, 1928.

§ 104 With information from E. M. W. Blokhuis.

§ 105 Goethe, *Farbenlehre*, **I**, 1, §§ 21, 22, and 52. Titchener, *Experimental Psychology*, **I**, 1, 29; **I**, 2, 47. *Nature*, **60**, 341, 1905. Helmholtz, *Physiologische Optik*, 3rd edn., **2**, 202. Goethe, *Farbenlehre*, **I**, 1, § 52.

§ 106 *De Natuur*, 1900. Goethe, *Farbenlehre*, **I**, 1, § 54.

§ 107 Goethe, *Farbenlehre*, **I**, 1, § 44. Discussions with Eckermann.

§ 108 Goethe, *Farbenlehre*, **I**, 1, § 46.

§ 110 Goethe, *Farbenlehre*, **I**, 1, § 30. *Philos. Mag.*, **4**, 427, 1828. *J. Brit. Astron. Assoc.*, **28**, 1918; **29**, 1919; **45**, 1935.

§ 111 K. Groes-Petersen, *Astron. Nachr.*, **196**, 293, 1913.

§ 113 *J. Opt. Soc. Am.*, **11**, 133, 1925.

§ 114 Goethe, *Farbenlehre*, **I**, 1, §§ 57 and 59. O. Meissner, *Z, Angew. Meteorol.*, **57**, 263 and 366, 1940. Helmholtz, *Optisches über Malerei*, Pop. Vorträge und Reden, p. 125. Leonardo da Vinci, *Trattato*, 1804 edn., p. 146. E. Schrödinger, in Müller-Pouillet, *Lehrb. Phys.*, **II**, 534, 1926.

§ 115 Goethe, *Farbenlehre*, **I**, 1, § 75. Chevreul, *C. R. Acad. Sci.*, **47**, 196, 1859. I. G. Priest, *J. Opt. Soc. Am.*, **13**, 308, 1926. *Das Wetter*, **20**, 69, 1903.

§ 116 *C. R. Acad. Sci.*, **48**, 1105, 1859.

§ 117   C. Martins, *C. R. Acad. Sci.*, **43**, 763, 1856.

Chapter 9

§ 118   Luckiesh, *Optical Illusions*, New York, 1922. Bragg, *Het Wonder van het Licht*, p. 49.

§ 119   *Pflüger's Archiv*, **39**, 347, 1886; **40**, 459, 1887. Later work of Basler.

§ 120   *Ann. Phys. (Pogg.)* **92**, 655, 1857. A. von Humbold, *Kosmos*, **III**, 75, 1799. *Handb. Phys.* **20**, 174. A. Müller, *Ann. Phys. (Pogg.)*, **106**, 289, 1859. *Nature*, **38**, 102, 1888.

§ 122   W. Metzger, *Gesetze des Sehens*, Frankfurt, 1936, chap. XI. Dante, *Inferno*, **31**, 136. Helmholtz, *Physiologische Optik*, 3rd edn., **3**, 209. J. J. Oppel, *Ann. Phys. (Pogg.)*, **99**, 540, 1856. Von Kries in Helmholtz, *Physiologische Optik*, 3rd edn., **3**, 209. *Proc. Brit. Assoc.*, 1848, p. 47. Basler, *Pflüger's Archiv*, **132**, 131, 1910.

§ 123   *Hemel en Dampkring*, **29**, 348, 380, and 413, 1931

§ 127   Harley, *Moon-lore*, London, 1885. Titchener, *Experimental Psychology.*

§ 128   Bernstein, *Z. Psychol.*, **34**, 132, 1904. G. Ten Doesschate, *Nederl. Tijschr. voor Geneeskunde*, **74**, 748, 1930. G. Colange and Y. Le Grand, *C. R. Acad. Sci.*, **204**, 1882, 1937. G. Ten Doesschate and F. P. Fischer, *Ann. Ocul.*, **176**, 103, 1939. L. Dunoyer, *C. R. Acad. Sci.*, **205**, 867, 1937.

§ 129   A. Müller, *Die Referenzflächen der Sonne und der Gestirne*, Braunschweig, 1918. R. von Sterneck, *Der Schraum auf Grund der Erfahrung*, Leipzig, 1907. E. Reimann, *Z. Psychol. Physiol. Sinnesorgane*, 1920. Dember and Uibe, *Ann. Phys.*, **61**, 313, 1920.

§ 131   Vaughan Cornish, *Scenery and the Sense of Sight*, Cambridge, 1935, chap. II.

§ 133   C. Flammarion, *l'Atmosphere*, 1888, p. 169. Edgar Allen Poe, *The Balloon Hoax.*

§ 134   E. Mach, *Erkenntnis und Irrtum*, Leipzig, 1905, p. 331. With information from Prof. E. H. Hazelhoff.

§ 135   O. Baschin, *Naturwiss.*, **7**, 510, 1919; **13**, 346, 1925. J. van der Bilt, *Hemel en Dampkring*, **7**, 56, 1909. Dember and Uibe, *Ann. Phys.*, **61**, 313, 1920. H. Stücklen, 'Zur Frage nach der scheinbaren

Gestalt des Himmelsgewölbes', dissertation, Göttingen, 1919.

§ 136   G. Ten Doesschate, *Nederl. Tijdschr. voor Geneeskunde*, **74**, 748, 1930. Pohl, *Naturwiss.*, **7**, 415 1919.

§ 137   Plateau, *Bull. Acad. Belg.*, **49**, 316, 1880. G. Ten Doesschate, *Nederl. Tijdschr. voor Geneeskunde*, **74**, 748, 1930.

§ 138   Vaughan Cornish, *Scenery and the Sense of Sight*, Cambridge, 1935, chap. II.

Chapter 10

§ 139   Poppe, *Ann. Phys. (Pogg.)*, **95**, 481, 1855. Larmor, *Proc. Cambridge Philos. Soc.*, **7**, 131, 1891. Bouasse, *Diffraction*, 1923, p. 415.

§ 140   Volz and Meyer, *Handb. Geophys.*, **VIII**, 943 and 1023. *Das Wetter*, **30**, 117 and 214, 1913; **55**, 404, 1938.

§ 141   Minnaert, *Physica*, **11**, 288, 1931. Flammarion, *l'Atmosphere*, 1888, p. 214. Observation by Brewster.

§ 142   *Philos. Mag.*, **17**, 61, 1883. *Z. Phys. Chem. Unterricht*, **4**, 275, 1891.

§ 144   Prins and Reesink, *Physica*, **II**, 49, 1944.

§ 145   *Nature*, **109**, 309, 1922. S. Thompson, *Nature*, **18**, 441, 1878.

§ 147   *Phys. Z.*, **10**, 965, 1909.

§ 150   *Philos. Mag.*, **29**, 456, 1890. E. van Everdingen, *Hemel en Dampkring*, **30**, 19, 1932. F. E. Volz, *Meteorol. Rundsch.*, **13**, 117, 1960. C. F. Brooks, *Mon. Weather Rev.*, **53**, 49, 1925. G. C. Simpson, *Mon., Weather Rev.*, **38**, 291, 1912. *Meteorol. Z.*, **39**, 33 and 324, 1922. *Hemel en Dampkring*, **1**, 349, 1903. *Philos. Mag.*, **17**, 148, 1883. Lepper, *Onweders en Optische Verschijnselen in Nederland*, **52**, 54, 1931.

§ 151   A. E. Heath, *Nature*, **97**, 6, 1916. W. J. Humphreys, *J. Franklin Inst.*, **207**, 661, 1929. *Hemel en Dampkring*, **6**, 145, 1908. *Nature*, **43**, 416, 1891. Clerk Maxwell, *Papers*, **II**, 160. *Sitzungsber. Akad. Wien*, **119**, 1057, 1910.

§ 152   Dijt, *Hemel en Dampkring*, **29**, 14, 1931.

§ 153   *Sitzungsber. Akad. Wien*, **119**, 1057, 1910. W. J. Humphreys, *J. Franklin Inst.*, **207**, 661, 1929.

§ 154   *Onweders en Optische Verschijnselen in Nederland*, **21**, 54, 1900; **24**, 160, 1903; **29**, 110, 1908. *Hemel en Dampkring*, **27**, 359, 1929. *Meteorol. Mag.*, **71**, 230. *Handb. Geophys.*, **VIII**, 1015.

§ 156   R. Meyer, *Die Haloerscheinungen*, Hamburg, 1929. M. Pinkhof, *Verh. Akad. Amsterdam*, **13**, 1, 1919. E. W. Woolard, *Mon. Weather Rev.*, **64**, 321, 1936; **65**, 4, 1937. S. W. Visser, *Handb. Geophys.*, **VIII**. C. A. van den Bosch, *Natuurk. Tijdschr. voor Ned.-Indië*, **92**, 39, 1932.

§ 157   C. A. van den Bosch, *Natuurk. Tijdschr. voor Ned.-Indië*, **92**, 39, 1932. S. W. Visser, *Versl. Akad. Amsterdam*, **25**, 1328, 1917; **27**, 127, 1918. *Hemel en Dampkring*, **15**, 17, 1917; **16**, 35, 1918.

§ 158   *L'Astronomie*, **68** 420, 1954. Visser, *Hemel en Dampkring*, **44**, 12, 1946. *Handb. Geophys.*, **VIII**, 1044.

§ 160   E. van Everdingen, *Hemel en Dampkring*, **16**, 97, 1918. *Onweders en Optische Verschijnselen in Nederland*, **39**, 66, 1918; **43**, 44, 1922. Visser, dissertation, Utrecht, 1936. *Hemel en Dampkring*, **20**, 39, 1922.

§ 165   *Hemel en Dampkring*, **20**, 39, 1922. Perntner-Exner, *Meteorologische Optik*, Vienna, Leipzig, 1922, p. 300. *Onweders en Optische Verschijnselen in Nederland*, **16**, 66, 1895. *Mon. Weather Rev.*, **48**, 506, 1920.

§ 167   E. van Everdingen, *Onweders en Optische Verschijnselen in Nederland*, **28**, 77, 1907. C. Schoute, *Hemel en Dampkring*, **7**, 1, 1909. K. Stuchtey, *Ann. Phys.*, **59**, 33, 1919.

§ 169   C. F. Squire, *J. Opt. Soc. Am.*, **42**, 782, 1952.; **43**, 318, 1953. R. Schütze, *Meteorol. Z.*, **55**, 265, 1935.

§ 170   E. van Everdingen, *Hemel en Dampkring*, **31**, 1933; **34**, 177, 1936. Neuberger, *Meteorol. Z.*, **52**, 232, 1935. S. W. Visser, *Hemel en Dampkring*, **34**, 114, 1936; **34**, 309, 1936; **40**, 307, 1942; **41**, 33 and 95, 1943; **41**, 82, 1943. *Optische Verschijnselen*, 1943. C. W. Hissink, *Hemel en Dampkring*, **4**, 64, 1906. *Hemel en Dampkring*, **24**, 390, 1926; **30**, 207, 1932. *Gerlands Beitr. Geophys.*, 1934. White, *Nature*, **154**, 517, 1944. H. Berg, *Meteorol. Z.*, **52**, 227, 1935. *Onweders en Optische Verschijnselen in Nederland*, **58**, 84, 1937. Visser and Alkemade, *Hemel en Dampkring*, **52**, 92, 1954.

§ 171   E. Barkow, *Meteorol. Z.*, **33**, 545, 1916. *Hemel en Dampkring*, **30**, 19, 1932. *Onweders en Optische Verschijnselen in Nederland*, **60**, 115, 1939. C. W. Hissink, *Hemel en Dampkring*, **9**, 13, 1911.

§ 172   C. A. Nell, *Hemel en Dampkring*, **7**, 41, 1909.

§ 174   M. Pinkhof, *Hemel en Dampkring*, **38**, 32 and 230, 1940. *Z. Angew. Meteorol.*, **57**, 95, 1940. *Bull. Am. Meteorol. Soc.*, **25**, 188, 1944. *Nature*, **154**, 491, 1944. Archenhold, *Nature*, **154**, 433, 1944.

§ 175   *Meteorol. Z.*, **27**, 113, 1910. *Hemel en Dampkring*, **38**, 78 and 79, 1940. M. Minnaert, *Hemel en Dampkring*, **26**, 51, 1928.

§ 176   Listing, *Ann. Phys.*, **122**, 161, 1864. Meyer, *Das Wetter*, **42**, 137, 1925.

§ 177   K. B. Blodgett, *J. Opt. Soc. Am.*, **24**, 313, 1934.

§ 179   Schlottmann, *Meteorol. Z.*, **10**, 156, 1893. C. F. Brooks, *Mon. Weather Rev.*, **53**, 49, 1925. With information form Prof. J. A. Prins and E. W. H. Blokhuis. Wood, *Physical Optics*.

§ 180   Zocher, *Z. Allg. Anorg. Chem.*, **149**, 203, 1925.

§ 181   *Rep. Brit. Assoc.*, **42**, 45, 1872. *Nature*, **47**, 364. *Z. Meteorol.*, **12**, 410, 1877. *La Nature*, **21**, 58, 1893. Ricerche Specola Vaticana, **4**, 55, 1958.

§ 182   Fizeau, *Ann. Chim. Phys.*, **63**, 385, 1861. Rayleigh, *Philos. Mag.*, **14**, 350, 1907; *Papers*, **V**, 410.

§ 184   R. Meyer, *Meteorol. Z.*, **27**, 112, 1910. G.C. Simpson, *Q. J. Theor. Appl. Meteorol.*, **38**, 291, 1912. C. F. Brooks, *Mon. Weather Rev.*, **53**, 49, 1925. Köhler, *Meteorol. Z.*, **40**, 257, 1923. Visser, *Versl. Akad. Amsterdam*, **52**, 1943. Penndorf and Stranz, *Z. Angew. Meteorol.*, **60**, 233, 1943.

§ 185   Donle, *Ann. Phys.*, **34**, 814, 1888. K. Exner, *Sitzungsber. Akad. Wien*, **76**, 522, 1877; **98**, 1130, 1889. J. A. Prins, *Hemel en Dampkring*, **38**, 244, 1940. J. J. M. Reesinck and D. A. de Vries, *Physica*, **7**, 603, 1940. Musschenbroek, *Introd. ad Philos. nat.*, **II**, § 2450, 1762. S. W. Visser, *Hemel en Dampkring*, **38**, 109, 1940.

§ 186   A. Gullstrand, in Helmholtz, *Physiologische Optik*, 3rd edn., **I**, 192. Exner, *Wiedem. Ann. Phys.*, **9**, 239, 1880. Von Laue, *Sitzungsber. Akad. Berlin*, 1144, 1914. H. A. Lorentz, *Versl. Akad. Amsterdam*, **26**, 1120, 1918; *Collected Papers*, **4**, 125. Goethe, *Farbenlehre*, **I**, nos. 91 and 92. L. Ronchi, Toraldo di Francia, Zoli, et al., in G. Ronchi, *Atti Fundazine*, 1951–1955.

§ 187   *Nature*, **37**, 440, 1888. *Q. J. Theor. Appl. Meteorol.*, **61**, 177, 1935.

R. Mecke, *Ann. Phys.*, **61**, 471, 1920; **62**, 623, 1920. Kiessling, *Meteorol. Z.*, **1**, 117, 1884. W. H. Köhler, *Meteorol. Z.*, **46**, 164, 1929.

§ 188   W. Schmidt, *Meteorol. Z.*, **33**, 199, 1916. W. Milch, *Meteorol. Z.*, **43**, 295, 1926. Tyndall, *Philos. Mag.*, **17**, 244, 1883. *Meteorol. Z.*, **55**, 313, 1938. W. Peppler, *Z. Angew. Meteorol.*, **56**, 173, 1939.

§ 189   H. van der Linden, *Hemel en Dampkring*, **1**, 3 and 248, 1903. A. Bracke, *Nuages irisés*, Mons, 1907. C. F. Brooks, *Mon. Weather Rev.*, **53**, 49, 1925. *Z. Angew. Meteorol.*, **60**, 185, 1943. H. Köhler, *Meteorol. Z.*, **46**, 161, 1929. Ruskin, *Modern Painters*, **I**, part 2.

§ 190   C. Störmer, *Geofysiske Publikasjoner*, **9**, no. 4, 1931; *Beitr. Geophys.*, **32**, 63, 1931. *Nature*, **145**, 221, 1940. Mohn, *Meteorol. Z.*, **10**, 82, 1893; *Vid. Selsk. Forh.*, 1893, no. 10. Slocum, *J. R. Astron. Soc. Can.*, **28**, 145, 1934.

§ 191   *Q. J. Theor. Appl. Meteorol.*, **39**, 157, 1913. E. Maey, *Meteorol. Z.*, **39**, 229, 1922. Benvenuto Cellini, *Autobiography*, book I, chap. 128.

§ 192   *Nature*, **90**, 621, 1913. Van Lommel, *Ann. Phys.*, jubilee volume, 10, 1874.

Chapter 11

§ 195   A. Heim, *Luftfarben*, Zürich, 1912. J. Plassman, *Meteorol. Z.*, **48**, 412, 1931.

§ 196?? A. Heim, *Luftfarben*, Zürich, 1912. Vaughan Cornish, *Geogr. J.*, **67**, 506, 1926. Haldane, *The Philosophy of a Biologist*, Oxford, 1935, p. 52.

§ 198   R. Wood, *Philos. Mag.*, **39**, 423, 1920.

§ 199   *Meteorol. Z.*, **41**, 43, 1924; **45**, 367, 1928. Spanenberg, *Ann. Hydr.*, **71**, 93, 1943.

§ 200   C. Dorno, *Physik der Sonnen- und Himmelstrahlung*, p. 116. Ruskin, *Elements of Drawing*, **XV**, 35.

§ 201   *Phys. Rev.*, **26**, 497, 1908.

§ 202   M. Minnaert, *Hemel en Dampkring*, **29**, 1, 1931. Ruskin, *Modern Painters*, **III**, 349.

§ 205   *C. R. Acad. Sci.*, **47**, 450, 1858. *Meteorol. Z.*, **6**, 1889. F. Busch and C. Jensen, *Tatsachen und Theorien der atmosphärischen Polarisation*,

Hamburg, 1911. Plassman, *Ann. Hydr.*, **40**, 478, 1912. *Wetter*, **34**, 133, 1917. Jensen, in Kleinschmidt, *Handb. Meteorol. Instrumente*, 666, 1935.

§ 206   F. Busch and C. Jensen, *Tatsachen und Theorien der atmosphärischen Polarisation*, Hamburg, 1911. Helmholtz, *Physiologische Optik*, 3rd edn., **2**, 256. T. Mendelssohn, *Rev. Faculté des Sci. Istamboul*, **3**, 2, 1938. Haidinger, *Ann. Phys.*, **67**, 435, 1846. Brewster, *Ann. Phys.*, **107**, 346, 1859. A. Hofmann, *Wetter*, **34**, 133, 1917. Stokes, *Papers*, **5**.

§ 208   Vaughan Cornish, *Geogr. J.*, **26**, 506, 1926. F. Richarz, *Meteorol. Z.*, **25**, 19, 1908.

§ 210   C. Wiener, *Nov. Act. Leop.*, **73**, 106, 1900

§ 213   G. M. Byran, *Mon. Weather Rev.*, **64**, 259, 1936. *Meteorol. Z.*, **31**, 257, 1914. Löhle, *Z. Angew. Meteorol.*, **60**, 269, 1943.

§ 214   M. Minnaert, *Hemel en Dampkring*, **29**, 89, 1931. Davis, *Science*, **76**, 274, 1932.

§ 216   W. E. Knowles Middleton, *Visibility in Meteorology*, Toronto, 1941. Sebastian, *Beitr. Geophysik*, **45**, 35, 1935. F. Löhle, *Sichtbeobachtungen*, Berlin, 1941; *Meteorol. Z.*, **55**, 54, 1938.

§ 217   *Meteorol. Z.*, **7**, 1890.

§ 219   Perntner-Exner, *Meteorologische Optik*, Vienna, Leipzig, 1922. P. Gruner and H. Kleinert, *die Dämmerungserscheinungen*, Hamburg, Grand, 1927. P. Gruner, *Handb. Geophys.*, **8**, 432 and 526, 1939. A. Heim, *Luftfarben*, Zürich, Hofer, 1912. Von Bezold, *Ann. Phys.*, **123**, 240, 1864. C. Combier, *La Météorologie*, **16**, 117, 1940. P. Gruner, *Beitr. Phys. Freien Atmos.*, **8**, 1, 1919.

§ 220   Perntner-Exner, *Meteorologische Optik*, Vienna, Leipzig, 1922. C. Combier, *La Météorologie*, **16**, 117, 1940.

§ 221   Smosarski, *C. R. Acad. Sci.*, **219**, 491, 1944. *Wetter*, **9**, 1892.

§ 222   J. Dubois, *C. R. Acad. Sci.*, **222**, 671, 1946; **226**, 1180, 1948. P. Gruner, *Helv. Phys. Acta*, **5**, 351, 1932; *Beitr. Geophys.*, **51**, 174, 1937.

§ 223   *Z. Angew. Meteorol.*, **54**, 1937.

§ 224   *Mon. Weather Rev.*, **42**, 503, 1914.

§ 225   A. H. Borgesius, *Hemel en Dampkring*, **17**, 145, 1920.

§ 226   *Astron. Nachr.*, **220**, 15, 1923. Dorno, *Meteorol. Z*, **34**, 246, 1917. *Hemel en Dampkring*, **10**, 156, 1913. *Nature*, **91**, 681, 1912. *Ann. Soc. Meteorol. France*, **53**, 1903. Dorno, *Abh. Preuss. Meteorol. Inst.*, **5**, 1917.

§ 229   P. Gruner and H. Kleinert, *Die Dämmerungserscheinungen*, Hamburg, 1917, p. 6. M. Wolf, *Astron. Nachr.*, **203**, 387, 1915.

§ 230   F. Schmidt, *Das Zodiakallicht*, Hamburg, 1928. *Publ. Kwasan Obs.*, **1**, no. 3, 1931. *Hemel en Dampkring*, **38**, 422, 1940; **41**, 239, 1943.

§ 232   *Astron. Nachr.*, **196**, 269, 1913. *Die Himmelswelt*, **34**, 95, 1924.

Chapter 11

§ 234   Fournet, *C. R. Acad. Sci.*, **47**, 189, 1858. Osthoff, *Mitt. Ver. Fr. Astron.*, **10**, 136, 1901. J. Plassman, *Meteorol. Z.*, **8**, 421, 1931. *Hemel en Dampkring*, **31**, 209 and 271, 1933. *Meteorol. Mag.*, **67**, 1932 to **69**, 1934. C. Wirtz, in R. Henseling, *Astronomisches Handbuch*, Stuttgart, 1921. Bottlinger and Schrödinger, *Naturwiss.*, **13**, 1925.

§ 235   *C. R. Acad. Sci.*, **177**, 515, 1923.

§ 237   La Cour, *Overs. Dansk Vidensk, Selsk. Forh.*, **75**, 1871. Bravais, *Ann. Phys. (Pogg.)*, **77**, 156, 1849. *Nature*, **29**, 104, 1884. Vaughan Cornish, *Geogr. J.*, **67**, 518, 1926. G. F. Tydeman, *Hemel en Dampkring*, **19**, 113, 1922.

§ 238   W. D. Bancroft, *Chem. News*, **117**, 197, 1919; *J. Frankl. Inst.*, **187**, no. 3. M. Pollock, *Light and Water*, London, 1903. Von Aufsess, *Ann. Phys.*, **13**, 678, 1904. C. V. Raman, *Proc. R. Soc.*, **101**, 64, 1922; *Nature*, **110**, 280, 1922. Sjoulejkin, *Phys. Rev.*, **22**, 85, 1923. K. R. Ramanathan, *Philos. Mag.*, **46**, 543, 1925.

§ 240   Wittstein, *Ann. Physik*, **45**, 474, 1858.

§ 241   Ruskin, *Modern Painters*, **III**, 304.

§ 242   Sjoulejkin, *C. R. Leningrad*, **1**, 494, 1935.

§ 243   *Nature*, **84**, 87, 1910. *Ann. Hydr.*, **30**, 429, 1902.

§ 244   *Arch. Sci. Phys. Nat.*, **17**, 186, 1904; **20**, 101, 1905.

§ 245   *C. R. Acad. Sci.*, **108**, 242 and 337; **109**, 412, 1889. E. O. Hulburt, *J. Opt. Soc. Am.*, **24**, 35, 1934. C. V. Raman, *Proc. R. Soc.*, **101A**, 64, 1922.

§ 246   W. Ule, *Peterm. Mitt.*, **38**, 70, 1892.

§ 247   Ruskin, *Modern Painters*, **III**, 504, 505, and 665, and appendix.

§ 248   K. Kalle, *Ann. Hydr.*, **67**, 22, 1939. Forel, *Bull. Soc. Vaudoise Sci. Natur.*, **13**, 73. C. V. Raman, *Proc. R. Soc.*, **101A**, 64, 1922. *Physica*, **11**, 368, 1931.

§ 249   Ruskin, *Modern Painters*, **III**, 526.

§ 250   Richard, *Wetter*, **34**, 69, 1917.

§ 255   Ruskin, *Modern Painters*.

§ 256   Vaughan Cornish, *Geogr. J.*, **67**, 506, 1926.

§ 257   *Nature*, **90**, 621, 1913. Russell, Dugan, and Stewart, *Astronomy*, **1**, 173.

§ 258   Ruskin, *Modern Painters*. Angström, *Geogr. Ann.*, 1925.

§ 263   *De Kampioen*, Feb. 1940, p. 43.

Chapter 13

H. Molisch, *Leuchtende Pflanzen*, Jena, 1904.

§ 265   *De Zee*, 1910–1912; 1920–1926.

§ 268   *Nature*, **88**, 377, 1912.

§ 269   A. J. M. Garjeanne, *De Levende Natuur*, **14**, 163, 1909. Dufour, *C. R. Acad. Sci.*, **51**, 31, 1860.

§ 273   *Ann. Phys.*, **89**, 620, 1853. W. Müller, *Erzbach Abh. Naturw. Ver. Bremen*, **14**, 217, 1897. *Album der Natuur*, 1897. *Meteorol. Z.*, **17**, 505, 1900. *Kosmos*, **5**, 270, 1908. *Wetter*, **20**, 46, 1903; **33**, 18 and 71, 1916.

Appendix A

A. A. Nijland, *Astron. Nachr.*, **160**, 258, 1902. *Science*, **66**, 507, 1927.

Index